# ARTISTIC RELATIONS

# ARTISTIC RELATIONS

Literature and the Visual Arts
in Nineteenth-Century France

*Edited by*
Peter Collier
*and*
Robert Lethbridge

YALE UNIVERSITY PRESS
NEW HAVEN AND LONDON   1994

Set in Sabon by SX Composing Ltd., Rayleigh, Essex
Printed in Great Britain by St Edmundsbury Press

**Library of Congress Cataloging-in-Publication Data**

Artistic relations: literature and the visual arts in nineteenth-
   century France/edited by Peter Collier and Robert Lethbridge.
      p.    cm.
   Includes bibliographical references and index.
   ISBN 0–300–06009–2
   1. Art and literature — France — History — 19th century.  2. Arts.
French.  3. Arts. Modern — 19th century — France.  4. Ut pictura
poesis (Aesthetics)  I. Collier. Peter.  II. Lethbridge, Robert.
NX549.A1A78   1994
700'.944'09034 — dc20                        94–4503
                                                     CIP

A catalogue record for this book is available from the British Library

# Contents

# Contents

# List of Illustrations

## List of illustrations

# Acknowledgements

In a collective volume of this kind there will always be those who assistance remains unacknowledged. Amongst those we can thank are: our contributors, for their enthusiasm for, and commitment to, this project; the Yale readers who made valuable suggestions; Robert Baldock for his encouragement and advice; our editor Candida Brazil, and Patty Rennie, who sensitively master-minded the editing and production process; Meryl Tyers who scrutinized every chapter; Elinor Dorday who translated Pierre Bourdieu's; Kate Tunstall for her creative design of an index more important than most; Beatrix Bown for the daunting task of computerizing it; Anita Ogier and Heather Henchie for their secretarial help; and Peter Bayley, as head of the University of Cambridge's Department of French, who made available the funds to allow us to secure the book's illustrations.

PJC
RDL

# Introduction

## *Representations*

This book seeks to map out the relationship between literature and the visual arts in nineteenth-century France. It is an area which has been the subject over the last few years of a number of specialized monographs and is inseparable from the interdisciplinary perspectives being developed in both teaching and research. In particular, literature and painting are increasingly being seen in relation to the broader background of cultural studies. An exemplary moment in this shift of direction might be said to be the publication of the first number of the journal *Word and Image* in 1985.

Within a largely chronological structure the book looks at most of the major writers and painters of the period. It provides information that is essential to an overview of the main paradigms of creative practice and also provides more closely focused analyses of the relationship between texts and images. We do not claim to launch some all-embracing theory of this field of study, and our introductory purpose is obviously incompatible with an exhaustive survey of each and every aspect of the sister arts at this time.

Nonetheless, we are not entirely passive followers of the new art history and the new modes of literary theory. While our study draws on theoretical approaches opened up by semiotics, Marxism, psychoanalysis, and feminism, it is not our intention to duplicate some of the specialist studies which have adopted these perspectives. The book is, however, the first major work to address the full variety of different kinds of relationship between nineteenth-century French literature and art. We remain aware that we have explored those relationships in terms of an agreed corpus of central figures, although one of the implications of our book may well be that readers start to call into question the conventional canon and its hierarchies.

Germaine Greer's chapter, for instance, brings into sharp relief the partial view that we have of artistic practice as it is traditionally retailed by the official histories. As far as the latter are concerned, Pierre Bourdieu poses no less fundamental a question in inviting us to rethink whether cultural fields are as autonomous as they are habitually described. Such questions have to be asked from within an understanding of how the period itself redefines what Baudelaire famously signals as 'correspondances'. We therefore felt that what was needed in the first instance was an authoritative introduction to the methods and substance of this comparative field, tested across the range of the standard canon, not least because no other such book so far exists.

While one of the most illuminating critical moves of the new art history has been to juxtapose paintings and contemporary discourse, the contributors to this book approach the relationship between the arts from within their own expertise as literary scholars. Literary perspectives themselves have been enriched by the awareness that texts can no longer be studied in isolation from other discourses. But to admit this is not merely to accept that other modes of cultural production should be taken into account, as the emphasis on film studies in our own age confirms. To do so is to be made increasingly aware that literary texts cannot be viewed independently of visual art; for not only is this part of a shared cultural context but it constitutes one of the informing conditions of verbal expression. Our book looks at the nineteenth century in France, which arguably provides in embryo all the varieties of images and discourses of the twentieth century. In its own right, however, the complex relation between the visual and the verbal in nineteenth-century France provides a privileged area for the study of relations which continue to preoccupy us today.

We need to elaborate the empirical context of such relationships. This means exploring contacts between writers and painters, personal affinities and interchanges; but these contacts have to be viewed within the social, technical and intellectual frames which, far from being a mere background, inform the artistic practice of painters and writers during the period in question. As Michael Moriarty's chapter demonstrates, no account of the relationship between literature and the visual arts is complete without reference to these coordinates. He looks at institutional frameworks such as the press and the Salon system in order to underline the fundamentally altered status of the nineteenth-century artist in relation to his public. Subsequent chapters look more closely at phenomena as diverse as book illustration, lithography and printing (Ségolène Le Men), technical advance in colour analysis (Bernard Howells), developments in photography (Eric Homberger) and portraiture (Michael Tilby). These pragmatic considerations are inseparable from a heightened consciousness of the visual.

What has been termed the 'democratization' of artistic production has far-reaching consequences. The period sees a massive increase in the

2

number of paintings available for viewing, not merely at the Salon but also in the private exhibitions to which painters have increasing recourse. There is a corresponding proliferation of texts about the visual arts, not just because of the number of newspapers which contract a series of review articles about the annual Salon, but also because for aspiring writers a journalistic apprenticeship becomes the norm (Gautier, Nerval, Baudelaire). From the point of view of the writer this can be largely explained by economic determinants; but he is perfectly aware of the newly public nature of reading as an activity. The café scenes of so many novels and paintings of the period testify to the position now occupied by the newspaper in the dissemination of ideas, opinions and information. Contemporary critics are themselves conscious of the threat posed to their authority by the relativization of values, the prioritization of originality and the innovations encouraged by post-Revolutionary individualism. One consequence is an urgent and continual reassertion of critical authority. The studies by Robert Lethbridge and James Kearns underline the way in which writers adopt a mediating role both defining their own aesthetic position and, more problematically, articulating the intentions of visual artists. In response to public incomprehension the critic assumes the role of translator, providing a language with which to discuss new visions and values; but a painter such as Manet, for example, dramatizes a dialectic of assimilation and resistance.

Comparisons between literature and the visual arts nevertheless need to be approached with caution. Too often there is a metaphorical slippage which tends to conflate different techniques in order to arrive at synonymity, rather than identify those differences which are the basis of any thoughtful process of comparison. Nineteenth-century artists were themselves, of course, explicitly engaging in various kinds of comparison. David Kelley looks at the transposition of common themes and motifs between such painters and poets as Delacroix, Gautier and Baudelaire. Roger Cardinal takes the case of a single artist, Victor Hugo, who attempts to create the visual equivalent of his own writing. In particular, Baudelaire's theory of 'correspondances' suggests that the senses are all interrelated, and that the mind and our perceptions are also infiltrated by these sensory relationships. Thus colour takes on the ability to express emotional and spiritual values, as foregrounded in the stanza of 'Les Phares' devoted to Delacroix. Rimbaud's poem 'Voyelles' goes a stage further in creating new correspondences. The very material presence of language is endowed with the power to evoke visual experience, and such potential substitutions allow him to explore a rich network of connotations both sensual and moral.

It seems to us instructive that towards the end of the century it is precisely those experiments with the visual properties of language which prefigure the twentieth century's rethinking of how to analyse sign systems. David Scott shows how Mallarmé's *Un coup de Dés* represents a symptomatic moment when the visual and expressive dynamics of language interacting with the medium of the white page start to generate meaning. In his reading of one of Rimbaud's *Illuminations* (the very title of which gestures towards the visual in its allusion to 'painted plates'), Roger Little reveals how this new poetic language is unsettling, since it inverts the conventional process of signification and sets up a process of visualization by sliding from signifier to signifier. Taken to its logical extremes, as Mary Ann Caws demonstrates, this frees us from familiar habits of reading and viewing so that a poem by Mallarmé or a painting by Seurat will overflow the limits of the text and the icon and aspire to the status of music.

The systems of interpretation proposed by nineteenth-century artists and writers are determined by very specific contexts and creative practices. Even the metaphors used by Baudelaire (Nature as a 'universal dictionary', for instance, or Delacroix as the 'poet' of painting) are potentially misleading. We can only begin to interpret them if we acknowledge Baudelaire's debt to Romantic theories of creativity, taken from Coleridge and Poe, which raise the writer's imagination to a divine level, and also the nineteenth-century status of the poet, still seen by major figures like Victor Hugo as Shelley's 'unacknowledged legislators of the world'; by contrast the painter has a marginal status, although it is one of the features of the nineteenth century that the novelist increasingly imposes his views on the public, while the painter loses much of the little authority he had left.

We cannot therefore merely assume that there is a given set of analogies which we can revamp through the twentieth-century social sciences. For a semiotician, who sees painting as above all a communicative language, it is tempting to apply the linguistic model, and arrive at tendentious analogies, where the phoneme, for example would parallel the single brush-stroke. Without wishing to reject such attempts to establish a comparative grammar of the different arts, we should bear in mind the deeper formative models of narrative and image-making which often lie disguised behind even overt attempts to cross frontiers between media. Novels have their own traditions of visual description which may not coincide with pictorial developments. Moreover, other kinds of writing such as poetry have inherent features which are different again. For example, the whole question of self-consciousness has to be seen rather differently in poetry, where the speaker constantly announces his presence and position, as opposed to sculpture, where the artist may signal the presence of his trace without necessarily symbolizing the act of speech, as Peter Collier argues in his chapter on Rodin and Valéry. Throughout this book we have taken care to note the specific differences in artistic expression that the different media elicit, not only the differences in visualization and consciousness just suggested, but also more fundamental divergences in the modes of expressing time and place, as Peter Collier shows in his chapter on Delacroix, Géricault, Byron and Baudelaire.

The implication of the viewer or reader within the construction of meanings has, of course, become one of the central concerns of twentieth-century literary and art criticism and theory. But even as we exploit modern theories, we should recognize on the one hand that they owe much to the kind of nineteenth-century experiments we have been discussing, and, on the other hand, that it would be wrong not to remain alert to other kinds of theoretical ambition developed during the nineteenth century. Not the least significant is the increasingly close relationship between the three arts – literature, painting and music – in the pursuit of a non-representational art, or rather, an art that could transcend the limitations of language and imagery.

We therefore have to remain alert not only to conceptual questions – how ideas are conveyed, whether visual symbols convey information in ways comparable to verbal argument – but also to the way in which material properties of the work are organized into stylistic qualities of rhythm, tonality, harmony. Processing an image or a text raises questions of the successive and the simultaneous, and the possibility of translating a sense of duration. There are problems of conveying time in an image as opposed to a text, and this is linked to the instantaneous perception of the image as opposed to the chronological processing of the text. Increasingly in the nineteenth century, Renaissance visual conventions of translation of successive moments into spatial sequences, or even a complete narrative of historical scenes, disappears in favour of the depiction of emblematic, pregnant moments, divorced from narrative evidence, which becomes the province of the novel or of photography.

But it is doubtless no bad thing if, even in the twentieth century, we are forced to acknowledge that there is not a generally agreed set of terms of reference or a stable critical platform from which we should approach the ways in which the nineteenth-century artists themselves understood and developed the comparative process. Indeed, it would be naive and unhelpful to suggest that there existed some neat series of comparisons based on a grammar of the visual arts or a series of fixed visual equivalents to textual practice. One of our aims in this book is to contribute to the ongoing debate as to what kinds of analytical tools and critical discourses it is most helpful to exploit in rethinking these key nineteenth-century relationships – not least because they lead into debates on twentieth-century culture which they can help illuminate.

At its simplest, we can start with an inescapable relationship between the arts, based on their mutual grounding in certain texts which provide a fund of prestigious narratives at the root of our Western culture (the Bible, classical mythology). Despite historical variants, there has long been a general consensus on which subjects are worthy of pictorial representation, since they are recognizable within a cultural community sharing knowledge of the same myths, legends, stories and values (to be found represented in church windows and altarpieces, for instance, or used as the basis of tragedy and lyric poetry). A cultural ideal finds its message reinforced by recourse to such universals. The nineteenth century is a period of exceptional flux and revolt in this respect. An emblematic topos like a shipwreck may still be operative in Victor Hugo (see Roger Cardinal's chapter), Géricault, Delacroix, Byron and Baudelaire (see Peter Collier), and in Mallarmé (see David Scott), but it has become an increasingly unstable and enigmatic motif, rather than an instantly recognizable symbol. All kinds of cultural symbolism, in fact, tended to change after the French Revolution. No symbolic grid, whether religious or not, was able to command a central or exclusive position. Two very obvious examples would be the demise of cruci-fixions and depictions of gods and goddesses – if not necessarily of pseudo-classical nymphs – and the rise of new cultural imagery, such as Orientalism or city scenes, since reason and history seem to show that culture is driven by action and events rather than by faith and symbol. One of the most striking features of nineteenth-century art is the crisis into which are thrown the normative reference points of the collective imagination – as Robert Lethbridge shows in the contemporary inter-pretation of accessories like the notorious cat in Manet's *Olympia*.

Indeed, the founding symbol, such as the shipwreck, readily located in Homer and Dante, starts to question its own significance, not only as a unitary symbol, but as the product itself of what has been called, in literature, 'intertextuality'. Throughout the history of painting and writ-ing their modes of representation have taken account of intertextual, and interfigural, relations with previous pictures and texts, and between the different media. And even in the nineteenth century a rebellious poet like Baudelaire will use a medieval topos (in 'Danse macabre', discussed by David Kelley), while painters are trained through the principle of copying casts of classical statues in the atelier and copying Old Masters in the Louvre. Germaine Greer shows how revolutionary it seemed for women artists to seek to copy the human form direct rather than imitate its idealized Greco-Roman artistic copy. As the century develops, the re-lation becomes more oblique, sometimes parodic – Ann Jefferson analyses Stendhal's conscious rejection of artistic description that tries to compose a second-hand artistic scene, and reveals his preference for a language that expresses the unstable emotions of the writer or viewer. Paddy O'Donovan notes how self-consciously the Goncourts attempt to recreate a visually artistic style of writing, rather than merely narrate the story of the artist. One might multiply examples, from Zola's composite portrait of the painter, Claude Lantier, in *L'Œuvre*, to Flaubert's interplay of the failed painter, Pellerin, and Impressionist narrative viewpoint, in *L'Education sentimentale*. There arises, in the nineteenth century, an extraordinary awareness of codes, while the models themselves have become less explicit. Baudelaire daringly mingles Molière's *Dom Juan* with Dante's *Inferno*, arguably in order to reject the moral implications of the symbolism of both authors, as Peter Collier shows, and at every stage the invocation of pictorial models becomes increasingly problematic: Mary Ann Caws looks at the way in which the imagery of Mallarmé becomes difficult to visualize, as it seems to ironize any pictorial recuperation and divert it towards rhythm and desire.

Thus Mallarmé's *Un coup de Dés* develops a trope that is partly visual, partly an asymbolic performance of the materiality of language, and thus an originally religious allegory of cannibalism in Dante is reactivated in paintings by Géricault or Delacroix and poetry by Byron in deliberately ironic reference to ways in which contemporary history denies the sort of moral truth that earlier texts symbolized. As the century proceeds, many of the literary and pictorial images that were based on narrative modes in general seem to recede in favour of different kinds of vision, whether those of everyday life, as T.J. Clark has argued in his *The Painting of Modern Life*, or the inner visions of the mind, as explored by Roger Little in his chapter on Rimbaud's *Illuminations*, or the depths of the subconscious made visible in the Symbolist texts and images scrutinized by Timothy Mathews. Even such great mythical figures as Don Juan and Orpheus undergo a transformation, as Peter Collier shows in his two chapters, arguing that their modern exploitation is dependent on an ironic and self-conscious interplay of intertextural and interfigural cross-referencing. In these mythical figures as well as in other archetypal figures – the nude as reviewed by the photographer (see Eric Homberger), the portrait as analysed by the scientifically inspired writer (see Michael Tilby) – there is a tendency both to move closer towards figures of everyday life, and yet simultaneously to call into question the act of creativity itself, as the artist's or writer's position is enacted in the choice and the working of such figures. The basic language of poetry, as well as of Symbolism and Impressionism, shifts during the century from being a language of symbolic representation towards becoming an act of exploration, plunging down into the very conditions of representation.

We should not forget that, in a more general sense, the distinction between the verbal and the visual is less clear-cut than generic categories suggest. Literary description of the external world is predicated on the assumption of an optical experience. And this is particularly true in the nineteenth century. If we associate much of the period with Realism, such an aesthetic can itself only be properly understood by invoking an intellectual climate dominated by Positivism. The latter is founded on the premise that scientifically verifiable *observation* is the only legitimate instrumentation for exploring reality. Realist writing implies an all-*seeing* point of view, making visible what is habitually out of sight. The novelist himself may remain, in Flaubert's phrase, 'visible nulle part'. We recognize, nevertheless, that the overview has been delegated to privileged observers in the shape of fictional characters whose function is to relay to us what they see, gifted as they often are with prodigious eyesight. It is not by chance that they are posted at windows and climb to topographic viewing-platforms. The panorama is not just a metaphor. For description which moves away from metaphysics and the vicissitudes of the inner life is optical in conception. Stendhal defines the novel as a roving mirror. Zola develops his 'Théorie des Ecrans' in 1866 around the ideal of transparency. Whether or not it can be realized is almost beside the point. The counter-imperatives of the relative, the partial and the unreliable do not of themselves problematize the basic principle of representation: that what is described simultaneously highlights the place from which things are seen.

Phenomenological truisms apart, it can also be argued, as Roland Barthes does in *S/Z*, that what he calls 'le modèle de la peinture' is the essential *structuring* paradigm of all descriptive writing. Even the most totalizing of mimetic projects is subject to a segmentation rectilinear in design. The focus is a frame; the narrative is organized as a series of tableaux; the overarching vision of Balzacian dimensions makes of individual texts the analogous subdivisions of the larger picture. Barthes considers this so pervasive a relational move that he concludes that the hierarchy between verbal and pictorial descriptive codes is a false one.

On the other hand, the limits of such a potential equivalence can be gauged by thinking about the technique of *ekphrasis*. The literary description of a real or imaginary work of art seems the most concrete of analogies, not only through its overt transcription of a visual achievement but also because of its detachable (*ek-*) status. In nineteenth-century texts, *ekphrasis* may have a number of different functions, ranging from the reinforcement of referential illusion to the mirroring perspectives afforded by the *mise-en-abyme* of the work which contains it. Zola's *L'Œuvre* is exemplary in many of these respects, filled as it is with descriptions of paintings. But it is also true that unless such descriptions refer us to real images with which we are already familiar, the reader's visualization of fictional pictures remains approximate at best and usually so incomplete as to be indistinguishable from countless others. And this is equally the case in art criticism prior to the availability of complementary reproductions. *Ekphrasis* even as

8

practised by Diderot in his *Salons* is testimony to his own verbal pleasure in responding to the pictorial. When literary figures undertake such
criticism on a more systematic scale, as they do in the nineteenth
century, the description of a painting is often less a verbal equivalent of
it than a self-sufficient and virtuoso linguistic performance.

It is to be reminded that the notion of *ut pictura poesis* is an unstable
alignment of the verbal and the visual. Modern attention to that relationship necessarily takes its departure from the body of Renaissance
and Enlightenment theory and practice which was built up around
casual or fragmentary utterances in classical times by Simonides, Horace
and others; and it is usual to cite Lessing as the prime mover against
those traditions. The reshaping, questioning and rejection of *ut pictura
poesis* does not alter the fact that in advocating that painting should
apsire to the condition of poetry, such an analogy between the arts presupposes both a challenge to, and the acknowledged superiority of, the
literary. Such a rivalry is implicit in much of the relationship between
literature and the visual arts in the nineteenth century. And alongside the
Romantic invocation of 'la fraternité des arts' and Baudelaire's oft-
quoted dictum that the best commentary on a painting would be a
sonnet, we need to remember that when Cézanne read *L'Œuvre* he
broke off a forty-year friendship with Zola and that Degas was convinced that the underlying motive for Zola's novel was the writer's need
to reassert an artistic hierarchy in which painting occupied a secondary
position.

That secondary position is most obviously exemplified by the process
of illustration. Yet even in its most subservient form, illustration of the
printed text, as Ségolène Le Men argues, it starts to develop a new
power. New techniques of lithography and printing allow the printing of
luxury illustrated editions of texts to claim an artistic status which was a
reaction to the mass entertainment industry that popular fiction was
tending to become. The text was able to become once more a visually
attractive, almost a physically pleasurable, object. The illustration also
allowed the artist to appropriate the visualization, perhaps to some extent the meaning, of the text. Le Men shows how in some cases the
illustrator became the prime mover, spurring publishers into commis-
sioning texts as a support for the images which the public desired. For
publishing became a major commercial activity in the nineteenth
century. Readers of illustrated reviews were encouraged through illustrations to become readers – if only of newspapers and reviews and
serialized novels. The illustration seems to have promised to transcend
the divide between high and low culture of previous centuries.

And yet despite or because of this, the process of illustration was felt
by some writers to be a dangerous limitation of the private imagination.
Flaubert was overtly hostile, Stendhal, as we have seen, tried to render it

impossible. Increasingly, the novelist, whether Huysmans or Zola, Stendhal or Flaubert, tried to provide his own apparatus for visualization, inviting each reader to create a private and unrepeatable inner vision, through a largely Impressionist style of writing. And in the case of poets such as Rimbaud and Mallarmé, this inner vision, intermingling traces of all kinds of inchoate impressions and symbols, became the prime goal of the poet.

More typical still of the interaction between the arts in the nineteenth century, perhaps even its major cultural contribution, was the principle of 'transposition'. Transposing is a metaphor taken from music, and its premise seems to be that in the first instance it is not possible or desirable to illustrate a text or comment on a picture, but that the comparative activity should be more of a recreation of one art using the specific procedures of the other than an analytic or critical response. Thus transposition is deliberately neither a description nor merely a repetition; it is a creative reworking, a deliberate *mis*reading, which emphasizes difference rather than similarity. It refers back to the artistic specificity of the original (Baudelaire's and Delacroix's Tassos are poetic in a different way in each different medium) as David Kelley argues – there are different resources for expressing mental and emotional experience in the different media. The original starting-point is often left behind – neither Rodin's nor Valéry's Orpheus, according to Peter Collier, has much to do with retrieving a beloved from the underworld, as both artists try to expand the possibilities inherent in their media: introducing self-consciousness into sculpture or material texture into poetry. Indeed, one of the essential features of the nineteenth-century transposition is that it announces and explores its own procedures, rather than simply reworking similar subjects. The appropriation of the subject may be quite self-conscious, as in Zola's thematic expansion of Renoir's *Balançoire* in *Une Page d'amour*, or disguised, as in many of Gautier's poems where the effort to generate pictorial or sculptural effects intentionally makes it seem that there is no original. At the most elementary level, the nineteenth-century transposition engages with certain new common subjects (the voyeuristic representation of prostitution for instance, explored more voluptuously in Manet's *Nana* than in Zola's ironic novel; the anecdotal riverside entertainments of Zola's lower middle classes in *Au Bonheur des dames* or *Thérèse Raquin* inspire a whole world of pleasure in Renoir; the café transforming the social subject matter of painting with its gaslight and its socialization of the street as well as the night, whereas in *L'Assommoir* it is taken as a metaphor for the degradation of an entire civilization).

In fact, the urge to transpose between the arts runs so deep in the nineteenth century that it invades critical discourse itself – the critical text often provides a vital service of mediation between the image and the poem. During the nineteenth century, as David Scott and James Kearns show, the function of art criticism slips from that of a prose description of the visual to being a transposition filtered through the emotions of the critic who invites his reader to become a surrogate artist, recreating the work in alternative terms. Baudelaire's claim that the most successful criticism of a painting might be a sonnet has to be seen in this light. Certain poems by Gautier or Baudelaire, as David Scott and David Kelley show, seem to attempt such a rewriting. But it could also be argued that Baudelaire was trying to place himself in a position where he could reconcile the viewpoint of the writer of the sonnet with that of the reader. For there is potentially something suspiciously hermetic and arrogant about suggesting that we need to be artists ourselves in order to understand art. The answer seems to be that, since few Salon-goers or newspaper readers wrote sonnets, the critic would have to create on their behalf an imaginary sonnet, conjured through his pen, mimicking the recreative experience while avoiding the imposition of passivity on the reader, who might object to reading a prefabricated sonnet.

The structure of this book accommodates this gradual movement away from representation of an unproblematic kind. In other words, in the second half of the century we are no longer offered the finished work for contemplation. What Michael Fried, in his *Courbet's Realism*, calls 'theatricality' foregrounds the very conditions of the process of artistic production, implicating the reader or viewer in this process. Corresponding to this is the emphasis on the subjective. And, what is more, this communication of inner feelings is given expression without having to pass through a secondary symbolic language of representation.

With the wisdom of hindsight we can see how this movement is itself related to the larger cultural context in which the artist operates. Intellectual influences, on the one hand, include that of Taine, notably his *Théorie de l'intelligence* (1870), and Hegel (through Vera's translations), as well as the developments of contemporary psychopathology and research on aphasia. From Baudelaire to Valéry, it can be argued, the problem of how to conceive the relationship between language and optical experience is so uneasily resolved that it was perhaps inevitable that both poets and painters should use, however clumsily, the diction of the ontology and the epistemology of perception. On the other hand, and at the same time, social and technological change invalidates the writer's or painter's claim to be the privileged recorder of the real. Walter Benjamin has analysed Baudelaire's paradoxical response to the irruption of photography, emphasizing its tendency to push Baudelaire into seeking out fragments of reality in his *Petits poèmes en prose*. As the century progresses we find that the attempt to provide photographic records of the real, as exemplified by Courbet or Zola, yields to a retreat from this totalizing temptation. Even Balzac, let alone Flaubert, had perhaps never

11

quite succumbed to the extreme temptation to pack their novels with detail in order to give the impression of a total reality available to the reader's gaze, but had rather sought what Barthes has called 'l'effet de réel', the inclusion of apparently unmotivated detail giving the impression of an overflow of brute unmediated reality, threatening the artistic mediation of the text. But there is a deeper current of withdrawal from the confident positing of external reality beyond the text altogether that Realism implied.

Paradoxically, all the scientific advances that led the nineteenth-century artist into attempts at a fuller picturing of reality led him also inwards to study his process of observation too. From the promethean attempt to survey the whole of the real social world in Balzac we move to the attempt to capture fleeting impressions of the modern soul observing itself in Baudelaire, or in Laforgue's *Derniers vers*. From the sweeping purview of the universal observer, as it were guaranteed by inhabiting a shared social space of agreed moral values and communicable signifiying systems (Christianity, monarchy, artistocracy, the Academy, Beauty, for instance) at the end of the eighteenth century, we arrive at the end of the nineteenth inside the mind observing the flickering formations of its inner visions – Monet's water lilies, Mallarmé's snatches of visualized images in *Un coup de Dés*, floating away from the wreckage of descriptive sense.

PJC
RDL

# PART I

## *SOCIAL CONTRACTS*

# Structures of cultural production in nineteenth-century France

## Michael Moriarty

The modernist axioms that the value of an artistic or literary production is not contingent on the intrinsic interest of the object, if any, represented, and that aesthetic responses and judgements are not contingent on ethical or political ones, presuppose the autonomy of an aesthetic sphere. In the contemporary context, Pierre Bourdieu has argued that this autonomy is constituted in social practice, through the socially differentiated formation of tastes.[1] Historically, the emergence of the autonomous sphere as an apparent given of experience can be seen as dependent on social and cultural mutations taking place roughly speaking between 1830 and the end of the century.[2] Their net effect is that the variety of artistic and literary production no longer subserves the varied interests of a single elite public, but the specifically identified and targeted interests of different groups within what is constituted as a mass public. Producer and consumer are no longer connected through diverse institutions of civil society, but by the workings of an impersonal market. (The very obviousness of the terms in which we think of these developments – 'art', 'literature', 'the author' – is itself a product of this history.)[3] In what follows, I shall begin by treating artistic and literary production separately, in order to show what is specific to each field, the better to exhibit the eventual parallels in their evolution.

Artistic production in the ancien régime had been dominated by the Académie Royale de Peinture et de Sculpture, founded in 1648. The Académie artist had a place in a hierarchy of members, his paintings in a hierarchy of genres: history painting at the top, then portraits, then landscape, then genre. He was trained to observe a body of artistic canons, and obliged to acquire a scholarly familiarity with ancient history and myth: which lifted him above his former level as a craftsman, a mercenary. He was thus equipped to glorify the monarchy partly by the very excellence of his art, but also by the ideological content his training enabled him to convey.[4] There was thus, in theory, a satisfying symmetry between the dominant production relations of art and the means of production, the Académie producing the artists and the monarchy providing the commissions. Indeed the Academician might paint for anyone other than the King only by special dispensation. This restriction was relaxed by the end of the seventeenth century, as a private commercial market in painting grew alongside the official structure of royal commissions; but the Académie's preeminence in the art world survived this development, all through the eighteenth century. Only Academicians might exhibit at the great biennial Salons, so that the Académie structure both regulated the production of art and channelled its consumption. Through the Salons, however, a public sphere of artistic discourse was formed: unofficial Salon reports, which grew in number from the mid-eighteenth century, tinged art criticism with coded political implications, impugning the social order through its products; and artists like David reacted to these responses.[5] But this in itself moved art and the response to art beyond its original elite public, represented in the concrete requirements of individual patrons, and brought it face to face with a broader public, the critic serving as a vital shaper and mediator of the public's response.[6] In this way, the Salon prefigured future developments.

During and after the Revolutionary period, the Académie and the Salons were reorganized several times, usually in response to changes in political régime.[7] But their continued dominance became increasingly problematic for artists. Private exhibitions, charging for admission, of the work of a single artist or a group, were rare in the first part of the nineteenth century, despite experiments by David between 1799 and 1804. The custom grew, however, because access to the Salon was precarious, normally depending on satisfying a panel of selectors.[8] In a completely open Salon, like that of 1793, with 1,462 exhibits, or 1848, with 5,362, it was harder for an individual work to catch the eye.[9] But when selection prevailed, the artist was subject to the jury's preference or caprice. As in 1843 or 1846, artists of established reputation, such as Théodore Rousseau and Corot, could be turned down, sometimes for political reasons, sometimes on account of aesthetic prejudice.[10] The critic Delécluze complained that the Salon functioned as a perpetual qualifying examination. In a petition to Louis-Philippe in 1847, many artists stressed the harmful influence of exclusion on a career: we hear of buyers of pictures which turned out to be rejected by the jury actually insisting on a refund.[11]

The decline of the Académie-Salon system, from the middle of the nineteenth century, was not principally due to an artists' revolt against hidebound traditional doctrine: as Albert Boime has shown, the Académie contributed greatly, if perhaps inadvertently, to the movements often seen as most opposed to it.[12] It is, however, true that certain of the

Académie's presuppositions about the status and nature of art, and the formation of the artist, came under pressure from technological change. Changes, first of all, in painting materials, which bypassed the need for long training in their preparation, and thus blurred the distinction between professional and amateur. Time-consuming preparation of canvases and paints disappeared: the tin paint tube also made paints easier to transport, thus facilitating the growth of *plein air* painting, vital to the development of the Impressionist aesthetic; rail transport made accessible a wider variety of outdoor sites.[13] New processes of producing images emerged: of the first in date, lithography, T.J. Clark has written that 'lithography, even more than the photograph, was the first step in industrializing the arts, the beginning of the age of mechanical reproduction'.[14] Stendhal complained that painters were beginning to paint with an eye to lithographic reproduction from the start.[15] The lithograph certainly contributed to the emergence of freer, more spontaneous draughtmanship, the contrary of the painstaking methods of the Académie training.[16] It met publishers' needs for a cheaper form of reproduction to meet the demands of an expanding market: it was cheap enough for mass-circulation newspapers. And it generated new kinds of artistic specialist: the travelling sketchers who satisfied the 1850s vogue for picturesque views in lithographic form.[17]

But photography was the decisive newcomer. In 1849 100,000 daguerreotype portraits were supposedly produced in Paris alone. Such portraits were not cheap at first, ranging from fifteen to a hundred francs; but cheaper production techniques brought the price down to within the range of a worker by the 1860s. Like lithography, the photograph affected the technique of painting itself. Painters could use photographs instead of working from sketches or from life.[18] And the experience of the photograph actually shaped the kinds of images painters produced; paintings that aimed at photographic accuracy are perhaps a less interesting example of this than those that adopted new compositional techniques like the off-centre arrangements and amputated images of Impressionism.[19] The immediacy and modernity of the photograph were values that could be realized in the painter's image of the city.[20]

But probably more important in the decline of the Académie-Salon system was the fact that it no longer functioned well as a link between artist and purchaser. The State continued to act as a patron. Napoleon I and Louis-Philippe attached great importance to the ideological role of art: Napoleon III commissioned scenes of French victories for prominent display in the Salon.[21] But the symbiotic relationship between State and Académie no longer functioned so well. A distinction emerged between 'official' art, promoted by the State, and 'academic' art, conforming to the Académie's preferences.[22] The Second Empire's commissions showed indifference to the promotion of the premier Académie genre, history painting in the traditional sense.[23] As a source of income for the artist, State patronage came under pressure from an expanding private sector. The fate of art under the Second Republic was significant of the future. Hopes that the State would sponsor an artistic revival that would both reward excellence and promote political and social enlightenment were frustrated. The government's Bureau des Beaux-Arts continued to exercise State patronage in a piecemeal and dictatorial fashion. It bailed out individual artists whose livelihood had been jeopardized by the collapse of the art market in the aftermath of 1848, but there was no re-organization of public artistic patronage, and artists' pleas for greater control of their own affairs were ignored.[24]

Above all, by the mid-nineteenth century, the Académie-Salon system was no longer satisfactorily mediating between the painter and a public that had expanded down the social hierarchy, and that was demanding pictures for domestic consumption.[25] The individual painter could hardly trust to the Salon as a reliable stimulus to future commissions: even if his work were accepted, it was competing with that of the other 3,000 painters operating in Paris at the time. The system focused on individual pictures, and could not take account of the painter's need for a regular middle-class income, suitable to his probable background and expectations as a professional man.[26]

To secure a position in the market, some genre painters specialized in the production of particular types of scene, like Rosa Bonheur and Troyon with their paintings of animals.[27] For Bonheur this adjustment to a market was a particular economic necessity, given a background and lifestyle that denied her inherited income or financial security in marriage (her father was a poor drawing-master).[28] But the crucial change in the relation between individual artists and specific fractions of the potential buying public was the gradual displacement of the Académie-Salon system by what Harrison and Cynthia White have called the dealer-critic system.[29]

When painting was organized by guilds, a painter had been his own dealer. Specialist dealers appeared in the late seventeenth century, and gradually came to play an autonomous and essential role in the French art market; by the late eighteenth century they were the big buyers at sales of important collections.[30] By the 1860s there were sometimes up to three art auctions a day in Paris.[31] Now, from the mid-nineteenth century, the influence of the dealers became paramount.

For the young painter the favour of a dealer could ensure recognition and a livelihood. Some dealers would support a painter with a monthly quasi-salary in return for promised works. To buy up the whole of a producer's output, as Durand-Ruel did that of several Barbizon painters, was part and parcel of a logic of speculation, from which the new system offered dealers the opportunity to profit. Unlike the Académie system, the dealer-critic system focused on artists not paintings: the isolated picture was of little use to a dealer, for its price was too variable and unpredictable, whereas the name of an artist could represent a reliable market value. But at the same time this had advantages for the artist too. Not being tied to the three-week Salon season, or to the requirements of State commissions, and able to supply anyone of sufficient wealth to purchase pictures, the dealer-critic system could command a bigger market than the Academic-governmental structure, and equally importantly it could better incorporate the requirements of the artist's career.

To promote and channel demand was part of the function of the critic, integral to the new system. The disappearance of neoclassical orthodoxy left room for a wide variety of critical standpoints, which could accommodate the variety of contemporary artistic production. Baudelaire appreciated this from the outset of his critical career, assigning the critic the role of mediator between the bourgeois public and the artistic expression of a temperament.[32] Within the logic of this twofold relationship, the critical rhetoric of the unrecognized genius came into play, to sublimate the speculative logic. To say all this is to deny neither the quality of the paintings caught up in this process nor the artistic enthusiasm and discernment of the major dealers such as Durand-Ruel. It is to point out, however, that the aesthetic judgement in this context is, whether consciously or not, a judgement also of the commercial viability in the short or long term of the artistic product.[33] Theodore Zeldin suggests that collectors were often driven by genuine passion rather than economic motivations;[34] yet they could not withdraw the pictures from the economic circuit: their passions, like those of Balzac's sublimely disinterested Cousin Pons, made money for others, if not for themselves.

In the dealer-critic system, the individual painter is the object of evaluation, isolated from any intrinsic relationship to a master or pupils (as in the guild system) or to a 'school' within which, in the Académie system, he derives his identity in relation to a set of doctrines and models.[35] Any grouping of painters henceforth derives its identity as such from a common relationship to a particular market. The artist's assumption of his status as an intrinsically independent producer was stigmatized by Baudelaire: 'L'état actuel de la peinture est le résultat d'une liberté anarchique qui glorifie l'individu, quelque faible qu'il soit, au détriment des associations, c'est-à-dire, des écoles.'[36] This passage throws further light on Baudelaire's understanding of the function of the critic: it is to separate out from the mass of individual producers the artist of authentic conviction and temperament.[37] This understanding of criticism responds exactly to the needs of artist and public as they are constituted by the emergent entrepreneurial system of artistic production.

The new system provided better for the artist's needs, and yet, by handing over economic responsibility to the dealer, preserved the imaginary status of painting as a pure, essentially non-commercial, activity.[38] But it could involve a new kind of personal dependence of the artist on the dealer. The Académie system at its best gave the artist a public identity, independent of any individual client. As the Whites observe, the Impressionists' dealer Durand-Ruel had on the contrary recreated in effect the role of the Renaissance princely patron; the painters' letters to him frequently indicate the reality of this dependence and undermine their expressions of hostility to the bourgeoisie.[39]

The fortunes of the Impressionists were bound up with the development of this system, and the decay of the Académie structure.[40] The events of 1863 reinforced their alienation from the Salon system. That year, about 3,000 artists submitted about 5,000 works. Sixty per cent, an unprecedented proportion, were rejected. Napoleon III personally intervened to set up a secondary exhibition, known as the Salon des Refusés, where artists could, if they chose, display their rejected offerings. But public ridicule merely confirmed the judgement of the jury.[41] Despite the bitter attacks on *Le Déjeuner sur l'herbe*, which at least raised his standing with young painters outside the Académie, Manet, unlike his colleagues, continued to attach importance to the Salons.[42] In 1873, he obtained his first great Salon success since 1861, with *Le Bon Bock*. Monet, Sisley and Pissarro had submitted nothing, and two submissions of Renoir's had been rejected. Another, successful, Salon des Refusés was held, where the Renoir pictures were favourably received, but it must have seemed perverse to continue to challenge the Académie structure head on: *Le Bon Bock* had arguably owed its success to its perceived affinities with Dutch Old Master paintings, a kind of compromise with the academic taste. As much as the rejection of Renoir, Manet's success in 1873, Rewald suggests, seemed to confirm that the best policy for the Impressionists in future was to ignore the Académie-Salon structure. Instead, in the following year, they held a group exhibition, where they received their baptism from a hostile reviewer.[43] Such shows, even by the negative reactions they aroused, helped to endow the group with a specific, marketable identity which dealers could turn to good effect.

From this perspective, the history of art in nineteenth-century France is thus the displacement of a hitherto dominant quasi-State institution from the centre of artistic production, which becomes regulated by a purer market structure, where the twofold mediation between painter and buyer is exercised by the dealer, operating on commercial principles, and the critic, who is inserted in the capitalist world of newspapers and periodicals. In the literary world, the point of departure is different, but the end result much the same.

Whatever its founders and patrons may have hoped, the Académie

Française had never enjoyed the same influence on literary production as the Académie Royale de Peinture et de Sculpture exerted on art. The claims of literature to the status of pure, non-mercenary activity were grounded somewhat differently. Much literary production in the Grand Siècle took place outside a market structure: it was practised as an amateur activity or remunerated non-commercially by royal or aristocratic patrons. The decline of such patronage in the eighteenth century and after rendered the writer more directly dependent on the market.

But although between the end of the ancien régime and the end of the Bourbon monarchy the overall trend in book production was upwards, the publishing industry was restricted by a combination of government controls and economic factors. Fearful of the spread of seditious ideas, both the First Empire and the Restoration restricted access to the trade by· requiring booksellers and printers to obtain a certificate (*brevet*) vouching for their political reliability, and sought to limit the number of printers. The industry was undercapitalized, financing a great part of its operations by credit (through *billets à terme*); it was thus particularly vulnerable to financial crises, and one such in the late 1820s caused a spate of bankruptcies, even among major figures in the trade. Its access remained restricted to a narrow market. A novel in the standard format (two 8vo volumes or three to five 12mo ones) would cost fifteen francs: more than a third of a worker's monthly pay. Only the middle bourgeoisie and upwards could afford such prices. The *cabinets de lecture* that made books available to some that could not afford them (but not to workers) stimulated but also limited the demand for texts.[44]

In this context, booksellers typically steered with caution. Low print runs, commonly 1,000 copies, excluded high profits on individual titles, but minimized risks. Reeditions of the classics were more popular than new works, as the bestseller figures show.[45] But there are two social implications of all this that deserve attention. In such a climate, the author was unlikely to grow rich from publication, but was therefore, paradoxically, less dependent on the bookseller, who in the first half of the century usually came from a lower social class.[46] Then again, print runs being so generally low, the distinction between 'mass' and minority writing, on which the modern distinction between 'non-literature' and 'literature' depends, had little scope to emerge: some of the most popular authors (Scott, Hugo) were among the most prestigious.[47] Both these situations were overturned by developments in the middle of the century: the combination of an expanded potential book-buying public and technological innovation, the latter making it possible to capitalize on the former.

The nineteenth century saw a massive expansion of literacy over the levels of the ancien régime.[48] It is useful to think in terms of literacies, a variety of relationships to printed material, rather than a supposedly homogeneous literacy;[49] hence of the potential not just for expanding the existing reading market, with its shared norms and interests, but for addressing new markets. Balzac would have agreed; he saw the potential provincial market as the key to his proposed reform of the book trade. The very success of the *cabinets de lecture* suggested that there was a massive gap between the reading and the buying public that could be profitably bridged: Emile de Girardin estimated that a novel sold in 1,000 copies was read by 40,000 people, who could and should be induced to become buyers themselves.[50] Secondly, it became technically possible to boost print-runs, while diminishing the unit cost of the book, owing to a combination of cheaper paper (produced mechanically in continuous rolls), faster presses (powered by steam, and integrating the various phases of the printing process into a single mechanism) and more economical methods of producing the text (the stereotype).[51] Publishers eventually responded to this double conjuncture: in 1838 Gervais Charpentier started a series of cheap editions of French and foreign classics. These were followed by the *romans à quatre sous*, illustrated, and produced in print-runs of 10,000 or so, through which a public of artisans and petty bourgeois could encounter the novels of Balzac, Hugo and Sand.[52]

The change was not just that established authors like these could be brought before a wider market. Since the print-run could now be calibrated to the demand of a specific market, new work had to be classified as suitable for minority or mass production. The minority/mass distinction was thus constructed in publishers' practice: and it tended to coincide with, and to reinforce, a symbolic hierarchy of genres, the most prestigious forms (such as poetry) being identified with the least popular. From around 1830 to the end of the century, the industrialization of book production and the fragmentation of the reading market go hand in hand.[53]

But the relationship between authors and publishers was modified partly as a result of this. Instead of negotiating a lump sum payment for the right to exploit an individual work over a definite period, authors might hand over their complete work, past and/or future, in return for the security of a fixed income, as did Zola.[54] As with the purchase by a dealer of a painter's whole output, the rationale was that each individual work is more readily identified and marketed in relation to others by the same producer. When both parties agree a rate of payment proportional to the number of copies sold, such an agreement covering future production as well, the transition from a more artisanal mode of production working on narrow but reliable profit margins to a more speculative industrial mode in which both author and publisher are implicated has been fully made. But the author is now more dependent on the publisher's capacities. In this age of individualism, artistic and literary production is a quintessentially collaborative enterprise: never more so than in the production by teams of writers (Dumas père had sixty-nine known assistants) of never-ending stories, in which, as Christophe Charle asserts, the very notions of author and work seem to dissolve.[55]

Literary production cannot be separated from the growth of the newspaper industry. Under the ancien régime, this latter was held back by censorship, restraints on competition through exclusive *privilèges*, and technical difficulties. But when censorship was lifted, temporarily, by the Revolution, newspapers become important political tools. Press freedom was severely restricted under the Empire, but enshrined in the Charte of 1814, though with precensorship by royal officials. Under the Restoration the press was a vital instrument of bourgeois ideological hegemony, opposition papers accounting for three-quarters of total circulation. Periodic attempts by the monarchy to counter this by censorship, alternating with periods of relaxation, could not prevent the Press from ultimately playing a significant role in its downfall.[56]

Under the July Monarchy, a major and largely successful attempt to bring newspapers to a wider public was made by Emile de Girardin and his rival Armand Dutacq.[57] In 1836 they founded the dailies *La Presse* and *Le Siècle* respectively, halving the usual subscription of eighty francs to forty, the difference being paid for by advertisements. Girardin, though not so much Dutacq, shifted his paper's focus away from politics – and literary and artistic culture were among the fields that profited (so was crime reporting). He recruited major literary figures like Hugo, Balzac, Dumas, Gautier (his art and theatre critic), thus wedding literature and art to the fortunes of capitalist enterprise. (As for crime, there were specialist publications also to cover that, such as the *Gazette des tribunaux*, which provided sources for the narratives of both *Le Rouge et le Noir* and, less directly, *Madame Bovary*.)[58] But Girardin tied literature to journalism in another way, by creating the newspaper serial or *roman-feuilleton*.[59] This, for a time, multiplied the economic opportunities for the novelist. In June 1842 the *Journal des débats* published the first episode of Sue's *Les Mystères de Paris*, which ran until October 1843. Sue was paid 26,500 francs for this: more than six times what, a few years before, Girardin had estimated a fashionable novelist could make from a single work. The new editor of *Le Constitutionnel*, Véron, bought the rights to Sue's follow-up, *Le Juif errant*, for 100,000 francs, boosting his falling circulation from 3,720 to 24,000. Not only did the *roman-feuilleton* afford the writer a massively expanded public (and until Second Empire restrictions a platform for ideological intervention); writing for newspapers could become, as in Zola's case, an integral element of literary production, publication in book form following swiftly on the appearance of the serial.[60]

Inasmuch as journalism both increased writers' financial resources and shaped the work they produced, it appears as an intrinsic element of literary production, part of the general process of the subjection of culture to capitalist imperatives.

It is worth considering the impact of this process on the gender aspect of recruitment to the cultural professions. Women could take advantage of the proliferation of art schools outside the Académie structure (by 1872 there were twenty art schools for women in Paris) and from changes in technology and taste that rendered long professional training (in the art and history of antiquity, the production of finish according to Académie precepts, and the preparation of materials) superfluous.[61] Serious painting could now be combined, not without tension, with a conventional female lifestyle.

No similar emancipation took place in literature, where a particular female lifestyle, that of the salon, had since the ancien régime directly or indirectly involved women in literary production. Women were still hampered as writers by the educational obstacles to their accumulation of cultural capital. In both fields, the scope of female practitioners was restricted by gender-ideological constraints on their adopting certain dispositions and practices seen as integral to the artist's lifestyle. As feminist art historians have noted, the Baudélairean model of the painter of modern life, who strolls through the city absorbing himself in the ebb and flow of the crowd, which applies importantly to the writer as well, is a masculine one: to leave home alone, to stroll by herself where her fancy took her, was simply unthinkable for the middle-class woman. It was towards the domestic space that women Impressionists like Berthe Morisot and Mary Cassatt principally turned their attention; but this, as Griselda Pollock argues, should be understood not as the reflection of an essential 'femininity', either of the artist or of the space, but as '[tracing] the construction of femininity across the stages of women's life'.[62] Their pictures might be seen as exploring the paradox whereby in order to depict the women's domestic space the woman artist has to detach herself from her own place within it. Similarly, the woman writer could not adopt certain avant-garde literary identities – that of the *poète maudit* or the Naturalist observer of reality's seamiest side – and was thus debarred from the prestige accruing to such innovations.

These social and economic aspects of literary and artistic production I have mentioned are not simply part of a 'background' external to the works themselves. Firstly, they developed in ways that changed the terms of the contemporary understanding and valuation of the work of art or literature, and ultimately literary and artistic practice itself. As Ann Jefferson shows, technological development shaped the language of representation: writing or painting could be justified or condemned through comparison with technological processes.[63] Sand's likening of the novel to a machine that produces a transfer (*décalque*) of reality is an affirmation of the artist's freedom: if the image is unpalatable, she is not to blame.[64]

Conversely, the photograph can provide the model of bad representation. Baudelaire's criticism of photography inspired Benjamin's famous notion that the age of mechanical reproduction brings about the decline of the aura of associations that cluster round an object, because its literality leaves no work for the imagination.[65] For Baudelaire, in the *Salon de 1859*, photography fulfilled the wishes of those who believed that art was no more than the exact reproduction of nature, ignoring its spiritual imaginative dimension. There was an ideological edge to the outburst, too: the suspicion that photography was being seized on by democrats as a means of spreading the taste for history and painting among the people, and that its influence on art could only take the form of an encroachment of the folly of the multitude on the domain of the impalpable and the imaginary.[66]

Secondly, the pressures exerted by the social structures of cultural production are inscribed on the text or image by the formal and discursive procedures by which it establishes a specific relationship with its public or publics.

The classicism of the ancien régime was essentially a body of doctrines and values serving to gear artistic practice to the requirements of a public existing inside or close to the Court. More important almost than the specific content of these norms was the presumption of their general acceptance. The social transformations of France alluded to here radically jeopardized the link between artistic or literary production and an elite clientele, generating a mass, though a socially divided, public for texts and images. In so doing, they destroyed the notion of an artistic or literary orthodoxy, manifested in a particular public, against which all works could be measured. The official catalogue of the Salon of 1793 had already stated that in future 'there will no longer be style or academic manner, but in their place the true and the natural in a thousand forms, in a thousand different characters, multiplied to the infinite from an inexhaustible source'.[67] This was a utopian prophecy of developments that individual artists would in fact find more problematic. Lacking a socially agreed or imposed code to which to refer, they had to negotiate their relations with their public afresh, almost in every work.

In so doing, they inevitably came to grips with the logic of speculation, and its concomitant requirement of perpetual innovation. In art Old Masters changed too slowly in value, and were too expensive, whereas innovative unfamiliar painting, unlikely to sell well at first for this very reason, could be acquired cheaply by the dealer as an investment for the future.[68] Artistic innovation responded to the needs of an entrepreneurial bourgeoisie whose social and academic dominance emancipated them from the need felt by their predecessors to equip themselves with traditional symbols of social and cultural prestige: they thus contributed to the proliferation of new styles alongside those academically approved.[69] For his part, the publisher tended to secure his own position in the more dynamic market by assembling a stable of authors, linked by some readily identifiable tendency that would secure the attention of a specific public. Hence the intimate association between particular publishers and particular literary schools. Again, the parallel with artistic production is evident. The budding author is thus induced to situate his work in some definite relation to the market and to the appropriate publisher, whether he seeks to attain a mass market or a happy few.[70] Without these developments it is impossible to grasp the imperatives of modernist innovation, quite alien to the art of earlier periods.

The Académie artist and the writer of the Grand Siècle precisely wanted their relationship with Raphael or Virgil to be visible, most of all when they aspired to improve on their predecessors. The founding gestures of modernist art – the decisive break with immediate predecessors, identified as caught up in degraded mass patterns of consumption, and the suspension of reference to the content and values of daily experience, precisely because that experience is identified as a mass form of perception – alienate the artist from the existing market. Yet such innovation is also the path to recognition by the market that has actually engendered the perception of people as masses.

Benjamin encourages us to ask not 'What is the *attitude* of a work to the relations of production of its time?' but 'What is its *position* in them?'; and he suggests that the work is positioned by its technique, which aligns it with or against the existing bourgeois relations of production.[71] In this context, the point is not just that *La Cousine Bette*, first published in *feuilleton* form, turns that form to aesthetic effect (the short chapters and the need to keep all the characters in the reader's memory contribute to dramatic shifts of focus between groups, powerful montage-effects from the juxtaposition of remote contexts, the maintenance of a complex plot, whose intricacy both fosters a sense of mystery and enforces the theme of society as a machine of which the workings are only partially visible to participants). It is also that, as Christopher Prendergast argues, *La Cousine Bette* adopts the antithetical moral structure of the popular melodrama, as if for a mass *roman-feuilleton* readership; and then proceeds to dissolve it into 'a purely amoral conflict of different interests and passions'.[72] The work thus summons from amongst the general readership of the *roman-feuilleton* a reader capable of questioning his or her expectations, and in so doing distinguishes itself from the mass literary production in which it risks being absorbed.

If *La Cousine Bette* can be seen as undermining the expected responses of part of its readership, the formal devices of *Illusions perdues* had called into question the possibility of any valid relationship between text and public. It does so partly by its combination of metaphor and metonymy – literature is tainted by contact with journalism, which is equated with prostitution, or with a labouring job where the editor is the contractor (*entrepreneur*);[73] partly by its self-reflexivity as a representation of the conditions of representation.[74] If literary activity, as the narrative suggests, is determined by journalism, where does this leave Balzac's own novel? If Lousteau tells Lucien the truth about literature out of self-interest, where does this leave Balzac's status as a truthful narrator?[75] If all human relationships are shaped by unequal or dishonoured contracts, can the resultant corrosion of values leave intact the primal contract between the novelist Balzac and his readers? The public is represented in the novel as anonymous, amorphous, gullible: how can Balzac's public be exempted from this representation?

Art and literature are presented as outlets for frustrated energy, on a par with journalism itself and 'les plus étranges excès'.[76] This self-reflexivity is not, I think Prendergast is quite right in saying, posed in the ludic mode of, say Diderot's *Jacques le fataliste* or Gide's *Les Faux-monnayeurs*. For Balzac affirms a faith in certain incorruptible absolute values, such as the Cénacle profess: but it is doubtful, the text itself seems to suggest, that such values can ever be embodied in unequivocal fashion. Prendergast convincingly argues that 'the desire of the narrator to establish himself as a centre of authority within a discursive hierarchy is . . . serously compromised by a process of fluctuation in which the meanings and values of words appear to change from one context to another'.[77] and Balzac's reactionary politics and their problems can thus be seen as inscribed in the text in precisely this combination of the affirmation and undermining of authority.

The techniques of Courbet's painting are subversive, but in a different way from Balzac's. He incorporates elements from popular art (rather than the mass art of the *roman-feuilleton*), and it is not the popular elements that are the target of subversion, but the responses of the affluent connoisseur.[78] 'The critics did not object to the exploitation of popular art . . . as a source of imagery and inspiration. . . . But to adopt the procedures and even the values of popular art – that was profoundly subversive.'[79] It suggested that Courbet's picture was addressed not to the connoisseur, but to 'a different, hidden, public': hidden in the sense that the Salon critics could seldom explicitly acknowledge it, except in such terms as these, from Thackeray's account of the Salon of 1841: 'Genteel people . . . do not frequent the Louvre on a Sunday. You can't see the pictures well, and are pushed and elbowed by all sorts of low-bred creatures.' He identifies, no doubt with splenetic or comic exaggeration,

two hundred common soldiers . . . fifteen hundred *grisettes*, two

27

thousand liberated shop-boys, eighteen hundred and forty-one artist-apprentices, half a dozen of livery servants, and many scores of fellows with caps and jackets, and copper-coloured countenances and gold ear-rings and large ugly hands, that are hammering or weaving or filing all the week.[80]

Compare this with the following outburst against Courbet: 'les louanges étranges décernées à M. Courbet ont eu pour premier organe certain populaire aviné qui envahit les banquettes du Salon Carré'.[81] The approval of the drunken man of the populace is then taken up, according to the critic's scenario, by art students. Social and institutional hierarchies are thus jeopardized, for the time being at any rate, by the image's self-positioning with regard to its viewers. As T.J. Clark argues, Courbet was seeking to prolong the procedures of popular culture itself, its transformations of materials supplied by the dominant culture, by using popular materials in his own images and in so doing to 'stay within the understanding of a mass audience – to forge images with a dual public, and a double meaning'.[82]

The aim here has been to point to certain implications of nineteenth-century changes in the social situation of artistic and literary production and consumption. In the first third of the nineteenth century, their situation was in many ways not radically different from what it had been under the ancien régime. The public was restricted to a social elite of aristocrats and the more prestigious sections of the upper bourgeoisie: relations with that public were mediated by institutions (in the case of painting: the Académie), and in any case by aesthetic-ideological norms, surviving from the pre-Revolutionary period. The challenge to these from Romanticism was initially qualified by its political associations with reactionary nostalgia. The cultural sphere had not yet been fully penetrated by the logic and structures of capitalism. When this happened, the scope of art and literature was greatly extended, and they achieved a partly illusory autonomy, the obverse of their dependence on the market and its representatives, publishers and dealers.[83] In the process, writers' and painters' understanding of their art was quite transformed, as they learned to live with a new divorce between literary and material standards, popularity and privilege; as the choice between conservatism or innovation became intrinsic to their enterprise. Very often, formal complexity in their works is the trace of such social tensions.

## Suggested reading

Baudelaire, Charles, 'Salon de 1846', 'Salon de 1859', 'Le Peintre de la vie moderne', in *Curiosités esthétiques, L'Art romantique*, ed. H. Lemaître, Classiques Garnier (Paris: Bordas, 1990).

Boime, Albert, 'Entrepreneurial patronage in nineteenth-century France', in *Enterprise and Entrepreneurs in Nineteenth- and Twentieth-century France*, ed. Edward C. Carter II, Robert Forster and Joseph N. Moody (Baltimore and London: John Hopkins University Press, 1976), pp. 137–207.

————, *The Academy and French Painting in the Nineteenth Century*, 2nd ed. (New Haven and London: Yale University Press, 1986).

Bourdieu, Pierre, *Les Règles de l'art* (Paris: Seuil, 1992).

Clark, T.J., *The Absolute Bourgeois: Artists and Politics in France 1848–1851* (London: Thames and Hudson, 1973).

————, *Image of the People: Gustave Courbet and the 1848 Revolution* (London: Thames and Hudson, 1973).

————, *The Painting of Modern Life: Paris in the Art of Manet and his Followers* (London: Thames and Hudson, 1985).

*Histoire de l'édition française*, ed. Henri-Jean Martin and Roger Chartier, 4 vols (Paris: Promodis, 1982–76), vol. II.

Holt, Elizabeth Gilmore, *The Triumph of Art for the Public 1785–1848: The Emerging Role of Exhibitions and Critics* (Princeton: Princeton University Press, 1979).

————, *The Art of All Nations 1850–1873: The Emerging Role of Exhibitions and Critics* (Princeton: Princeton University Press, 1981).

Nochlin, Linda, *Women, Art and Power, and Other Essays* (London: Thames and Hudson, 1991).

Pollock, Griselda, 'Modernity and the Spaces of Femininity', in *Vision and Difference: Feminity, Feminism and the Histories of Art* (London: Routledge, 1988) pp. 50–90.

Prendergast, Christopher, *The Order of Mimesis* (Cambridge: Cambridge University Press, 1986).

Rewald, John, *The History of Impressionism*, 4th edn (London: Secker and Warburg, 1973).

White, Harrison C., and White, Cynthia, *Canvases and Careers: Institutional Change in the French Painting World* (New York: John Wiley and Sons, 1965).

# 2

# *The link between literary and artistic struggles*

## Pierre Bourdieu
## (*translated by* Elinor Dorday)

In order to understand the collective transformation which led to the creation of the figures of the writer and of the artist through the formation of relatively autonomous social universes, in which economic necessities are partially forgotten, we have to step beyond the boundaries which any division into specialities and levels of competence imposes: for, as long as one is confined to the limits of a single tradition, whether literary or artistic, the essential factor will remain incomprehensible. Because the various steps on the road towards autonomy were taken at different moments within these two universes, in accordance with different economic or morphological changes, and also in relation to authorities which are themselves different – such as the Académie breakthroughs made within the artistic world, and vice versa, in order to increase their own independence'.[1]

The formation within society of autonomous fields of production proceeds hand in hand with the forming of specific principles of perception and appreciation of the natural and social world (and equally of literary and artistic representations of this world); that is to say, it proceeds in tandem with the development of a strictly aesthetic mode of perception, which places the principle of 'creation' in the representation itself, and not in the object which is being represented. This process is nowhere more vigorously affirmed than in the ability to portray low and vulgar objects from the modern world in an aesthetic manner.

If it appears to be impossible to make sense of the innovations which have led to the creation of the figure of the artist and of modern art itself unless they are placed within the context of all the fields of cultural production taken as a whole, it is because the transformations which have occurred within the fields of art and literature have done so at staggered intervals. These intervals have allowed writers and artists, like athletes in a relay race, to benefit from previous advances already made, at different times, by their respective avant-gardes. Thus certain discoveries, made possible by the particular logic of one or other of the two fields, have become merged, and appear in retrospect as complementary aspects of a single historical process.

I have analysed elsewhere the history of the battles which painters – particularly Manet – had to wage in order to gain their autonomy from the Académie. I have also analysed the process whereby the universe of the artist ceased to function as a hierarchical *apparatus*, regulated by a particular body, in order to turn itself gradually into a *field* of competition for the monopoly over artistic legitimacy. The process which leads to the formation of such a field is one of *institutionalized anomy*, where no one may claim the role of absolute master and possessor of the *nomos*, the principle of legitimate vision and division. The symbolic revolution, of which Manet was the instigator, eliminated the very possibility of reference to any ultimate authority, to any sort of supreme court, that might be capable of solving all disputes concerning art. In this way, the centralized and monotheistic nomothete (long embodied by the Académie) yielded to a competition between plural and unspecified gods. The challenge to the authority of the Académie gave new impetus to the apparently finished and completed historical progress of an artistic production which had been shut up inside a closed world of predetermined possibilities, and opened up a newly infinite universe of possibilities for exploration Manet completely undermined the social foundations of the fixed, absolute viewpoint of artistic absolutism (just as he totally undermined the idea of a privileged position being reserved for light, which would henceforth be in evidence everywhere on the surface of objects): that is to say, he instituted a plurality of points of view, something which is engraved upon the very existence of a field. (Here one may well ask whether the act – which has often been noticed – of abandoning the sovereign and almost divine point of view in the writing of the novel itself should not be related to the appearance of a plurality of competing perspectives within the field.)[2]

However, in the course of their struggle against the Académie, the painters (and in particular those rejected the Salons) were able to fall back on the comprehensive fiction, launched by the Romantic movement, of the image of the artist in conflict with society, a rebel whose originality is measured by the misunderstanding to which he falls victim, or by the scandal which he provokes. However, they also received direct support from writers, liberated as these latter were from the authority of the seventeenth century, but at the price of attributing to them a limited function which was, in any case, defined from without. Writers transmitted to artists an exalted image of the heroic break which they were in the process of accomplishing and, above all, they raised into the realm of discourse those discoveries which the artists were then making on a practical level, notably in terms of lifestyle.

Following on from Chateaubriand (who in *Les Mémoires d'outre-tombe* exalted the artist's stoic suffering of poverty and his spirit of devotion and self-denial), the great Romantics – Hugo, Vigny, Musset – found that defending the martyrs of art gave them many opportunities to give voice to their hatred of the bourgeoisie, or to their own self-compassion. Here, the very image of the artist cursed by Fate – an element which is central to this new vision of the world – hinges directly upon the example of generosity and self-sacrifice offered by artists to the entire intellectual universe. Thus we have Gleyre refusing to accept any fees from his students, Corot coming to the aid of Daumier, Dupré renting a studio for Théodore Rousseau's use, and so on, not to mention the heroic suffering of so many in the face of misery and poverty, or the supreme sacrifice of life itself for the love of art – exalted but sinister existences, which are depicted in the *Scènes de la vie de bohème*, as in all novels of this genre (take Champfleury's novels, for example).

Disinterest as opposed to self-interest, nobility of spirit as opposed to baseness, generosity and daring as opposed to miserliness and prudence, pure art and pure love as opposed to mercenary art and mercenary love – from the Romantic period onwards, the opposition asserts itself everywhere. First of all in literature, with numerous contrasting portraits of the artist and the bourgeois – Chatterton and John Bell, the painter Théodore de Sommervieux and the old draper Guillaume in *La Maison du chat-qui-pelote*, and so on – but also, and above all, in the form of caricature, with the likes of Philipon, Grandville, Decamps, Henri Monnier or Daumier denouncing the *bourgeois parvenu* beneath the features of Mayeux, Robert Macaire or Monsieur Prudhomme. And doubtless no one contributed more than Baudelaire (whose first recorded written works are the *Salons* of 1845 and 1846), towards elevating the image of the artist at once as a solitary character who, like Delacroix, asserts himself as a 'dandy', as an aristocrat indifferent to society's honours and who looks only to posterity,[3] and also as a saturnine character doomed to suffer melancholy and misfortune.

Writers elaborate the theory of the totally separate economy of this separate world when, like Théophile Gautier in the preface to *Mademoiselle de Maupin*, or Baudelaire in the *Salon de 1846*, they produce with reference to painting the first systematic formulations of the theory of art for art's sake: this singular way of living through art, whose roots lie in an art of living that rejects the bourgeois lifestyle, notably because it is founded upon the act of refusing any social justification for art or the artist himself.

It is significant that the idea of art for art's sake should have arisen with reference to the *Roland furieux* by the sculptor Jean Duseigneur (or Jehan du Seigneur), which was exhibited at the Salon of 1831, for it was in fact at the home of this particular artist, in the rue de Vaugirard, that the group comprising Borel, Nerval and Gautier, referred to by Nerval as the 'petit cénacle', would regularly meet, and whose members, in an effort to shun the extravagances of the *Jeune France*, would later come together on more solemn ground, at the rue du Doyenné. Gautier – a painter turned writer (like Pétrus Borel and Delécluze), and therefore predisposed to play the role of intermediary between the two spheres – was the most 'pictorial' of writers and the 'flawless master' of the young generation (so reads the dedication of *Les Fleurs du mal*) and he would express the vision of art and the artist which was to take shape within this group. This was a vision which centred upon the freedom to develop intellectual creativity, even if this meant offending public taste, conventions or rules: it implied hatred and rejection above all others of those whom the painters dubbed grocers, philistines or bourgeois, and the celebration of the pleasures of love and the sanctification of art, which they considered to be the second creator, after God. By associating elitism and anti-utilitarianism, the artist sneered at conventional morality, religion, duties and responsibilities, despising everything which could possibly conjure up the idea of any service which art might have to render society.

Tebaldeo in *Lorenzaccio* is such a figure: the only free spirit left in a universe of corruption, he alone is capable of giving some sort of meaning to the world, of exorcizing evil and transforming life by virtue of artistic contemplation and creation. He is the artist who asserts himself in the face of the Académie, and whom the ill-will of the official institutions serves only to make still greater. He is the artist who represents the perfect incarnation of the 'creator', a passionate spirit, driven by the energy and potency of his extraordinary sensitivity and his unique capacity for trans-substantiation. This world which we refer to by the global term 'Bohemia', but which is so diverse and polarized even within itself, is the setting for a formidable experiment, which Lammenais calls 'spiritual debauchery'. As a result of this experiment, a whole new *art de vivre* is invented: the bohemian way of life ceases to be merely a phase, a passing moment of freedom granted to bourgeois adolescents, in order to evolve, very gradually, into a complete lifestyle in its own right. Nonconformist clothing and make-up are, in fact, merely the most visible aspects of a heretical break with all the conventions and propriety belonging to the bourgeois way of life. Thus the *Jeune France* find themselves expelled from the house rented by Pétrus Borel, because their neighbours complain about them sitting naked in the garden, busy following the teachings of the Evadnists, a sect which favoured the spiritual emancipation of women.

However, like an 'exemplary prophecy' in Max Weber's sense of the term, the artist's way of life does offer writers in return a model of the pure artist which they are in any case trying to invent and establish. And pure painting, freed from the obligation to serve some purpose, or even to mean anything at all, which they set up in opposition to the Académie tradition, contributes towards realizing the possibility of 'pure' art. Artistic criticism, which holds such an important place in the creative lives of writers, no doubt offers them an opportunity to discover the truth about their own methods and artistic plans. What is in fact involved is not just a redefining of the functions of artistic activity, nor is it the mental evolution which must take place in order, firstly, to conceive all those types of experience hitherto excluded from the academic order of things – 'emotion', 'impression', 'light', 'originality', 'spontaneity' – and secondly to reappraise the most familiar words in the traditional lexicon of art criticism – 'effect', 'sketch', 'portrait', 'landscape'. In fact, what it concerns is the creating of the conditions for a new belief, one capable of giving a meaning to the art of living in that topsy-turvy world which is the world of the artist. The painters who were making the break with the Académie and with the bourgeois public would doubtless not have managed to achieve the transformation which was so vital to them, without this help from the writers. For these latter, strengthened by their specific skills as professional interpreters, and reliant upon the traditional break with the 'bourgeois' social order that had been established in the literary field with the coming of the Romantic movement, were predisposed to assist in the task of ethical and aesthetic conversion then taking place among the artistic avant-garde, and to bear the symbolic revolution on to its ultimate realization by setting down as explicitly stated and accepted principles, with their theory of 'art for art's sake', all the necessities of the new economy of symbolic goods.

However, in the course of defending heretical painters, the writers themselves learned much that would serve their own cause. Thus the liberty which painters (especially Manet) afforded themselves, by affirming what Joseph Sloane calls the 'neutrality of the subject'[4] – that is, the rejection of any hierarchy between objects, as well as of any didactic, moral or political function whatsoever – was bound to have some reciprocal effect upon the writers, for, although long freed from the constraints of the Académie, writers were more directly subject to demands to deliver a 'message' since, as employers of language, it was more difficult for them to revoke all communicative function.

The revolution that was to lead to the formation of separate artistic universes which seemed to take refuge in the purity of difference that was their defining characteristic took place in two separate phases. First of all, it was a matter of freeing painting from the obligation either to fulfil a social function, respond to a commission or a command, or serve a cause. In this phase, help from the writers played a determining role. Thus it was in the name of painting which, as compared to written or spoken language, has no obligation to deliver any message, that Zola was to denounce the didactic use which Proudhon wished to make of Courbet's painting:

> What! You have writing, you have the spoken word, you are able to say anything you wish, and yet you are going to look to the art of lines and colours for teaching and instruction. Come, for pity's sake, remember that we are not made up of reason alone. If you are a practical man, then leave it to philosophers to do the instructing, and leave painters the right to give us emotions. I do not believe that you should demand of an artist that he teach, and, in any case, I categorically deny the instructive effect of a painting on the morality of the masses.[5]

Manet, and all the Impressionists who followed, went well beyond that, repudiating all obligation not only to serve a cause, but even to say anything at all. So much so that in the end, in order to carry their work of artistic emancipation to its extreme, they would have to free themselves from the writer himself, who (as indeed Pissarro said of Huysmans) 'judges in his capacity as a writer of literature, and so for most of the time sees only the subject of the painting'.[6] Even when, like Zola, they defended themselves by affirming the specificity of the pictorial mode, writers were liberators but at the same time alienators. All the more so in that, with the end of the Académie's monopoly over consecration, these 'taste-makers' had become 'artist-makers', who, by means of their discourse, now had it in their power actually to sanction something as a works of art. And so, barely as yet liberated from the institution of the Académie, the painters – and Pissarro and Gauguin more than any – now had to undertake to free themselves from the literary hacks, who were at this stage (just as in they heyday of Académie criticism) relying upon their artistic work in order to draw attention to their own artistic taste and sensitivity, even going so far as to superimpose or substitute their own commentaries.

The affirmation of an aesthetic which makes the pictorial work (and indeed all works of art) into an intrinsically polysemous reality – and one which is therefore impossible to reduce to simpler terms in any glossary or exegesis – doubtless owes a great deal to this desire of the painters to free themselves from the grip of the literary hacks. This does not, however, preclude the fact that in their effort to liberate themselves, they were able to find weapons and tools of thought in the literary camp, most notably among the Symbolists, who, at about the same time, were refusing all transcendence of the signified in relation to the signifier, thus making music into the purest form of art.

The story, as told by Dario Gamboni,[7] of the relations between Odilon Redon and his critics, especially Huysmans, is a perfect illustration of the final struggle in the war for liberation which the painters had to wage in order to win their own autonomy and affirm the irreducibility of the pictorial, artistic work to all types of discourse (as opposed to the famous *ut pictura poesis*) or – which boils down to the same thing – its infinite and limitless accessibility to all possible forms of discourse. Thus was completed the long task which led from the Académie's absolutism – which presupposes the existence of an ideal truth to which both creation and contemplation of the work should confirm – through to subjectivism, in which each may create or recreate the work in his own way.

Doubtless it is only with Duchamp, however, that the artists were to arrive at a strategy which would allow them to use literature without being used by it themselves, and thus to escape from the relationship of structural inferiority into which they had been placed – both in relation to creators of metadiscourse, because of their own role as creators of objects which are by their very nature inarticulate, and first and foremost in relation to themselves. This strategy consisted in methodically denouncing and thwarting all attempts to annex the artistic work by means of discourse, and doing this not just in the structure and in the construction of the work itself, but also by way of an anticipated or even a retrospective metadiscourse (for instance in an obscure and disconcerting title). All this, of course, was accomplished without discouraging exegeses of the work; quite the opposite, in fact, for this was still just as necessary as before if the work of art was to achieve a full social existence.

The movement of the artistic and, as a direct reaction, of the literary fields towards a greater level of autonomy was accompanied by a process of *purifying* the mode of expression whereby each art or genre directed itself more and more towards what defined it as such, above and beyond the socially accepted and recognized exterior signs of its identity. The painters abandoned literature – that is, the 'topic', the 'anecdote', everything which could evoke any intention of reproducing or of representing, in short, of *speaking* – in the interests of the pictorial, considering that the picture should adhere to its own, specifically pictorial rules, which should stand independently of the object represented. Similarly, the writers rejected the pictorial and the picturesque (such as were to be found in the work of Gautier and the Parnassians, for example) in favour of the literary, invoking instead music, which carries no meaning, as opposed to message and meaning, and, with Mallarmé, they ruled out the use of the plain words of simple reportage, the language of representation, discourse which merely denotes and naively indicates a referent.[8]

This means that, from one purge to the next, the struggles which took place in the two separate fields led to the gradual isolation of the essential principle of the defining factor of each art and each genre in itself: the 'literariness' as the Russian formalists called it, or the 'poetic', that which distinguishes poetry from prose. In this way, in free verse, for example, by causing secondary characteristics like rhyme and rhythm to disappear, the history of the field has only allowed something resembling a highly concentrated extract to remain (as in the work of Francis Ponge, for example), made up of those properties best suited to produce the poetic effect of making words and things less banal – the *ostranenie* of the Russian formalists – without having to resort to techniques socially designated as 'poetical'. Each and every time that one of these relatively autonomous universes establishes itself, whether it be an artistic or a scientific field or one of their specialized areas, the historical process thereby instituted plays the same role of extractor of quintessence, in such a way that the analysis of the history of the field is in itself the only legitimate form of analysis of that essence.[9]

The formalists (and notably Jakobson, well-versed in phenomenology), anxious to reply as methodically and coherently as possible to traditional questions which critics and teachers ask of the genres (theatre, novel, poetry), have satisfied themselves, like any other tradition of thought on 'pure poetry' or 'theatricality', with constituting as a transhistoric essence something that is, in reality, no more than a sort of *historical quintessence*, that is, the product of the long, slow process of historical alchemy that accompanies the process of self-determination of the fields of cultural production.

The long battle fought by the painters to free themselves from any form of supreme authority (even that of State patronage, surely the most neutral and eclectic of all), and to break away from 'subjects' imposed on them, had thus revealed the possibility – and simultaneously the necessity – of a cultural production completely free from all direction or external imperative, one capable, moreover, of discovering within its own boundaries the vital principle of its own existence and necessity. In this way, the fight had played a part in showing the writers (who, either by exalting the struggle or by analysing it, had helped it to be carried on) the possibility of a freedom thenceforth made available and thus obligatory for anyone wanting to adopt the role of the artist, the writer and, above all, the intellectual.

How can one avoid supposing, in fact, that Zola was using the inevitable identification suggested by the homology of position to claim for himself the same freedom that he demanded for the artist? In stating that the artist is answerable only to himself, that he is entirely free with regard to moral and social purpose (which, it must be remembered, provoked great scandal and forced Zola to leave the staff of *L'Evénement* in 1866), he affirms, more radically than had ever been done previously, the right of the artist to his own, personal impressions, as well as to his subjective reactions: thus 'pure painting', rid of its duty to bear meaning, becomes a means of expression of the artist's own individual sensitivity, and of the originality of his conception. In short, to

cite the famous catchphrase, it becomes a 'corner of creation seen re-
fracted through a temperament'. Zola did not admire Manet's work for
its objective realism – which is what Champfleury defended it for – but
because it reveals the specific character of the painter himself. Similarly,
when he pleaded at great length in favour of *Germinie Lacerteux*, he
fêted not so much the naturalness and naturalism of its descriptive passages, as the 'free and lofty manifestation of a personality', the
'individual, characteristic language of a soul' and the 'unique product of
an intelligent understanding', refuting all pretensions to measure in
terms of ethical or aesthetic rules a work which sets itself 'above morality and beyond all sense of decency and purity'.[10]

Moreover, how can one fail to see that by this reaffirmation of the
power of the creative individual (which was without parallel since
Delacroix), and of his right to free self-determination – a right which entails the critic's or the spectator's right to emotional comprehension,
with no preconditions or presuppositions – how can one fail to see that
through this, Zola was merely clearing the way for the radical reassertion of the freedom of the writer later, in fact, to be found in his *J'Accuse*
open letter and his militant stance over the Dreyfus Affair? The right to
view things subjectively, and the claim to freedom to denounce and con-
demn the irreproachable violence of the Reason of State, in the name of
private and personal duty, are in fact one and the same thing.[11]

Achieving – in spectacular style – this necessary freedom, which had
become progressively more possible within the cultural field of cultural
production, Zola intervened in the political field not under the aegis of
an authority which was strictly political in nature, but in the name of the
specific authority which he had won for himself in the cultural field. The
very affirmation of a specific necessity, such as that made by art qua art
or, even better, that made by form qua form (whether political, musical
or poetical), does in effect imply taking a fundamental liberty with regard to all the necessities which constitute other fields, when considered
as specific entities, such as the obligation to calculate interest rates,
taken from economics qua economics, as soon as it claims to extend to
all spheres of activity, or that Reason of State, a characteristic of politics
qua politics, that is to say as *Realpolitik*, which was defined in opposition to theology (and the theory of the divine right of monarchs,
encumbered as this is by external obligations), and, most of all, in opposition to morality.[12] It is this liberty which forms the foundations of the
intellectual's possibility of expressing himself as just that – an intellectual – in the domain of politics and morality.

*The link between literary and artistic struggles*

## Suggested reading

*The link between literary and artistic struggles*

## Suggested reading

Bourdieu, Pierre, *Distinction* (London: Routledge, 1984).

———, *Les règles de l'art* (Paris: Seuil, 1992).

Gamboni, Dario, *La plume et le pinceau* (Paris: Minuit, 1989).

Hanson, Anne Coffin, *Manet and the Modern Tradition* (New Haven and London: Yale University Press, 2nd ed., 1979).

Sloane, J.C., *French Painting between the Past and the Present: Artists, Critics and Traditions from 1848 to 1870* (Princeton: Princeton University Press, 1951).

Zola, Emile, *Mes haines* (Paris: Fasquelle, 1923).

# 3

## 'A tout prix devenir quelqu'un': the women of the Académie Julian

### Germaine Greer

The case for Rodolphe Julian as a pioneer who greatly advanced the cause of women artists was put in February 1881 in *La Citoyenne*:

> Nous avons des écoles de dessin de la ville très suffisantes pour celles qui se destinent à l'industrie mais nulles au point de vue vraiment artistique, ou bien deux ou trois ateliers à la mode où les jeunes filles riches s'amusent à faire de la peinture … Heureusement les expositions annuelles sont là et les derniers salons ont démontré que ces femmes si dédaignées sont de vaillantes élèves et portent haut et ferme le drapeau de l'école libre, l'Atelier Julian qui leur a ouvert ses portes.[1]

When these words were written by 'Pauline Orell', the 'annual exhibitions' had been showing women's work for more than a century. Anne Vallayer-Coster, Adelaide Labille-Guiard and Elisabeth Vigée-Lebrun were the best known members of a respectable group of eighteenth-century French women artists whose work was valued in the same terms and at the same rates as the work of their most distinguished male colleagues. David's uproarious throng of students included a significant number of women; a significant number of his students, male and female, taught women in their turn, as did an equally significant number of his colleagues. About half of the professional painters of the late eighteenth and early nineteenth century taught, and about half of them taught women, either in the women's homes, in ateliers hired for the purpose, or in their own studios. Some had few female students, some hordes. Some taught noblewomen, others the daughters of artisans, others both. Fathers and brothers remained important teachers of women painters for most of the nineteenth century; fathers and brothers also sent women to work in the studios of colleagues whose specialities were closer to the women's preferences. From 1800 to 1830 women's work was never less than 14 per cent of the total shown in the Salons; in 1855 the proportion sank to 6.7 per cent and continued to bump along

40

at more or less the same level for twenty years. In 1880 it jumped up to 12.5 per cent, as a result of changes in the organisation of the Salon, not because of the existence of the Académie Julian.[2]

The women whose work was noticed in the Salon of 1880 are representative in their heterogeneity if nothing else. Euphémie Muraton-Duhanot[3] was the only woman to win a medal, and that a third class medal, for a painting of 'un banc de jardin chargé de roses'. The only master acknowledged by Mme Muraton was her husband, Alphonse Muraton. For the rest, it was as the *Gazette des Femmes* complained in 1878, 'toujours les mentions honorables lorsqui'il s'agit de talents féminins!'[4] Six of forty 'mentions honorables' went to women, to Harriet Backer, Uranie Colin Libour, Virginie Demont-Breton, Fanny Fleury, Noémie Guillaume, and Emilie Leleux. Harriet Backer, after training at the Stockholm academy, when she travelled to Paris had chosen to be taught by Bonnat, Gérôme and Bastien Le Page. According to Bénézit, Uranie Colin Libour had been taught by P. Rude, L. Muller and Bonvin, two of whom appear to have been misnamed. She may have been taught by the sculptor, François Rude, but it seems more likely that she was in fact taught by his wife, the painter Sophie Rude Frémiet. Colin Libour's work was first shown in the Salon of 1861 and last in 1889; pupils of hers had been exhibiting for many years. Twenty-one-year-old Virginie Demont-Breton was being trained by her father, Jules Breton; in the succeeding three years she went on to win the third class medal, the second class medal and to be declared *hors concours*. Both Fanny Fleury Laurent, who had been exhibiting since 1864, and Noémie Guillaume Bocquet listed as teachers Henner and Carolus-Duran.[5] Emilie Leleux Giraud had first trained with Lugardon in Geneva, then with Léon Cogniet, and lastly with her husband, Armand Leleux.

In every Salon for forty years, there had been an important number of works by Cogniet's pupils both male and female. More than seventy female 'élèves de Cogniet' can be traced in the Salon records, many exhibiting regularly for ten, twenty, even thirty years, which suggests that they were working full time as painters. Sophie Jobert exhibited regularly at the Salons between 1839 and 1870, Eugénie Grün Charpentier from 1840 to 1875, Ernestine Quantin Schwind between 1844 and 1879, Emma Roslin-Blanche from 1847 to 1881, Héloise Vuitel (also listed as Huitel in the livrets du Salon) from 1848 to 1885, Claire Mallon Masson between 1848 and 1880, Fideline Choel from 1849 to 1878, Félicie Schneider Fournier from 1849 to 1882, Laure Chatillon Delaune from 1851 to 1887 and Léonie Dusseuil from 1859 to 1880. Cogniet's most respected pupil was probably Nélie Jacquemart, of whom every commentator uttered that highest of praise, that you would never guess from the solidity of her technique that she was a woman.[6]

Before his death in 1880 Cogniet had been acknowledged a second-class painter who was, partly because of his tolerance and respect for others, a first-class teacher. There is little documentary evidence of his methods beyond an interesting series of paintings preserved in the Musée des Beaux-Arts in Orléans.[7] One, painted by Cogniet's older sister, Marie Amélie Cogniet, and exhibited in the Salon of 1831, shows a mansarde lit from a high window, with walls painted the usual reddish brown. The master stands, one foot on a mysterious ladder, with his paint-filled brushes in his hand, studying an enormous canvas showing an ambitious figure composition, while his lone female student assistant, herself holding a brush, huddles before it, trying not to obstruct his view. In the corner stands a storage rack with plaster casts on top, next to a folding screen, which implies the occasional appearance of the undraped model, as does the stove near-by, upon which stands a plaster replica of the Venus of the Belvedere. On the back wall alongside hangs a large picture of what appears to be a Hercules, a virtually naked male form in dynamic pose, embellished by airborne drapery. Almost unseen in the far corner a young man is sitting to work on his own canvas, while a small person in long skirts peeps in at the lower left-hand corner. The oddness of the composition, with all the figures in little, dotted about a great void dominated by the painted gesturing Hercules and the immobile Venus, makes its own wry comment upon the atelier Cogniet. While Marie Amélie was working on this picture, Cogniet painted the studio from the opposite point of view showing that the ladder led to the sill of the half-shaded high window where spare tabourets were stored. His picture is a tour de force of perspective composition, showing not only the arched ceiling, the window and the door to the leads standing ajar, but his sister standing to her easel in the corner opposite.

A third painting, also attributed to Cogniet, shows a ladies' atelier crowded with fashionably dressed women. Women who choose to train as professional painters are seldom if ever from the class that calls its females ladies, nevertheless ladies were expected to be able to take a likeness of a person, a house or a garden, though not usually in messy, smelly oils. Minor masters were often forced to take work as drawing masters in the houses of the chattering classes and some of their pupils, fallen upon hard times, had occasionally to turn accomplishment into livelihood. Abel de Pujol's atelier des dames of the 1820s was something of an innovation in that the ladies worked in a proper studio from plaster casts and models, but they appear to have been neither encouraged nor eager to exhibit their work.[8] Virtually the only record of the existence of Pujol's ladies' atelier is to be found in the three paintings made of it by Adrienne Marie Louise Grandpierre Deverzy, who became the second Mme Abel de Pujol. In the version exhibited in the Salon of

1822 the atelier was shown bustling with ladies in tight-bodiced long-sleeved silk dresses, some sitting, some standing to their work, others clustering around the handsome young maître enthroned with a student's drawing upon his knee. Only one or two appear to be studying the model who is sitting for a formal portrait in evening dress.[9] Such pictures were the best advertisement a fashionable atelier could have and the good looks of the maître an important consideration. Cogniet's women's atelier is different in that the teacher, who is showing a student how to make up a palette, is either Cogniet's wife, Caroline Thévénin, herself from a painter family, or her sister Marie Anne Rosalie Thévénin, who exhibited in the Salons between 1842 and 1881, winning three medals. The pictorial evidence seems to show that, with the help of the women in his family, Cogniet ran a ladies' atelier form which he recruited pupils who would profit by intensive technical training.[10] His best female students have left durable works of good texture and colour based on sound if unadventurous principles of composition.

Nevertheless it is not Cogniet but his pupil, Rodolphe Julian, who has been canonized for services to women's art. A year after 'Pauline Orell' hailed him in *La Citoyenne* he was awarded the Légion d'Honneur, whereupon his delighted female students presented him with a huge bouquet. In 1903 Gabrielle Réval hailed him in *L'Echo de Paris* as 'un révolutionnaire dans l'enseignement artistique'; the cry was repeated in 1968 by Martine Hérold and, more surprisingly, by Catherine Fehrer in the *Gazette des Beaux-Arts* in 1984.[11] In order to understand how a champion of conservative academicism comes to be hailed as a radical, it is necessary to examine more closely the preconceptions of the author of the article in *La Citoyenne*. She dismisses as if with a sneer the 'écoles des dessin de la ville pour celles qui se destinent à l'industrie'; in fact women graduates of the Académie Julian regularly took part in the concours for positions in the city schools of design. Though 'Pauline Orell' might not appreciate the chance to earn an honourable living, many of her female contemporaries saw in it their only hope of survival.

Since the time of Mme de Mirbel, porcelain painting had been an important means of support for women; while hundreds of practitioners of the 'vraiment artistique' were starving, Delphine de Cool[12] and her best pupils were enjoying not only riches, but prestige. In February 1882 De Cool who, as directrice of the Ecole de Dessin pour les jeunes filles in the first arrondissement for more than twenty-five years, taught hundreds of women, held a sale of her émaux de Limoges at the rue Drouot, where the top prices for copies after Rubens and Cabanel were in the thousands of francs.[13] In October 1879, *La Gazette des Femmes* reported: 'Les écoles de dessin de Paris comptent actuellement 6,370 femmes . . . Que de porcelaine decorée il va nous falloir casser si nous ne voulons pas voir toutes ces abeilles chômer.'

When the opening of seven more schools of design was announced in December 1879 the *Gazette des Femmes* asked tersely, 'Etait-ce bien urgent?' In November 1880 the *Gazette* reported without comment the suicide of a twenty-four-year-old porcelain painter called Marie Larsonneur. If porcelain painters had become a drag on the market by 1880, there was no demand whatever for the oil paintings that hundreds of women painters showed year after year. In May 1880 *The Artist* reported that 'there are in France at present 2150 lady artists, of them 107 are sculptors, 602 oil painters, 193 miniaturists, 754 ceramists and 494 water colour and fan painters, or pastel and crayon drawers'.[14] As Maximilienne Guyon, who entered the Académie Julian in 1883 when she was fifteen, remarked bitterly: 'J'ai vu, de mes yeux vu, mes camarades de chez Julian manger, elles aussi la vâche enragée, attendre les trois francs d'un dessin, les cent sous d'un portrait . . . Ah! le ventre creux, voilà par où s'est établie la première égalité entre l'artiste-homme et l'artiste femme!'[15] How to make a living was just one of the things that women did not learn at the Académie Julian.

'Orell' is quite wrong in implying that in the winter of 1881 the only alternatives to the Académie Julian were either city schools of design or 'ateliers des dames'. According to May Alcott, 'Messieurs Chaplin, Barrias, Duran, Cabanel, Jackson, Luminais, Bougereau, Robert-Fleury, and Lefebvre' all accepted women students. Of them only the last three were associated with the Académie Julian, Bouguereau only after 1880.[16] Chaplin's women's atelier was described by Arthur Baignières in the *Gazette des Beaux Arts* in May 1879 as 'un . . . des plus suivis' with, among its famous pupils, 'Mlle Delorme, Mlle Dubost, Mlle Claudie, Mlle Banuelos, Mlle de Challié, Mlle Petiet, Mme Ayrton, Mme Noble-Pigeaud . . . Mlle Barillot, Mme de la Villette'. Baignières left out, possibly because by this time she left exhibiting in the Salons to her élèves, Chaplin's most brilliant élève, Madeleine Lemaire, 'la Patronne', Proust's salonnière friend and benefactor,[17] whose frothy flower paintings still fetch tens of thousands of francs in the sale-rooms, Marie Lacroix-Gessler, known in art as Mme Anselma, and the Comtesse de Saux, famous in the Salons since 1855 as Henriette Browne, who had been brought to Chaplin's atelier by her mother when she was only sixteen.[18] Louise Jopling-Rowe, Chaplin's best-known English pupil, would have been unpleasantly surprised to have her celebrated self forgotten.[19] Less suprisingly Baignières omitted to name Eva Gonzalès and Mary Cassatt, who both worked for a time with Chaplin.[20] The women of the Chaplin atelier continued to distinguish themselves in the Salons until the end of the century, led by the universally praised and much premiated Louise Abbéma.[21] Perhaps because of the adoring attention lavished on him by generations of enthusiastic young women, Chaplin's own work, always decorative and often sentimentally pornographic, became more and more self-indulgent though hardly less popular. The

Académie Julian prided itself on strength, 'drawing by the masses'[22] and 'facture solide'.

May Alcott may have intended to list only the ateliers open to foreign women; even so she should have mentioned Carolus-Duran and Henner. She was also under the impression that Bonnat received only male pupils, with a sole exception, when in fact Bonnat taught dozens of women besides Harriet Backer. The explanation of Alcott's mistake is probably that Bonnat preferred to hand-pick his female students, who would have to work with him in his own atelier, his students' atelier being an unsuitable place for a woman.[23] Alcott's recommendation to her female readers was not the 'Academie Jullien' with its 'dirty close rooms' but the well-lighted and ventilated' atelier of another of Cogniet's pupils, Edouard Krug, who provided two daytime sittings as well as an evening one for one hundred francs a month, and whose professors visited each student for five minutes every day rather than once a week. Despite Alcott's unsolicited testimonial, of the women painters trained by Krug only a scant handful are known to history, which records literally thousands of 'Julians'.

If we consider the women whose work was singled out for praise by the reviewers of the Salon of 1880, we find that the female Julians did less than well. De Chennevières, writing in *La Gazette des Beaux-Arts*, went so far as to single out 'l'image déplorable de M. Léon Say par Mlle Beaury-Sorel, qui trouve dans le nouveau président du Senat un ennemi-né du musée du Luxembourg'.[24] De Chennevières praised, on the other hand, 'le charmant tableautin *les Peines de coeur* de Mme L. Enault, la femme de notre cher confrère'; Alix-Louise Enault, who was a pupil of Tissier and Willems, went on to win a 'mention honorable' in 1887. De Chennevières also singled out a small landscape with donkeys by Marie Cazin, touched by 'cette religion de la jeune artiste pour la manière de son mari', though she had been previously taught by Juliette Peyrol-Bonheur and Barge. As usual the Brittany seascapes of Elodie Lavillette, pupil of Corroler and Dubois, received warm commendation. The only foreigner whose work took De Chennevières's eye, besides Harriet Backer, was Marie Collart, who had trained in Brussells.[25] Pastel portraits by Eva Gonzalès, by Rudder's pupil, Mme McNab-Danglars, directrice of the Ecole de Dessin pour les Jeunes Filles in the ninth arrondissement, and by Madeleine Wymbs, pupil of Lebourcher and Flandrin, also came in for commendation, together with a self-portrait in fusain by Marie Ernestine Lavieille, who was taught by her father.

The astigmatism of 'Pauline Orell' is explained by the fact that behind her mask lurks Marie Bashkirtseff, twenty-some years old, passing as twenty.[26] Though to the unsympathetic she may have seemed a jeune fille riche merely playing at painting, she herself was convinced that she was an exception to every rule. Julian may not have realized what an asset was coming his way in September 1877 when Bashkirtseff turned up at the atelier in the rue Vivienne with her friend, Berthe Boyd, but it did not take him long to realize that the young woman's self-absorption, her desperate desire to 'be somebody' together with her social visibility, offered him opportunities that he should not squander. He began to give her a degree of personal attention that no female 'Julian' had ever had. While he played her full-time mentor and confidant she, all unwitting, became his unpaid publicist. Her qualifications included snobbery, intellectual and other, ignorance and arrogance. To this day she remains the most famous of the thousands of élèves de Julian though she is far from being the most competent woman artist the school produced.

The special treatment meted out to Bashkirtseff was not relished by the other women working in the atelier: disgusted by the Bashkirtseff legend, the English watercolourist Mary L. Breakell gave her own account of the Julian experience as it was lived by the Englishwomen of the Bashkirtseff era:

> We rose before it was light, and dressed ourselves with freezing fingers. We were out at 'first breakfast' in a humble *crêmerie*, drinking our hot chocolate in thick white bowls like mortars; crunching our crisp rolls with the worthy working folk of Paris in their blue blouses at the marble tables; then trudging bravely for an hour, through the snowy streets and leafless Elysian fields and boulevards (for it was bitter cold in Paris that winter of 1882) . . . We hardly ever arrived later than half-past eight o'clock in the morning, and we worked from that time till five, with an hour off for 'second breakfast' at midday, stimulated with ardent anticipations of success in the future – success commensurate with the long hours of our work and with our enthusiasm. It was a Bohemian, barny sort of place, that studio; merely a huge garret in the back quarter of some hotel of which I know not the name, and we entered from the arcade of the Passage by a small, mysterious doorway and a dark and narrow winding stair.[27]

The English girls began work from the model at once, as the other students drifted in. At 10 Julian would look in to check that all was in order. And some time afterwards, Marie Bashkirtseff would sweep in, drop her furs to the floor for the maid to pick up, and begin work. Following the precedent of Pujol and Cogniet, Julian suggested to Bashkirtseff that she paint a large piece showing his female élèves at work for the Salon of 1881. Bashkirtseff selected the angle she wanted and demanded that the wall separating Julien's sanctum from the women's atelier be taken down to give her space to work. At the same time Amélie Beaury Sorel, who was well known to be in love with the *patron*, was asked to paint the same subject from the opposite side of the room. The rest of the students were thus obliged to serve as models, to the detriment of their own work. Breakell found it torture, to be ordered to hold her pose and work at the same time, 'arranged in the usual school of art triple semi-circle round the model, ... huddled by each other's easels, cribbed, cabined and confined in the smallest of possible spaces'.[28]

According to Breakell the main figure in Bashkirtseff's picture (fig. 1) is the American student 'Alice B'.[29]

> Near by, in vivid contrast to her, stands Mlle de V., a high-born, well-corseted, starched, painted and stippled Parisienne, whose angular, incongruous presence in this picture of Bohemia might, in Julian's judgment (and perhaps in the eyes of fashionable Paris at the next Salon) add prestige and chic to his studio that would outbalance the inartistic blot her presence makes on the composition – in the eye of the artist. For the truth is she entirely spoils the picture.[30]

Only Bashkirtseff, it would seem, laboured under the delusion that what was going on was 'vraiment artistique'; 'prestige' and 'chic' are hardly to be reconciled with 'l'amour du travail et la passion de l'art', according to Julian rhetoric, 'les seules choses qui puissent faire aimer l'existence'.[31]

Breakell tells us that the other students in Bashkirtseff's picture included Madame Maignon, the wife of a 'mental specialist', the American, Anna Klumpke, who, after the death of Nathalie Micas, became the companion of Rosa Bonheur and inherited all her money, two Swedish girls who wore daggers at their sides, a Canadian cross-dresser and a stout Italian who smoked cigars.[32]

Bashkirtseff included in her canvas sixteen figures: Breakell thought that in all there must have been twenty-five students, 'counting those in the ranks, cooped up and cramped behind the others, with big palettes and sheaves of brushes obscuring them'. Julian got the exposure that he wanted, for both pictures were hung in the Salon. Amélie Beaury-Sorel had glamourized her picture not only by adding ferns and palms, but by placing the figure of Marie Bashkirtseff in the foreground, resplendent in a gown of 'white matelasse crinkled multitudinously in a thousand stitchings'. 'Ah! when that white vision ... gleamed ... like a white queen from some far, upper social world of *chic* and fashion – what a long-drawn sigh of wonder heaved the simple breasts of those girls in cotton *peignoirs* as they scraped their charcoal!' Though Bashkirtseff signed her big picture 'Andrey' it was exhibited under her name. Perhaps by that time she was beginning to realize that Julian was manipulating her. Once the publicity coup had been pulled off, distance crept between her and Julian, but her death and the publication of the *rifacimento* of her journals kept the legend alive, so that thousands of women the world over were convinced that the 'art life' was livable only in Paris and only at the Académie Julian.

Orell/Bashkirtseff believed that the Académie Julian played a crucial role in empowering women painters because it provided them with the opportunity to study the undraped model. 'On nous demande avec une indulgente ironie combien il y a eu de grandes artistes-femmes. Eh! Messieurs, il y en a eu et c'est étonnant, vu les difficultés énormes qu'elles recontrent. Parlez donc aux gens comme il faut d'envoyer leurs filles dessiner d'après le nu sans lequel il n'y a pas d'études possibles.'[33]

Tracing the history of the idea that '(s)he who cannot draw the nude can draw nothing' with its corollary that '(s)he who can draw the nude can draw anything' is beyond the scope of this discussion.[34] It would matter little if the emphasis upon becoming a 'grande artiste femme' rather than simply learning to paint was typical of Bashkirtseff only, but hundreds of women, about half of whom had travelled from far countries, even from the ends of the earth, spent thousands of woman-years and hundreds of thousands of francs in the ateliers of the Académie Julian without either learning to paint or becoming 'grandes artistes femmes'.

It may be said in Julian's defence that he had not initially intended to exploit the aspirations of naive women, for he had not originally intended to cater for females at all. According to George Moore, who entered the atelier in 1873 when the students were still treated as intimates by the patron, Julian hired Markouski's old dance studio in the Passage des Panoramas and a model to pose there in 1868, because he could not make a living any other way. Moore gives a vivid rendition of the way Julian charmed the first student to endure working in the atelier all by himself.[35] In 1888 William Rothenstein heard a rather different version:

> He himself used to tell the story of how, at his wits' end for a living, he hired a studio, put a huge advertisement, 'Académie de Peinture', outside, and waited day after day, lonely and disconsolate; but there was no response. One day he heard a step upon the stairs; a youth looked in, saw no one, was about to retire, when Julian rushed forward, pulled him back, placed an easel before him, himself mounted the model-stand – 'et l'Académie Julian était fondée!'[36]

With time Julian added another piquant detail about the first student: 'C'est lui, affirmait Julian qui lui porta chance: c'était un petit bossu'.[37]

Though George Moore was wrong in affirming that Julian was bred to be a shepherd (he was actually the son of a poor schoolmaster in La Palud, Vaucluse), he was evidently not wrong about his essential coarseness. When Julian opened his first 'atelier libre' he was thirty-one. The classic hagiographic account of his career tells us that while he was working as a salesman in a bookshop in Marseilles, he read voraciously and, fired by Balzac, decided to try his fortunes in the capital. He entered the atelier of Léon Cogniet, at the same time as Tony Robert-Fleury, Jean-Paul Laurens and Krug; the relationships he made there were the nucleus of the network that was to give him virtual control of the Salons by the end of the century and perhaps long before.[38] Cogniet had been removed from the presidency of the Ecole des Beaux-Arts in the shake-up of 1863, but the old-boy network was to remain intact until 1881 when control of the Salon passed once more into the hands of artists themselves. Hundreds of the individuals who now had the right to vote for the selection of the jury had been taught by Cogniet, and hundreds more had attended the Académie Julian. Rodolphe Julian seems to have maintained some kind of contact with all of them.[39]

After Julian had exhibited two drawings and six paintings in the same Salon des Refusés in 1863 in which Manet showed *Le Déjeuner sur l'herbe* and Whistler *La Femme en blanc* and was ridiculed along with them,[40] he abandoned all hope of making a living by painting or illustrating.[41] Instead he became a promoter, first of wrestling, 'la lutte romaine', and when he lost the considerable amount of money he had made doing that, he decided to merchandise art education. What the Académie Julian offered and continued to offer was training to prepare young Frenchmen to enter the concours for the Ecole des Beaux-Arts. From the beginning Julian exploited his contacts, first in securing the services of Gustave Boulanger, Jules Lefebvre, Tony Robert-Fleury and Bouguereau to criticize his students' work[42] and then in securing visibility for those students. Otherwise Julian organized his atelier on the same lines as all the other French artists' ateliers: students entered as *rapins* and graduated to the rank of *compagnons* or *anciens*; their teachers decided when they could leave off drawing from casts and begin to draw from life, when they might begin to use colour and if they might enter work for the Salon or for the competition for the Prix de Rome. Discipline and the day-to-day running of the studio were the responsibility of the *massier*, who collected the students' contributions to the masse and used them to pay for models and other running expenses. Pupils made a one-off payment for a tabouret and easel, which remained the property of the atelier. Anyone accepted as an entrant for the Prix de Rome was allowed to work in the ateliers at cut rates; laureates were invited to return to the ateliers, which were never closed, and work from the life without paying at all. Julian well knew that the *compagnons* and *anciens* in the atelier were, if anything, more important than the masters when it came to inspiring and directing students. In the case of any student he considered exceptionally gifted he regularly waived the fees. Julian also made sure that pupils knew of his connections with wrestling,[43] which aided him materially in keeping order.[44]

Though George Moore considered that Julian had begun with an entrepreneurial plan to take over the French art establishment, it seems more likely that he was at first surprised to see how easily the network of connections that spread out from the ateliers could be made to work in his interest. Moore tells us that Julian realized when the Ecole des Beaux-Arts had shut down temporarily after a bout of student uproar that, if he offered medals of his own, the students would flock to his academy. So the idea of the monthly concours with not only a medal but 100 francs as the prize was born. As the ateliers proliferated all were involved, women and men equally, but though women students outnumbered men by two to one, those among them who won prizes had usually to content themselves with 'mentions honorables'.

Hardly a year passed when one or more of the Julian professors, Jules Lefebvre, Tony Robert-Fleury, G. Boulanger and later William Bouguereau, did not serve on the Salon jury. Conversely it was in the professors' interest to see their pupils not only well represented in the Salons but among those premiated. According to Moore:

> The Salon had not enjoyed democracy for more than three years when it came to be noticed that all the best places were occupied by pictures by *les eleves de Julian* ... Julian had turned his business into a company, of which he was managing director at forty thousand francs a year; M. Bouguereau received ten thousand francs a year for his professional services, and it is said that more than one of the professors has money invested in the studio. Branch establishments had sprung up in every quarter of the town, eighteen in all, some of the larger ones numbering two hundred pupils ... A large proportion of these pupils could do a drawing that would pass muster; those who could not had drawings done for them, and so it came to pass that *les élèves de Julian* elected a jury devoted to their interests and headed by their own professors. In return for the honour paid them, the professors gave the best places to their pupils and covered them with medals. The more medals the more pupils, and so the studio waxed prosperous.[45]

Lovis Corinth has left a damning account of how the scam was organized. After the students had got the numbers of their entries to the Salon: 'They rushed to let the directors' office know their entry numbers, which Jules passed on to the teachers, in a register where their names were listed. By this means the latter could tell which pictures were by their pupils.'[46] There is no need for Corinth or Moore to labour the point that the system could not and did not involve foreigners, who had no voice in selecting the jury. In Corinth's account, one German 'Julian' loses his mind and dies soon after and another wanders through the rooms of the Salon looking for his picture only to find it hung so far up on the wall that it seems no larger than a postage stamp. A less partisan

1. Marie Bashkirtseff, *L'atelier Julian*, 1882 (Dnepropetrovsk Art Museum, Ukraine)
2. Anon., *Une académie de peinture*, late nineteenth century (Collection Académie Julian, Paris)

observer agrees: 'A la fin du siècle, on put accuser l'Académie Julian de favoriser une sorte de maffia, des professeurs et certains de leurs élèves s'épaulent réciproquement dans les élections au Jury du Salon et la distribution des récompenses'.[47]

In 1903 the Julian organization outdid itself, carrying off seven out of the ten Prix de Rome. By then there were 'Julians' scattered not only throughout Paris and provincial France, but throughout the art schools of Europe and America, busily promoting their own kind to the detriment of art education everywhere.

Though there were literaly thousands of women 'Julians', they were neither the warp nor the weft of the web of influence that Julian had woven out of his early contacts in the ateliers of Cogniet and Cabanel. He had no crusading concern to correct the deficiencies in women's art education. The truth seems to be that when his ateliers reopened after the war of 1870, a handful of American women walked in, paid their fees and the masse and for the use of their tabourets and easels, and sat down to work alongside the men.[48] May Alcott is not an entirely reliable source but there is some evidence to support her vague account of how the women's ateliers at the Académie Julian came to be set up. Alcott, writing in 1879, recalls:

> Then there is Jullien's upper and lower school, in Passage Panorama, where a student receives criticism from the first leading authorities, and is surrounded by splendidly strong work on the easels of the many faithful French, who for years have crowded the dirty, close rooms though I believe that the lower school, as it is called, no longer opens its doors to women, for the price, being but one half of that of the upper school, attracted too many. Also with better models, and a higher standard of work, it was yet found to be an impossibility that women should paint from the living nude model of both sexes, side by side with Frenchmen.
>
> This is a sad conclusion to arrive at, when one remembers the brave efforts made by a band of American ladies, some years ago, who supported each other with such dignity and modesty, in a steadfast purpose under this ordeal, that even Parisians, to whom such a type of womanly character was unknown . . . were forced into respect and admiration . . . M. Jullien himself confessing that if all ladies exercised the beneficial influence of a certain madonna-faced Miss N among them, anything would be possible.[49]

According to George Moore, when he went to the Académie Julian in 1873, there were eighteen or twenty young men studying there together with eight or nine 'English' girls, which seems unlikely. A painting of the class by Julian himself that was exhibited in the Salon of 1876 shows an undraped female model being drawn by a mixed class. Curiously, a small oil sketch signed Lancerotto, that was offered for sale by

Sotheby's in 1989, showing men and women working at easels side by side in a crowded atelier, is also dated 1876.[50]

Julian's picture was clearly intended as publicity for the atelier; the *patron* was not averse to a little sensation if that would be good for business.[51] What was not clear was whether the presence of women in the life class was good for business. There was no point in attracting a small number of odd foreign women at the cost of driving away a large number of Frenchwomen, whose families would not tolerate such impropriety. More important perhaps were the feelings of the male students, who were used to all kinds of suggestive and entertaining horseplay with the models both male and female and to letting off steam and relieving tension and boredom in all kinds of ways, most foolish and noisy, some violent. The last thing Julian wanted to do was to see his best students flee to rival ateliers to escape the inhibiting presence of respectable and not always young women.[52] The Frenchmen who opted to train as painters generally came from the lower middle class or lower;[53] the men and women who could afford to travel from America were usually fairly well-connected. Julian soon learned to stream his students, and did so with such adroitness that very few of them had any clear idea of the total number of ateliers, where they were or what went on in them.[54]

May Alcott's version of the founding of the women's atelier of the Académie Julian is borne out by the advertisements placed by Julian in *Le Moniteur des Arts* in January, March, April, May, June, November and December of 1877: 'Académie de Peinture pour Hommes. Modèle vivant. 27 Galerie Montmartre (pass des Panoramas). Académie pour Dames. Modèle drapé. Même galerie no 30. Professeurs: MM. Boulanger, J. Lefebvre, Tony Robert-Fleury, Bouguereau.' The upper school in the passage des Panoramas was organized upon different lines: the women had the services of a *bonne* or indeed two, for maids named Léontine and Marie are both supposed to have worked there for forty years or more. The *bonnes* did the work that was done in the men's ateliers by the *rapins*, cleaned the studios, kept the models' stove alight, ran errands for the young ladies, and took care of their outer garments. Although May Alcott cannot get Julian's name right, she was right about the fees the women paid, 700 francs a year against the men's 400, and probably right too about the quality of the models they got for their money.[55] Belloc, though she is generally a fan of Julian, points out that for twice as much money women got 'half the teaching received by the men working in his studios'.[56] More insidious perhaps was the difference in atmosphere between the strictly segregated schools, which was not simply a matter of tobacco smoke. Hooper is anxious to reassure her readers that the models maintained 'irreproachable correctness of language and deportment' and that the atmosphere was 'irreproachably cold and pure'.[57] Sutherland put it less favourably: the women's classes were so formal that in the presence of the master the women 'hardly dared breathe'.[58]

In October 1877 *Le Moniteur des Arts* was so disloyal as to give in answer to frequent inquiries from its female readers about 'un cours de dessin pour dames' the name of Mme Marie Nicolas-Drapier, 'professeur de la ville de Paris, élève de Chaplin' who offered 'étude d'après nature du modèle vivant' and had installed the same artificial lighting system as was in use at the Ecole des Beaux-Arts.[59] A month later under the same heading appeared an adjustment of the record: 'Tous nos lecteurs connaissent au moins de réputation, les cours fondés au passage des Panoramas par M. Rodolphe Julian ... L'atelier des dames, distinct de l'atelier pour hommes, est organisé avec un soin très particulier ...'

Clearly the mixed classes were no more. Julian had judged it best for business to reassure potential clients that in his ateliers young women would not necessarily be exposed to the sight of the naked human body at all, let alone in the company of ribald young men. Actually women in at least one of the ateliers for the Académie Julian were drawing from the nude or nearly nude for at least part of the day, but this was not something that Julian wanted Parisian mothers to know. In certain of his ateliers mothers were welcome to accompany their daughters and to stay with them as they worked; after Julian's death when his widow resumed the direction of the ateliers of the rue de Berri, she announced in *L'Académie Julian* that she would ensure that there the élèves would be made artistes without ceasing to be 'femmes du monde'.[60]

Julian was neither the first nor the only patron to offer women the choice of drawing from the undraped model, even in Paris where the idea was more shocking to the bons bourgeois than it was in London, Philadelphia, New York or Munich. In 1867 when Louise Jopling worked at Chaplin's studio, an otherwise unknown ex-student called Miss Besley provided for the 'serious' students an undraped model at 7 a.m.[61] May Alcott tells us that at the Atelier Krug the 'much discussed question of the propriety of women's studying from the nude [was] settled in a delicate and proper manner by the gentlemanly director', leaving her readers no whit the wiser.[62] There was of course nothing to stop serious women students from clubbing together to finance their own nude model. The official art-schools that allowed women access to a life class did so under strict conditions: they could not enter the room until the model was posed and they might not remain in the room if the drawing-master was present. What Julian offered to women was the chance to pose their own model and to secure the best viewpoint. The woman who produced the best work in a week was allowed to pose the model the next week, an unheard of liberty. The women were not expected to leave the room in the event that the master might actually see them contemplating nudity. When, one day in October 1877, Julian strode into the women's atelier while the nude model was still on the stand, Marie Bashkirtseff's friend, Berthe Boyd, was so upset at the implied offence to her modesty that she left never to return.[63] She would have been truly scandalized to discover that the studios were often so crowded that not all the students could get a view of the model, in which case Julian would put up two models, not always of the same sex.

Not even Julian, however, allowed his female élèves to contemplate the male genitalia; male models in the women's atelier were and remained throughout the history of the Académie Julian stoutly caleçonnés. Even so, the average Parisian bourgeois appears to have found the idea of the women's life class extraordinarily piquant. In his play *La Massière* (1905), which was set in the 'Académie Justinian', Jules Lemaître introduces a male model who has been banished from the ladies' atelier for blowing kisses to one of the pupils. He is brought back at the intercession of the heroine, played by Martha Brandès who studied at the Académie Julian in the 1880s and is supposed to figure in Bashkirtseff's painting. When told there is to be a male model, an ingenuous pupil simpers: 'Modèle homme, chouette! ... Moi, ça me fait toujours quelque chose ...'

A society lady accompanying her daughter to the Atelier Justinian is scandalized when the male model reenters clad only in his caleçon. She whispers a question into the massière's ear. 'Never,' the massière replies. In another rib-tickling routine Suzanne, the ingenue, does her amazing imitation of the 'trois manières de peindre', the French, the German and the English. And the maître is satirized for offering what was in fact the exhortation uttered ad nauseam in the ateliers Julian, 'Soyez virile'. Any suspicion of xenophobia or sexism on the part of the distinguished author and his adoring audience is borne out by the piece as a whole, in which the massière though purely loved for her spirituality and talent by the maître whose wife is jealous, avaricious and soulless, achieves that most enviable of destinies, marriage with the great man's son.

Julian's trump card in attracting eager, undemanding and docile female students to serve as milch cows to nourish his main enterprise was the occasional attendance upon his students of his *compagnon d'atelier*, Tony Robert-Fleury, winner of the Prix de Rome and of the Grand Médaille d'Honneur du Salon, before he was thirty-three. Robert-Fleury, who seems to have suffered from early burn-out, knew what was expected of him and played the part to the hilt. Cecilia Beaux entered the 'Julien cours' in the rue de Berri in 1888:

I began, of course, with an 'Academy', a full-length drawing. 'Tony' – that is Tony Robert-Fleury – was to criticize that week, and at the hour entered a young middle-aged and very handsome man, with a face in which there were deep marks of disappointment, his eyes, grey and deeply set, smouldered with burnt-out fires. As I observed him from behind my easel, I felt I had touched for the first time the confines of that which made France and Paris a place of pilgrimage. Into the room with him came something, not perhaps a quality of his own, but of what he had come from and lived in. The class, although accustomed to him, was in a flutter.

As Robert-Fleury sat looking at Beaux's drawing he began to speak in a manner that stirred her strangely, though she could not understand what he was saying. He was in fact quoting Corneille. Then, 'He rose, not having given me any advice, but bent his cavernous eyes on me with a penetrating but very reserved smile, and turned to the next.' Beaux was thirty-three years old and yet she did not see Robert-Fleury's corny act for what it was.[64]

The other half of the winning team in the women's classes at the Académie Julian was William Bouguereau. Late twentieth-century taste finds Bouguereau's work vulgar, false and sentimentally pornographic. In fact he drew wonderfully and could have painted just as well, if he had not been seduced by a false notion of photographic realism that dictated a hard, flat finish. In some quarters he was reverenced as a new Michelangelo; in others he was reviled as the most repellent of the peintres pompiers. The women who came halfway round the world to have him look at their drawings for a minute or two a week were all devotees.

> Si le maître a été vénéré et écouté par les hommes, on doit dire qu'à l'atelier de la rue de Berri on le considérait comme un demi-dieu; on avait un véritable culte pour lui. Jamais on ne se fera idée des reliques que les Américaines envoyèrent dans leur pays, et la plus précieuse etait un morceau d'allumette qui avait servi au grand homme; les dames arrachaient la cigarette qu'il avait poliment jetée avant d'entrer chez elles, en remettant son chapeau et son paletot à Léontine, la bonne . . .[65]

Reaction against Bouguereau's style of painting had been gathering for years, but the women of the Académie Julian remained utterly loyal.

If the combination of saintly Bouguereau and Byronic Robert-Fleury did not get the clients hooked, Julian was prepared to court his students himself. Cecilia Beaux remained under the impression that Julian knew 'nothing whatever about art' – a misconception which reveals how little attention Julian had actually given her work, especially when compared with his treatment of Marie Bashkirtseff. When Beaux moved out to her own studio in the rue Notre Dame des Champs, Julian realized that he had let a valuable contact slip through his fingers and took the trouble to visit her there: 'M. Julien had a few words with me, very serious and with some emotion, to which my beating heart, of course, responded. "Mademoiselle" he urged, "You must devote yourself to the expression of feeling." He would have had her believe that he feared that she would not 'adhere to the noble truth only'.

The success of the women's ateliers at the Académie Julian was easily copied; by 1886, according to one observer, Paris was crowded with ateliers des dames:

> A man must, as a rule, have a very decided talent before he will adopt a profession which demands more and gives less than any other ... But with women the case is different. There are numbers who, having just enough money to live quietly abroad, and pay the very moderate studio fees, discover that art is an excellent weapon to kill time withal; and that a studio makes a very pleasant club; that you can never tell if you have a talent or not until you try; that it is so nice to be able to paint pictures of your friends; and in fact that you might as well join Z's studio, just to see what it is like. This irrevocable step taken the victim rarely if ever recovers ...[66]

The author's saturnine view of the 'prevalence of the artistic mania' and 'the thoughtless manner with which it selects its victims' might be thought to sort ill with Bashkirtseff's plea for equality before the easel, but it shows a firmer grasp of the reality of the situation. Julian and the 'leading authorities' who worked for him found no difficulty in keeping women scratching away at their Ingres paper for year after year, heartened only by the occasional 'Continuez!' From 1880 onwards female students outnumbered the men, but in the monthly concours which was open to all the ateliers the prize of 100 francs seldom went to a woman. The insidious manipulation of female self-delusion is perhaps the most contemptible aspect of the Julian operation. Bashkirtseff sensed it, confided it to her journal but fell for it anyway, in her desperate need to think of herself as 'vraiment artistique'.

One of the most distinguished female pupils of the Académie Julian spoke rather sardonically of the teaching there in an interview for *L'Echo de Paris*: 'Dans les écoles, croyez bien que chaque élève se développe comme elle peut. Voyez chez Julian, est-ce que la leçon d'une heure par semaine, partagée entre cent élèves, peut exercer une influence directrice sur le talent d'une femme?[67]

When women were clamouring for the right to attend the Ecole des Beaux-Arts, they were struggling to board a sinking ship.[68] Nevertheless the convention among feminist art historians is to regard women's acceptance into moribund academies, an innovation which spread from the provinces to the centre, as a victory. One of the great enigmas of modern culture is that, as art education spread into every hamlet and hovel, art itself withdrew from the masses to become an arcane language spoken by a very few, extremely arrogant individuals and their patrons. Art education was brought into every hovel and hamlet by troops of dedicated people, the majority of whom were women.

> A young woman has studied with New York artists, themselves pupils of Carolus-Duran, Gérôme or Henner; has graduated at the Art Students' League or the Cooper Institute, or perhaps has drawn and painted in Paris and Munich; at twenty-five she goes to Wisconsin, Michigan or still further and she supervises drawing classes over large sections of those states.[69]

The devoted handmaidens of high art, who practically fainted if one of the great academicians should condescend to notice them, were the unwitting mediators of the denial of art to the many. They were taught and themselves taught a kind of 'fine art' that self-defining genius regarded with contempt and revulsion. Artists of both sexes were led up a blind alley by Rodolphe Julian, but only the women represented the experience to themselves and others as a liberation.

## Suggested reading

Cosnier, Colette, *Marie Bashkirtseff: un portrait sans retouches* (Paris: Horay, 1986).

Greer, Germaine, *The Obstacle Race* (London: Secker and Warburg, 1979)

Lethève, Jacques, *La vie quotidienne des artistes français au XIXe siecle* (Paris: Hachette, 1968).

Milner, John, *The Studios of Paris: The Capital of Art in the Late Nineteenth Century* (New Haven and London: Yale University Press, 1988).

Weinberg, H. Barbara, *The Lure of Paris: Nineteenth-century American Painters and their French Teachers* (New Yorkand London: Abbeville Press, 1991).

Yeldham, Charlotte, *Women Artists in Nineteenth-century France and England* (New York and London: Garland Publishing Inc., 1984).

# PART II

## *VISUAL FRAMEWORKS*

# *Writing the arts: aesthetics, art criticism and literary practice*

## David Scott

To understand why there were so many nineteenth-century French writers on the arts involves investigating Romantic aesthetics and art criticism and recognizing the challenges they posed to literary writers, especially in view of their awareness of the post-Renaissance tradition of the rivalry of the arts. For central to Romantic aesthetics was the concept of excess: beauty in art is not only in the subject, concept or intention of the work, but also in the multiple suggestive reverberations produced by its material form. Writers were quick to grasp the opportunity this offered to creative writing. As art critics they set out to describe the effects of this visual excess in the plastic arts and as writers or poets to recreate a literary equivalent of it. This was to be achieved not only by explicating the work's content – an exercise verging on the pleonastic given that the subject of the painting or sculpture was in many cases already literary – but also by seeking out analogous areas of feeling or thinking which were then elaborated in juxtaposition with painting or sculpture. Since creative writers, the Romantics included, were most concerned, ultimately, with form, this in turn led them to reflect on formal equivalents and to explore the degree to which literature (and especially poetry) was analogous to painting and sculpture in the way they organize their subject matter.

A coherent expression of Romantic aesthetics appeared quite late in France. Though a French translation of Lessing's *Laocoon* had been published in 1802, the impact of Coleridge's writings on Poetics and the Imagination filtered in only very slowly – and very often through the intermediary of third parties, such as Mrs Crowe.[1] Charles Baudelaire was the first French writer cogently to articulate aesthetic theories which took into account German and English ideas on the Imagination as well as contemporary developments in literature and the visual arts. But the *Salon de 1846* and the *Salon de 1859* essentially expressed the ideas of a poet in the context of art criticism, not the writings of a philosopher in a treatise on aesthetics. Earlier aesthetic theorists such as Quatremère de Quincy, Victor Cousin and Théodore Jouffroy were aware of Lessing's comparative study of literature and the visual arts as well as classical aesthetic thought, but were mostly out of touch or sympathy with contemporary art. They tended therefore to tinker with classical or eighteenth-century ideas with only superficial reference to Romantic concepts of the Imagination, rather than fully to rethink aesthetics in the light of nineteenth-century artistic practice. Nevertheless, some interesting formulations emerge from their writings, especially those of Cousin and Jouffroy, which point to significant later developments.

It is in their attempt to justify a hierarchy of the arts that Cousin and Jouffroy tend to offer their most interesting insights into the emerging Romantic aesthetics. Cousin's argument for the superiority of literature in the first edition (1836) of his famous treatise *Du Vrai, du Beau et du Bien* is significant in this respect since it reveals the paradoxes of art as they come to be better appreciated in Romantic aesthetics. Poetry is both precise and vague, finite and infinite. Words in poetry are both material and immaterial; as clearly definable as lines and colours, but infinitely more suggestive; they are both the simplest and the richest expression of the absolute. How is it that the finite is able to express the infinite, the simple the absolute? And how is it that a phenomenon as apparently indeterminate as poetry can be judged superior to the other arts? The answer Cousin suggests, although he does not fully clarify his position, is that poetry, like music (for Cousin, the second in the hierarchy of the arts), appeals to 'les idées favorites de notre imagination'.[2]

These ideas, it seems, are neither fully containable nor fully definable: when expressed in terms of words, they overstep the bounds of literal meaning (the finite, the precise) and yet part of their charm is that they retain a certain specificity. The intention bestowed on them by their author need not necessarily define the reading of them by their receiver and, more significantly still, they do not have to be defined in the formal or generical terms of their kind. Indeed, when they are performing at their best, they are most aptly defined in terms of other arts. Thus, the greatest paintings are described as 'de la pure poésie' (*Du Vrai, du Beau et du Bien*, 280) and the most vivid poetry compared to the visual arts. It is implied not only that the imagination, insatiable in its demand for satisfaction, yearns for ideas or sensations beyond those inherent in the phenomena in question, but also that it is prepared to create new syntheses – on a formal, semantic or generical level – to achieve the required level of fulfilment. That this is in particular the case with poetry is made clear by Cousin when he argues that poetry, of all the arts, is most able to benefit from the resources of the others: 'Avec la parole, la poésie arrive à peindre et à sculpter; elle construit des édifices comme l'architecte; elle imite, jusqu'à un certain point, la mélodie de la musique. Elle est, pour ainsi dire, le centre où se réunissent tous les arts . . . '('Using words, poetry can both paint and sculpt; like an architect, it can build edifices; like a musician, it can create melody. Poetry is, so to speak, the centre at which all the arts meet . . .') (*Du Vrai, du Beau et du Bien*, 290).

But how is poetry, 'l'art par excellence', able to create the sensual and physical aspects of experience that play such an important role in the activation of the imagination in the plastic arts? Cousin, unwilling to make the transition from aesthetic theory to an examination of artistic practice, does not have much to say on this point. Théodore Jouffroy, on the other hand, is prepared to investigate a little further, at least in theoretical terms, the extent to which language is able to exploit the resources of the other arts. In answering the question 'Comment les descriptions poétiques mêmes parviennent-elles à nous émouvoir?' Jouffroy stresses the importance of an alliance between form and content in which the artist is as concerned with the former as with the latter: 'L'artiste ne doit pas tant faire comprendre l'invisible que le montrer; et le montrer, c'est le revêtir de formes matérielles.'[3] The implication here, though again, given Jouffroy's essentially theoretical stance, it is not fully brought out, is that the poetry of artistic expression resides as much in the form of the work, in its material existence, as in the ideas governing its conception. Language then must be considered as much from a material as from an intellectual point of view. Or as Jouffroy himself puts it in a memorable formula: 'La littérature doit être matérielle et non métaphysique' (*Cours d'esthétique*, 299). In other terms, words themselves, as much as the ideas they ostensibly convey, have a fundamental role to play in the creation of what Jouffroy calls 'l'émotion esthétique', that is, the imaginative response of the reader/receiver in relation to the poetic text. That this response to poetry could be governed by visual stimuli, and this on a literal, sensual, as well as on a metaphorical level, is implied but not fully spelled out by Jouffroy. Once again, it will only be so by writers who, less concerned with theoretical issues per se, are more attentive to their responses to the art object itself and more concerned to explore the problems of expressing in writing their reactions to it.

It is interesting in this respect to compare the responses of an artist such as Delacroix to moments of inspired perception of reality or of the work of other great artists with those of a (more or less) contemporary aesthetician such as Quatremère de Quincy. The Romantic conception of the art object as a producer of an imaginative surplus, vividly borne out by Delacroix's experience as recorded in his *Journal*, is rejected or supressed by Quatremère. In a passage celebrating the achievements of Rubens as a painter, Delacroix writes that 'le succès dans les arts n'est point d'abréger, mais d'amplifier, s'il se peut, de prolonger la sensation, et par tous les moyens'[4] and confirms 'ce besoin de l'homme d'éprouver à la fois le plus d'émotions possible' (*Journal*, 373). Quatremère, on the other hand, asserts in his *Essai sur la nature, le but et les moyens de l'imitation dan les beaux-arts* 'l'impossibilité morale où nous sommes, de recevoir deux impressions à-la-fois';[5] his inability to perceive synthetically and imaginatively becomes the basis of the principle on which he goes on to establish his aesthetic theories in the *Essai*, in which he affirms that 'chaque art est moralement et physiquement restreint à l'unité d'objet dans son imitation, comme à l'unité de sujet dans son ouvrage . . .' (*Essai*, 48).

The paradox of the simultaneously material and immaterial qualities of the art object that Cousin and Jouffroy had allowed in their theoretical writings is viewed far more suspiciously by Quatremère, who places 'la partie sensitive' and 'la partie imaginative' of the mind in watertight compartments. Delacroix, on the other hand, will not hesitate to reassert, at least in the context for painting (a certain skepticism persists in Delacroix, as we shall see, with regard to the scope of poetic language), the intangible nature of aesthetic emotion: 'Ces figures, ces objets, qui semblent la chose même à une certaine partie de votre être intelligent, semblent comme un pont solide sur lequel l'imagination s'appuie pour pénétrer jusqu'à la sensation mystérieuse et profonde dont les formes sont en quelque sorte l'hiéroglyphe' (*Journal*, 372). The work of art is thus able to satisfy a number of mental requirements: 'l'image offerte aux yeux non seulement satisfait l'imagination, mais encore fixe pour toujours l'objet et va au-delà de la conception' (*Journal*, 285).

The implications of this awareness for the question of the synthesis of the arts or of different genres are fully realized by Delacroix who, like Hugo also in his *Préface de Cromwell*, anticipates Wagner, when he sees theatre as being a confirmation of the human need to explore the fullest possible range of ideas and emotions (*Journal*, 373). This position was the diametrical antithesis of that taken up by Quatremère, who elevates to the status of a natural law the idea that the differences between the arts must be observed: 'Montrons donc la réalité des barrières qui doivent exister entre les arts d'imitation morale, ou les différents genres de poésie; et faisons voir que la nature y ayant aussi posé des limites, leur transgression, de quelque manière qu'elle ait lieu, est une transgression des lois naturelles' (*Essai*, 31)

It is curious that lip service to these 'barrières' will continue to be paid in the 1830s and 40s, even by French writers who were increasingly concerned to exploit correspondences between the visual arts and literature on a practical and creative level. Théophile Gautier was one of the first of these and in many ways exemplifies the ambiguous situation of the artist in this period in France whose statement of position in theoretical terms is very often not in synchronization with his practice. Gautier

3.  Tony Johannot, frontispiece of *L'Artiste*, 1831

started out his career as a *rapin* in the painter Rioult's studio but, partly inspired in 1829 by Victor Hugo's collection of poems *Les Orientales*, turned thereafter to a career as a professional writer, although he continued to paint throughout the rest of his life.[6] His practical experience in the studio, as well as refining his visual perceptions, taught him much about the technical processes of art and there is little doubt that this training was to have a profound impact on his development as a writer. So that although, in a passage of 1831 attributed to him, he suggests, reflecting Cousin and others' thinking that, '*L'ut pictura poesis* est une vieille bêtise qui pour avoir tantôt deux mille ans n'est guère plus respectable pour cela. La peinture et la poésie sont de choses diamétralement opposées',[7] his creative writing as an art critic and a poet provided a bridge between artistic production and literary practice that had a significant impact on the development of correspondences between the arts in France.

This development of the possibility of inter-art correspondences was predicated in part on a new concept of the artist, one that implied the widening of the term to include the writer and the musician on the same footing as the painter and sculptor. This concept is exemplified in what was to be one of the longest-lasting and most influential of nineteenth-century literary reviews, *L'Artiste* (1831 to 1904, edited by Gautier in the 1850s), whose title vignette in 1831 (fig.3) united the figures of a painter, sculptor, poet and musician. It took for granted that writers and painters were imaginative and creative individuals who aimed at comparable goals in their different media and who could learn much from each other on a technical and practical as well as on an intellectual level. This cross-fertilization was echoed in *L'Artiste* by the frequent juxtaposition of art criticism and poetry, and of images and text, and implied a challenge in particular to the writer. For although in the vignette of 1831 the dominant position in the image is taken by the central, standing figure of the painter – the sculptor is a sketchy presence in the background and the writer and musician are seated to the right and to the left of the picture – in practice, in *L'Artiste*, the writer had a key and double function: to criticize and to promote the visual arts, and to offer original creations in the terms of his own medium, that of language.

For literary writers, excellent art critics that they sometimes were, it was often difficult entirely to separate these two functions. This difficulty is clearly stated by Baudelaire in his *Salon de 1846* in which he stresses that criticism should be entertaining and poetic, not cold and mathematical. If writer and painter were both artists, it was logical that their responses to both nature and the arts should be artistic: 'Ainsi le meilleur compte rendu d'un tableau pourra être un sonnet ou une élégie' (*BOC*, 11, 418). This idea perfectly suited nineteenth-century writers, anxious to reassert the preeminence of their medium in the fraternal struggle between literature and the visual arts, but it was less popular among the painters themselves. Delacroix's distrust of Baudelaire as an art critic and misunderstanding of his achievement as a poet are documented in his *Journal* (see 175 and 582).[8] His attitude is based on his fear that his paintings were being upstaged by the art-critical writings ostensibly about them. Delacroix's comments on Gautier's art criticism also make this clear: 'Il [Gautier] prend un tableau, le décrit à sa manière, fait lui-même un tableau qui est charmant, mais il n'a pas fait un acte de véritable critique' (*Journal*, 515–16). Though an avid reader and great admirer of literature of the past, Delacroix never seems to have been in tune with contemporary poetry, especially that of Gautier and Baudelaire, both of whom were a generation younger than himself. This distrust of their writing, in verse or in prose, is reflected in a letter to Théodore Thoré, an art critic with no literary pretensions, to whom Delacroix felt able therefore to express his scepticism about literary art criticism: 'On nous juge toujours avec des idées de littérateurs et ce sont elles que l'on a la sottise de nous demander. Je voudrais bien qu'il soit aussi vrai que vous le dites que je n'ai que des idées de peintre; je n'en demande pas davantage.'[9]

Delacroix's unease may have been in part a result of his obscure awareness that literary art criticism was, at bottom, less about art and more about how writing, in attempting to come to terms with the visual image in the arts, develops strategies for foregrounding its own suggestive and visual potential. This process is perfectly exemplified in the art criticism of Gautier and Baudelaire, and nowhere more so than in the context of their writings on the artists they most admired. In his *Salon de 1847*, for example, Gautier's elaborate account of Thomas Couture's striking canvas *Romains de la Décadence* or *Orgie romaine*, although it says little that would not have been appreciated by the artist himself, nonetheless activates literary or poetic energies that go beyond the picture itself. Gautier's account, for example, of Couture's juxtaposition of human figures and marble statues rapidly transcends literal description to become an artful elaboration of the figurative potential of certain literary expressions:

> des statues, aux physionomies sévères, aux attitudes solennelles, représentant les grands Romains des époques glorieuses, assistent, témoins impassibles, du haut de leur piédestal, aux débauches de leurs descendants dégénérés; on dirait qu'un éclair d'indignation brille dans leurs yeux blancs, et qu'un sarcasme de marbre crispe leurs lèvres sculptées.

> statues, whose severe countenances and solemn postures represent the great Romans of the imperial age, stand high on their pedestals, passive witnesses to the debauchery of their degenerate descendants; a spark of

indignation seems to shine in the blank orbits of their eyes while their sculpted lips seem pursed in an expression of stony reprobation.[10]

This amplification of the image's metaphorical potential is even more daringly applied to the 'live' participants in the scene when the poet/art critic transposes the attributes of the marble statues to those of the living woman. For transcending her role as personification of Rome, the Messalina figure in Couture's painting is transformed in Gautier's account into a fragment of sculpture from the Parthenon, half-clothed in marble draperies fashioned by Phidias, with the bust of a statue, flesh of stone and marmoreal brow. The text becomes in fact a poetic extemporization on one of Gautier's favourite themes – that of writing being analogous to scupture in marble, in which the word's literal, figurative and aesthetic connotations are explored in a display of linguistic virtuosity that in effect obliterates Couture's painting.

The fact that, much to Gautier's approval, Couture should choose to set his painting in the context of a quotation from Juvenal establishes a literary aura for its viewing which other literary art critics will also seek to exploit when writing on painting. They were greatly encouraged to do this, of course, by the inherently literary content of much French painting in the first half of the nineteenth century which, even in the case of an artist as original as Delacroix, continued to observe the academic conventions in relation to the hierarchy of the arts, which placed 'history' painting (that is of Greek mythological or Christian subjects) at the top. A temptation of literary art criticism for a while would then be to explore the literary content of the picture, to treat it as a version of a text that had been translated by other artists or writers, past or contemporary. Its aim would be itself to become a further reading of the myth or image, one predicated on the picture in question, but also showing an awareness of the history of its previous literary or painterly incarnations. It would do this above all by focusing on the relatively vague or ill-defined areas of the painting, raising questions precisely about what was absent or missing from the work. In this way literary art critics opened up a field of poetic reverie that would also be explored by them in terms of poetry.

An example of this process is offered by Baudelaire's response, in his *Salon de 1859*, to Delacroix's painting *Ovide chez les Scythes* in which his lyrical reaction to the work is placed in the context of a number of other poetic texts treating the 'Ovid in exile' theme. First mentioned is Chateaubriand's evocation of Eudore's discovery of Ovid's tomb in *Les Martyrs* in which Chateaubriand himself cites the first verse of the elegy by Ovid inscribed on his grave. These texts are followed by the notice accompanying Delacroix's painting in the Salon which is finally followed by the poet/critic's response to the painting:

Tout ce qu'il y a dans Ovide de délicatesse et de fertilité a passé dans la peinture de Delacroix; et, comme l'exil a donné au brillant poète la tristesse qui lui manquait, la mélancolie a revêtu de son vernis enchanteur le plantureux paysage du peintre. L'esprit s'y enfonce avec une lente et gourmande volupté, comme dans le ciel, dans l'horizon de la mer, dans des yeux pleins de pensée, dans une tendance féconde et grosse de rêverie (*BOC*, II, 636).

All the delicacy and inventiveness of Ovid has been recaptured in Delacroix's painting; just as exile crowned the famous poet with the sadness he hitherto lacked, so melancholy has clothed the painter's lustrous landscape with its magical varnish. The mind plunges into it with leisurely and voluptuous pleasure, as into the heavens, into a maritime horizon or into eyes full of thought, in a mood fertile and pregnant with reverie (*BOC*, II, 636).

Here Baudelaire has not even attempted a literal description of the painting nor analysed its structure or *facture*. As an account it is repetitive, not to say pleonastic, and some of the images it evokes are not in the painting. This is beside the point, however, for what Baudelaire is offering his readers here is not art criticism, but a generalized concept of the poetic, the favourite themes, indeed, of his own poetic repertoire, evoked here as a series of literary equivalents to the images proposed in Delacroix's painting. As a text, then, it operates fundamentally in juxtaposition with the object it purports to be describing and establishes, in the process, an autonomy that will be consciously exploited by Baudelaire and others in their writing which, although outside the Salon context, is still inspired by the visual arts.

Although the images of Romantic painting and sculpture were to provide an important stimulus to contemporary poetry,[11] it was an awareness of how the methods and effects of the visual arts could be adapted to formal developments, especially in verse, that would have the greatest impact on inter-art correspondences. Here two questions arose. The first was the nature of the relationship between the aesthetics of painting and that of literature. The second was that of how the language of literature and poetry, benefiting from the example of painting and sculpture, could be made more plastic, more visual in its appeal. Taking the aesthetic question first, it became clear to literary art critics that the beauty of a picture lay in the overall harmony of the object itself and in the suggestive properties of its formal features. Baudelaire consistently stressed, in his account of the impact of Delacroix's pictures on him, their abstract qualities, qualities that could be appreciated before the subject of the painting was grasped (see *BOC*, II, 425, 592, 594–5 and

753). Colour and the plastic qualities of paint were perceived as providing the key formal and expressive elements in pictorial art. On the one hand they were seen to be able to harmonize the various parts of a picture through a system of tonal correspondences, while on the other they were also able to articulate feeling, mood or tone (*BOC*, II, 625). Colour was recognized as being in itself a kind of language, a way of thinking: '[La couleur] pense par elle-même, indépendamment des objets qu'elle habille' (*BOC*, II, 595).

It was this perception of the relative autonomy of colour in Romantic painting which, confirming intuitions that were beginning to declare themselves in the context of prosody, suggested to nineteenth-century poets and writers the possibility of instituting a similarly aesthetic approach to literary and poetic composition. The linguistic and prosodic equivalents to colour harmonies in painting were perceived increasingly in the phonetic harmonies, rhymes and other formal devices which created unity of feeling or tone in literature. The 'aesthetics' of prosody became then, for poets from Gautier onwards, an area as rich in poetic resources as the subject or theme of the text. Gautier, like Hugo in *Les Orientales*, often chose his rhymes before he had fully decided on the subject of his poem just as the Romantic artist sometimes selected harmonious colours before getting to work on his canvas and in this way allowed his choice of pigments to influence the development of his subject. In modifying the classical notion of an essentially linear mode of composition, writers increasingly began to conceive of literature in plastic and spatial terms.

Gautier, for example, attributes to the words in Baudelaire's poetry the same material, sensuous qualities that Baudelaire perceived in the colours of Delacroix's paintings: '[les mots ont] en eux-mêmes, et en dehors du sens qu'ils expriment, une beauté et une valeur propres'.[12] By the same token, Baudelaire admires in Gautier's handling of the prosodic resources of French verse the way he introduces 'systématiquement et continuellement la majesté de l'alexandrin dans le vers octosyllabique', achieving 'la fusion du double élément, peinture et musique, par la carrure de la mélodie, et par la pourpre régulière et symétrique d'une rime plus qu'exacte' ('the fusion of the two elements, painting and music, by integrating melodic structure and rhyme's regular and symmetrical splashes of crimson') (*BOC*, II, 126). This conception of poetics was summarized and confirmed by Théodore de Banville in his *Petit Traité de poésie française* of 1872. Asserting poetry's primacy in the hierarchy of the arts and underlining its ability to synthesize and incorporate into itself their aural and plastic qualities, Banville uses terms and ideas derived from the aesthetic theory of Cousin and Jouffroy:

[La Poésie] est à la fois Musique, Statuaire, Peinture, Eloquence; elle doit charmer l'oreille, enchanter l'esprit, représenter les sons, imiter les couleurs, rendre les objets visibles, et exciter en nous les mouvements qu'il lui plaît d'y produire; aussi est-elle le seul art complet, nécessaire, et qui contienne tous les autres ...

[Poetry] is simultaneously Music, Sculpture, Painting and Eloquence; it should delight the ear, enchant the mind, reproduce sounds, imitate colours, make objects visible, and inspire in us all the moods it seeks to express; thus it is the only complete and perfect art, containing all others ...[13]

The plastic qualities of the word as sign were of course pursued not only in nineteenth-century verse but also in prose writing. Once again, it was art criticism that provided the bridge between the most plastic of the arts – painting and sculpture – and one of its most abstract forms – language. The Goncourt brothers were the first to develop fully the potential of prose as an artistic medium with their *écriture artiste*, in which literature was able to create a sense of the material presence of the object comparable to that achieved in the visual arts. Their stress on the material quality of painting as an art in their essay on the Exposition Universelle of 1855 is stronger even than that of Baudelaire in the context of Delacroix. In it they argue that painting should be 'l'animation matérielle d'un fait, la représentation sensible d'une chose', whose principle function is that of 'la recréation du nerf optique'.[14] Painting for them is a material art, daughter of the earth, its aim, as Chardin shows in his still lifes, to recreate 'la vie inanimée des choses' (*L'Art du 18e*, 82), or as the sculptor Carpeaux contrives in his female busts, 'la spiritualité matérielle de la créature féminine' (*L'Art du 18e*, 247).

Literature's function in relation to painting, for the Goncourts, is not merely to take elements of itself back from painting in the form of narrative, history, subject or any other form of content, but to try to recreate some of the sensations it draws from its raw material. Its function would be similar in relation to nature. In their art-critical and other writing, the foregrounding of the object and of its sensual qualities is achieved through a number of formal and stylistic techniques including nominalization, the promotion of the noun at the expense of other parts of speech. Another technique is the use of adjectives in a relationship of juxtaposition, like two adjacent pigments on the canvas or two crayon marks on the paper: 'le tapage des zinzolins et des chevelures blondes' (*L'Art du 18e*, 68) and 'des entrecroisements de hachures noires et de hachures rouges' (*L'Art du 18e*, 77); then there is the creation of a syntax reproducing not a logical order of relationships but the order of *sensations*: 'Et en cercle, petites mules et hauts talons sur le carreau noir et blanc, paniers et basques ça et là sur les bois dorés aux formes rondis-santes, autour du clavecin sonore, radieux des fantaisies de quelque Gillot, la belle compagnie écoutait' (*L'Art du 18e*, 132). Additionally and simultaneously, the Goncourts constantly stress the formal qualities of the words they use (parallelism of structure, similarity of sound, patterns of repetition) to enhance the sensual and material impact of the experiences they convey. The effect their style produces is close to that evoked by Mallarmé writing more generally on the poetic function of syntax: 'Un balbutiement, que semble la phrase, ici refoulé dans l'emploi d'incidentes multiplie, se compose et s'enlève en quelque équilibre supérieur, à balancement prévu d'inversions.'[15]

Mallarmé's writing, even more than that of the Goncourts, extends the plastic aspect of language while at the same time expanding its symbolical potential. The form/content paradox is thus further deepened in Mallarmé's poetry, which promotes both the materiality of the word as sign and its metaphorical transparency. This is achieved by developing further two areas of potential: the reintegration of sensation into the thinking process, and the foregrounding of the page or book as part of the medium of writing (in prose or in verse). For Mallarmé, words only take on their full significance when they appear on the page; the latter is not simply a neutral support but a symbolic field activated by the text's imprint. The poet, consciously or unconsciously, composes the blank areas of the page as carefully as the words themselves. The conventions of prosody had helped him do this in the past; in the age of free verse and prose poetry, he is simply more conscious of the process. The relation between object and word (or sign) is seen then as being reproduced in that between word (signifier) and concept (signified). The signified(s) of the words are buried in the page surrounding them as well as in the relationships established by syntax or other means within the text.

This process is illustrated by Mallarmé's poem *Un coup de Dés* in which both pictorial and prosodic space have been reintegrated into the text – the first in the form of the margins and form-dictated line lengths of the text, the second in the mobilization of the totality of the page as a theatre for visual as well as linguistic activity. In this way, relations both between the linguistic elements themselves and between words and the page become highly charged, often proposing simultaneously two contrary modes of apprehension – one spatial and graphic, the other linear and logical. The spatial organization of the picture is reflected in the page 'designs' of *Un coup de Dés* – which Mallarmé described as 'Au fond, des estampes'[16] – both in the textures and sizes of the eleven type-faces employed and in the semi-representational forms proposed by some pages. The logical structure of the text is shown in the way the linguistic elements interact, even if they do not use the linear model of

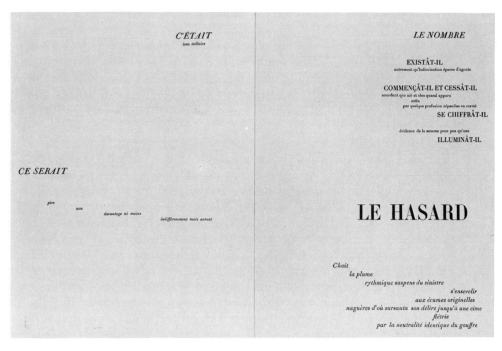

CÉTAIT
*issu stellaire*

LE NOMBRE

EXISTÂT-IL
*autrement qu'hallucination éparse d'agonie*

COMMENÇÂT-IL ET CESSÂT-IL
*sourdant que nié et clos quand apparu*
*enfin*
*par quelque profusion répandue en rareté*
SE CHIFFRÂT-IL

*évidence de la somme pour peu qu'une*
ILLUMINÂT-IL

CE SERAIT

*pire*
*non*
*davantage ni moins*
*indifféremment mais autant*

LE HASARD

*Choit*
*la plume*
*rythmique suspens du sinistre*
*s'ensevelir*
*aux écumes originelles*
*naguères d'où sursauta son délire jusqu'à une cime*
*flétrie*
*par la neutralité identique du gouffre*

4. Stéphane Mallarmé, extract from *Un coup de Dés jamais n'abolira le hasard*, 1897

conventional prose. This becomes clear in Mallarmé's use of typography (fig.4).

The use of different typographical series on the same page and the institution of a problematic relationship between them (aggravated by the spatial as opposed to rigorously linear layout adopted) makes it possible for Mallarmé to present several lines or levels of thought at the same time. To this extent, *Un coup de Dés* represents an extension and refinement of his customarily parenthetic style of writing. Whereas, however, in most Mallarmean prose, the main clause may be fragmented or suspended over as much as a paragraph, in *Un coup de Dés* it becomes a matter of pages. The massive capitals which, continuing the title of the poem, become its main proposition are spread over four sheets while the institution of the various different series in smaller Roman capitals and in lower case Romans and italics has the effect of spreading out the simultaneous development of several different but related sets of ideas over a number of pages. Mallarmé here is attempting to illustrate diagrammatically the complex processes of human thought, to express the irregular and sensuous meanderings of reverie as well as the more consistent and consequential logic of rational thinking. In

73

other words, he is trying to construct in visual as well as linguistic terms a plausible diagram of the mind. Mallarmé's project, then, in *Un coup de Dés* is a logical, if radical, development of nineteenth-century French aesthetics and poetics, as it contrives to convert language into a medium that is both figural and textual, or, to use Jouffroy's terms, material and metaphysical.

This ambition, shared with Mallarmé by a number of French writers in this period, to exploit simultaneously in one hybrid creation the characteristics of two or more different art forms, is also evident in the generic ambiguity of *Un coup de Dés*. For this text is a *poème en prose*, a genre the potential of which, in the second half of the century, was increasingly explored by poets – Baudelaire and Rimbaud, as well as Mallarmé – seeking to combine both the lyrical properties of language's formal harmonies and the more flexible registers of prose. Once again, the Imagination, in seeking to transcend the bounds of a given framework – formal or generic – sought to keep options open in two or more worlds of expression. The relationship between the development of the prose poem and writers' interest in the visual arts is particularly significant in this respect: from Aloysius Bertrand's *Gaspard de la Nuit* of 1842, with its subtitle *Fantaisies à la manière de Rembrandt et de Callot*, through Rimbaud's *Illuminations* of the 1870s, with its proposed subtitle of *Coloured Plates*, to Mallarmé's *Un coup de Dés* of 1897, the prose poem developed as a means both of exploring the visual structures of the plastic arts and of recreating, formally and typographically, the graphic dimension of texts. Once again, then, imaginative excess in one form or genre is recuperated by the utilization of functions of another.

The implications of this phenomenon for formal or generical classification are, of course, problematic. This may have been one of the reasons for Quatremère de Quincy's reluctance to overstep the bounds of the arts as they had become established in neoclassical European theory and practice. For if all categories are, at bottom, arbitrary, if the imagination is freest when liberated from conventional restraints, what was the function of aesthetics? What even Quatremère's writings demonstrate, however, though not as eloquently or illuminatingly as those of the poets and art critics who followed him in the nineteenth century, is that it is in exploring the tensions between generical, formal or other categories – painting and literature, poetry and prose, line and colour – that the creative and the critical imagination alike are actively mobilized. It is in this respect, especially, that French nineteenth-century works which confront correspondences between literature and the visual arts constitute an exemplary field for comparative study.

## *Suggested reading*

Christin, A.–M. (ed.), *L'Espace et la lettre. Ecritures, typographies*, Cahiers Jussieu no. 3 (Paris: UGE/10–18, 1977).

Florence, Penny, *Mallarmé, Manet and Redon: Visual and Aural Signs and the Generation of Meaning* (Cambridge: Cambridge University Press, 1986).

Lyotard, Jean-François, *Discours, figure* (Paris: Klincksieck, 1971).

Scott, David, *Pictorialist Poetics: Poetry and the Visual Arts in Nineteenth-century France* (Cambridge: Cambridge University Press, 1988).

Souriau, Etienne, *La poésie française et la peinture*, Cassal Bequest Lecture (London: Athlone, 1966).

Thévoz, Michel, *L'Académisme et ses fantasmes* (Paris: Minuit, 1980).

# 5

## *The problem with colour. Three theorists: Goethe, Schopenhauer, Chevreul*

## Bernard Howells

Painting, or more accurately, Drawing, has always possessed in Perspective an unshakeable foundation. All this part of art can be demonstrated, like geometry . . . Chromatics or the part that concerns colours has so far lacked a pictorial theory and lacked any rule except for the criteria of taste and genius or perhaps of visual habit . . . All this part is in the strangest confusion.

Castel[1]

Colours . . . are not only an ornament we should be sorry to lose, but are also a means of assisting us in the distinction and recognition of external objects. But the importance of *colour* for this purpose is far less than the means which the rapid and far-reaching power of the eye gives us of distinguishing the various relations of *locality*.

Helmholtz[2]

'All form depends on drawing (*Zeichnung*). It is drawing and drawing alone which makes painting in general an art, just as it is colour which makes it painting' (Schelling).[3] The first, Schelling adds, gives us truth, to which the second adds the supplementary illusion of material reality. 'Drawing is the essential', writes Kant: the 'allure' (*Reiz*) of colour gratifies the senses but does not belong to the beautiful because it cannot be the object of disinterested contemplation, i.e. of judgements of *pure* taste; colour in painting is restricted by the requirements of beautiful form and ennobled only by the latter.[4] Judgements of this kind give some idea of what Baudelaire was up against when he undertook his 'partial, passionate, political' defence of Delacroix and colour in the *Salon de 1846*[5] 'partial', 'political' and therefore 'just', in Baudelaire's historicizing perspective, because he was aware that the contemporary line/colour debate was the tip of the iceberg, part of a clash of values in which colour had been the victim of a quasi-systematic repression. He thought that European art in the mid-century was at a critical turning-point ('Il est vrai que la grande tradition s'est perdue, et que la nouvelle n'est pas faite')[6] and that its future, if it had one, lay in the emancipation of colour. To understand Baudelaire's 'passionate' intervention we need to grasp, in its widest context, the kind of thinking that lay behind the academic mistrust of colour. It is difficult for us in the modern period, which accepts the autonomy of colour in painting or sees it as an integral part of form, to enter into that value-system which traditionally relegated it to the lowest position – below line and below chiaroscuro – as the least essential of the three 'parts' of art. It is not simply pictorial values which are at stake in this hierarchy. In it are imbricated other hierarchies which define a certain moment of humanism: reality/appearance, depiction/impression, knowledge/sensation, rational/irritational, public/private, human/natural, male/female (it is a minor topos of nineteenth-century manuals that line is male, juridical, sufficient for the representation of *form*, especially of the highest form, the human form, and destined to exercise a strict control over the promiscuities of colour – female – associated with the evocation of *flesh*).[7]

It is not my aim here to review the polemic which continued in the nineteenth century to pit the '*coloristes*' against the '*dessinateurs*', Delacroix against Ingres, as it had pitted Rubens against Poussin, the Venetians against Raphael. Nor do I intend to examine, except incidentally, Baudelaire's position within it. I wish to look outside art history altogether and track the repression of colour into an area where it is all the more startling because least expected – in three theoretical works of the first half of the century which set out to investigate colour in a scientific or philosophical way: Goethe's *Theory of Colours* (the didactic part of the *Farbenlehre*, 1810), Schopenhauer's *Vision and Colours* (*Über das Sehn und die Farben*, 1816 and 1854) and Chevreul's *De la loi du contraste simultané des couleurs*, 1839.[8] The exposition of these three texts is intended to give some idea of the problematics of colour. At the same time I propose a reading of them which demonstrates how each in its own way works from premises or returns to conclusions which perpetuate a long-standing philosophical devaluation of colour seen as a secondary aspect of the visible, separable from and subordinate to the spatial. The same demonstration could have been continued with Helmholtz. But it may be more useful, instead, to look back to earlier science and make some preliminary remarks which relate the status of colour to the doctrine of qualities and to the Aristotelian/Newtonian controversy.

We read, in *The Oxford Companion to Art*, that 'throughout the greater part of the history of painting colour was regarded as no more than a decorative adjunct to the essential delineation of shape'.[9] 'Shape' includes not just line but, especially from the Renaissance onwards, the rational representation of objects in three-dimensional space, hence, in art-terms, chiaroscuro and perspective, both claimed as part of 'le dessin' – a term translated sometimes by 'drawing' or 'line' or 'draughts-manship', sometimes by 'design'. 'Dessin' was not distinguished from the wider 'dessein' (*disegno* in Italian) until the eighteenth century, and continued to draw much of its prestige from the latter's association with the idea of a rationally planned universe whose perfection was bodied forth in art. The privilege accorded to 'le dessin' in neoclassical doctrine and, conversely, the Romantic revalorization of colour as the affective element in painting are closely connected to the traditional distinction between primary and secondary qualities which received a new lease of life with the rediscovery of Democritus in the Renaissance and was criti-cal in the growth of scientific rationalism and, indirectly, of pictorial aesthetics. The primary qualities (extent, volume) are those without which the idea of objects is unthinkable – the geometrical (measurable) properties of matter which are the basis of the causal, space-time description of the world given by classical mechanics. Colour on the other hand (like taste, warmth) is a secondary quality – an 'aesthetic' quality in the original sense of being dependent on the sentient human organism, intermediate between the objective and the affective, only loosely tied to objects (in Newton's view not a quality of objects at all) and not amenable to abstraction.

The hierarchy of primary and secondary qualities remains operative in what Baudelaire called the analytical 'méthode double' or 'méthode suc-cessive'[10] of academic painting (draw first, colour second) which privileges 'le dessin' as (theoretically) amenable to the control of an exact general science (geometry) and therefore of a proper pedagogy, unlike colour which is abandoned to the intuition of individual 'genius'. Line, so the academic argument goes, constitutes in itself an adequate (if schematic), coherent and universally intelligible image of reality. At the other end of the scale, colour is only *strictly* necessary for the repre-sentation of inorganic substances (precious stones, different metals and so on). In this scale of necessities, 'form', equated with 'le dessin' at the expense of colour, trails with it something of its scholastic ontological definition: that without which the existence of a thing is impossible (*forma dat esse rei*). Baudelaire sought to neutralize then invert this hier-archy, arguing that we analyse the visible into colour and line in order to facilitate execution, but there are no lines in nature, only the juxtaposi-tion of coloured masses, so that 'forme et couleur sont un'.[11] Line separates artificially objects and parts of objects from each other; it creates stable conceptual identities and emphasizes the psychological distance between perceiver and perceived. Colour on the other hand blurs the distinction between objects and between subject and object; it corresponds to knowledge in the sense of coalescence rather than abstraction.

As the middle-term of the hierarchy, chiaroscuro is inevitably problematic – claimed by the 'coloristes' to be part of colour, which is naturally light or dark (see De Piles)[12]; claimed as part of drawing by the 'dessinateurs' because, as the minimal condition for representing solids 'in the round', it is considered part of the 'essential delineation of shape' and can be adequately represented (and taught) by a rationally gradated system of monochromatic shading. Castel makes a typical claim for the priority of chiaroscuro, as part of drawing, over colour when he writes:

> Painting is perfectly able to do without colours in representing objects; but it cannot do without chiaroscuro, because it cannot do without drawing. Chiaroscuro can do without colour; but colour cannot do without chiaroscuro; chiaroscuro is the basis, colour merely an accident. Whichever colour you take, it has its degree of chiaroscuro; whilst degrees of chiaroscuro are not necessarily tinged with colour.[13]

This hierarchy survives intact in the bulk of nineteenth-century aesthetic and pedagogic manuals, even in Helmholtz,[14] or else it is only very grudgingly modified. For Charles Blanc, who did more than any other art critic of the century to reveal Delacroix and Chevreul to the Impressionists, 'le coloris n'est autre chose que le clair obscur nuancé'.[15] For Bracquemond, beleaguered by Impressionism in 1885, colour retains simply 'l'apparence momentanée des choses ... indépendante de leur forme'[16] whose permanence is adequately defined by contour, light and shade alone.

Formulae like Castel's and Blanc's alert us to a complex issue underlying aesthetic polemics and one which belongs as much to science as to art – the Aristolelian/Newtonian controversy, particularly as it concerns the relation of chiaroscuro to colour.[17] Put simply and abstractly, the priority of chiaroscuro over colour could find some kind of justification in Aristotelian theory which saw colour as the product of varying mixtures of light and dark, or white and black, and which arranged the hues in a tonal scale going from the darkest (usually blue) through the median colours (red and green) to the lightest (yellow). Variations in the number and arrangement of the hues need not concern us here.[18] By showing that, on the contrary, white resulted from the mixture of 'homogeneal' coloured lights which alone were 'primary' and that the spectrum corresponded not to a tonal scale but to a scale of refrangibilities, Newton unsettled the residually Aristotelian basis of painterly theory. Blanc's phrase 'le coloris n'est autre chose que le clair obscur nuancé' is a statement of aesthetic priorites which conceals an Aristotelian definition of colour, closer in fact to Goethe than to the Newtonian Chevreul. I wish to show now how Goethe's Aristotelian interpretation of colour actually devalues rather than revalues its chief object.

# *Goethe*

Goethe's account of colour presents itself, self-consciously, as a phenomenology which seeks to protect the reality of immediate sensuous experience from reductive abstraction. The senses have direct access to knowledge, not just to 'secondary phenomena' but to 'primordial phenomena' (*Urphänomene*) – a term by which Goethe aims to suggest a reality, still concretely apprehended but nevertheless a sufficient principle of explanation (or 'idea'), which exists at the boundary of human knowledge and beyond which we cannot go without stepping into the void of the inhuman.[19] Colour is the secondary phenomenon, explainable only in terms of the *Urphänomen* of light and dark which, like the other primordial phenomena governing nature (e.g. magnetism or electricity), is a polarity, a 'double property, which is in fact but a principle of reunion' (295). Goethe's theory of the generation of colour-appearances, like his studies of the morphology of animals and plants, reflects his belief not only in the unity of mind and world but also in the possibility of a unified view of nature – 'to refer a boundless empiricism to one centre' (293) – which rests on the characteristic premiss of *Naturphilosophie* that nature is a hierarchically organized totality.

'Physiological colours' – colours which are not there in nature but appear subjectively in accordance with the law of complementarity, for example in after-images of various sorts – provide 'the foundation of the whole doctrine' (1). Hitherto seen, for the most part, as 'extrinsic', 'casual', 'adventitious', as 'imaginary spectres' (1) or 'temporary visual defects' (22), they are, for Goethe, 'the necessary conditions of vision' (2), distinct from but actually confirmed by pathology. Goethe's importance lies in the keenness with which he grasped this point, not in the construction he subsequently put upon it. From the premiss that light and darkness put the retina in opposed states (total activity or total inactivity), he develops the proposition that

> In the act which we call seeing, the retina is at one and the same time in different and even opposite states . . . [In this way] we at once perceive all the intermediate gradations of chiaroscuro, and all the varieties of the hues (5) . . . The eye cannot for a moment remain in a particular state determined by the object it looks upon. On the contrary, it is forced to a sort of opposition, which, in contrasting extreme with extreme, intermediate degree with intermediate degree, at the same time combines these opposite impressions, and thus ever tends to a whole, whether the impressions are successive, or simultaneous and confined to one image (13).

Goethe's Aristotelianism becomes apparent in the way he goes on to suggest that the production of the hues is dependent on and intermediate between the fundamental contrast of light and dark – as, for example, in his observation that when we close our eyes after looking at a dazzling white object, the after-image goes through a series of colour-transformations from yellow through red then blue to darkness (16, 17). Goethe's observations are all made to converge towards the 'important leading phenomenon' (63) that, whenever and however colour makes its appearance, it is always associated with shade: 'Colour itself is a degree of darkness (*skieron*); hence Kircher is perfectly right in calling it *lumen opacatum*' (31), a 'subduing of light' (130).

'Physical colours' (Goethe's second category) are close to and 'have but little more reality' (56) than physiological colours and, for that reason, despite their vividness (*emphatici, speciosi*) have also been deemed 'transient', 'fugitive', even 'false' (56). They are 'colours in a progressive and mutable, but not in a final or complete, state' (57) because they do not belong properly to objects, as 'chemical colours' do in Goethe's view, though they are produced 'objectively' under certain conditions which all involve the intervention of material mediums or the interference of material objects. Colours may be produced incidentally by reflection (*catroptical* colours) which involves a 'subduing of light' (160). They appear (in the case of *paroptical* colours) in the shadow produced at the edges of objects – at their boundary with light (164). But they are first and foremost connected with colourless mediums (*dioptrical* colours) – which brings us to the puzzle of Goethe's experimental disagreement with Newton.

It is part of Goethe's concern with 'concreteness' that he refuses to consider light as an abstract source. What we see, even in the case of the sun or the hole in Newton's 'window-shut', is a circumscribed object or luminous image: 'In the act of seeing, generally, it is the circumscribed visible which chiefly invites our observation' (90). This is another 'leading premise' and I will argue that it involves a tacit promotion of the original delimited shape which entails a devaluation of the coloured image derived from it. To take a typical experiment: when Goethe viewed a white surface bounded by black from close-up through a prism, he records that violet then blue appear to one side, yellow then orange to the other, the surface in-between remaining uncoloured. When a black surface bounded by white is similarly viewed, these pairs simply exchange places. Discriminating between hues was, Newton conceded, a matter where 'Sense is Judge'.[20] Granting Goethe's right to claim that the first colour in Newton's spectrum was not a 'true red' (*Purpur*) but a yellow-red (*Orange*) and ignoring his account of how 'true red' is produced as a median colour, Goethe's *initial* observation is not irreconcilable with Newton. But his interpretation and subsequent refinement on it *are*. Goethe assumed the hues were produced by the admixture of light and dark at the boundaries where a white surface was displaced by refraction over a dark one, or vice versa. This was precisely the kind of misinterpretation Newton warned against repeatedly as typical of 'vulgar' (i.e. Aristotelian) optics.[21] As Goethe's contemporaries pointed out, what he had observed was perfectly explainable in Newtonian terms: 'The appearance of white in the centre, according to the Newtonian theory, arises from each line of rays forming its own spectrum. These spectra, superposing each other on all the middle part, leave uncorrected (unneutralized) colours only at the two edges'.[22] In arguing that the hues were produced by superimposition of white on black Goethe was, Helmholtz showed, treating a displacement he himself describes as 'apparent' as if it were real.[23]

The nub of the matter is that refraction for Goethe meant essentially displacement and dislocation of shape: 'Objects seen through mediums more or less transparent do not appear to us in the place which they should occupy according to the laws of perspective . . . This deviation from the law of right-lined vision is known by the general term of refraction' (76, 77). The deviation is only apparent, of course, and colour only appears if the boundaries of the object or surface can be seen. As with reflections and shadows, colour is therefore associated with 'mere accessory images . . . secondary dimmed and darkened' (139, 140), analogous and allied to those 'secondary images' which are the shadows of bodies, and produced when the 'primary image' is made to deviate by the interference of a corporeal medium from geometrical rectitude.

'Colours', Goethe writes elsewhere, 'are the actions and sufferings of light', in its contest with darkness[24] – the flickering on the wall of Plato's cave, we might say. What motivates his indignation with Newton is not some experimental disagreement but the fact that *Opticks* topples white light from its 'primordial' or pristine position, making it 'a middling colour . . . a mean between Colours . . . equally capable of being tinged with any colour whatever'[25] – its original status usurped by the variety of 'primary', simple, 'homogeneal' rays that produce the sensation of the hues. All hierarchies are thereby inverted:

> We look upon the mistake that has been committed [by Newton] in the investigation of this subject to be a very serious one, inasmuch as a secondary phenomenon has been placed higher in order – the primordial phenomenon has been degraded to an inferior place; nay, the secondary phenomemon has been placed at the head, a compound effect has been treated as simple, a simple appearance as compound (73) . . . We repeat that we cannot admit it [colour] to be an elementary phenomenon. On the contrary, we have traced it to an antecedent and a simpler one; we have derived it, in connection with the theory of secondary images, from

the primordial phenomenon of light and darkness, as affected or acted upon by semi-transparent mediums (102).[26]

Another category of physical colours – *epoptical* colours, that is the changing progression of colours observable in bubbles, films or thin laminated plates under pressure – is, for Goethe, the very symbol of colour's transience and mutability, of the fact (already implicit in complementarity) that 'where colour exists at all, the whole scale is soon called into existence' (188). No colour can stand on its own. Baudelaire saw in this 'relative existence'[27] of colour the secret of the colourist's 'magic'. On the other hand it is the stuff of the warnings issued by academic critics against the threat which colour-behaviour poses for the individuality of forms: 'En présence de la couleur active, aucune matière colorée ne peut prétendre à une individualité propre'.[28]

Goethe took the view that 'Sense is Judge' to its limit. Colour-theory (like organic chemistry and biology, which occupy the highest positions in the Romantic hierarchy of sciences) is a department of science 'independent of geometry' (286), to which optics unfortunately became attached through 'other laws of vision which the mathematician was legitimately called upon to treat' (lx) (i.e. perspective). What distinguishes colour from other phenomena in physics which also depend on polarity is its immediate aesthetic relevance (297), its direct impact – like that of music (298) – on the senses, and, through these, on the mind. The meaningfulness of colour is not a matter of learnt response, but of what Baudelaire would have called 'correspondance'. Colours in the outside world are already 'familiar' to the eye, which accepts with pleasure the fact of having its potentiality determined thereby towards a given state (305). Colours which sense recognizes as distinct are distinctly significant ('characteristic' in Goethe's terms). At the same time they stimulate the eye to 'produce the complemental hue' (317), showing that 'nature tends to emancipate the sense from confined impressions by suggesting and producing the whole' (319, 320). Combinations of colours are arranged diagrammatically by Goethe in a hierarchy (see fig.5) The relation of opposite colours (the diagonals) results in 'pure, harmonious, self-developed combinations, which always carry the conditions of completeness with them' (321). Combinations represented by the chords of the circle are less satisfying, because lacking an element of the desired totality (321). Neighbouring colours are too close to each other for their combination to be more than faintly significant or 'characteristic'.

Spontaneity/necessity, specificity/universality, emancipation/completeness are, then, built into the aesthetic experience produced by colour. But, at the same time, the ability of colour to stimulate affective impressions 'without relation to the nature or form' of objects confers

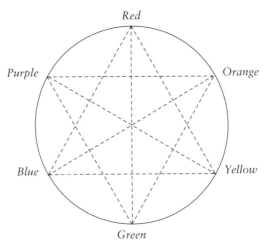

5. Goethe, diagram of colour combinations, from *Theory of Colours*, trans. Charles Eastlake, 1840

upon it, in art, a problematic freedom. 'Expression' dictates how an artist exploits the 'characteristics' of colour. Uncertainty in expression (what Baudelaire calls 'doubt'[29]) leads either to weak colour or to motley. Colour is all the more vulnerable to 'uncertainty' in that 'light and shade are already defined in the drawing, and are, as it were, comprehended in it, while the colour still remains open to selection' (344). In other words, tied to affect and partly untied from form, colour enjoys a flexibility which is the privilege of the peripheral. The absence of colour (as in some monochromatic paintings of antiquity) is a 'violent abstraction' and the neglect of colour in favour of abstract line (for example in the representation of draperies) is one of the 'pernicious prejudices of art' (338). But at the same time chiaroscuro affords a 'picturesque completeness' (332) and retains its privilege as an artistic procedure vindicated by Goethe's own theoretical premises: 'The separation of light and dark from all appearance of colour is possible and necessary. The artist will solve the mystery of imitation sooner by first considering light and dark independently of colour, and making himself acquainted with it in its whole extent' (331).

## Schopenhauer

Schopenhauer thought of himself as Goethe's most 'fervent defender' (5). *Vision and Colours* is an early work, related to *The Fourfold Root*

84

*of the Principle of Sufficient Reason* rather than to the more distinctive Schopenhauer of *The World as Will and Representation*. In it Schopenhauer attempts to wed Goethean colour-theory to Kantian epistemology – a marriage of incompatibles, in Goethe's view. Schopenhauer judged Goethe to have provided a methodical phenomenology of colour but not a *theory* in any proper sense, i.e. an account of colour phenomena unified under a single general concept.[30] That concept, for Schopenhauer, was the bipolar physiological activity of the retina. Goethe, he argued, had emphasized the distinction between 'physiological', 'physical' and 'chemical' colours in such a way as to obscure the truth that all colours are, strictly speaking, physiological – a function of the retina's dynamic response to stimulus. 'Physical' and 'chemical' colours are simply shorthand for referring to different categories of external stimuli. The first concern of colour-theory is with the subjective *sensation* of colour, not with its objective external *causes* (21–22) Any account of the latter must be congruent with the former. Only by understanding the effect (the modification of the retina's activity) is it possible to arrive at a proper understanding of the cause (the corresponding modification in the source) and so bring the objective aspect of colour-science into harmony with the subjective.

Schopenhauer distinguishes between the 'extensive', 'intensive' and 'qualitative' divisions of the retina's activity, which operate simultaneously and conjointly in ordinary vision (62). The 'extensive' division – the fact that stimulus can fall on different (or the same) parts of the retina – only affects colour specifically where after-images, optical mixing and so on are concerned. Response to degrees of light and dark produces an 'intensive' (measurable) division of the retina's activity. White light requires its total 'intensive' activity, darkness results in its inactivity, shadow (and, as we shall see, colour) requires its partial activity – as in Goethe. But white, black and the intermediary shades of grey are not colours properly speaking The sensation of colour involves the 'qualitative' division of retinal activity (25) – something distinct from but closely related to and dependent upon the *partial* 'intensive' activity, since the colours only appear in what Leonardo called the 'middle zone' between the extremes of light and dark and have inherent tonal values which can be quantified and arranged in a scale, or expressed as a relation of simple fractions. Each of the 'essential six' hues represents a certain fraction of the retina's total response to white light; its complement, spontaneously generated in the case of after-images and so on, makes up the remainder to a total of one (34):

| Black | Violet | Blue | Green | Red | Orange | Yellow | White |
|-------|--------|------|-------|-----|--------|--------|-------|
| 0 | ¼ | ⅓ | ½ | ½ | ⅔ | ¾ | 1 |

This is clearly a version of the familiar Aristotelian scheme, laid on its side and expressed numerically. How or why the 'intensive' division of the retina's activity becomes translated into a 'qualitative' activity which produces the sensation of colour is never explained but simply ascribed without further ado to an inherent physiological capacity.

The important thing is that colour is always produced by the division of activity into two equal or unequal qualitative 'halves', and any account of the external causes of colour must be congruent with this bipolarity. Goethe's derivation of the colours from the admixture of light and dark produced under certain conditions, satisfied the requirement; Newton's seven (or five) primary homogeneal rays of different refrangibilities did not. The Newtonians, in Schopenhauer's view, were incurable realists obsessed with 'objectivity' (34, 51) – as if there were really a fixed (odd) number of coloured rays 'out there' in nature causing directly corresponding sensations in the eye. So they inevitably lapse into discussing colour as if it were resident like some chemical property in the ray itself. Newtonian theory 'considers each colour simply as a *qualitas occulta (colorifica)* of one of the seven homogeneal lights, gives it a name, and leaves it at that' (40). Such a view, Schopenhauer argues, ignores the *active* role of the retina, requires us to believe that colours are 'presented completely formed to the eye' (68) and ultimately posits some kind of 'harmonia praestabilita' (68, 69) between the human sensory apparatus and the world. On the contrary there are (as Runge's coloursphere suggests) an infinite number of colours with no fixed divisions; the rays of light are infinitely divisible (as Newton acknowledged) and to this corresponds the infinitely divisible activity of the retina. *But the division is always into two parts*: 'Colour always appears as duality, because it is the qualitative bipartition of the activity of the retina. From the point of view of chromatology it is absolutely impossible to speak of isolated colours, but only of pairs of colours.' (35) Newton was right (as against Goethe) to claim white could be reconstructed from colours, but wrong to think all seven (or five) were required.[31] Given the right 'energy' and 'purity', the sensation of white can be produced from any two complementaries (by 'physical' but not by 'chemical' mixture). On the other hand, Goethe was, in Schopenhauer's view, more right than wrong: right to believe that the external cause of colour must be 'attenuated light' (72); wrong to believe that white could not be reconstituted from prismatic hues, and wrong, paradoxically, like the Newtonians, by excess of 'objectivity'. Goethe refused to accept the possibility of reconstituting white because of the darkness (*skieron*) present in all colours. His mistake was to imagine the *skieron* was present in an objective sense, whereas it simply originates, according to Schopenhauer's theory, in the 'fraction' of the retina's capacity which remains inactive. Goethe's account of physiological colours was exemplary but it is significant that his account of physical colours did not tally with it. For example, his physical opposites – yellow/blue, which derive from the alleged polarity of light and dark in nature – do not correspond to his physiological complements which are yellow/violet and blue/orange (71) (see Fig. 5). This mismatch is symptomatic of a fundamental misapprehension: there is no polarity of light and dark *in nature*, only light, its gradations, its absence. Polarity properly understood is the prerogative of the retina's activity. Goethe's 'primordial phenomenon' was a misplaced concept: 'The only real primordial phenomenon [*Urphänomen*] is the organic ability of the retina to allow its nervous activity to be divided into two qualitatively opposed halves, sometimes equal sometimes unequal, and to allow these to be manifested successively' (73).

Schopenhauer's physiologism is a philosophical position that did not require him to have a scientifically exact notion of physiology. His 'qualitative division' of the retina's activity is a bit of theoretical guesswork inspired by Goethe and incompatible with the trichromatic receptor theory developed by Young about the same time, which became the basis subsequently (in Helmholtz) of a properly scientific physiological optics. Schopenhauer's 'fractions' are also guesswork, typical of the ambition to describe colour 'logically', and bring it within the purview of proportion. But Schopenhauer did not intend his fractions as an *explanation* of colour. Arithmetic cannot account for sensation. 'Où le calcul commence, l'intelligence des phénomènes cesse' (90 – in French in the text), he writes of the French propounders of wavelength-theory. To take up a distinction he elaborates systematically: calculation and concepts do not belong to primary, immediate, intuitive knowledge, but to abstract secondary representation.[32] Nor can the 'fractions' be empirically demonstrated. But the fact that the 'essential six', though rarely encountered in a 'pure' state, have always been universally identified and recognized as such, even if they have received different names (32, 33), is an indication in favour of some kind of subjective but universal norm of colour discrimination: 'an a priori norm' (34), 'an ideal, an Epicurean anticipation [*prolepsis*] independent of experience' (33), 'analogous to the regular geometrical figures which do not present themselves absolutely perfectly in reality, but which can be perfectly known and understood by us with all their properties' (33). Much seems to be being claimed for colour here, but the appearance is deceptive. Schopenhauer's 'fractions' do not constitute some kind of Pythagorean arithmology of colour or even a properly quantitative theory.[33] The three primaries traditionally distinguished by painters and scientists give rise automatically to a system of paired opposites – the 'essential six' which correspond to a rational division easy to grasp, universally recognized and expressible as simple fractions (69) – but the six are no different from any other colours one cares to imagine; *all* colours can be paired. The only 'a priori norm' is in fact the *duality* of the retina's activity.

Schopenhauer's vocabulary ('a priori norm' etc.) is part of his attempt to use Goethe's colour-theory as a useful introduction to Kantism and in the process colour is in fact downgraded rather than elevated. Colour-theory interests Schopenhauer to the degree that it illustrates the shift away from a naive realism which takes the 'objective' uncritically as absolutely 'given' (vi) towards an acknowledgement of the subjective conditions of knowledge which science must come to terms with. Colour is a 'subordinate problem' (iv) within the general theory of vision, elaborated most fully in *The Fourfold Root of the Principle of Sufficient Reason* and subordinate in its turn to a Kantian-type epistemology. This introductory function explains why Schopenhauer simultaneously claimed his colour-theory to be central and marginal to his overriding philosophical concerns (iv).

How important is colour to knowledge of the world? Perhaps inevitably the question surfaces most clearly in the problematic section on 'chemical colours' where Schopenhauer pays the price for his anti-Newtonism. 'Physical colours' (spectra and so on) at least have the intelligibility of occurrences. 'Chemical colours' Schopenhauer is forced to declare 'unintelligible' (67). Dismissing Newton's refrangibilities, he severs the 'chemical' from the 'physical', deprives himself of an explanation of surface-colours and is driven back to invoking some Aristotelian 'qualitas occulta' (74) in a way that causes his own physiologism to waver: colour seems held captive in bodies 'like a spellbound prince' (76). Marked colour-changes often correspond to minimal real change; conversely colour may be 'completely identical in utterly dissimilar things' (40); so it bears no 'constant relationship with the internal essential properties of the object' (75). Its unreliability as an indicator confirms its subjective nature but makes it problematic for knowledge:

> All this confirms on the one hand the predominantly subjective nature of colour as evinced by my theory, which has always been felt – witness the old adage 'des goûts et des couleurs il ne faut pas disputer', and also the well-proved 'nimium non crede colori', because of which colour has become almost the symbol of deception and inconstancy, so that it has always been considered dangerous to rely on colour. For this reason one must be wary of attaching too much significance to colours in nature (75, 76).

Locke, says Schopenhauer, places colour at the top of the list of secondary qualities but no philosopher has ever considered colour to be 'a real, essential, constitutive element of bodies' (40). Colour is 'a particular and subordinate part of the world of objects' (19), to which it is attached only in a 'secondary and mediate fashion' (65), 'clothing visible bodies at best like a superfluous addition' (19).

But whether viewed as a secondary quality of objects or considered under the heading of subjective sensation, colour seems unable to shake off the stigma of supplementarity. Why the retina should be so made that the division of its activity produces the 'extra' sensation of colour is, Schopenhauer writes, a question belonging, like so many in physiology, to final causes 'as if, through colour, we possess an extra means of distinguishing and recognizing things' (73) which can already be sufficiently distinguished by light and shade, as the daguerreotype 'proves' (65) and as people with twilight vision can testify. 'All intuition', Schopenhauer repeats, 'is intellectual' (7), and '*space* is the form of all intuitive perception, i.e. of *that* apprehension in which alone *objects* can, properly speaking, present themselves'.[34] Colour assists in a supplementary fashion in the determining of spatial relations. As such it occupies a 'middling' position in the hierarchy of sensations from which the understanding infers the objective world – higher than taste, smell and hearing which 'remain subjective . . . [because] their sensations point to an external cause, but yet contain no data for determining its *spatial* relations'[35] but lower than touch ('the most radical and thorough sense'[36]) and lower than the other capacities of vision which furnish the essential data (size, shape, position and so on) for our geometrical construction of reality.

# Chevreul

The story of Chevreul's discovery of the 'law of simultaneous contrast' is instructive: it arose out of investigation of the 'misbehaviour' of colour. Appointed, as an eminent organic chemist, to supervise the dyeing processes at the Gobelins tapestry works, he received complaints from customers about the quality and apparent inconsistency of some of the colours used, particularly the 'défaut de vigueur' (iii) of the blacks in some cases. Extensive investigation convinced him that the problem was not due to any material deficiency or chemical change but to an optical effect brought about by the proximity of other hues. He was finally able to formulate a law which brought satisfactorily together under a single umbrella his own observations as well as the various phenomena of induced colour, familiar enough to painters and scientists, and the concepts of complementary or opposite colours associated with them since the eighteenth century. And he brought this body of theory into line with Newton, narrowing the gap between Newtonian theory and painterly practice.

Chevreul's law can be stated in several ways. One is that juxtaposed colours modify each other mutually in a way that tends to recreate the conditions for the production of white light. When opaque coloured bodies reflect light they absorb some rays and reflect others, the sum total of reflected and non-reflected rays being white. The complement of colour A consists of all those ingredients of white light absorbed and so not reflected back to the eye by A. Complementary colours are therefore defined as 'deux lumières diversement colorées' which 'prises dans une certaine proportion' reconstitute white (4). The spectrum represents light divided into colour groups. This is necessarily a rough grouping; the rays in any one group are not all identical, and coloured bodies which reflect back to the eye a dominant colour are also reflecting some rays corresponding to other colours – hence the variety of different reds, greens and so on. A green body, for example, is also reflecting some red light (as well as blue, yellow) which modifies its greenness, and vice versa. When a green surface A and a red surface B are juxtaposed the green in A eclipses the secondary green in B, or in Chevreul's terms, renders it 'inactive' (11) (and vice versa). The result is that the red surface appears to lose whatever green it contained and become more red, the green surface more green. If red and yellow are juxtaposed, the red appears less yellow or tends to violet (because of the blue which is also present); the yellow appears less red or tends, for the same reason, to green. In short each colour appears to lend its own complement to its neighbour. Or, to give the law its more usual formulation: the mutual modification always involves the optical suppression of the common ingredient and appears to heighten the difference between the juxta-posed surfaces: 'When the eye sees simultaneously two contiguous colours, it sees them as dissimilar as possible, both with respect to their optical composition and the height of their tone' (11).

Modification involves tone as well as hue and it is not uniform; it is strongest on either side of the line of demarcation where it may actually appear as a zone of a different colour, and it weakens progressively as the eye moves away from the divide. This has considerable implications for the representation of form. Juxtaposed colour-surfaces gain in contrast but lose in sharpness of delineation and, because tonal contrast is also involved, may give an unintended three-dimensional appearance. *Strict* juxtaposition is not necessary: modification occurs, only in a weaker form, when surfaces are not contiguous, provided they are viewed *simultaneously* or *successively*. Chevreul even distinguishes a third category: 'contraste mixte' – a mixture of the successive and the simultaneous, whereby the complementary attendant upon the image of one surface may be projected onto and modify the colour of a new sur-face presented to the eye (40) – a trick of colour which can mislead painters badly (and displease tapestry-buyers) if they concentrate their gaze too long on a surface of one colour (a local colour).

Chevreul's aim, like Goethe's, was to introduce rule into the unruly. His account of the [mis]behaviour of colour draws attention to the way colours deceive and distort or 'lie' – appear to the eye when seen to-gether or under a given illumination differently from what they are 'in themselves', i.e. seen singly or locally in unbiased light. A painter must understand how the deception works, if he is to reproduce the colours of nature successfully. He must know, for example, that under an orange illumination yellows or reds will appear enhanced, greens or violets will be impoverished and neutralized. A portraitist might therefore need to dissuade a lady from sitting in a favourite green dress in a sunlit room, or else modify the green on his palette, or use an accessory or back-ground coloured in such a way as to help rectify the distortion. He will take steps to counteract the ill-effects of 'le contraste mixte', whch can result in 'un coloris terne' (151). He will be alert to the pitfalls of juxta-posing different tones of the same colour in such a way as to give the impression of relief where none was intended or, conversely, he can 'model' – produce an effect of chiaroscuro by just such a juxtaposition (what Baudelaire calls 'le modelé des coloristes'[37]): 'Juxtaposer deux teintes plates de tons différents d'une même couleur, c'est produire du clair-obscur' (157). To obtain a grey with a very delicate rosy tint (as in some shot-silks) he need not mix the pigments on his palette – it is suffi-cient to place the grey next to a green which will lend its complement (red) to it.

Chevreul's brilliant investigation of optical mixing arose, paradox-ically, out of a desire to safeguard local colour, then went way beyond this. But his fundamental aim remained the rectification of colour, not its emancipation. Colour is not an end in itself but is subordinate to other aesthetic considerations, governed by the hierarchy of genres. Apart from landscape and still-life, colour (and the utility of the law of contrast) comes into its own in portrait (160, 161) and interiors (165) where it is associated especially with the critical choice of *accessories*. The diversity of colours and accessories is a *distraction* which stops the spectator's eye coming to rest on the subject (162) – a distraction the portraitist may usefully exploit if the physiognomy of the model is 'com-mon' or 'blemished' (162). On the other hand, where the subject is 'noble' the use of colour will need to be mitigated and focus on the phy-siognomy of the sitter is better achieved (as in Van Dyck) by tonal means within a restricted colour range, i.e. by 'harmonie de gamme' and 'har-monie de nuances' rather than by 'harmonie de contraste' (161, 162).[38] These observations apply *a fortiori*, Chevreul notes, to historical paint-ing which seeks to draw attention to the physiognomy of participants in a remarkable action. Knowledge of the law of contrast here helps the painter work within a restricted range of hues by enabling him to choose those that will not be too distorted or lose too much by juxtaposition. In short, the higher up the hierarchy of the genres one goes, the less important colour becomes and the greater the need to control its potential misbehaviour, its proneness to 'accident'.

In the last analysis, the problem is that (unlike sound) colour has no 'special existence' (538) – to use a formula of Chevreul's which recalls Blanc's and Bracquemond's complaints about colour's 'lack of individuality' or 'impersonality'. Colours depend on, are memorable, and therefore contribute to meaning only by association with recognizable objects or forms: 'In every case where most persons are agreeably affected by the sight of associated colours, *those colours speak to them through the form which they clothe*' (538) (my italics). Chevreul's view of the aesthetic impact of colour is, on this score, niggardly in comparison with Goethe's or Baudelaire's. There is of course a pleasure in pure colours and in their combinations 'lors même qu'elles ne rappellent par leur délimitation aucun objet déterminé' (535), but colour cannot constitute a meaningful language in the way music does because meaning is discursive and depends on the ability of the memory to recall a complex successive order:

> In language it is the succession of words which makes up the sentence; in music, melody is nothing else but a succession of various sounds; and harmony or the coexistence of several concordant sounds only really means something musically because of the sounds which have preceded it or are to follow; in a word I find the essential character of *significant* sounds to lie in their succession and in the faculty we have of recalling and reproducing them in that order of succession, whether they concern language or music (536).

Castel's *clavecin oculaire* was doomed to failure because one cannot memorize a sequence of colours, in any meaningful way, apart from identifiable objects:

> Nearly every person confuses colours with the objects in which they appear; and it is true to say that colours only exist for most people insofar as they depend on some material form, since, far from being able to view colours to the exclusion of objects, most people on the contrary see them as fixed in objects, like one of the essential qualities of bodies, so that if the memory preserves the recollection of colours, the latter are always attached to the form of some material object (537).

Chevreul's contribution to Impressionism is one of the ironies of nineteenth-century art history. Imagining colour to be an essential quality of objects is, he maintains, a widespread illusion. The impulse to recognition is primary (part, no doubt, of our biological survival equipment);

through memory it attaches colour to the identification of objects and in this way makes it tributary to meaning. The practised eye *can* view colour apart from objects (what Chevreul calls 'absolute colour') but this is a sophisticated attitude requiring the suspension of a number of visual and mental habits – his complaining customers were sophisti- cated, discerning people. The painter needs to perfect himself in 'absolute colour' just as he needs to study abstract geometry if he wants to master linear perspective (166). But Chevreul clearly had no wish to disturb the function of object-recognition which ties colour to form, or to question its subordination to representation and legibility in painting. Unlike Goethe and Schopenhauer he approached colour-theory osten- sibly without any philosophical axe to grind but forearmed nevertheless with a set of ideological assumptions about art and knowledge which were precisely those Baudelaire, in the *Salon de 1846*, wanted to chal- lenge. Chevreul's aesthetics belong to academic neoclassicism,[39] but his colour-theory, in other hands, helped further what Wölfflin described as 'the most decisive revolution art history knows'[40] – the emancipation of colour from line and finally from representation, the conversion of means into end which led, in the modern period, to the full autonomy of the art-object.

## Suggested reading

Gage, John, *Colour and Culture: Practice and Meaning from Antiquity to Abstraction* (London: Thames and Hudson, 1993).

Kemp, Martin, *The Science of Art* (New Haven and London: Yale University Press, 1990).

Lichtenstein, Jacqueline, *La Couleur éloquente: Rhétorique et peinture à l'âge classique*, Coll. Idées et Recherches (Paris: Flammarion, 1989).

Sherman, Paul D., *Colour Vision in the Nineteenth Century: the Young-Helmholtz-Maxwell Theory* (Bristol: Adam Hilger Ltd, 1981).

Westphal, Jonathan, *Colour: A Philosophical Introduction*, 2nd ed. (Oxford: Blackwell, 1991); a response to Wittgenstein.

Wittgenstein, Ludwig, *Remarks on Colour*, ed. G.E.M. Anscombe, trans. L. McAlister and M. Schättle (Oxford: Blackwell, 1977).

# 6

# *Book illustration*

## Ségolène Le Men

'Nous voulons des vignettes, le libraire veut des vignettes, le public veut des vignettes; trois exigences à satisfaire: arrange-toi comme tu pourras':[1] with these words, an author of the 1830s addresses his brother, the artist decorator who is supposed to draw a 'vignette' for his novel. The vignette craze arose suddenly during the July Monarchy, and started the fashion for illustrations which changed the appearance of books and magazines until the end of the nineteenth century: how, why and when did this happen? Among the various factors which helped to promote book-illustration, technical developments have to be stressed, as well as sociocultural phenomena which are linked to the rise of the reading public, and to the emergence of new and distinct editorial professions. In the history of French book-illustration, the July Monarchy stands out as the crucial period, and the year 1835 as a turning-point between a period when the image was rare and a situation where it became common: the whole function and status of the illustration changed during this period.

## *The conditions of nineteenth-century book-illustration*

The fashion for illustration occurred when a set of technical inventions made the conjunction of texts and images in modern editions possible and cheap. Thus 'livres à figure', which in the past had been de luxe editions, were replaced by 'livres illustrés', advertised as 'éditions de luxe à bon marché'. It depended also on the great changes affecting both the publishing world and the audience of readers and book-owners.

## New techniques

Many inventions affected the printing world between 1750 and 1880 – the production of paper, the techniques of typography, the printing machines and bookbinding techniques – changed, became more mechanical, and introduced an industrialized publishing world. Simultaneously, the search for new ways of producing images was a recurrent quest of the nineteenth century, which ended by radically changing the conception of the reproducible image, described by Walter Benjamin as the image 'in the age of mechanical reproduction'.[2] Three techniques dominated the printing market during the July Monarchy: wood-engraving, steel-engraving and lithography.

Wood-engraving gave a fresh impetus to the old wood-cut technique which had been used in Renaissance illustrations. The engraving was done on the end-grain of small boxwood blocks with a line-engraving tool, the graver or burin; the design could thus be very precise and compete with metal-engraving; it had the advantage of being included in the typography, as a printing-process in relief.[3] The use of stereotype, and later, in 1839, the invention of electrotype, solved the problem of wear. Although small in-text vignettes also remained in fashion, large illustrations, as required for illustrated magazines or for inset plates, could be achieved only by joining a number of single blocks in a composite block.

Steel-engraving allowed much larger printing runs than copper-engraving. As an intaglio process, it involved the use of separate plates within the illustrated books, except in rare cases when the text also was engraved, as in *Chants et Chansons populaires de la France* (Paris, Delloye, 1843). It had a smooth, transparent tonality, which recalled watercolours, much appreciated in the Romantic age, whereas wood-engraving approached the graphic quality of pen and ink sketches. Usually, steel-engraving had etched areas, and combined line and stipple or sometimes stipple and mezzotint. And finally, lettering was done by a lettering engraver.

Lithography was a chemical process based on the fact that grease repels water: the drawing is inscribed on the stone in ink; the chalk stone is moistened with water; the surface is rolled over with printing ink, which will adhere only to the marks drawn. A special press is required to transfer the ink on to the sheet of paper; thus the illustration required a separate printing from the text. Lithography remains truest to the original, as it allows any type of graphic original to be reproduced with accuracy, whatever instrument may have been used to execute it, pen, pencil or brush: 'la lithographie est le dessin lui-même; on y trouve la main, le crayon, la pensée de l'auteur; . . . c'est un miroir qui réfléchit et multiplie l'original' ('lithography is pure drawing; it contains the hand, the pencil and the thought of its creator; . . . it is a mirror reflecting and multiplying the original').[4] In contrast to endwood-engraving, which was confined to a minute area, lithography made larger formats possible: therefore it was used by newspapers, or for 'voyages pittoresques'. It also contributed to the rise of the illustrated poster.

Each of these techniques implied the development of new skills and new professions. They were inseparable from the formation of related industries and the organization of markets. All three techniques were imported from neighbouring countries, but lithography, which came from Bavaria, was adapted more readily by French industry than the two others: invented in 1796 by Senedelder in Munich, lithography was introduced to Alsace in 1800 by Anton André, a music publisher, and later to Paris in 1814–16 by Engelmann and Lasteyrie; many lithographic workshops (including those of Delpech, Giroux, Aubert and Lemercier) existed during the Romantic period. The two other techniques had to fulfil conflicting requirements: on the one hand, the public was enchanted by the 'English style', but, on the other hand, industrial and commercial competition between France and England was strong.'[5]

In the last quarter of the eighteenth century, Thomas Bewick (1753–1828), from Newcastle, showed how tiny wood-engraved vignettes could be used for book-illustration. During the continental blockade, a leading publisher and printer from Paris, Ambroise Firmin Didot, imported the technique to France by inviting Charles Thompson, an engraver from London, to settle in Paris and train pupils.[6] During the July Monarchy, other British wood-engravers[7] either came to Paris, or were commissioned to do engravings for French publishers, or sold them vignette models by catalogue. Before 1835, only a handful of French engravers had mastered the technique (Porret, Brevière); by the end of the July Monarchy, many French signatures were appearing,[8] and in 1847 there were 39 Parisian workshops, employing 193 people, which also worked for foreign countries, mainly Russia, Spain and Italy.[9] the most famous firm was known by the monogram 'ABL' (Andrew, Best and Leloir).

Steel-engraving also came from England, although the invention was American.[10] It was linked to the development of bank-note engraving, which was faced with the problems of forgery and of producing very large print-runs, at little expense.[11] In 1822, Warren produced the first regular steel-engraving.[12] Charles Heath and the Findens operated the main workshops, where up to four artists could contribute to a single plate. The 'gravures anglaises' were imported into France by French printsellers and soon became fashionable; they were sold for instance by Aubert, who advertised them in *La Caricature* in 1830. They were also exported by English publishing companies.[13] After 1825, French publishers had started issuing illustrated books with English steel-engravings, by Westall, for example, or Corbould. Meanwhile, steel-engraving became the early speciality of the Johannot brothers who illustrated, after Devéria, *Satyre Ménippée*, in 1824; they became famous for their illustrations of Fenimore Cooper (1826–30) and Walter Scott (1830–2): steel-engraving was thus associated with British literature, or British book-forms, in the case of 'keepsakes'. Made up of short pieces of literature, interspersed with steel-engraved plates, these gift-books were aimed at the 'salons' or women's 'boudoirs' and given as New Year presents; the *Keepsake Paris-Londres* proves the intercultural trend[14] of the Romantic illustrated book: '[les éditeurs] ont voulu joindre à un choix de ces belles *vignettes anglaises*, qui ont porté si haut la réputation des graveurs de LONDRES, des *Nouvelles inédites* dues à des écrivains distingués de PARIS, unissant ainsi, pour les faire valoir l'une par l'autre, en outre de leur mérite respectif et incontestable, la littérature *française* et la gravure *anglaise*' ([the publishers] have sought to combine a selection of those beautiful English vignettes, which have so enhanced the reputations of their London engravers, with some unpublished stories by distinguished Parisian writers, thus uniting French literature and English engraving in such a way that they not only display their unquestionable respective merits, but also bring out each other's qualities').[15] At that time, French signatures could also be found in the steel-engraved plates of the books published by Perrotin and Furne, who specialized in history and literature, but Théophile Gautier recalled that the publishers commissioned texts for English plates: 'c'était l'usage alors d'aller demander aux littérateurs encore heureux d'être imprimés un bout de vers ou de prose pour servir de texte à ces splendides illustrations des Robinson, des Cousin, des Finden, des Westall, des Roberts et des Prout' ('it was the custom then to ask some writer, who was gratified to see his work printed at all, for a snatch of verse or prose to serve as a text for these splendid illustrations by the likes of Robinson, Cousin, Finden, Westall, Roberts and Prout').[16]

The term 'illustration', or 'illustré par', with a pictorial meaning, was printed in italics in the 1830s, as a neologism which came from England: as a French word, 'illustration' normally referred at that time to an illustrious person. Only when the famous magazine *L'Illustration*, characterized by its wood-engraved vignettes, was founded in 1843 (following the example of the *Illustrated London News*) did the expression, explained in the first article of the magazine, become more familiar: 'l'essor extraordinaire qu'a pris depuis quelques années l'emploi de ce genre d'illustrations (la gravure sur bois) semble l'indice d'un immense avenir. L'imprimerie n'a plus seulement pour fonction de multiplier les textes: on lui demande de peindre en même temps qu'elle écrit' ('the extraordinary ascendency which the use of this type of illustration (wood-engraving) has achieved over the last few years seems to promise a stupendous future. Printing no longer serves only to reproduce texts: it

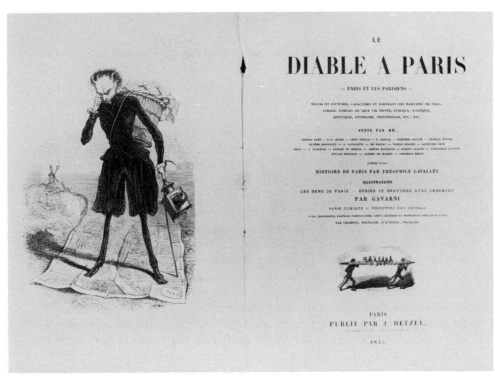

6.  Paul Gavarni, frontispiece, and Bertall, title-page vignette, for *Le Diable à Paris*, Vol. I,
    Paris, J. Hetzel, 1845

is also called upon to paint as well as to write').[17] Book-illustration was
acknowledged by this time, when it had become very common, and
linked to the development of magazines; soon it started to be treated by
the literate class as a vulgar art, invaded by photo-mechanical processes,[18] and it even took on pejorative undertones in the last quarter of
the century, when the pictorial arts tried to free themselves from literature and subject matter.

## Changes in the publishing world

The profession of publisher came to be defined as such during the first
half of the nineteenth century;[19] earlier, the role was not clearly defined
and belonged either to the printer or to the bookseller. The importance
of this new role was especially clear in the field of illustrated books.
There, the publisher acted as a coordinator – at the same time as the

musical conductor started to take on this role too – he had to construct each book as a new enterprise involving the writer, the illustrator, the engraver, the printer of the text, sometimes the printer of the plates, and the draughtsman who transferred the original drawing on to the wood-block. The painter-illustrator Gigoux (1806–94) recalls how the publisher Dubochet behaved in 1835: 'dès les premières livraisons du *Gil Blas*, Dubochet avait entrevu une entreprise excellente. Aussi ne me quittait-il plus de la journée. A peine mon bois était-il esquissé qu'il le portait à la gravure, sans me laisser le temps de le finir. . . . Ce Dubochet était d'une dureté excessive pour ses pauvres graveurs' ('with the very first issues of *Gil Blas* Dubochet had realized what a successful business he could create. So from then on he never let me out of his sight. As soon as I had finished sketching the design of my wood-block, he would take it away to be engraved, without giving me time to finish it. . . . That man Dubochet was dreadfully hard on his poor engravers') (*Causeries sur les artistes de mon temps*). After 1835, illustrated books tended to become collective works, inspired by the formula used for magazines, which made the role of the publisher even more important. He had to finance his project, as well as decide its typographical and visual aspect. Romantic publishers combined the functions of publisher and editor: in this respect Hetzel was the most representative, and in the frontispiece of *Le Diable à Paris* (1845, fig. 6), Gavarni (1804–66) drew a caricature of him in the place traditionally devoted to the portrait of the author. In the 1840s, large teams of illustrators, engravers and authors were involved; the title-page named some of them.[20] Sometimes the publisher listed them gratefully on a dedication page, which simultaneously stressed the importance of his own participation.[21]

However, the 'éditeur à images' or 'éditeur de pittoresques' (Renduel, Furne, Perrotin, Dubochet, Curmer, Hetzel . . .) could appear only once the profession of 'illustrator' was acknowledged. Tony Johannot (1803–52),[22] Grandville (1803–47)[23] and finally Gustave Doré (1832–83)[24] contributed to the definition of this profession, which appeared to the artists as an alternative or a complement to the difficult life of the painter. Of the Devéria brothers, Achille was described as earning money as an illustrator so that Eugène could live as a painter; Gigoux drew his illustrations for *Gil Blas* at night and painted *The Death of Leonardo* for the Salon during the day. After 1838, three painters, Meissonier (1815–91),[25] his brother-in-law Steinheil (1814–85) and Trimolet (1812–43), earned their living together as illustrators, so that every three months one of them could spend one month painting.[26] The illustrator had also begun to compete with the author; and around the time when the 'espèce gendelettre', described by Balzac in the *Monographie de la presse parisienne*, was starting to make an impact, and the Société des gens de lettres, founded in 1838, was starting to defend the rights of writers, the layout of names in title-pages and posters registered this rivalry; Grandville, Gavarni and Doré even reversed the expected hierarchy between writer and illustrator: Hetzel, for instance, published in the *Scènes de la vie privée et publique des animaux* by Grandville (1842), and the *Œuvres choisies* by Gavarni (1846), where the illustrator was treated as the author. This was the end of an evolution announced in the title-vignette of *L'Artiste* by Johannot, which displayed the sister arts in a 'salon' around the painter facing his easel (fig.3): all the different forms of expression contributed to artistic sensitivity, but above them all stood the visual arts. Fifteen years later, Gavarni referred to this founding vignette: in the frontispiece of his *Œuvres choisies* he stood at his easel, but alone. The illustrator had the status of a painter, and this painter had replaced the author.

## The quest for readers and book-owners

The nineteenth century was a century of mass literacy, punctuated by educational laws (Guizot in 1833, Falloux in 1850 and Ferry in 1882–3): the expansion of schooling was greater in the 1820s and the 1830s than at any other time in the century; there were one million boys in primary schools in 1830, and two million by 1848.[27] Beyond inculcating the rudimentary skills, developing a taste for reading among the 'new readers' was felt to be crucial: pictures were part of a strategy which aimed at attracting them to the book as object, and to a written culture. Among the illustrations, representations of readers occurred frequently, particularly in frontispieces, where the reading situation was given as an indication of how to approach the book: in the illustrated ABCs, for instance, frontispieces showed the reading lesson; in books of tales, Mother Goose's spindle was often replaced by a book;[28] and in the title-vignette of popular 'novel-magazines' (*journaux-romans*), the worker was shown reading in the evenings by lamplight.[29]

The campaign to promote reading was addressed to the public at large (referred to by the ambiguous notion of 'le peuple'); distinct readerships, mainly women and children, were also acknowledged. Each of them offered a large market to the publishers and requires specific types of literature, which appeared at first in instalments, in the form of magazines, *Journal des dames, Journal des demoiselles, Journal des enfants*, and later on as specific types of book.[30] This specialization became increasingly important over the course of the century. In the case of children, for instance, 'libraires d'éducation' (educational booksellers) appeared during the Restoration; the ritual of school prize-giving created a very large market in cloth-bound illustrated books, which became, from the July Monarchy until the end of the century, the speciality of publishers in the provinces, for example Mame in Tours, Lefort in Lille, Mégard in Rouen. Hetzel started a collection entitled 'Nouveau Magasin des enfants' in 1843, at a time when he also ran a collection called the 'Bibliothèque des dames du monde'; during the Second Empire he became a famous 'éditeur pour les mioches', publishing Jules Verne in his magazine founded in 1864, *Le Magasin d'Education et de Récréation*, and contributing to the invention of children's albums based upon images: 'pourquoi les marchands de livres mettent-ils autre chose que des images dans les livres?' his heroine, Mademoiselle Lili, wondered.

Illustration was also linked to the recognition of reading as a leisure activity: the distinction between illustrated and non-illustrated books is thus related to the creation of a daily timetable where work-hours are clearly spearated from leisure hours; this leisure time could be devoted to entertainment, or to self-instruction, and reading illustrated books could foster either 'education' or 'recreation'. In the case of children's literature, schoolbooks tended not to be illustrated, whereas 'home-books' were (as were the books given as prizes, thus building a bridge between school and home).

Images were considered as part of the process of acquisition of knowledge: 'le monde capitaliste industriel fonde son pouvoir sur l'empirisme qui fait de la réalité une référence absolue, et sur les connaissances expérimentales qui permettent la maîtrise de la nature'[31] ('the world of capital and industry founds its power on empiricism, which makes reality its absolute reference, and on scientific enquiry, which opens up the conquest of nature'). The origins of this pictorial pedagogy, based on the 'object lesson', where the image is a substitute for the true object, may be traced from the *Orbis Sensualium Pictus* by Comenius (1658) to Locke's sensualism adopted in France by Madame de Genlis, or to the plates of Diderot's *Encyclopédie*. Edouard Charton for instance, born in 1807, was convinced of the importance of pictures in the acquisition of knowledge and in the 'popularisation' of science, technology and the arts. He kept this aim in mind throughout his life: he was the editor of the *Magasin pittoresque* in 1833, then the cofounder of *L'Illustration*, and finally the director of the *Tour du monde*, an illustrated travel journal, in 1860, and of the 'Bibliothèque des merveilles', an encyclopaedic collection, both published by Hachette. Significantly, he had started his career in journalism as chief editor of the *Bulletin de la Société pour l'instruction élémentaire* in 1829, and had become a disciple of the Saint-Simonist doctrine, which linked industrial capitalism to humanitarian ideals.

The increase in reading ability did not imply that more people would buy books: books and newspapers were expensive in the first part of the century; readers borrowed them from 'cabinets de lecture'.[32] Publishers were also confronted with cheap Belgian pirate editions, which competed with the official editions of the 'nouveautés littéraires'. Along with lowering prices, illustration was a means of changing habits and increasing the book-owning readership. In the shop-window, the 'vignette' printed on the illustrated cover of the book showed how exciting the novel was supposed to be. Inside, illustrated posters attracted buyers; these posters described the way the books were sold in weekly or monthly parts to which one could subscribe by way of newspaper subscriptions.[33] Before Christmas, publishers issued illustrated catalogues to advertise their new titles.[34] Thus, the image was part of an advertising stragegy, which was noted, and mocked, in one of Grandville's last books, *Un Autre Monde* (1844).[35]

In order to compete with the habit of reading in cafés and cabinets de lecture, the illustrated books of the July Monarchy addressed other aspects of social life, which were domestic, and linked to the salons: lithographic albums of the 1820s had introduced the habit of browsing through pictures collectively during receptions, and illustrated books adopted this concept. For instance, Grandville's 1828 album *Les Métamorphoses du jour*, with its human animals, which helped create the fame of its author, inspired one of the most famous illustrated Romantic books, *Scènes de la vie privée et publique des animaux* (Hetzel, 1842), and later on was itself issued in the form of an illustrated book (Havard, 1854) and reprinted (Garnier, 1869). Commenting on one of Grandville's lithographs, *Mœurs aquatiques*, Balzac showed how a collective reading, based on such pictures, occurred in the social circle of the salon.[36] The printer Aubert sold (and even lent) these albums which were looked at 'around the table'.[37] Thus, even if it seemed clear that pictures would attract more readers, the illustrated book was not yet conceived in terms of 'mass media': it opened up to a large middle class a medium which was traditionally reserved for the upper classes, and the social life of the salons.

## The development of the illustrated book

The history of the Romantic illustrated book has to be considered in two stages, the first when the illustrative image was rare, and the second when it became frequent. The change came suddenly, in 1835, when Dubochet issued *Gil Blas* by Le Sage with six hundred vignettes engraved on wood after Gigoux, although it had been foreshadowed in 1830 by the fifty vignettes of Charles Nodier's *Histoire du roi de*

*Bohême et de ses sept châteaux*, illustrated by Porret's wood-engravings after Tony Johannot.

## The experiments of the 1820s

Each of the illustrative techniques was used in different types of books at this time: steel-engraving was for novels, keepsakes and travel books, while lithography was used for albums, and in the *Voyages pittoresques et romantiques dans l'ancienne France* (edited by Isidore Taylor, Charles Nodier and Alphonse de Cailleux), which were published in twenty-two volumes between 1820 and 1878.[38] In 1828, Delacroix's lithographs to Goethe's *Faust* remained an isolated creation, but they influenced many Romantic vignettes, especially those of Tony Johannot for *Le Voyage où il vous plaira* (Hetzel, 1843).

For the technique of wood-engraving, which was to become the major one for the illustrated book, the 1820s were an experimental phase when minor changes prefigured later developments: for instance, the tail-pieces, engraved by Thompson for volumes four and five of the *Hermite de la Chaussée d'Antin* (1814), represented the first use of end-wood engraving in book-illustration. Balzac was involved, as a printer, in this new technique. Monnier had stayed in London where he was influenced by Cruikshank, who was the first professional 'illustrator' in England. Devéria and Boulanger, who were friends of Hugo, illustrated his early poetical works. They introduced the new art to the salons.

## The 'Romantic vignettes' (1828–35)

Under this title, Champfleury[39] described the first flowering of the Romantic illustrated book, and recorded mainly the books which included a wood-engraved 'vignette' on the title-page or an etched frontispiece. There it symbolized the meeting of art and literature, and was linked to the idea of the sister arts developed by the Romantic circles, where painters and poets met socially:[40] 'au temps dont je parle, le crayon était vraiment confident de la plume, et complice aussi. La vignette se faisait en même temps que la page'[41] ('during this period, the pencil was on the most intimate terms with the pen, truly aiding and abetting it. The vignette was drawn while the page was being written'), wrote Asselineau who was also referring to the frontispiece etchings by Nanteuil. In his sketchy, witty manner, Tony Johannot, inspired by Hugo's *Préface de Cromwell*, favoured paroxysmal situations and grotesque figures. The black and white contrast allowed by the technique suited the atmosphere of the Romantic drama. The vignette could also be sentimental or melancholic. It figured as a banner for Romantic publications, during the Romantic battle.

At a time when the July Monarchy allowed the press relative liberty, and when competition between publishers, constantly threatened by bankruptcy, intensified, the vignette became a 'must' in the 'nouveautés littéraires' printed between 1830 and 1835, with a peak in 1833; advertised by *L'Artiste* and by *La Caricature*, who reproduced in their columns the small wood-engraving by Henri Porret[42] after Tony Johannot, these book novelties, published by Gosselin, Ladvocat and Urbain Canel, were aimed at the same upper-middle class and mostly Parisian audience as the lithograph-illustrated magazines.

However, the noun 'vignette', in contemporary vocabulary, had a double meaning, as illustration developed in two opposite directions, both of which are found in the work of the brothers Johannot. On the one hand, it referred to the wood-engraved in-text vignette, and on the other hand, to the inset steel-engraved plates, often grouped into illustrative 'suites' or sequences. Asselineau and Champfleury took only the first type into account: it consisted of a small narrative sketch without a linear outline, and became a symbol of the Romantic fragment[43] as opposed to the closed totality of the rectangular painting, to which the second type belonged. This explains the frequent parallel between 'tableau' and 'vignette' which occurs in contemporary art criticism. The floating shape of the in-text vignette mirrored the image perceived by the reader on reading the text. Bewick used the rococo ornamental formula of the vignette without definite border lines mainly in tail-pieces – which he deliberately spelled 'tale-pieces', thus underlining the change from ornament to illustration – and the first page of *Jane Eyre* proves how receptive the public was to this new concept. Thus, the new pattern of reading could be compared to a 'spectacle dans un fauteuil', or a magic lantern projection,[44] and the illustrator played the role of a privileged viewer who acted as an intermediary between author and reader. Vignettes of the second type, the plates in 'suites', were devoted to the main 'subjects' or episodes recorded in the texts; 'suites' were sometimes issued without text, in order to be located at the right place in the book by its owner, regardless of the edition. Such an analysis of a text into its narrative stages belonged to a tradition of the print market: it recalled the series of prints by Hogarth, at the time when the genre of the novel was coming into being. It was also rooted in the neoclassical series of prints by Flaxman, or in the painted illustrations of Boydell's Shakespeare gallery.[45] In France, the 'suites par quatre' or 'par huit' existed in the Parisian eighteenth-century copper-engraved imagery of the 'rue Saint-Jacques', and were adapted later for lithography.[46] During the nineteenth century, 'suites' occurred in the decorative arts of panoramic wall-paintings and of patterned plates. Introduced by the Johannots for their illustrations of Byron, Scott and Cooper, 'suites' were used in conjunction with modern English literature. They came with complete works by popular contemporary writers, like the songs of Béranger, or the complete works of Delavigne, or large publishing projects, like the *Musée de la Révolution* issued by Perrotin in 1835, and thus subtitled: 'collection de sujets dessinés par Raffet et gravés par Frilley, destinée à servir de complément et d'illustration à toutes les histoires de la Révolution (Thiers, Montgaillard, Mignet, Lacretelle, etc.)' ('a collection of scenes drawn by Raffet and engraved by Frilley, destined to complement and illustrate a variety of Revolutionary histories (by Thiers, Montgaillard, Mignet, Lacretelle, etc.)').

## The illustrated book and the instalment-system (1835–48)

When the publisher Dubochet, in association with Paulin and Hingray, started *Histoire de Gil Blas de Santillane*, in a collection which was to publish illustrated versions of the masterpieces of literature, he was overwhelmed by the success of the enterprise: he had first commissioned from the painter Gigoux a hundred 'vignettes', then three hundred more, and then yet another two hundred; finally, he sold over 15,000 copies of the book which had new runs in 1836 (by Paulin) and 1838 (by Dubochet). The publisher was able to adjust immediately to the demand of the audience, because the book was issued in instalments, sold at forty centimes each. This was to become usual with illustrated books, which thus became akin to a periodical, with texts divided into regular parts, in the manner of a feuilleton.[47]

From then on, the two types of vignette were combined and used within the same books. The in-text vignette was not only kept on the title-page, but appeared frequently in the text of the instalments. The in-set vignette (or plate) could also be engraved on wood. It was printed on a separate sheet of thick paper, inserted in each part or every two parts. When the book was complete after one or two years, it was sold as a whole by the publisher, for the New Year: the customer could either buy it, or bind the instalments, the last of which included the frontispiece, the summary and the list of plates as an indication to the bookbinder.[48] The separate plates could thus become regular illustrations, or prints to be framed or pinned on the wall. These variations in the forms in which books were brought and consumed are a typical feature of the publishers' editorial policy during the July Monarchy: it helped them to attract a very large public.

The quantity of images being published grew so much that Beraldi spoke of 'museums of images'. There were more and more engravers,

illustrators and publishers, producing more and more illustrations, especially as the laws of September 1835, which prohibited political
caricature, obliged some of them to turn from the press to the book. Prolific artists produced thousands of illustrations. A cumulative process
had started, as the publishers reused illustrations that came from earlier
editions, or bought vignettes by catalogue: as time passed, they had so
many vignettes in their collections that they commissioned only a few
new ones when they issued new editions. Some illustrated books had
thus been reissued over half a century (like the ones issued by Furne), or
the plates could be adjusted to suit a new text, either by the publisher or
by the owner. This phenomenon is striking when one surveys the illustrated editions of *Notre-Dame de Paris*: the illustrations appear as layers
which visually build up the successive readings of the novel.[49] Some
books seem to have been conceived from vignettes, like the *Dictionnaire
pittoresque* published by Aubert in 1839. This practice of 'réemploi' (re-
cycling) has been overlooked, since book-collectors search only for the
first printing of an illustration. But it was very common.

The circulation of the same vignettes from text to text gave a kind of
memory to the images. One may perceive how a 'language' of illustrations was built up historically by using a genealogical method, which is
close to the one Catherine Velay-Vallantin claims for the study of the
history of the 'conte' or tale.[50] Some pictorial 'archetypes'[51] derived from
stereotypes; they were borrowed from various sources, mainly popular
imagery, Revolutionary caricatures, the early Romantic vignettes, recent
political caricatures, and Romantic painting. For instance, Gavarni's
frontispiece for *Le Diable à Paris* (1845) showing Hetzel as a lame devil
was inspired by Monnier's vignette for *Le Livre des cent et un* (1830). A
large number of the texts devoted to book-illustration figure on the list
of bestsellers identified by Martyn Lyons;[52] most of them were linked to
a conventional set of images, to which every new illustrator referred, trying out variations in the manner of the oral story-teller: Bluebeard
raising his hand over his wife, Don Quixote and the windmills, Paul and
Virginie crossing the river. . . . These images could also be transferred to
a new context; part of the pleasure for the reader was then to recognize
them. Thus, Johannot's vision of Quasimodo (1830) or *Notre-Dame de
Paris (The Hunchback of Notre-Dame)* not only was a constant theme
in all the illustrations of the novel (right up to the cover of a recent comic
by Gotlib), but also haunts a number of other books, from the children's
novel by Desnoyers, *Les Aventures de Jean-Paul Choppart*, to the illustration of *L'homme qui rit* by Daniel Vierge. This 'language' of
illustrations shared by the reader and the illustrator helped images to
fulfil their role of adapting given texts for new audiences: oriental tales
for the French public, literary texts for 'le peuple', adult literature for
children. . . . Illustration helped to cross boundaries between cultures,

nationalities, social classes and ages. This tendency increased during the course of the century, though some could not accept it: Champfleury regretted that the 'image-makers' (imagiers) had seen Doré's illustrations. The major achievements of Romantic book-illustration were reprinted in cheap popular editions with two columns after 1850.[53] Thus, books selected their public by their material aspect (format, typography, paper) rather than by their images, which were forged from a common language.

The instalment-system introduced some tension between the overall structure of the book and its fragmentary structure. The 'feuilletonesque' (serial) succession of the instalments introduced a special kind of image, an image of 'cutting' ('la coupure'), to which Louis Reybaud refers wittily in his novel *Jérôme Paturot à la recherche d'une position sociale* (1845), a pastiche illustrated by Grandville.[54] The aim is to maintain the reader's eagerness to know the rest of the story by the choice of a very impressive and strange image: by a blackly humorous visual pun, the 'cutting' shows a decapitated head, bleeding and convulsive: 'Mais quelle était cette tête! Quelle était cette main!' asks the text, before the illustration under which the 'feuilleton' formula appears: '(à suivre)'. 'Voilà, môsieur, ce que j'appelle arrêter un feuilleton', the publisher comments on the following page. 'C'est-à-dire que, sur deux millions de lecteurs, il n'en est pas un seul qui ne voudra savoir ce que c'est que cette tête!'

Concurrently with the constraint of the 'cutting' image, the illustrations had to foreshadow the organization of the whole book: according to tradition, different kinds of illustrative spaces were distinguished – the initial picture (frontispiece, or title-page vignette), the sequential pictures (in-text vignette or plate) and the final picture (tail-piece); further divisions of the text, like parts or chapters, were underlined in the same way, although the initial picture could also be a head-piece and/or an illustrated letter. Each book respected these conventions, but it also developed its own rhythm, by reproducing a similar outlook from instalment to instalment. For instance, the publisher Hetzel, in *Le Diable à Paris*, created an alternation between series of plates by Gavarni, thematic pages of sketches by Bertall, and the flow of the illustrated text: he gave a kind of polyphony to the book which at first sight seemed to lose its unity. The visual perception of the written text implied by illustration seemed to revive the ancient art of memory, a branch of rhetoric by which one learned to remember an oral discourse through a sequence of pictures assigned to specific spaces (loci): 'Le livre est comme un édifice dont le frontispice est souvent une enseigne et dans lequel, une fois introduit, il lui [the reader/viewer] faut donner successivement une attention égale aux différentes salles dont se compose le monument qu'il visite, sans oublier celles qu'il a laissées derrière lui, et non sans chercher à l'avance, dans ce qu'il connaît déjà, quelle sera son impression à la fin du voyage'[55] ('The book is like a building whose frontispiece is often a sign, and where, once he has entered, the reader/viewer has to pay attention equally to the different rooms which make up the monument he is visiting, without forgetting those he has left behind, nor yet without guessing in advance, from what he has already discovered, what his final impression at the end of the tour will be'), wrote Delacroix. Fundamental to the art of memory was the reference to architecture, which belongs to the etymology of many French words related to illustration: 'frontispice', 'bandeau', 'cul-de-lampe' . . . Romantic illustrated books made this etymology visible in many cases, for instance in the illustrations for *Notre-Dame de Paris*, where there is a link between the metaphor of the illustrated book as a cathedral and the argument of the novel. The metaphor of travel mentioned by Delacroix is conveyed by the poster, the frontispiece and the first head-piece of *Le Voyage où il vous plaira* (1843). Illustration may also compare the book to an organic structure, either a body (as it is suggested in the English words 'head-piece' and 'tail-piece'), or a growing plant: in that case, the etymological reference is to the word 'vignette', meaning the little vine-shoots which decorated the borders of illuminated Gothic manuscripts. The use of visual metaphors, here applied to the definition of the process of illustration within the book, belongs to the rhetoric of the Romantic illustrated book; it had been crucial to the language of caricature, from the Revolution to the beginnings of the July Monarchy, and was probably derived from it.

The system of Romantic book-illustration was also based on the definition of three kinds of pictures, to which the subtitles of the books or the summaries of the plates referred. In chapbooks, constantly reused woodcuts provided the book with a kind of shop-sign, which allowed the reader to identify rapidly the group to which the chapbook belonged; the picture of the boat, for instance, referred to travel literature. This generic function was present in the early versions of the title-page vignette, where the vignette was the banner of Romanticism, and where each of the categories ironically featured by Gautier in the Préface to *Mademoiselle de Maupin* could be recognized on sight, from the vignette. After 1835, the generic function was attributed rather to the inset plates, which were classified into three major varieties, each of which was linked to a genre of the illustrated book: the 'type' was related to the 'physiological' literature, where social types and professions were described in collections which built up a panorama of modern life in the 1840s. The other two varieties were the 'view' (*vue* or *site*), linked to the *Voyages pittoresques* and to travel literature, and the 'scene' (*scène*), linked to fiction (mainly novels and plays) and to history. These three notions developed within the history of prints, literature and painting: types, for instance, belong to the tradition of street cries, whose popular imagery goes back to Bouchardon and, earlier still, to the Carracci brothers; the texts related to them have their own literary tradition, from the *Tableau de Paris* by Mercier to La Bruyère's *Caractères*. Thus, 'physiological literature' was based on the intersection between these two traditions.[56]

The notion of 'type' is extremely symbolic, as it also raises the question of the nature of prints in relation to the monetary market: the medical meaning stressed by the word 'physiologie' has hidden the numismatic one, where 'type' is opposed to 'token'. Like the print, the type is coined, and many copies may be issued. A series of equivalences unifies the social type, the print-market, and the money-market, in the representations offered by illustrated books at a time when Guizot was inviting the French to make money their priority: 'enrichissez-vous par le travail et par l'épargne'.

Romanticism tried to cross the boundaries between expressions and genres: the illustrated book in itself exemplifies this feature, as does the visual form of the 'tail-piece' vignette which could appear in any place. The way in which many books mixed views, scenes and types and sometimes combined them within the same plate or vignette is further evidence of this trend. This happened mainly in novels, which is precisely the literary genre which refers to all the others.

Two years after the first printing of his novel *Notre-Dame de Paris*, Victor Hugo introduced two 'forgotten' chapters, which added a philosophical meaning to the sentimental love novel or Gothic novel he had already written: in the chapter 'Ceci tuera cela' of his 'medieval novel', he shows how the printing press is bound to 'kill' the language of architecture, which was based on images. This novel was precisely the one which was illustrated more often than any other during the nineteenth century, as if the publishers and illustrators were trying to demonstrate ironically that everything had happened the other way round, and that the development of the press and the 'Gutenberg galaxy' had helped increase the power of images. And indeed, new techniques, imported from neighbouring countries, made illustration possible within the context of the industrialized printing world; the increase in literacy changed the dimensions of the audience, and the presence of images was perceived as an attraction; the editorial field was reorganized, and the professions of illustrator and of publisher came of age. 'Illustration', after the experimental period of the 1820s, grew up between 1830 and 1835 in conjunction with Romanticism; after 1835, the use of illustration became more frequent; its function was to adjust a given text to its readership, and to facilitate coexistence between the instalment-system and the concept of the book as a whole. 'Illustration' thus became not an adjunct to a text but an increasingly familiar language in its own right.

## Suggested reading

Adhémar, Jean, et Seguin, Jean-Pierre, *Le Livre romantique* (Paris: Editions du Chêne, 1968).

Bezucha, Robert J., 'The Renaissance of book illustration', in *The Art of the July Monarchy, France 1830 to 1848*, Exhibition catalogue, Museum of Art and Archeology (University of Missouri, Colombia, 1990), pp. 192–213.

Bouchot, Henri, *Le Livre à vignettes au XIXe siècle* (Paris: Rouveyre, 1891).

Brivois, Jules, *Bibliographie des ouvrages illustrés du XIXe siècle, principalement des livres à gravures sur bois* (Paris: Rouquette, 1883).

Champfleury [Jules Husson], *Les Vignettes romantiques* (Paris: E. Dentu, 1883).

Chartier, R., et Martin, H.-J. (eds), *Histoire de l'édition française: Le Temps des éditeurs, Du Romantisme à la Belle époque*, vol. III (Paris: Promodis, 1985).

Ray, Gordon Nicholas, *The Art of the French Illustrated Book 1700 to 1914*, 2 vols (New York: Pierpont Morgan Library-Cornell, 1982).

# 7

## 'Telle main veut tel pied': Balzac, Ingres and the art of portraiture

## Michael Tilby

In Balzac's *Comédie humaine* references to painters and paintings abound. A similarly obsessive naming of works of art and their creators on the part of many another writer might justifiably be seen to indicate a rare understanding of the visual arts and a highly developed artistic sensibility. In the case of Balzac, the significance of these references is at once more diverse and less profound.

It was principally through his various fictional artists that Balzac expressed his theories on the nature of the creative process. In contrast, his ready evocation of their real-life counterparts and of the Old Masters who were for them compulsory subjects for study was, in one respect at least, merely a facet of his all-consuming fascination with the life of the modern city. Napoleon's equal commitment to patronage, propaganda and pillage had ensured that painting and, above all, its public exhibition was now a prominent feature of Parisian life and, as such, a requisite element of Balzac's totalizing vision. More specifically, the single atelier or gallery, no less than the heterogeneous annual Salon, by offering a selection of works for appraisal and possible purchase, made the visual arts the most obvious meeting-place of artistic endeavour and the social and economic reality of which that endeavour in a post-Revolutionary, post-Imperial world was inextricably part. As Balzac was quick to appreciate, painting in the new bourgeois world of which he was the chronicler had entered the mainstream of public life and thereby exhibited to the spectator dimensions that fell outside the traditional realms of aesthetics or moral purpose.

In another respect, Balzac's instinctive comparisons with the art of painting reflected his desire to seek compensation for an unpalatably material world in an overtly idealist perspective, undeterred by the capacity of the material world always to reassert itself. In imitation of Scott, his ready adoption of the painter's point of view was most commonly a means of denoting superlative beauty, as in the case of the impact of the young peasant girl in *La Rabouilleuse*, Flora Brasier, on both the elderly Doctor Rouget and the admirable young painter, Joseph Bridau,[1] or in his general description of Florine in *Une Fille d'Eve*.[2] Again following Scott, he would frequently accompany such references to beauty with the rhetorical lament that the writer lacked the means the painter had at his disposal to do justice to the visual quality of a striking scene or human appearance. In an early novel that relies heavily on conventional references to painting, *La Femme de Trente Ans*, he specifies that, whereas the spectator of the painted portrait is able to experience directly the individual's inner turmoil through 'les tons du teint' and 'l'air de la figure', the 'poet' has to fall back on elaborating the dramatic causes themselves.[3]

In many such instances Balzac is content to refer to 'un peintre' or 'les peintres'. If a particular painter is named, the choice may not be as significant as might at first be supposed. A reference to a specific artist may be replaced in a later edition of the text by one to a quite different artist, without there being a corresponding change to the description it accompanies. Thus in *La Rabouilleuse* an initial reference to Ingres is replaced subsequently by one to his rival Delacroix,[4] while the reference to Gérard in the description of Madame Firmiani is later replaced by one to Ingres, who is now seen as the obvious painter to capture 'la fierté du front, la profusion des cheveux, la majesté du regard, toutes les pensées que trahissaient les couleurs particulières du teint'.[5]

The substitution of Ingres for Gérard in *Madame Firmiani* took place in 1842 and can be seen as a reflection of Balzac's determination to forsake his natural affinity with the Imperial school of painters in order to confer a more authentic modernity on his earlier compositions when they came to be incorporated in the *Comédie humaine*. Ingres was now firmly established as the supreme portraitist of the age, or, as Baudelaire put it, 'le seul homme en France qui fasse vraiment des portraits'.[6] Nevertheless, in the context of portraiture, a rapprochement between Balzac and Ingres is, superficially at least, compelling. They were recorders of the same social world: Ingres's sitters, whether his Imperial subjects or those who achieved prominence during the July Monarchy, could so easily have been the models for characters in the *Comédie humaine*.[7] More significant still are the qualities that unite them as creative artists. One of Ingres's most fervent admirers, Charles Du Bos, ascribed to them the same ability to combine the individual and the type: 'le portrait tout ensemble individuel et générique; un être particulier, et en même temps toute une profession et toute une époque'.[8] Both indeed constitute prime examples of a new approach to the art of portraiture, one that was widely practised in both portrait painting and the literary description of character.

The new tradition was rooted in the art of physiognomy popularized by the Swiss pastor, Johann Caspar Lavater.[9] Lavater's belief that the character of each individual was imprinted upon distinct facial features and that these could be 'read' scientifically enjoyed a particular vogue between 1775 and 1810, but its influence continued to be felt by creative artists in France for several decades to come, revealing itself both in their theories and practice and in the language of much contemporary art criticism. Baudelaire, a convinced Lavaterian, was still operating loosely within this tradition when he spoke, in *Le Peintre de la vie moderne*, of the distinctive character of every age: 'Chaque époque a son port, son regard et son sourire'.[10] Lavater's conviction that there was a unique harmony discernible in every individual physiognomy extended to gesture, gait and setting, this last dimension making him a particular source of stimulus for Balzac in his determination to convey to the reader the character of an individual's abode.

That every individual represented a harmonious whole was borne out, Baudelaire maintained, by the way an apparently familiar voice, though it be found to belong to someone unknown to us, is nonetheless accompanied by the very gestures and mannerisms of the person we thought we had recognized.[11] This, he continued, was why Lavater had drawn up a catalogue of noses and mouths that could not exist in tandem, and why he had found fault with earlier artistic representations of human physiognomy. Lavater, he admitted, may have been wrong in respect of specific details, but his basic principle remained sound. To this principle Baudelaire gave the striking formulation: 'Telle main veut tel pied; chaque épiderme engendre son poil.'

The extent to which Lavater influenced nineteenth-century approaches to the representation of the human figure, both visually and in terms of personality and character, is immediately discernible in Sainte-Beuve's concept of the 'portrait littéraire', the features of which illuminate considerably the context in which Balzac and Ingres were both working. Sainte-Beuve's method sought to highlight 'le rapport de l'œuvre à la personne même, au caractère, aux circonstances particulières'[12] and was rooted in a desire to isolate the unique combination of factors responsible for what T.S. Eliot would later call the 'individual talent'. He possessed what he regarded as the novelist's boundless curiosity, and believed that minute details were the sole means of access to 'l'intime vérité'. Not that this implied a lack of discrimination: what he sought was not 'l'anecdote futile' but 'celle qui caractérise'.[13] Irving Babbitt, contrasting him with Taine, maintained that 'a greater particularizer ... than Sainte-Beuve never lived'.[14]

For all Sainte-Beuve's antipathy towards Balzac, he shared the latter's belief that the species was to be apprehended through the detailed study of its individual members. 'Un individu bien observé', he maintained at one point in his *Port-Royal*, 'se rapporte vite à l'espèce qu'on n'a vue que de loin et l'éclaire.'[15] As a modern, he was, like Lavater, the enemy of idealization and of purely generalized traits. He considered his concern to be with the natural and with the real and therefore saw it as his task to preserve wrinkles and warts. Comparisons with the visual arts suggested themselves to him with some regularity, and it has been well observed that 'his characters appear to us not as abstractions but in their bodily presences, with their physical mannerisms, their gestures, the sound of their voices'.[16] Nowhere is this more apparent than in a passage on his general method that appears in his portrait of Diderot. What brings a portrait to life and banishes mere analysis, he insists, is the capturing of 'le tic familier, le sourire révélateur, la gerçure indéfinissable, la ride intime et douloureuse qui se cache en vain sous les cheveux déjà clair-semés'.[17] Such a procedure was destined to become a refrain in contemporary references to the art of portraiture in both literature and painting. Within Sainte-Beuve's own work it is exemplified, for example, by the 'Lavaterian' anecdote featuring the fingernails of the writer and academician Joseph-François Michaud: 'Michaud était journaliste jusqu'au bout des ongles. Il les avait fort noirs, les ongles. Sa femme disait de lui: "Quand il va au bain il met des gants de peur de se laver les mains."'[18]

Balzac's description of Judge Popinot in *L'Interdiction*, a passage beloved of Henry James, provides a splendid example of the extent to which his fictional portraits derived from a similar practice:

> If nature, therefore, had endowed M. Popinot with an unprepossessing exterior, the magistracy had not embellished him. His frame presented a mass of conflicting lines. His massive knees, his large feet, his broad hands, contrasted with a sacerdotal face, which vaguely resembled a calf's head. Soft to the point of being insipid and but poorly lit up by two eyes ill-matched in colour, the latter was altogether anaemic. Split in two by a straight, flat nose, it was surmounted by a forehead devoid of any protuberance and decorated by two enormous ears, which bent awkwardly forward. His frail hair, thinly spread, exposed his skull in several irregular furrows. One feature alone commended this countenance to the student of physiognomy. The man had a mouth whose lips conveyed a divine goodness. They were good, substantial red lips, sinuous, moving, with a thousand folds, in which Nature had expressed the noblest of feelings, lips which spoke to the heart and revealed in the man intelligence, clear thinking, the gift of second sight and an angelic cast of mind; therefore you would have quite failed to understand him in judging him solely by his sunken forehead, by those eyes that lacked all warmth, and by his pitiful appearance. His life was in harmony with his physiognomy; it was full of secret endeavours and concealed from view a saintly virtue.[19]

In contrast to the more one-dimensional portraits to be found in Scott's

Waverley Novels, Balzac's description of Popinot offers an immediate impression of individuality and distinctiveness, and resists being slotted into our personal gallery of familiar faces. It offers an interpretative challenge, discoveries to be made ('secret endeavours'), and it is explicitly the skills of the student of physiognomy that are required. There is, in the best Lavaterian tradition, harmony within the irregularity, as well as a prominent feature (the 'substantial red lips') that is expressive precisely as a result of the contrast it presents with our stereotyped sense of an everyday face. This is a face to be contemplated, its expressiveness not easily exhausted. It is, moreover, a portrait that literally speaks to the spectator. James was tempted to conclude that Balzac's portraits 'shape themselves under his pen as if in obedience to an irresistible force'. The more analytically-minded reader will focus on the way the myriad details give us a sense of the whole man, his life, and his relationship with the material world of which he is part, rather than with the timeless world of nature that is Scott's idealized context.

These new principles of literary portraiture had their very clear parallel in contemporary portrait painting and above all in the work of Ingres. Although certain of Ingres's contemporaries complained that his classicism interfered with the truthfulness of his portraits, and although the painter turned to ancient classical models as well as to Raphael for the poses he gave to such contemporary figures as Madame Moitessier and Madame d'Haussonville (see fig. 7), his concern with the individual in his contemporary context remained supreme. To that extent he could be said to satisfy the requirements laid down by Hegel in his *Aesthetics*:

> A portrait must be an expression of individual and spiritual character. This nobler element in a man, which the artist introduces into the portrait, is not ordinarily obvious in a man's features. Therefore, if the artist is to bring out the sitter's character, he must have seen him in several situations and actions, in short been well acquainted with him, got to know his manner, hear his speech, and noticed his sort of feelings.[20]

The phrase 'not ordinarily obvious' can be linked to Hegel's distrust of the deterministic dimension of Lavater's theories.[21] Elsewhere, however, he notes, in a formulation that could have been Lavater's own: 'if today a portrait is to be made of an individual belonging to his own time, then it is essential that his clothing and external accessories be taken from his own individual and actual environment'.[22]

A concern with individual psychology was not, of course, the exclusive invention of the Romantic age. As Philip Conisbee has shown, in France 'the intimate and psychologically penetrating type of portrait flourished especially from the early 1740s onwards', Maurice Quentin de la Tour's 'quick and merciless eye' being singled out by him in this respect.[23] As late as 1863 we find Sainte-Beuve being drawn to la Tour's

7. Jean-Auguste-Dominique Ingres, *Madame la comtesse d'Haussonville*, 1845 (Frick Collection, New York)

'vivants et parlants portraits'.[24] As for the Goncourt brothers, they had no hesitation in seeing la Tour's pastel portraits in broadly Lavaterian terms: 'il fait en prodigieux physionomiste, le portrait du caractère dans le portrait de l'homme. Les visages pensent, parlent, s'avouent, se livrent.'[25] But a comparison of Ingres's portraits and a representative eighteenth-century portrait prized for its ability to render the sitter's individuality, Aved's *Madame Crozat* (1741; Musée Fabre), suggests that in the latter example the sitter's individuality, rather than pursued for its own sake, is subordinated to the activity in which she is engaged and to the particular set of values thereby represented. It is manifestly a moral portrait, one that seeks our unquestioning approval of the sitter.

The individuality of Ingres's female portraits is sharply differentiated from such eighteenth-century practice. Exuded by every detail, not just by the physiognomical features, the individuality remains an end in itself. The spectator immediately senses that the clothes are the sitters' own, and that they emphasize the life of the bodies within. In Ingres's portrait of Madame d'Haussonville, the objects on the table behind her seem incontrovertibly her possessions.[26] This is cleverly suggested, not only by their heterogeneity and by their random display, but also by the rich chromatic echoes set up between them and the countess's costume and accessories. The result is a harmonious whole that gives us the impression of a tangible yet indefinable personality revealed with great immediacy. Gautier was one critic who was particularly alive to Ingres's ability to convey an impression of uniqueness of personality. Commenting on the effect of Ingres's portrait of Madame Rothschild, he enthused: 'l'œil brille, éclairé par une repartie prête à jaillir de ses lèvres. C'est une conversation spirituelle, commencée dans la salle de bal ou au souper, qui se continue; on entendrait presque ce que dit l'interlocuteur hors du cadre.'[27] In all these portraits by Ingres our curiosity about the sitter excludes all question of approval or disapprobation.

Contemporary responses to Ingres reveal the extent to which a Lavaterian perspective in portraiture had permeated the prevailing critical discourse. Although Baudelaire counted himself an admirer of Ingres's 'boldness' – Ingres was for him 'l'homme audacieux par excellence'[28] – it was explicitly on Lavaterian grounds that he castigated Ingres's art for its allegedly idealizing tendencies. According to such a view, Ingres sought artfully to disguise nature's apparent imperfections. Hence the critic's objection to 'une armée de doigts trop uniformément allongés en fuseaux et dont les extrémités étroites oppriment les ongles', when Lavater would have deduced from the subject's broad chest and muscular forearm that these fingers should have been considerably more square.[29] It was Ingres's invariable deference to the example of Raphael that was seen by Baudelaire as the cause of his failure to respect the syntax of authentic portraiture. In short, he was charged by him with imposing on his sitters 'un perfectionnement plus ou moins complet, emprunté au répertoire des idées classiques'.[30]

It is certainly possible for the strict Lavaterian to catch Ingres out, as in his substitution of his wife's hands for those of his infinitely restless sitter, Madame Marcotte. Yet Ingres's practice is much closer to Lavaterian principles than Baudelaire at times suggested. The 'particularizing, individualizing tendency of his drawing'[31] unites him with both Lavater and Sainte-Beuve. Gautier specifically praised Ingres's ability to render the human physiognomy in its 'individuality and characteristic details . . . to come to grips with the thoughts behind the features and sometimes to sum up a whole age and a whole class in a mere head standing out against a vague background'.[32] Baudelaire himself highlighted the expressive function Ingres had given to the overcoats of Molé and Cherubini.[33] Their *redingote* and *carrick* respectively are no mere accessories but part of the individuality of the portrait. As Lavater had put it, 'Stimme, Gang, Stellung, Gebärdung, Kleidung – alles an dem Menschen ist physiognomisch.'[34] It was precisely such innovations that some of Ingres's contemporaries found difficult to accommodate. Even Baudelaire was treading a thin line between admiration and ridicule when he maintained with regard to the overcoats that 'M. Ingres . . . ne recule devant aucune laideur et aucune bizarrerie'.[35] The uncompromising champion of Delacroix, Théophile Silvestre, who, together with the Goncourts, was the most vociferous of Ingres's detractors, was indeed quick to deride Ingres's approach to costume, claiming: 'tous les membres de l'assemblée que l'artiste a fait comparaître devant le public sont visiblement tyrannisés par leurs vêtements'.[36] But whether such details attracted admiration or derision, they were everywhere recognized as one of the dominant features of Ingres's innovative approach.

Harmony remained the goal of all artists working in the Lavaterian tradition. A. Le Go, in his review of the Salon of 1833, advanced his theory of a progression between Ingres's portrait of Madame Devauçay (1807) and his portrait of Monsieur Bertin (1832, fig. 8) and saw it precisely in terms of a greater understanding of the harmonious principles of physiognomy.[37] In the case of the earlier portrait, the mouth, the cartilage of the nose and the relief of the cheeks are out of keeping with the 'l'expression suave' of the rest, whereas in the portrait of the newspaper proprietor, 'tout est d'accord'. Le Go drew his reader's particular attention to Ingres's alertness to Bertin's 'irrégularitiés naturelles': one eyebrow higher, one eyelid lower, than the other. The effect was still harmonious, and his conclusion shows just what Ingres's contemporaries had been led to expect from a portrait:

The harmony of the two sides of the face is perfect. With what skill the wateriness of the eyes is rendered, using that transparent veil which characterizes so well the mental dimension of a certain time of life. With what skill also the variations in the relief replace the skin tones, where M. Ingres, obliged to admit his weakness as a colourist, emphasizes so clearly the form of those parts on which the layers of flesh are super-imposed. And those hands, see how perfectly they conform to the nature of the head and to the proportions of the body. What felicity, what truth, I should say, in the pose of the entire man! Here indeed is one of those portraits where the individuality of the original is so clearly accentuated that on seeing it you recognize not just the man but his entire personal habits as well.

So far removed was such a portrait from conventional notions of 'le beau' that the young Gautier was initially nonplussed by the artist's real-ism. Yet his regret that Ingres had not stuck to the nude, or at least, to subjects drawn from antiquity, did not blind him to the extent to which Ingres had attributed expressive potential to 'un pli de gilet et de re-dingote'.[38] When some twenty years later the portrait was reexhibited in the Universal Exhibition of 1855, his unambiguously positive assessment of it revealed that he had now learnt to respond to the potential of such an unconventional use of prosaic detail:

> To an external likeness of the sitter, he adds an internal likeness. Beneath the physical portrait he gives us its moral counterpart. Is there not an en-tire epoch to be discovered in the magnificent pose of M. Bertin de Vaux, leaning his fine, strong hands, like a bourgeois Caesar, on his powerful knees, with all the authority of intelligence, wealth and a self-confidence that is his due? What a well-ordered mind, how clear-sighted and mascu-line the gaze! What serene affability surrounds that magnificent, guileless mouth! Replace the frock coat by a fold of purple and you would have a Roman emperor or a cardinal. As he is here, he is the *honnête homme* under Louis-Philippe, and Dr Véron's six volumes have nothing more to say about that age now past.[39]

Gautier's reevaluation of the Bertin portrait can only have been en-couraged by the praise it had received from Baudelaire in *Le Salon de 1845*. For Baudelaire, it remained the most audacious, alive and modern of all Ingres's portraits.

When Gautier came to consider Balzac's approach to portraiture, his appreciation was conducted in ways that are strikingly reminiscent both of Sainte-Beuve's concept of the 'portrait littéraire' and of his celebra-tion of Ingres's achievement in his portrait of Bertin:

> this deep understanding of the modern world left Balzac, it has to be said, comparatively unreceptive to plastic beauty. ... Ideal beauty, with its

8.  Jean-Auguste-Dominique Ingres, *Portrait de Monsieur Bertin*, 1832 (Musée du Louvre, Paris)

pure, serene lines, was too simple, too cold, too uniform for that complex, involved and diverse genius. The characterful pleased him more than *style*, and he preferred physiognomy to beauty. In his female portraits, he never failed to introduce some indication, a crease, a wrinkle, a pink blotch, a hint of tenderness or weariness, an obtrusive vein, some detail indicative of life's bruises that a poet, tracing the same picture, would most surely have suppressed, no doubt wrongly. ... Where a lesser writer would have produced a portrait, Balzac creates a living figure.[40]

With due allowance made for the more restricted range of possibilities open in practice to the portrait painter, it would indeed appear that Gautier sensed a close affinity between Balzac and Ingres as two artists responding to the same fundamental tenets of the Lavaterian tradition.

That Balzac was consciously working within the Lavaterian tradition is clear at every turn. Lavater is named by him on numerous occasions. Within *Eugénie Grandet* (in the preface to which he terms himself a 'peintre littéraire'), there is a Lavaterian description of the three Cruchots, which, for all its emphasis on their unattractiveness, possesses, in its harmonious use of expressive detail, a significant resemblance to Ingres's 'Monsieur Bertin': 'They presented a perfect mixture of awkwardness and senility. Their faces, as faded as their threadbare coats, as creased as their trousers, seemed worn out, wizened, and puckered.'[41] A further rapprochement with Ingres, and one that reinforces the extent to which, *pace* Baudelaire, Ingres can be said to belong to a broadly Lavaterian tradition, may be made with regard to the way costume is seen by Balzac to function as a language. The assumption is expressed explicitly by him in the context of a description of Marie de Vandenesse in *Une Fille d'Eve*, in which 'la toilette' is said to be 'une manifestation constante de la pensée intime, un langage, un symbole'.[42]

There was, then, much in Ingres's art of portraiture that might have been expected to 'speak' to Balzac. Still further reasons for such an expectation can be adduced, starting with the predilection Balzac and Ingres shared for Raphael. A further parallel existed in that both Balzac and Ingres found fame in a sphere other than that which corresponded to their primary aesthetic or intellectual aspirations; they were compelled to exploit the realms of portraiture and the novel for economic reasons. The comparatively low esteem of portraiture is emphasized, or rather exaggerated, for satirical effect, in Balzac's story *Pierre Grassou*, in which the eponymous artist's mediocrity is forcefully contrasted with the genuine creativity of Joseph Bridau. Portrait painting is largely associated by Balzac with the self-image of the newly successful bourgeoisie and is seen thereby as an undisguised commercial transaction. Grassou is made to enjoy undeserved success as the 'portraitiste attitré' of the bourgeoisie. It is not just the ridiculous Vervelle family (how comically different they are from the Rivière family painted by Ingres!) who seek immortality through his brushes and palette; Grassou's consistently representative sitters also include Monsieur, Madame and Mademoiselle Crevel (see *La Cousine Bette*).

It may therefore come as a surprise to discover that the *Comédie humaine* contains very few references to Ingres. As has been noted already, the invocation of the portraitist's talents in *Madame Firmiani* was a later substitution. Still more surprisingly, it is the sole reference to Ingres as a painter of portraits; the other, sporadic, references are to 'La Grande Odalisque', 'Saint-Symphorien' and 'Le Vœu de Louis XIII'. When Balzac depicts Marie de Vandenesse, it is not Ingres but Sir Thomas Lawrence who is invoked.[43] It is left to the Goncourts' Madame Mauperin to insist upon having her portrait painted by Ingres.[44]

A number of diverse reasons may be adduced to explain Balzac's reticence with regard to the painter who was, at the level of subject matter at least, his most obvious counterpart among visual artists. Firstly, we should not assume on his part an intimate familiarity with Ingres's work. Leaving aside the drawings done during his Roman sojourn, Ingres was not a truly prolific portraitist, and his work, apart from an occasional showing at the Salon or other exhibition, most commonly remained in the hands of his sitters. Théophile Silvestre relates how it was with considerable reluctance that Ingres contributed to the charity exhibition at the Galerie Bonne-Nouvelle in 1846.[45] It was after Balzac's death that the Universal Exhibition of 1855 occasioned the extensive articles that Baudelaire and Gautier devoted to Ingres. Familiarity with works that were not on public display in this period depended largely on the availability of engravings, and Baudelaire, we may note in this connection, was led to deplore the delay in the appearance of the fine engraving that Henriquel Dupont had made of Ingres's portrait of Bertin.[46]

The fact remains that Balzac's tastes in painting were not advanced. In the words of Malcolm Easton:

> By upbringing he would not have been one to sympathize outright with the revolution in painting initiated by Gros, in 1804, and culminating in the work of Delacroix, twenty to twenty-three years later ... he had grown up with the standards of taste accepted by the petty bourgeoisie from which he sprang, and never altogether departed from them. This is apparent in his rather mechanical references to Raphael as the final canon in visual judgements, as also in a bourgeois fondness for the Dutch school. Among moderns, he preferred Guérin and Girodet.[47]

A case in point is provided by Balzac's portrait of the young Pierrette, in the course of which she is compared to a figure in Léopold Robert's painting, *L'Arrivée des Moissonneurs dans les Marais Pontins*: the child-cradling young woman who is described by him as '[une] figure raphaélique'.[48] Here Balzac deliberately chooses for comparison a painting that had been *the* success at the Salon of 1831 and which was considered by Sainte-Beuve to be Robert's masterpiece.[49] But it also represented Balzac's personal taste. His copy of Mercuri's engraving of the picture was a treasured possession; *Pierrette* was literally composed with it before his eyes.[50] Robert was not an advanced painter and Sainte-Beuve was right to question the validity of the comparison between Robert and Ingres that was frequently made as a result of their shared devotion to the memory of Raphael.[51] It is therefore indicative that of the two 'Raphaélisants', it should be to Robert that Balzac was drawn. The fact that he should have looked outside the genre of portraiture for an artistic representation with which to compare one of his own portraits points furthermore to the limited usefulness for his purpose of specific portraits, since his characters were designed to be individualized types endowed with a much greater power of suggestion than that possessed by any one specific counterpart from the real world.[52]

Portraiture in the *Comédie humaine*, moreover, possesses essentially negative connotations. Balzac's overt references to it are almost invariably made in relation to the striking of shallow, insincere or ridiculous poses. Crevel is thus immortalized by Grassou in his ludicrously inappropriate Napoleonic pose. When the reader of *La Cousine Bette* first meets him, the National Guard officer is described mockingly as inspecting himself in the mirror: 'il se regardait dans la glace, par-dessus une vieille pendule Empire, en se passant lui-même en revue'.[53] Back home in his own, more opulent surroundings, the Grassou portrait performs the same function as the Hulot mirror, but with the added reassurance that the reflection will always live up to expectation. Balzac's satire nonetheless varies in its severity. A reference to portraiture can often be no more than a means of ensuring that a critical distance from the character is established, as when Raoul Nathan is described with his 'bras croisés sur sa poitrine comme s'il posait pour son portrait, magnifique d'indifférence pour toute la salle, plein d'impatience mal contenue'.[54] His habitual pose is alleged to be that rendered famous by Girodet's portrait of Chateaubriand.[55] The comparison with a public figure thus becomes a highly specific device to signal affectation. In all such examples, the simulation of the sitter's pose is seen as a reflex reaction, a counterfeit act that offers an image akin to the copies of masterpieces that Grassou naively provides for the wily Elie Magus. The acquisitive society of the July Monarchy is, like so many Messieurs Vervelle, unable to distinguish the fake from the real. In *La Rabouilleuse*, the genuine artist, Joseph Bridau, finds himself unable to complete his portrait of his reprobate brother, a portrait that his mother desires presumably as a means of deluding herself about his true nature. The sureness of his artistic eye makes it impossible for him not to see the real Philippe.

As far as Ingres's specific practice is concerned, the consciously painterly quality of his portraits may also be regarded as being of limited stimulus to the author of the *Comédie humaine*, whose needs as a novelist remained essentially very different. Ingres's art is manifestly not one of self-effacement. The spectator is constantly aware of the artist's response to his sitter, a response that Baudelaire characterized admirably in his phrase 'servilité d'amoureux'.[56] For Ingres, the portrait remained first and foremost an aesthetic creation. The undisguised delight he took in his medium would lead Du Bos to regard his work as 'peinture pure' in the best sense of the term ('l'acception non point limitative mais au contraire infiniment riche et variée').[57] This was a dimension of Ingres's art that naturally caused some to question the extent to which his portraits represented a true likeness. Edmond About, for example, maintained that if nine-tenths of those who saw an Ingres portrait would instantly recognize it as a likeness of the sitter, every single one of them would exclaim: 'C'est un portrait de Monsieur Ingres.'[58] Admirers and detractors alike focused on Ingres's concern with artistic perfection. Silvestre alleged that his painting went against the fundamental law of art, namely its requirement to be 'human', and he complained that the spectator ended up suffocated.[59] The Goncourts, while making an exception for Ingres's male portraits, derided his 'peinture porcelainée'.[60]

As for those who delighted in Ingres's work, they described its effect in terms of enchantment. Sainte-Beuve marvelled at the 'mille intentions savantes' that emerge from a close inspection of his painting and thereby banish the misleading initial impression of 'un ton assez uniforme'. He concluded that 'on ne peut plus en détacher les yeux'.[61] Of Madame Devauçay's eyes, Gautier maintained 'ils vous suivent, ils vous obsèdent, ils vous charment, en prenant le mot au sens magique'.[62] In all such cases the reported effect is diametrically opposed to the kind of interpretative activity that Balzac felt was the required response to the complex set of signs present in any material reality. As Jacques Rivière would later say of the sensuousness of the 'lignes délicieuses' that compose an Ingres painting: 'Elles ravissent jusqu'à faire perdre la pensée.'[63] Expressed in this way, it would be difficult to imagine an artistic experience less calculated to appeal to the author of the *Comédie humaine*. The literary parallel that suggests itself instead is with Flaubert. Du Bos singled out in this connection the description of Madame Renaud in the first *Education sentimentale*.[64] But in *Madame Bovary* too, in such descriptions as that of the aristocratic occupants of the ballroom at La Vaubyessard, Flaubert delights in the allure of surfaces and treats us to the legitimate artistic counterpart of Emma's enfeebling fetishism. In many such instances there is a particular fascination, akin to that of Ingres, with the relationship between the body and its clothes.

In the final analysis, precise examples of portrait painting could, at best, be of only limited usefulness to Balzac the novelist, despite the fact that his practice may be regarded as rooted in beliefs and principles derived from a 'scientific' context that he shared with Ingres. An illuminating illustration of the highly individual direction in which his art of portraiture developed within the Lavaterian context is provided by the particular case of his extensive description of Nathan in *Une Fille d'Eve*. Nathan has often been regarded as the most composite of all the characters in the *Comédie humaine*, as far as actual models are concerned. In addition, part of the description of him in *Une Fille d'Eve* has been shown to have been closely modelled on Gautier's description of his fictional painter Onuphrius, whose story is one of those related in *Les Jeunes-France*.[65] Yet this was a description to which Balzac made a number of changes. These have been seen exclusively in terms of him incorporating aspects of his own appearance and experience, thereby causing Nathan to emerge as still more of a composite figure. But an obsession with precise models has obscured the fact that Balzac's modification of the original reveals a fundamentally different approach to the description of individual characters by the two authors concerned.

Gautier's Onuphrius is a straightforward caricature of a typical member of the self-consciously eccentric Jeunes-France set. His creator's humorous description reduces him to a jerky machine whose 'démarche incertaine' is described as 'entrecoupée d'élans subits, de zigzags, ou suspendue tout à coup'.[66] In the eyes of the conventional onlooker, he is said to be either 'un fou' or 'un original'. As will be seen, caricature is just one of the models that Balzac exploits in his much more complex linguistic portrait.

It is significant that Balzac follows closely only the middle section of Gautier's description and that he does not begin his act of 'plagiarism' with Gautier's opening section, which is concerned precisely with Onuphrius's physiognomy and general appearance. Gautier's portrait of his character in these initial paragraphs is rooted in a few simple ideas, such as Onuphrius's cultivation of the appearance of a Giotto or Cimabue angel and the contrast apparent in his features between youth and old age, and would not have satisfied Balzac as it stood. It is not, as has generally been maintained, that this section of Gautier's description was simply ignored by Balzac. Various features of his opening depiction of Nathan can be traced back to isolated details in the original, but this only serves to highlight Balzac's indifference to its essentials. If Onuphrius's premature aging is the starting-point for the harrowed countenance that Balzac gives to his character, the development in terms of the theories of creativity and self-destruction explored by the novelist in his 'romans et contes philosophiques' indicates the latter's need to go beyond the merely picturesque. As for the elements in Gautier's portrait that Balzac is content to retain, they are transformed as a result of being incorporated in a description that is much longer than the passages borrowed and which, as a result, is responsible for the portrait as a whole being instantly recognizable as Balzacian in its complex diversity.

More specifically, and in contrast to Gautier's original, Balzac's portrait of Nathan is Lavaterian, even down to the anecdote of the journalist's unkempt fingernails, which recalls uncannily Sainte-Beuve's reference, already quoted, to Michaud's fingernails. Nathan's clothing, worn rather than merely adorning his person, is, in true Lavaterian fashion, an extension of the personality readable in his physiognomy. The portrait also contains the key notion of harmony: 'Ses vêtements semblent toujours avoir été tordus, fripés, recroquevillés exprès pour s'harmonier à sa physionomie.' Then, in the very midst of a passage closely modelled on Gautier's text, the novelist introduces a further Lavaterian observation with regard to Nathan's gait and conversation ('sa conversation . . . imite l'allure de son corps'), which in turn produces the conclusion that 'la toilette du moral était donc alors chez Raoul en harmonie avec son vêtement'.

Balzac's description of Nathan undoubtedly offers certain obvious parallels with a painted portrait. Firstly, this is the description in which Nathan is described as affecting the pose rendered famous by Girodet's portrait of Chateaubriand. As has been seen, the concern to highlight the relationship between the sitter's body and his clothes was a particular feature of the Ingres portrait. Nathan's pose, we are told, was struck quite simply 'pour déflorer les plis réguliers de chemise', though Balzac goes on to provide additional animation, observing that the writer's tie was 'en ce moment roulée sous les convulsions de ses mouvements de tête, qu'il a remarquablement brusques et vifs'; the comparison drawn is with thoroughbred horses restless in their harness. Most strikingly of all, Nathan is singled out as one of that minority of men who stand out instantly in a drawing-room, forming 'un point lumineux où vont tous les regards', in the manner, one might suggest, of certain portraits that exert a magnetic appeal from their position on a crowded gallery wall.

Yet it is Onuphrius's caricatural movement that Balzac retains most closely from Gautier's original, though, characteristically, he builds upon it in his own distinctive way. The wit, the distorted *mot* from *Le Misanthrope*, the comparisons with a heron's legs and a crab's pincers are his own fertile inventions. What is remarkable, therefore, in his portrait of Nathan is its composite nature as far as *techniques* are concerned. What the reader is offered is not purely an emulation of the art of the portraitist nor merely an example of caricature. It is an amalgam, a constant shift from one to the other, just as there is a continual hesitancy between an impression of the character as an individual (it is stressed that he is at pains to avoid resembling another) and an appreciation of him as a representative of the Jeunes-France and of his profession. It is not, however, a simple oscillation between two distinct approaches to the representation of the infinite interpretability of external appearances. Portraiture and caricature may traditionally have been seen as complementary,[67] but here, instead of representing straightforward alternatives, they form a continuum, as a result of which Balzac's dynamic art of visual characterization is able to indulge in a range of subtle differences of emphasis in between.

The fact remains that if nineteenth-century portraiture has its origins in the Lavaterian tradition, so even more does the caricature of that period. It was of the caricaturist Daumier that Baudelaire wrote: 'Il a un talent d'observation tellement sûr qu'on ne trouve pas chez lui une seule tête qui jure avec le corps qui le supporte. Tel nez, tel front, tel œil, telle main.'[68] In other words, the art of both the portraitist and the caricaturist has a common source in an eye for the unique personal characteristic. The Balzacian continuum between portraiture and caricature thus has its external counterpart in the world of contemporary aesthetic theory. The representation of physiognomy, gait and gesture in both portraiture and caricature turns on the same subtle question of where the individual becomes the idiosyncratic. The reader of About's imaginary account of how Ingres set about producing a portrait could be forgiven for wondering whether the critic was in fact describing a caricaturist at work:

> He studies a face and forms an idea of it. True or false, this idea is personal to him. He says to himself: 'This man has the face of a Roman emperor, or that man has the appearance of a fox, a lion, or a monkey.' According to the particular case, he enlarges the mask at the expense of the skull, or he gives a rounder shape to the head, ruffles up the mane of hair, or lengthens the arm; he throws into relief the salient feature of a physiognomy, exaggerating its character, and erasing its insignificant features. In a word, he creates an entirely new man.[69]

Gautier, likewise, insisted that Ingres's style was characterized by 'l'exagération dans un principe vrai des détails extérieurs'.[70] The fundamental similarity of the principles behind nineteenth-century portraiture and caricature is moreover accentuated by the fact that attempts to translate examples of these art forms into words show language to be a blunt instrument incapable of rendering the distinctiveness of a visual masterpiece.

127

The paucity of references by Balzac to Ingres may, then, tell us something about Balzac's artistic taste, but it cannot be taken to indicate that the two creative artists adopted fundamentally different approaches to the art of portraiture. Their practice, for all their declared prejudices, was resolutely modern and was rooted in the same belief that the distinctive detail was the interpretative key to the unique complexity of the whole, this attachment to the specificity of the individual case being paralleled by the highly conscious art of the 'portrait littéraire' elaborated in the same period by Sainte-Beuve. But just as Sainte-Beuve could admire the work of the one (Ingres) and abhor that of the other (Balzac), so the broad similarities of approach of the two 'portraitists' still allowed their individual practice to differ considerably, to the extent that the literary 'equivalent' of Ingres was, in some important respects, Flaubert rather than Balzac.

The Lavaterian tradition, as has been seen, could allow a diversity of artistic practice and aesthetic effect. A portrait by that avowed Lavaterian, Girodet,[71] remained sharply distinguishable from one by Ingres, to say nothing of a caricature by Daumier. Yet a comparison of Balzac and Ingres also throws into relief the equally obvious fact that portraiture in the novel, for all its affinities with the contemporary visual arts, by no means functions in an identical way. Balzac's frequent evocation of painting does not constitute an attempt to present the reader with an experience akin to a confrontation with the work of a visual artist. It does not seek to reproduce the untranslatable and mesmerizing effect created by the painter or sculptor. Instead, whereas an Ingres portrait is there for us to behold directly, the novelist must assume the function of the reader's surrogate spectator of the real, that of its commentator as well as its creator. Whereas an Ingres portrait is for us a finished simulacrum of the real, the Balzacian description offers us the much more tentative spectacle of the artist at work.

## Suggested reading

Adhémar, Jean, 'Balzac et la peinture', *Revue des Sciences humaines*, avril–juin 1953.

Baltrušaitis, Jurgis, *Aberrations. Quatre essais sur la légende des formes* (Paris: Olivier Perrin, 1957).

Easton, Malcolm, *Artists and Writers in Paris: The Bohemian Idea 1803–1867* (London: Arnold, 1964).

Snell, Robert, 'Gautier critique d'Ingres' in *Théophile Gautier, L'Art et l'artiste*, Colloque international, 2 vols (Montpellier: Université Paul Valéry, 1982).

Tytler, Graeme, *Physiognomy in the European Novel: Faces and Fortunes* (Princeton, NJ: Princeton University Press, 1982).

# 8

## The model's unwashed feet:
## French photography in the 1850s

### Eric Homberger

The generic term 'photography' began to replace 'daguerreotype' in common usage in the 1850s. The succession of techniques, each enthusiastically boomed by practitioners and advocates, long continued; but with the stabilization of the term the confusing early chapters in the emergence of photography came to an end. Until recent work by Jonathan Crary, it is a story largely assumed to have been driven by technological innovation; in the hands of its leading historians photography has been regarded, as Peter Galassi observed, as a 'child of technical rather than aesthetic traditions'.[1] Perhaps this assumption is best recorded in the catalogue for an Arts Council exhibition of early photography: 'The origins of photography lie in the two sciences chemistry and optics.'[2] It will be useful to retrace the steps which led to the perfecting and simplification of photographic technique by the middle of the nineteenth century – not only to suggest the preeminence of France by the onset of the Second Empire, but to emphasize the significance of realism for the early period of photography. Thus we shall see more clearly the changing significance of photography for the great 'realism debate' of the 1850s.

The history of photography usually begins with the search of draughtsmen, architects and amateurs for drawing aids. As early as the sixteenth century the phenomenon of the camera obscura was known. A box with a plate of glass on the rear or top admitted light through a small hole in the front (as early as the 1550s it was found that a lens could greatly sharpen the image) which allowed a reversed image to appear on the glass plate. By the nineteenth century the camera obscura could be as large as a desk placed within a tent. A draughtsman could sketch the image thrown upon a piece of white paper by a lens and mirror. The camera obscura was more than an ingenious toy. The principles behind its operation were widely known, and suggested to the thoughtful a philosophic metaphor for the way mankind draws truthful inferences about the world. The observer, trapped in a 'dark room' and with dutiful thoughts of Plato's parable of the cave, recorded on paper the reversed images of the external world and sought to interpret its full nature. As a model for perception, this was at once passive and seemingly objective. It was only with the developments in the study of vision in the early nineteenth century that the subjective dimensions of perception and its physiological contexts became more widely grasped. The camera obscura 'model' disintegrated in the nineteenth century amidst a profusion of artists and scientists who emphasized the profoundly subjective nature of vision.[3]

The faithful accuracy of the camera obscura joined with an experimental interest in photo-chemistry in the eighteenth century. It had long been observed that the nature of certain chemical substances, particularly silver salt, changed when exposed to light. For decades amateur experimenters, tormented by the evanescence of the sharp, intriguing images revealed by the camera obscura, tried to find a way to fix (that is, to save permanently) the images recorded on the glass plate. Their best efforts continued to darken and eventually were nothing more than a plate of impenetrable black. Thomas Wedgwood and Sir Humphry Davy failed to fix such images with silver nitrate in 1802.

The idea of sun-writing, of capturing the very likeness of nature, was a Promethean desire to steal the fire of heaven and turn it to the betterment of mankind. In 1816, while Mary Shelley was reading Humphry Davy's *Discourse Introductory to a Course of Lectures on Chemistry* (1802) and his *Chemical Philosophy* (1812), and contemplating her own fable of science and ambition in *Frankenstein or The Modern Prometheus* (1818), Joseph-Nicéphore Niepce (1765–1833), an enthusiastic experimenter, took the first primitive photographs in his farm courtyard. Using sheets of paper sensitized with chloride of silver, exposed to light by the use of the camera obscura, Niepce recounted in his 'Notice sur l'héliographie' how he tried various substances and materials: copper-coated plates used by engravers, silver-plated sheets of copper, lithographic stones, and glass plates in combination with light-sensitive materials such as bitumen asphalt and other light-sensitive varnishes. He also experimented with iodine vapour to 'develop' a latent image and discovered that oil of lavender would dissolve the unexposed bitumen, leaving a faint image. The resulting plate could then be bathed in acid, engraved and printed on to paper.

Niepce's first photograph was made in 1826, though it was not rediscovered until 1952. Photography effectively begins as a technical step towards greater precision in engraving.[4] In 1827 Niepce met Louis Jacques Mandé Daguerre (1787–1851), who had also been experimenting with the camera obscura and attempting to fix images with silver chloride paper. Their partnership was formed in 1829. Niepce died without seeing any results from his efforts; his wife and son were forced to

131

sell the family property to pay the debts incurred by his researches. Daguerre had worked as a scenic artist and was the proprietor of the famous 'Diorama' of Paris, a theatrical exhibition of large (15 × 23 yards) illusionistic paintings on both sides of theatrical gauze depicting various buildings and locations in the city. By manipulation of the light source (from front, rear or combination) a near-perfect illusion was achieved. In 1823 Daguerre opened a Diorama in Regent's Park, London, which survived as an attraction until 1851. He experimented with the light-sensitive iodide of silver (silver salt) in 1831 and accidentally discovered four years later that the vapour from a few drops of mercury enabled more sensitive images to be developed with shorter exposure times (20–30 minutes). He had stored away an exposed plate, and found, several days later, that it had emerged bearing a distinct picture. By trial and error he eliminated a range of substances and chemicals until he came upon mercury vapour – a few drops from a broken thermometer. He did not succeed in permanently fixing images until in 1837 he used a solution of common salt in hot water.

Seeking to publicize the 'daguerreotype', Daguerre failed to find a private entrepreneur to finance development of the invention. The *democratic* possibilities of the daguerreotype strongly appealed to him. Everyone could make their own views. It promised something for everyone – artists, leisured classes, ladies.[5] François Arago (1786–1853), physicist, astronomer, perpetual Secretary of the Academy of Sciences, and leader of the Republican opposition in the Chambre des deputés, announced the invention of photography on 7 January 1839. In his 'Rapport à la Chambre des députés' of 3 July 1839 he stressed the profound usefulness of the invention for learning and science. It could have been used to preserve pictorial records in Egypt, now lost, and would in the future make a great contribution to the survey of historical monuments. With unprecedented speed and registration of detail, for which one person was sufficient to do the work which formerly took many hours of exacting labour, the invention would have a beneficial effect on art (and also the economy). Like Daguerre, Arago emphasized the democratic simplicity of the procedures: 'Daguerreotype calls for no manipulation which anyone cannot perform. It presumes no knowledge of the art of drawing and demands no special manual dexterity. When, step by step, a few simple prescribed rules are followed, there is no one who cannot succeed as certainly as well as M. Daguerre himself.'[6] Details of the process used were announced on 19 August at a public meeting. The French government bought the rights from Daguerre and gave them to the public. In return for the surrender of his rights, he was awarded a pension for life.

The third stage in the early evolution of photography was achieved by William Henry Fox Talbot (1800–77), a polymathic English gentleman who was an experimenter, linguist and Member of Parliament in the 1830s. A man with strong amateur interest in science and technology, Fox Talbot experimented with the camera lucida in 1835 to find ways of fixing images using light-sensitive paper. By 1839 he submitted a paper to the Royal Society in London claiming priority for the invention of photography. The images he produced were reversed, and soon faded. He discovered that reversed images could be used to create a 'correct' image by reexposure of the negative to the sun on top of another sensitized sheet of paper. Fox Talbot's images were made by the use of paper bathed in a solution of sodium chloride, and then dipped into a silver nitrate solution, the chemicals bonding together to form a light-sensitive silver chloride solution that sank into the fibres of the paper. With thirty minutes required for exposure, his times were inferior to Daguerre's. In 1840 Fox Talbot discovered the possibility of developing a *latent* image, with a short exposure time, by use of gallo-nitrate of silver. He called this method 'Calotype' (from the Greek *kalos*, beautiful) or 'Talbo-type'.[7]

The situation of photography in the 1840s was dominated by two rival techniques: the daguerreotype and the calotype. The daguerreotype used polished silver-plated copper plates, usually $6\frac{1}{2} \times 8\frac{1}{2}$ inches. Sensitized by vapour of iodine, they were exposed manually to light by the operator, who then placed the exposed plate in a box with heated mercury which would 'develop' the latent image into a visible one on the silver surface. The plate was then bathed in a bath of sodium chloride to fix the image. When dried, it was framed behind glass and sealed to prevent discolouring due to rust and oxidation. The daguerreotype's detailed image, argued Janet Buerger,

> is unlike any other picture. It gives the effect not of a representation of the subject, but of the subject itself – Nature per se staring out at the observer. The impression is not of a picture sitting on the surface of a canvas or a piece of paper, or even on a piece of metal, but of a true spatial existence, distilled for repeated experiences by the viewer. This immediacy of reality was a quantum leap beyond that provided by the calotype.[8]

The limitations of the daguerreotype were equally striking. Long exposure times were required, which thus as if by magic emptied street scenes of pedestrians and vehicles. The technique gave little opportunity to the operator to shape the appearance of the final image; the surface was mirror-like and hard to see; the pictures were laterally reversed; and each image was unique. The cameras used by daguerreotypists were large, and the complete equipment of plates, spirit lamp, mercury box and bottles of chemicals posed problems for operators. Complete outfits were offered by opticians in Paris for between 250 and 400 francs.

Nonetheless, the daguerretotype satisfied a hunger for self-representation, and promised a new age of accurate images. It was the detail of early photographs which affirmed their moral and material utility. When in 1841 John Ruskin first heard of the daguerreotype from Dean Liddell of Christ Church (whose daughter Alice became a favorite model for Lewis Carroll), friends in Paris sent him examples of the early products. He believed he was the first in England to have seen Daguerre's work. By 1842 he was arguing that complex artistic problems of chiaroscuro and aerial perspective could be greatly aided by the daguerreotype. The American painter Samuel F.B. Morse, who introduced the daguerreotype into the United States, argued that it would not only improve the work of artists, it would also educate public taste:

> It will ease the artist's task by providing him with facsimile sketches of nature, buildings, landscapes, groups of figures ... scenes selected in accordance with the peculiarities of his own taste ... not copies of nature, but portions of nature itself ... the public would become acquainted through photography with correctness of perspective and proportion, and thus be better qualified to see the difference between professional and less well-trained work.[9]

Edgar Allan Poe, writing in a New York journal in January 1840, praised the daguerreotype for its stunning detail and accuracy: it was '... *infinitely* more accurate in its representation than any painting by human hands'.[10]

The calotype, perfected by 1841 with significantly shorter exposure times than daguerreotypes, was protected by Fox Talbot's jealously guarded copyright. Commercial use was limited because he would only grant licences on the payment of a substantial sum. The calotype inevitably had less appeal to commercial operators than to enthusiastic amateurs. Fox Talbot's *The Pencil of Nature* (1844–6), which consisted of 274 copies of 24 hand-made 'original' examples of the calotype, were sent gratis to photographic societies. He did not regard photography as an art; rather, he shared the views of Daguerre and Arago that the photograph was something useful for scientists and a valuable help to artists. Calotype images were recorded on paper and possessed many advantages over the daguerreotype. The impressive achievements of Adamson and Hill in Scotland as portraitists using the Fox Talbot technique did much to strengthen the impression of its superiority over the daguerreotype. But it could not rival the latter in commercial applicability. As the photographic industry developed in Europe and the United States, the division between the subtle images possible with the calotype and harsher, more purely mechanical applications of the daguerreotype drew ever wider.

With the perfecting in 1847 of the techniques for impregnating paper with light-sensitive substances by Louis-Désiré Blanquart-Evrard (1802–72), a cloth merchant who had been instructed in the calotype by his local chemist, the era of the daguerreotype symbolically ended. (It remained widely used throughout the 1850s: *The Daguerreian Journal* was first published in New York in 1850, and a year later 700 daguerreotypes were shown at the Great Exhibition at Crystal Palace in London; 21 million daguerreotype plates were manufactured in France alone that year.[11] In Blanquart-Evrard's atelier in Lille, between two and three hundred prints could be made in a single day's work. Fox Talbot's factory in a garden shed in Reading could not begin to achieve such productivity. It was a technical and commerical triumph for French photography, and through the 1850s France led the world in innovation and quality of work. There was a dramatic upswing in the scale of photographic activity in France after the revolution of 1848, which only slowed down with the depression in 1857.[12] Blanquart-Evrard used albumen from chicken eggs to make the emulsion adhere to the surface of the photographic paper; he also perfected the use of toning agents, like gold salts, which gave his prints a nut-brown richness that also resisted fading. The first photographically illustrated book, Maxime du Camp's *Egypte, Nubie, Palestine et Syrie: Dessins photographiques recueillis pendant les années 1849 et 1851* (1852), used the calotype process as modified by Blanquart-Evrard. The volume consisted of 125 calotypes printed by Blanquart-Evrard, mounted on card, with a short text. Gustave Le Gray, an enthusiastic experimenter with technical processes, began working with *papier ciré sec*, a dry waxed photographic paper (coated with silver salts and beeswax) which was lightweight and highly portable.

The perfection of new techniques, publications such as Du Camp's, and the impact of the Crystal Palace exhibition did much to make 1850 the beginning of the modern age of photography. (The death that year of Daguerre, who had given up photography in 1840, and the invention of the collodion process by Frederick Scott Archer, intensify one's sense of 1851 as a symbolic turning-point.) The Société Héliographique, which largely represented the interests of 'art photography', was founded in Paris in 1851, with the active suport of Le Gray, Le Secq and Eugène Delacroix; the society's journal, *La Lumière*, was edited by Ernest Lacan, whose *Esquisses Photographiques* appeared in 1856. In the same year the Commission des Monuments Historiques established a Mission Héliographique. Five photographers (Baldus, Bayard, Le Secq, Le Gray and Mestral) were selected to travel in different areas of France to document the condition of important antiquities. Although the project was suddenly and mysteriously ended and little survives from its work, the experience of the mission gave French photographers a commanding position worldwide in architectural photography.

When the rebuilding of Paris began in earnest with the appointment of Baron Hausmann as prefect of the Seine in 1853, the leading photographers of the era (including Marville, Nègre and the Bissons) were soon involved in large-scale projects recording a Paris that was being transformed almost beyond recognition. Le Secq, like so many other intellectuals, lamented the destruction of so much of what made Paris distinctive. The neighbourhood where he lived as a child was among those largely demolished. But he declined to place himself among those most determinedly opposed to the regime which came into being with the plebiscite which inaugurated the Second Empire on 21–22 November 1852. A fondness for the picturesque and a sentimental and romantic dislike of the more aggressive forms of modernity did not necessarily mean that he took sides in the political disputes. The physical transformation of the city was clearly an important part of the Emperor's plan for social reform.[13] And for photographers Haussmann created some of the grandest urban perspectives in the world, and photographic images were in great demand. Le Secq completed an album of twenty-two photographs of the centre of Paris during 1852 and 1853, concentrating on the structures planned for demolition and the old Paris street scenes which were soon to be lost.[14]

By the Exposition Universelle in 1855, the daguerreotype had largely vanished from commercial use. The lavish display of photographs organized by the Société Française de Photographie, which greatly enhanced the reputation of photography, coincided with the rejection by the jury of the Exposition des Beaux-Arts of Courbet's *Un enterrement à Ornans* and *L'Atelier* (fig. 25). The realism of photography, its triumphant promise in the early 1840s, was now increasingly used as a term of dismissal and abuse. John Everett Millais's *Christ in the Carpenter's Shop* (exhibited at the Royal Academy in 1850) had been received with a fierce denunciation. The details – St Joseph's dirty fingernails, the 'low' environment – offended religious sensibilities. Courbet's *Un enterrement à Ornans* was criticized by Etienne-Jean Delécluze for resembling a 'faulty daguerreotype'. His is a slightly more ironic remark than may at first appear: to make up for the low admission charges of twenty sous he planned for his Realist exhibition at 17 Avenue Montaigne, Courbet hoped to sell photographs of his pictures to the visitors. There is perhaps no need to retrace the insulting and hostile reception which greeted Courbet in 1855; the reality of Courbet's work was felt to be brutal, a negation of the ideal.[15]

While, as Scharf argues, the photographic standard of sharpness increasingly became the yardstick against which pictorial representations were judged, photographers – criticized for the 'biting sharpness' of their images – sought devices to soften them. In the hope of making photographs more 'artistic' photographers sought to make them less realistic.

Le Gray's seascapes were manipulated; that is, assembled from different images.[16] As Henry Peach Robinson (*Fading Away*, 1853, using five negatives) and O.G. Rejlander (*Two Ways of Life*, 1856) had demonstrated in England, the 'composite' photograph, made from as many as thirty different negatives, freed the photographer's vision from the clumsy realism of what could be actually seen, and it also liberated them from the technical limitations of their cameras and equipment. Such work, which soon attracted the label 'pictorialism', sought conclusively to demonstrate that the photographer was not merely someone who was capable of operating a machine, and that the photograph itself was no mere mechanical reproduction of the visual world. The path was now open towards the art photography movement of the 1890s, and its ornate, subjective vision.

In the repeated efforts of mid-nineteenth-century photographers to escape the harsh clarity of their own technology, and also to win social and cultural respectability, they emulated the stylistic practices of painting. The staging of genre photographs became one of the staples of 'artistic' commercial activity in Paris. Commercial studios, with their carefully arranged poses, props and lighting, set the standard for a painterly aesthetic in early photography. Ever more elaborate attempts were made in the 1850s to reproduce the chiaroscuro of academic painting, and to follow the genres of the fine arts. The 'Etude académique' (see fig. 12), 'Etude d'après nature', 'Etudes variées' were soon established categories among the 'Etudes photographiques.' The visual quality of these pictures often astounded contemporaries: their detail, accuracy and life-like rendition of tone and mass, such as the still-life photographs of Charles Aubry from the 1860s, were at once felt to herald a new era in the advance of visual accuracy. The photographic studio of Alexis Gouin at rue Louis-le-Grand in Paris specialized in coloured daguerreotypes of nudes. Madame Gouin, and her daughter (who married the photographer Bruno Braquehais) mastered the art of 'refined colouring' and Mme Gouin marketed boxed sets of colouring material (12 tubes of paint and six brushes for 15 francs).

But photographs of naked women were unsettlingly detailed and in the increasingly conservative atmosphere which followed the establishment of the Second Empire in 1852, it was necessary to represent the women in the photographs as occupying a traditionally understood role, that of artists' models (thus asserting the analogy between artist and photographer). Several practitioners of nude photography created photographic narratives of daily life, as though the model had paused briefly while undressing before the bath. Julien Vallou de Villeneuve specialized in semi-erotica in a domestic setting recreated in his studio. Courbet used de Villeneuve's nude studies, as well as that of other photographers, for his *L'Atelier*, *Les Baigneuses* and other works from the 1850s. Other photographers, such as Guglielmo Marconi, worked

9. Gustave Le Gray,
*Nu, c.* 1849 (Société
Française de
Photographie, Paris)

10. J-F. Boitouzet,
*Nu au miroir*, 1855
(Bibliothèque Nationale,
Paris)

11. Billon, *Nu*,
calotype
stéréoscopique, 1861
(Bibliothèque
Nationale, Paris)

12. Bruno
Braquehais, *Nu.
Etude académique*,
calotype, 1854
(Bibliothèque
Nationale, Paris)

with nudes within the traditional range of academic poses and classical props.

In this effort to win respectability, the ragged edges, socially and aesthetically, of these images were occasionally left visible. Early in his career as a photographer Gustave Le Gray opened an atelier in a factory building at 7 chemin de Ronde de la Barrière de Clichy. It was there, in 1849, in a corner of the wooden-floored structure, that a model posed on the floor, her torso rising perhaps a foot to the wall at the end of the room. A piece of paper lay casually at her side. The sole of the model's right foot was directly in view, with her left foot held at an angle. Both feet are positively filthy (fig. 9).[17] J.-E.-Fr. Boitouzet's *Nu au miroir* (1855, fig. 10), which has a model sitting on a draped bed, dramatically reveals a similar casualness before the detailed problems of creating an adequate artistic illusion. Above the piece of fabric which serves as a backdrop for the model, there is a casually thrown blouse. At the model's feet are her homely, well-worn slippers. The ostensible subject of the photograph is a vignette on the problem of copying nature: by the side of the naked model is a mirror (carefully placed to give us another view of her left breast) and a small statue of a similarly undressed woman in a somewhat different pose.[18] A similar 1865 photograph by Paul Berthier (1822–1912), *Etude d'après nature no. 1*, is constructed before the discoloured wall of the studio. The overweight model sits on a draped couch, turned away from the camera. Her legs are intertwined, revealing her dirty feet. On her leg there is a circular bruise.[19] An anonymous pornographic stereoscope, made before 1870, is of a naked model, legs akimbo, who wore nothing but her leather shoes and stockings rolled down to her knee. The effect is obscene, though perhaps neither lascivious nor erotic.[20]

The unwashed feet and bruises, the lowered stocking and scuffed leather shoes, tell us much about the *bohème* world of young Parisian artists, their models and *grisettes*. They also hint at the large and highly visible world of commercial sex in Paris, and of the sexual availability of maids, servant-girls and other young women. Christine Roux, the original of Murger's Musette and a familiar figure in bohemian circles in Paris in the early 1840s, posed for the sculptor Clésinger and was the subject of one of Nadar's first nude studies.[21]

The trade of commercial photography was insecure; bankruptcies were commonplace, and virtually from its invention 'erotic' photography was an important element in the trade. By the 1850s stereoscopes (see fig. 11) and tinted images of nudes commanded a fair share of the market, reminding us of the nagging commercial insecurity of photographers trying to sustain a business upon the often meagre earnings available from commercial work. Le Gray was, perhaps supremely among his contemporaries, dedicated to becoming an instructor of good photographic practice. He had served his professional apprenticeship in the class of Paul Delaroche in the early 1840s, copying still lifes, statuary and the work of other painters. Le Gray would be a Delaroche for his own students, and for a host of interested amateurs who flocked to his studio for tuition before a journey. Before Maxime Du Camp's voyage to Egypt in October 1849, he attended Le Gray for lessons (and unhappily found in Egypt that his own chemical preparations produced work notably inferior to his tutor's). But the income generated by commercial photography only enabled him to hire a model from the poorest class – perhaps a domestic servant or laundress. In a drawing class, the detail would be ignored as the students were ever instructed to attend to the ideal, and to observe form and proportion; in a photograph the grimy sole, the slippers and filthy heel cannot be ignored.

The controversy which followed the uncertain results of his students was conducted largely in terms of whether Le Gray's methods were too complex and exacting, too personal and even too impressionistic. The camera was a truth-telling machine, celebrated for its accuracy. But sometimes the details were disturbing, intrusive and irrelevant. To the disappointment of those who saw the photograph as a powerful adjunct to the new science and rational spirit of the day, Le Gray's work often revealed underlying aesthetic principles and elements of fantasy (Charles Nègre on Le Gray, May 1851: ' . . . he reproduces effects that make us dream, simple motifs that move us and sites whose bold and powerful silhouettes astonish and even frighten us'[22]), rather than a dispassionate commitment to the factual description of the world. The project of truth-telling was felt to be intrusive, as well as being half-hearted and, as Crary argued, only partially accurate. Delacroix, who advocated the use of daguerreotypes for the training of the artist, maintained that the startling realism achieved was ' . . . still only a reflection of the real, only a copy, in some way false just because it is so exact. The monstrosities it shows are indeed deservedly shocking although they may literally be the deformations present in nature herself; but these imperfections which the machine reproduces faithfully, will not offend our eyes when we look at the model without this intermediary.'[23] The distinctive strengths of the photographic image have been transmuted, in little more than a decade, into a constant refrain in the doubts and hostile criticism of realism in the 1850s.

The realism of photography posed a series of uncomfortable problems for the realists themselves, and for their audience. Defenders of the new spirit demanded for painting and literature the same rights that mirrors had. Louis Napoleon's distasteful poke at the generous rump of Courbet's bather registered a complex rejection. Nude women remained a commonplace in painting, and the classical conventions governed expectations for the artist and audience. Aaron Scharf suggests that the Emperor was outraged because she was both proletarian and nude, a

washerwoman masquerading as a nymph.[24] What I am suggesting is that
the conventions had changed meaning since the advent of photography.
The gloss of the Ideal no longer seemed to possess its traditional power
when, before one's eyes, the unwashed feet and well-worn slippers of the
model insisted upon another kind of social reality standing behind the
image. Mid-century photographers worked vigorously to escape from
the nature of their own medium. They perfected their scene-making (no
more tell-tale signs to betray the illusion), used an abundance of signify-
ing props to reinforce the artistic traditions being alluded to. Most
importantly, they worked closely to maintain the notion that the occasion of photography was intrinsically dramatic. Despite tediously long
exposure times for portraits, the scene could be arranged and lit, as any
staged play; the occasion of photography was also a vast cultural screen
erected, before which the subject was *intended* to pose. A few notable
images deliberately represented their own construction (Olympe Aguado's *Self-Portrait in his own studio in Paris*, about 1855, and Pierre
Louis Pierson's image of the French heir-apparent on a pony, with
Napoleon III, about 1859); most sought assiduously to perfect the illusion.[25]

The explosion of interest in photography came towards the end of the
1850s, when Disdéri's cartes de visite caught the imagination of the
public. Each carte was a little social performance, combed and arranged
precisely to eliminate those tell-tale clues which had proven so disquieting earlier in the decade. Particular care was taken to eliminate
clues of provenance; we are all bourgeois now. In his essay on the Exposition Universelle of 1855, Baudelaire commented on the paintings of
David and his allies: ' . . . the whole of that truly extra-natural world [of
the paintings] was forever moving about, or rather *posing*, beneath a
greenish light, a fantastic parody of the real sun. . . .' [26] It was the photography of the early 1850s which made the *pose* a new tool for social
disguise, and also of cultural analysis. The low price of the cartes de
visite meant that *everyone* (except the poorest) had their opportunity to
join the posing throngs. Pocket-sized self-representation, and with a
choice of ten poses. Distinguished men of letters posed as decrepit
monks at Julia Margaret Cameron's studio; Baudelaire posed as a mis-
understood genius for Nadar; young children from the Oxford elite
posed as Neapolitan street waifs for Lewis Carroll; peasant women
posed as peasant women; the dead, even the victims of *la semaine san-
glante*, were carefully arranged for postmortem portraiture; artists were
posed – as artists, one after the other leaning on fluted column, within
the same ornate frame;[27] elderly men with beards were posed as alche-
mists or as Rembrandtesque studies; fruit was posed; landscapes
recomposed; professional tools like violins became mere props; figures
out of world literature, from Shakespeare and Cervantes, were artfully

reconstructed.[28] Every photographer's studio became an Aladdin's cave of helmets, statuary, telescopes, rich drapery, tassels, exotic clothing.

It is perhaps also easier to understand dandyism, and the brilliant series of portraits which were made of Baudelaire by Nadar and Carjat at this time, if the triumph of photographic artifice over 'nature' is placed in context. Nadar's great portraits belong to this world. Sarah Bernhardt and Mikhail Bakunin lean on the same well-worn column in Nadar's studio; Verdi and Alexandre Becquerel (*fils*) are photographed leaning on the arm of the same tassled chair. The self-portrayal of Nadar's subjects, largely impassive, become signs within a pattern of meaning constituted by his other subjects: the extravagances of the plump-legged 'Poules' from the Folies-Bergère, the performing dog, snake charmers, actors and actresses (Bernhardt as Harlequin), ballerinas and cartoonists. In the midst of Nadar's sobriety (a 'distinct abstemiousness', in the words of Roger Cardinal),[29] small details take on an inordinate significance: from the half-squint of Delacroix, Gautier's dissipated vanity, de Nerval's haunting fingers gently touching each other, the angle of Boulanger's *képi*, to Offenbach's louche self-amusement. Nadar gives us the enthronement of the Second Empire's posed culture, a culture of poseurs.

## Suggested reading

Baudelaire, 'The Exposition Universelle, 1855', *Art in Paris 1845–1862: Salons and Other Exhibtions*, trans. and ed. Jonathan Mayne (London: Phaidon Press, [1965]).

Galassi, Peter, *Before Photography: Painting and the Invention of Photography* (New York: Museum of Modern Art, 1981).

Gosling, Nigel, *Nadar* (London: Secker and Warburg, 1976).

Janis, Eugenia Parry, *The Photography of Gustave le Gray* (Chicago: Art Institute of Chicago and University of Chicago Press, 1987).

Rouillé, André, *L'Empire de la Photographe: Photographie et pouvoir bourgeois 1839–1870* (Paris: Le Sycomore, 1982)

——— *La Photographie en France: Textes et Controverses: Une Anthologie 1816–1871* (Paris: Macula, 1989).

Scharf, Aaron, *Art and Photography* (London: Allen Lane The Penguin Press, 1968).

# 9

## Manet's textual frames

### Robert Lethbridge

On a cartouche attached to the frame of Manet's *Lola de Valence*, Baudelaire's quatrain of the same title provides us with a moment in the relationship between literature and the visual arts which is, above all, symptomatic. It is usually considered as merely the poet's most enduring tribute to the painter. But it is of a different kind from the formal dedication to Manet of the prose poem 'La Corde'. For his precise instructions for the engraving of the verse within the etching after *Lola de Valence* also speak of the temptation to leave a mark, in the most literal sense, on the original painting: 'Il serait peut-être bien d'écrire aussi ces vers au bas du portrait soit au pinceau, dans la pâte, soit sur le cadre en lettres noires'.[1] It is perhaps not surprising that Manet should resist the first of these suggestions. To position Baudelaire's text outside the image was consistent with the convention of supplementing the title of a painting with an apposite quotation in the Salon *livret*. It was a practice not without risks, as Manet would find to his cost in the case of the stanza from Zacharie Astruc's 'Olympia' displayed in the catalogue for the Salon of 1865.[2]

A critical response deprived of the interpretative certainties of a classical or biblical reference seized on such textual commentaries as statements of intention. Authorial notoriety facilitated condemnation, even to the extent of relegating the painting itself to secondary importance. As Zola would write, in his 1867 study of Manet, 'quant à *Lola de Valence*, elle est célèbre par le quatrain de Charles Baudelaire, qui fut sifflé et maltraité autant que le tableau lui-même.[3] The fact that he could find very little to say about the latter other than through this poetic grid, cited in full once again, is not a strategy (or limitation) exclusive to the novelist as art critic. But it did confirm Manet's discernible anxieties about the appropriation of the visual by the verbal. Convention alone, in other words, is insufficient to explain why Manet felt able to alter the margin of an etching, but not to rework the pigment at the bottom of

*Lola de Valence* in order to accommodate Baudelaire's quatrain – which would have displaced his own signature. Beyond the exemplary physicality of the inscribed frame of this 1862 painting, it is with these sorts of spatial tensions that the present chapter will be concerned. For to explore the necessity of juxtaposing texts and images, as a means of understanding some of Manet's major works, is inseparable from the related contemporary question of artistic fields subject to what has been called, significantly, a process of 'mutual contamination'.[4] In this light, 'textual frames' are not just the completing context of literary tropes and allusions;[5] they are also a sectioning-off, it can be argued, given expression within a pictorial reassertion of the limits of the canvas.

That Zola should have reprinted the inscription is somewhat incongruous given the thrust of an essay at pains to discount the perceived link between the painter and the poet: 'Et je profite de l'occasion pour protester contre la parenté qu'on a voulu établir entre les tableaux d'Edouard Manet et les vers de Charles Baudelaire.'[6] It serves to remind us, however, of another 'textual frame' (as it were) elaborated around Manet, in the shape of an interlinked series of discourses, no less operative for being repeated, revised or denounced. In this respect too, of course, the particular focus on Manet is illustrative. Unable to predicate fully its meaning and effects, painting relies on critics to complete the communicative exchange with the spectator in those instances when the latter cannot find his own language to articulate an intuitive response. And it is hardly by chance that the mid-century sees these verbal intermediaries assuming an increasingly disproportionate role in the representation of the painter's work. The most basic condition of this mediation, as self-evident as it is easily forgotten, still pertained: prior to the availability of colour reproductions, the visual could only be translated, or traduced, in written invitations to visualize. From the point of view of the painter, the so-called 'democratization' of culture merely exacerbated the hierarchy of inferiority and dependence. Whether generated by modifications to institutional structures, by the instability of horizons of expectation, or by the widened remit of a newly diversified press,[7] the undeniable consequence, around and about the visual arts, was a proliferation of texts. Distrust, at its most extreme, could label such writing as parasitic. At the very least, 'la fraternité des arts' was a nostalgic invocation. 'La plume et le pinceau', as a recent study of Redon has demonstrated, were now more or less oppositional terms.[8] Even as literate a painter as Degas (to take yet another example beyond Manet) voiced this rivalry in his angry declaration that 'en un trait nous [peintres] en disons plus long qu'un littérateur en un volume', and in his alleged remark that Zola had written *L'Œuvre* 'pour prouver la grande supériorité de l'homme de lettres sur l'artiste'.[9]

The above generalizations are designed to put Manet in perspective. Another, which hardly needs underlining in a book such as this, is that French artists, throughout the nineteenth century, find in writers spokesmen and exegetes. One thinks of Delacroix and Baudelaire, or Courbet and Champfleury. Manet nevertheless remains a privileged case by virtue of the sheer number of such commentators. This is partly a function of a fortuitous centrality. His active career as painter, between the early 1850s and his death in 1883, exactly spans the major cultural shifts of the period – themselves reflected in his own changing styles. And he is in personal and creative contact during that time with virtually all the representatives of different, and often apparently incompatible, aesthetics. What vitiates any ideal of reciprocity is the barely disguised way in which these writers test their position against the painter's achievement; they use Manet to differentiate or assimilate their own imaginative and critical practice; they recruit or reject Manet; they seldom interpret his work other than in the service of their own reflections. Intersections subsequently aligned into a critical intertextuality could start with Gautier, Mallarmé or, in a later synthesis, Valéry. The advantage of developing those of Manet, Baudelaire and Zola, is that all the various 'textual frames' referred to so far can be superimposed to singularly illuminating effect.

This is not the place to challenge one of the great commonplaces of the history of art, namely that this or that painting by Manet is 'Baudelairean'. As Nils Sandblad wrote, a long time ago, 'the relationship between Baudelaire and Manet has been the subject of countless analyses'.[10] The directions of the latter continue to be determined by the relative weighting given to the compositional and symbolic features of Manet's pictures. At one end of this spectrum, his entire œuvre is seen to be informed by the influence of Baudelaire.[11] Even when scholarly cross-reference to *Les Fleurs du mal* is held in check, Manet's scenes of contemporary life can be related to Baudelaire's critical writing on the visual arts. At the other extreme, the formalist emphasis inherited from Zola has adopted an equally sceptical stance in respect of that 'parenté' his 1867 study denied. The vast majority of studies on Manet since that time have been unable to subscribe to Zola's polemical declaration that his paintings are 'without meaning'. It remains instructive to ask whether what Valéry was surely right to call 'quelque profonde correspondance'[12] between Baudelaire and Manet is not just enriching but integral to our interpretation of the latter.

Nineteenth-century juxtapositions certainly have to be treated with caution. When Charles Monselet, in the context of the Salon des Refusés, refers to Manet as 'un élève de Goya et de Ch. Baudelaire',[13] the associative move is as disingenuous as the crude caricature of poet and painter in *Le Charivari* of 15 June 1864. The same pejorative logic had

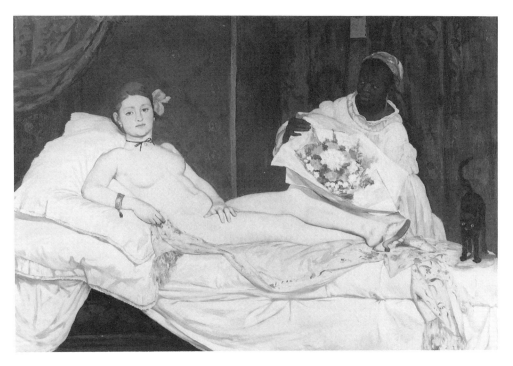

13.   Edouard Manet, *Olympia*, 1863 (Musée d'Orsay, Paris)

14.   Edouard Manet, *La Musique aux Tuileries*, 1862 (National Gallery, London)

resulted in *Le Buveur d'absinthe* being rejected by the Salon of 1859, supposedly at the instigation of Couture who believed it had been inspired by the section of *Les Fleurs du mal* entitled 'Le Vin'.[14] To 'champion' Manet, by contrast, was to sever him from such an invidious comparison; and this, at least in part, is the subtext of Zola's remarks: acknowledging a friendship, but not common themes, and silencing the notorious connotations of Baudelaire's 'bijou rose et noir' by transposing the formula to the tonal structure of *Lola de Valence*. Far more complex, as T.J. Clark has shown,[15] are the implications of Alfred Sensier's review of *Olympia* (fig. 13) in 1865. Here the notion of a 'peinture de l'école de Baudelaire exécutée largement par un élève de Goya' is resonant rather than classificatory; it is supported by lines from 'Le Chat'; and it is amplified by the quatrain from 'Les Phares' not only compounding Baudelaire and Goya, but also itself gesturing to a plate in *Los Caprichos* which bears a striking resemblance to *Olympia*'s admixture of realism and allegory.

It could be argued that to single out such insights is not without its own tendentiousness. But it does suggestively discriminate between, on the one hand, critical positioning and, on the other, textual framing. For it is now almost too easy to invert the reception of Manet in the 1860s by invoking Baudelaire in the interests of the painter's modernist credentials. This process is abetted by the recuperation of 'sources'. Specific parallels have been drawn between the colour and mood of *Le Buveur d'absinthe* and those singled out in *Le Salon de 1846*, and between the physiognomy of *La Chanteuse des rues* (1862) and the one described in Baudelaire's 'Les Promesses d'un visage'. Theodore Reff also cites other instances 'of Manet turning directly to Baudelaire's poetry for inspiration', notably in an unpublished drawing based on the 'Femmes damnées'.[16] The better-known example of *La Musique aux Tuileries* (1862, fig. 14) does nothing to lessen the potentially misleading nature of all such evidence. Baudelaire's anecdotal presence within this painting is hardly conclusive. At first sight, it might seem to confirm the story that he proposed the subject to Manet during their visits to the Tuileries gardens and, more interestingly, to point to affinities with 'Les Veuves'. It has recently been pointed out, however, that while the prose poem may be contemporary with the painting, they have very little in common; both are set in a park; but entirely absent from Manet's image are not only figures of bereavement but also the 'estrangement and dispossession' stressed in Baudelaire's text.[17] As instructive in their own right as such comparisons may be, they leave unattended the problem of a necessary complementarity.

The case of *Olympia* subjects this problem to a magnification at once less ambiguous and equally open to overdetermination. Even art historians most wary of speculative hypotheses agree that 'Manet *must have* thought of Baudelaire'.[18] For the painting's iconography provides irresistible compensation for the fact of the latter's departure for Brussels a year before *Olympia*'s appearance at the Salon of 1865. Little does it matter that, from there, the poet's famous question ('est-ce un chat, décidément?') could indicate his own ignorance of details of its execution between March and May 1863. Indeed, so permeated with textual allusions is *Olympia* now seen to be that the question itself is endowed with the possibility 'that he raised his eyebrows at the thought of such an overtly Baudelairean signature'.[19] Mallarmé, in 1876, was content to remark that the cat was 'apparently suggested by one of the prose poems of the author of the *Fleurs du mal*'.[20] By an unrelenting process of accretion, virtually no aspect of the painting has not been subsequently aligned to Baudelaire's themes and preoccupations. The most authoritative survey of the relevant scholarship unhesitatingly concludes that the courtesan's maidservant is 'a pictorial rendering' of 'A une Malabaraise' and that Olympia herself 'seems literally to illustrate' a number of other poems.[21] Those regularly cited include 'Une Martyre', 'Danse Macabre', 'Hymne à la beauté', 'Le Serpent qui danse' and, preeminently, 'Les Bijoux'. To an impressive list, Reff adds texts from *Les Fleurs du mal* devoted to the exoticism of Jeanne Duval as well as 'La Belle Dorothée' (*Petits Poèmes en prose*), 'which is exactly contemporary with *Olympia*'. His sustained demonstration that 'in addition to the nude figure, each of the other motifs in the picture – the Negress, the black cat, the bouquet of flowers – has its equivalent in Baudelaire's poetry' is persuasive; and that 'each of these motifs adds another dimension to the meaning of the whole' is not in doubt.[22] This is not incompatible, however, with Beatrice Farwell's denial 'of any painting by Manet *depending* on any particular poem of Baudelaire'.[23]

For equivalence and superimposition are by no means synonymous. The black cat at the courtesan's feet, for example, needed no recognition as an intimately Baudelairean symbol to counter Zola's insistence on its episodic realism and its function within *Olympia*'s pictorial structure. The critics of 1865 who labelled the painting 'la Vénus au chat' or, even more derisorily, 'Le Chat noir' identified the feline as sexual surrogate of the female without recourse to *Les Fleurs du mal*.[24] As Reff has shown, Manet's substitution for Titian's lapdog itself summarized its meaning perfectly: the little white animal curled up contentedly on the bed of the 'Venus of Urbino' symbolized marital fidelity; the black alley-cat stood for promiscuity. Contemporary caricaturists all sensed the significance of the exaggerated size and rigidity of the tail, in depicting the cat as a diabolical, sexually aggressive creature.[25] It has also been argued that those who saw in the animal a darker, more malevolent meaning, inseparable from the nineteenth-century symbol of the Sphinx, may well have thereby made explicit Manet's own intentions. Nor is this the only aspect of *Olympia* explicable other than in specifically Baudelairean terms. Properly informing 'frames of reference' are those of popular imagery and pictorial tradition, whether in the parodic 'langage des fleurs' of Achille Devéria or the black slave of Delacroix's *Femmes d'Alger*.

To treat with extreme caution the notion that certain works by Manet 'illustrate' some of Baudelaire's texts (with the implication that the latter afford interpretative purchase on the paintings themselves) is not to devalue the creative interchange between artist and poet. It is to locate its pragmatic consequences less in visual quotation than in the Baudelairean aesthetic to which Manet responds. His letter to Degas (in 1869) asking for the return of *L'Art romantique* and *Curiosités esthétiques* is a rare instance of firm information about his personal library and reading habits.[26] But it is inconceivable that 'Le Peintre de la vie moderne' did not present him with the most direct of challenges. That Baudelaire's essay of 1859–60 singled out Constantin Guys was a fair reflection of criteria to which, at that time, Manet's work did not really conform. His subsequent change of direction, away from his so-called 'Spanish phase' and towards the potential beauty of the urban and the contemporarily prosaic, is testimony to the catalysing effect of his contact with Baudelaire's thinking. At the very least, there is a virtually synchronized redefinition of artistic ideals; but it is also in the light of Baudelaire's writing that some of Manet's paintings become less opaque.

Thus the *thematic* relation of *Le Buveur d'absinthe* to poems like 'Le Vin' or 'Le Vin des chiffoniers' is ultimately less revealing than the Baudelairean incongruities it asserts. It is an image of the socially down-and-out, transgressing the conventions of morally uplifting subjects; yet this is invested with distinction, through the silhouette of the dandy, top-hatted and self-contained, and of the urban *flâneur* who is both spectator and spectacle. In this sense, the painting exemplifies, literally and figuratively, the *intoxication* so central to Baudelaire's reflections on the poetic.

Similarly, *La Musique aux Tuileries* gains from being viewed in a wider perspective than as a possible transposition of 'Les Veuves'. For it engages with Baudelaire's *ideas* in altogether more complex ways. The most obvious reference to 'Le Peintre de la vie moderne' is its representation of the black frock-coats and top hats of contemporary Paris, the very markers of modernity. As well as this exploitation of prosaic detail as the raw material of an artistic composition, the painting is notable for its lack of focus in terms of drama and its eschewing of the didacticism to which Baudelaire objected in Courbet. Even its missing subject (the 'musique' performed by a band out of sight and out of picture) corresponds to Baudelaire's emphasis on an 'art pur'. In his terms again, it captures instead the spirit and the essence of modern life: not in its verisimilitude but through its imaginative structuring, conveying that confusion of the times within its formal shapes, perfectly matched to the expression of contradictory attitudes and poses. We can legitimately imagine the assembled literary figures conversing seriously in the shaded space behind the bustle, set against the frivolity of both infantile and adult games. The painting foregrounds boredom and concern, self-consciousness (the group on the left almost posing for their picture to be taken) and spontaneous abandon (the parasol), business and leisure, those rigid and yet attentive trees bending like the equally dark and apparently attentive gentlemen hovering over ladies in their Sunday best. To move from foreground to background, however, is also to encounter a kind of Baudelairean irony, as those differentiated human figures gradually lose their outline and distinctiveness, relegated as they are to the status of a sea of hats. What we have in *La Musique aux Tuileries* is Manet's own claim to be considered 'le peintre de la vie moderne'.[27] Without that implied critical frame it is difficult to conceive how one might begin to approach its calculated tensions. Nor is it too fanciful to suggest that the painting situates itself *in relation to* the discursive. Baudelaire and Gautier in conversation at the margin are the voices of antithetical judgements on Manet's achievement.

To invoke theoretical texts rather than poems does not justify, of course, the provision of Baudelairean solutions to each and every one of Manet's enigmas.[28] A case in point is Bradford Collins's study, unequivocally entitled 'Manet's *Luncheon in the Studio*: an Hommage to Baudelaire'.[29] It does not seem self-evident that all the painter's images of cats signal the acknowledgement of a debt.[30] And to detect in *La Maîtresse de Baudelaire* (1862) a reference to the poet's admiration for Delacroix (as *coloriste*) may be to take this process one step too far.[31] As far as homage is concerned, we need go no further than the numerous etchings of Baudelaire which Manet prepared between 1862 and 1869, his collaboration with Asselineau on a memorial volume, and the marvellously suggestive vignette design originally intended for one of the portraits to be included in that posthumous project.[32]

Interpolated caveats notwithstanding, the enhancement which Baudelairean juxtapositions propose can be better measured by comparing Manet's analogous contacts with Zola's writing. Differences of response can be accounted for by those of temperament and vision, aesthetic preferences and personal affinities. What is equally certain is that, at this particular historical moment, the novelist per se occupies a more competitive position vis-à-vis the visual arts than does the poet. The latter is in relative decline and hardly represents a threat to the painter's autonomy.[33] A writer like Zola, by contrast, brings into stark relief limited pictorial access to a mass public and economic power. There is no reason to doubt the sincerity of Zola's championing of Manet in this

15.  Edouard Manet, *Portrait d'Emile Zola*, 1868 (Musée d'Orsay, Paris)

period 1866–8; but neither would it be unfair to suggest that his polemical articles were designed to further his own reputation and proclaim his own aesthetic principles as much a those of the artist. Self-advertisement, in other words, was not the least compelling of his motives in adopting Manet's cause. And it is to these texts, rather than to Zola's imaginative writing, that Manet can be seen to respond most assertively. In this respect only, there are superficial similarities with his Baudelarean inscriptions.

Indeed, it would be possible to repeat our earlier argument to the effect that Manet's literary borrowings, in this case from Zola's novels, do not give to the paintings concerned a properly allusive dimension. The figure in *La Prune* (1877–8), for example, may seem to us to bear an uncanny resemblance to Gervaise Macquart in *L'Assommoir*, serialized between April 1876 and January 1877. This is not only unhelpful. It also serves to underline the fallacious nature of parallels established on the basis of common subjects; for the café scene is a veritable genre in which Manet's contributions have to be placed alongside those of Degas, Renoir, Gervex and Boldini. Potentially more revealing, but ultimately just as problematic, is the case of *Nana*, painted during the winter of 1876–7. While this obviously predates Zola's novel of the same name (planned in 1878 and the first instalment of which appeared in October 1879), there has been much scholarly juggling of chronology to justify the possibility that it was in fact inspired by episodes in *L'Assommoir* in which Gervaise's daughter begins her career as a Parisian 'cocotte'.[34] The consensus is that the painting owes only its title to Zola (shortly before its unsuccessful presentation to the Salon jury of 1877); and that it is considerably more likely that it was he who was inspired by Manet's image, both in the preparation of the later novel and its theatrical adaptation in 1881.[35]

Nowhere, however, is the self-sufficiency of Manet's art more fully articulated than in the portrait of Zola (fig. 15) exhibited at the Salon of 1868.[36] And it does so from within a *confrontation* with texts which frame this particular painting and, more generally, which seek to elucidate the significance of the painter's œuvre. The specific allusion, of course, is to Zola's *Edouard Manet, étude biographique et critique*.[37] The recognizable sky-blue cover of the pamphlet, at the right-hand margin, is both visually prominent and a focal point in the most literal sense. But the portrait represents the culmination of a series of exchanges between writer and painter initiated by Zola's pioneering defence of Manet in an article of 7 May 1866, included in his review of the Salon of that year. Only by reconstructing that dialogue is it possible to determine whether Manet was simply repaying a debt when he agreed to Zola's own suggestion to paint his portrait. For if the painting has been cited as evidence of Manet's 'penchant for calling attention to himself in concealed but insistent ways',[38] it constitutes a precise response to the less discreet emphasis in Zola's earlier studies of the artist.

In these, as Manet could hardly fail to note, Zola took the opportunity to write about himself, both directly and by implication. He underlined his own audacity and courage as a critic in daring to attack the arbiters of public taste, and referred to the hostility he would incur as a result of his admiration for Manet's work: 'on rira peut-être du panégyriste comme on a ri du peintre. Un jour, nous serons vengés tous deux.' In discussing Manet's critics, who had attacked the artist for his 'brutalités voulues' and his 'violences systématiques', Zola was in effect also answering those who had criticized his first novel, *La Confession de Claude* (1865), for 'la crudité de tons' and its 'hideux réalisme'.[39] To link his name with Manet's was, at one level, merely to display the opportunism characteristic of his exploitation of polemical journalism. In presenting Manet, however, not as the extraordinarily sensitive artist that he was, bitterly resenting his notoriety, but rather as a 'lutteur convaincu' engaged in a struggle to 'apprivoiser la foule', Zola's identification with the painter gives way to what is almost a self-portrait. To trace Manet's development from his reliance on tradition to the free expression of 'cette langue originale qu'il venait de découvrir au fond de lui' was to outline his own career as a writer. As Zola wrote, 'je fais d'une question individuelle une question qui intéresse tous les véritables artistes', in calling for 'une saine critique, non pour Edouard Manet seulement, mais encore pour tous les tempéraments particuliers qui se présenteront'. What is more, Zola offered his 1867 study of Manet as an example of his own critical method: 'Mon étude sur Édourd Manet est une simple application de ma façon de voir en matière artistique, et . . . je livre à l'appréciation de tous un essai où l'on jugera des mérites et des défauts de la méthode que j'emploie.' This is inevitably marked by the pseudo-medical jargon of two important texts contemporary with it, namely 'Un Roman d'analyse' (in *Le Figaro* of 16 December 1866) and his 'Deux définitions du roman' (prepared the same month) in praise of 'le roman analytique'. Zola's view of Manet as 'un peintre analyste', in January 1867, prefigures the notion of 'la peinture naturaliste' in his *Salon* articles of 1868. His own role as novelist and critic, and Manet's talent as an artist, would all be increasingly defined according to the criteria of a developing, if still inconsistent, naturalist aesthetic.

Zola's efforts to link his name with Manet in the public mind had continued throughout 1867. And it may be significant that Manet hesitated before finally approving Zola's suggestion to republish his January study in brochure form to coincide with the opening, on 24 May, of his private exhibition in the Place de l'Alma. At the very least, it is clear that the painter was uneasy about such blatant exercises in publicity. Another was Zola's attempt to persuade his publisher to bring out an illustrated edition of his *Contes à Ninon*. In a letter to Albert Lacroix of 8 May 1867,[40] he disclosed that Manet had agreed 'par reconnaissance, par sympathie' to provide the drawings for such a project; success was assured, Zola promised, owing to Manet's 'bruyante réputation' which could only be helped by the 'publicité énorme' expected to surround his exhibition. 'Nous désirons avant tout faire une œuvre *purement artistique*', he stressed; but, as he went on: 'Si vous m'accordez quelque expérience en matière de réclame, croyez à mes assurances; mon nom et celui de Manet sur une même couverture doivent tirer l'œil des passants et les forcer à s'arrêter'; and Zola concluded, in what is a revealing admission: 'jamais je n'ai si habilement travaillé à ma réputation qu'en cherchant à mettre le nom de Manet sur une de mes œuvres'.

It may indeed have been because that project finally came to nothing that Manet proceeded to paint Zola's portrait between November 1867 and February 1868. It could be argued that the painting had the same tactical function as Zola's earlier physical portrait of Manet, designed to counter the popular misconception of the artist as a 'rapin débraillé', 'une sorte de bohème, de galopin, de croquemitaine ridicule'. It was now Manet's turn, in other words, to present Zola to the public. And gratitude for the writer's support, it is invariably claimed, is not just circumstantial. The uncomplicated view of the painting is that in its general conception and internal reference to Zola's 1867 study of Manet, the portrait testifies not only to their friendship but also, like Fantin-Latour's grouping of contemporary artists, to a common commitment to a new aesthetic programme. Taken to euphoric lengths, 'on ne saurait mieux signifier la consubstantialité du scriptural et pictural'.[41] A more equivocal reading of the painting might start with Manet's own signature,[42] indexed by the writer's exuberant quill-pen which threatens to obscure this symbolic marker of his achievement.[43]

This is certainly an allusive painting. Such is its sophistication that the background reproduction of *Olympia* has been seen as a reference to Zola's preoccupation with the Fatal Woman in his fiction.[44] Here again, however, the essential framing text is a critical one. *Olympia*, Zola had insisted, was Manet's outstanding work, 'son chef-d'œuvre . . . la chair et la sang du peintre . . . l'expression complète de son tempérament'. In all his writing on Manet, no other painting is subjected to such extensive analysis. It was thus as appropriate for Manet to reproduce *Olympia* in a portrait of Zola painted in February 1868 as it had been for him to provide an etching of it for the latter's pamphlet nine months earlier. As far as this element of the portrait is concerned, Reff also suggests that in subtly shifting the courtesan's gaze towards the writer at his desk, Manet was able to express, 'with a visual wit altogether characteristic of him', both his own appreciation and Olympia's acknowledgement of Zola's efforts to defend her reputation.[45] Recognition of that significance remains profoundly double-edged. For it alerts the spectator to the multiple inscriptions which make of the portrait as a whole the most *eloquent* refutation of Zola's unwillingness to grant Manet a degree of intentionality.[46] It refers us back to the writer's attempt to deflect criticism from the painter's subject matter to the pictorial qualities of his work; and to his refusal to allow Manet to be identified with the imaginative expression of an outdated Romanticism. And, in the process, the painting takes issue with the implication that only writing can articulate meaning. What the portrait of Zola is not is a structure of colours. We know that Manet experienced such difficulties with language that he had to enlist Zola's help to prepare a text.[47] Not the least of the ironies of this particular painting is that Zola's own texts are transformed into a fan-like arrangement as stylized as the cropped images above them.

Even the highlighting of that cropping technique is declarative. It speaks of a complexity in his art which Zola had not really understood, registered in the collage of the upper right-hand corner of the portrait. *Olympia* is offset from, but inextricably related to, that composite design. The figure in the Kuniaki print pays the writer an equally qualified compliment. Broad shoulders enveloped in black are turned towards Zola in his frock-coat, and mirrored hands reinforce the allusion to the 'lutteur' the critic had characterized Manet himself as being. It is less clear whether the label returned is also one rejected as a definition of his own stance. But the print simultaneously completes Zola's commentary. Like the Japanese screen on the left, itself cropped, it points to a handling of perspective much admired by the painter but left unmentioned by Zola who fails even to spot the dividing screen in *Olympia*. The pictorial allusion to Velasquez's *Drinkers*, behind the copy of Manet's picture but not entirely out of sight, is another such reference to lacunae in Zola's texts. Most obviously it recalls Manet's admission that *Le Buveur d'absinthe* was a Parisian character painted with the technical simplicity he had discovered in Velasquez. Zola, by contrast, could see only 'une vague impression de Thomas Couture' in its 'intention mélodramatique'; and, more generally, his dismissive 'le peintre se cherchait encore' is out of sympathy with those creative contacts with tradition which Manet himself reasserts.

This failure, on Zola's part, to give to the art of the past its due weight is suggested by the open book he holds but does not read, and the spatial forms of which correspond to the rectangles above. It has been identified as a volume of Charles Blanc's *Histoire des peintres*. That Zola is not looking at it, as indeed his glance is turned away from every other pictorial influence on display, seems like further evidence of Manet's 'visual wit'. For this is a book which Zola never mentions in any context, let alone in the course of his interpretation of Manet. We do know, however, that it was one of the works most constantly consulted by the painter in his studio;[48] and that it was vital to his habits of composition precisely because it contained black-and-white illustrations of the Old Masters. Signalling Zola's absent reference, this reference-*book* organizes around itself a discourse of quotations, allusions and verbal signs open to our reading. While Zola looks away in non-recognition, the viewer can hardly ignore the structural centrality of this emblematic juxtaposition of text and image.

This counterpoint to Zola's texts about Manet is ambiguous enough to problematize the portrait's status as an icon of artistic reciprocity. While it may gesture towards solidarity and the power of massive inkpot and flamboyant pen, much in the painting moves in a less celebratory direction. Far from confirming his appreciation and assimilation of the visual arts, the portrait shows Zola in a world of images with which he seems to have no relation. The fact that he is surrounded by those reflecting Manet's activities and tastes, rather than his own, adds to that sense of his being awkwardly misplaced. Dangling eye-glasses suggest the perceptual blank of Zola's gaze, oblivious not only of images in hand and around him, but also of the portrait-painter. Nor is the characteristic Manet *éventail* into which the writer's books are recast the only aspect of the composition subordinate to the geometric imperatives of the whole. Even its human subject seems reduced to a pictorial function. The painting anticipates, in some ways, the mirroring surfaces of Manet's later work. For the image of the writer is positioned in a space of representation (pictures of pictures, images of words about pictures, the illusion of an illustration of the original) always at one remove from the reality it seeks to duplicate. And within it, Zola is framed, hemmed in by the painting's interlocking frames.

Underlying Manet's resistance to textual appropriation, we can thus discern a statement about his own art. It has often been suggested that he unconsciously transferred to Zola a large measure of his own physical distinction and sartorial elegance.[49] What the portrait might also be said to do is to invert Zola's ambition to 'mettre le nom de Manet sur une de mes œuvres'.[50] Here, in other words, we have the image of the writer and the name of the painter side by side. The latter's signature is framed by texts, and yet both Zola and his writing about the artist are firmly within Manet's pictorial frame. Those paradoxes inform the contemporary debate about the relative autonomy of literature and painting. And where Manet ultimately stands can be gauged by following the diagonals to an originality writ large, in the lettering dwarfing Zola's authorship, affirming his distance from what Baudelaire called 'des peintres littérateurs'.[51]

## Suggested reading

Clark, T.J., *The Painting of Modern Life: Paris in the Art of Manet and his Followers* (Princetown, NJ: Princeton University Press, 1984).

Finke, Ulrich, (ed.), *French Nineteenth-Century Painting and Literature* (Manchester: Manchester University Press, 1972).

Hyslop, Lois Boe, *Baudelaire: Man of his Time* (New Haven and London: Yale University Press, 1980).

Reff, Theodore, 'Manet's Portrait of Zola', *Burlington Magazine*, 117 (1975), pp.35–44

Sandblad, Nils, *Manet: Three Studies in Artistic Conception* (Lund: Gleerup, 1954).

Zola, Emile, *Ecrits sur l'art*, ed. Jean-Pierre Leduc-Adine (Paris: Gallimard, 1991).

# PART III

# MODELS OF REPRESENTATION
## FROM ROMANTICISM TO NATURALISM

# 10

## Newspaper and myth: migrations of the Romantic image

### Peter Collier

In one striking poem in *Les Fleurs du mal*, entitled 'Don Juan aux enfers', where Molière's Don Juan sails into Dante's Hell in a scene recalling a Delacroix painting, rather as if he has strayed on to the wrong film set, Baudelaire sets us the puzzle of disentangling the intertextual and interfigural migrations of the Romantic image. The figure and fate of Don Juan form an eternally powerful myth. The versions by Molière and Mozart are doubtless best known, but in the Romantic period Byron, Delacroix and Baudelaire contributed their interpretations, and as we trace their differing exploitations of the themes of shipwreck and cannibalism, sexual desire and political protest, and their rebellious morality, we discover the existence of an elaborate interplay between each other's images and texts.

Painted images have been inspired by written sources for a very long time. In the Middle Ages and the Renaissance, art provided visual equivalents for narratives from the Bible or from Ovid. In the secular age of the French Revolution and Empire, however, the most prestigious art drew on models taken from classical history – Livy's story of the three Horatii, which had already been dramatized in the seventeenth century by Corneille in *Horace*, was painted by David – no doubt taking the Roman as an example for the French Republic. If, however, at the end of the eighteenth and the start of the nineteenth century, history starts to displace scripture and mythology as the privileged discourse originating official painting, that history may as well be contemporary narrative as classical or neoclassical writing. The triumph of contemporary history, moreover, could be seen in paintings by Gros or Vernet of Napoleon's battles, based on eye-witness accounts. In fact the focus on history and current affairs was to become one of the hallmarks of the Romantic movement, although the Romantics also tended to use contemporary literature as inspiration. Delacroix takes many major subjects from Byron's writing (such as La Mort de Sardanapale), as

161

16.  Théodore Géricault, Le Radeau de la Méduse, 1819 (Musée du Louvre, Paris)

17.  Eugène Delacroix, La Barque de Dante, 1822 (Musée du Louvre, Paris)

Byron himself draws on subject matter from current affairs (for example, Greece). Delacroix's *La Liberté guidant le peuple* (1830) mingles realistic observation with the symbolic figure of Marianne. Hugo and Musset tried to offer major critiques of Restoration politics in plays such as *Hernani* (1830) and *Lorenzaccio* (1834), set in medieval Spain and Renaissance Florence respectively, although the censor was not fooled. The different strands are united in Delacroix's *La Grèce sur les ruines de Missolonghi* (1826).

Two of the most notorious and public images of the Romantic movement were directly inspired by the written word – one by newspaper reports and a subsequent pamphlet, the other by a medieval poem. Géricault's monumentally scandalous canvas, *Le Radeau de la Méduse* (fig. 16), exhibited at the Salon of August 1819, was inspired by eyewitness accounts, published in 1817, by A. Corréard and H. Savigny, survivors of the shipwreck of the *Medusa* in July 1816, which became a political cause célèbre because of suspicions that the incompetent captain, Hugues Duroy de Chaumareys, had been given command of a ship on account of his Royalist sympathies rather than any professional qualification.[1] Delacroix's *La Barque de Dante* (fig. 17), on the other hand, which was acclaimed by critics and public alike at the Salon of 1822, was a direct representation of a literary text, Canto VIII of Dante's *Inferno*. Dante and Virgil sail across the Styx, assailed by the frenzied figures of the drowning and damned.[2]

Neither of these two paintings, however, was merely an illustration of a written narrative. Géricault has not chosen the most obviously dramatic moment, that of the shipwreck itself, nor even the most scandalous element of the adventure, the survivors' foray into cannibalism, but rather the moment of reversal of fortune, the moment of pathos when hope turned to despair, as the survivors spied a distant ship, which tragically proceeded to ignore them. A process of cumulative suspense, easy enough to convey in consecutive linguistic narrative, has to be transposed into a simultaneous visual conflict, by pitting a vast pyramid of bodies against a tiny ship, for instance. Different stages of the drama – the mutiny of the sailors, the cannibalism, the false hope, and the rescue – are collapsed into one composite image.

Certainly Romanticism was a kind of Realism before the invention of the term. Géricault had conversations with Corréard and Savigny themselves, after reading their pamphlet; the carpenter of the *Medusa* made him a scale model raft, and when he went to select his canvas in February 1818 he bought a mammoth piece 7 metres by 5, whose length was the exact width of the real raft (7 metres by 20), making it a 1:4 reduced model. He stocked his studio with pieces of decomposing bodies lifted from the local morgue, and, alongside his professional models, he persuaded Corréard and Savigny themselves to pose, camping hyper-real versions of their own characters.[3] There is political comment implicit in the painting, too, through the placing of a black man at the apex of the picture, reminding the viewer that the mission of the *Medusa* was to carry soldiers out to colonize Senegal, and that the French nation was involved in enslavement, despite the theoretical abolition of the slave trade under the French Revolution.

Delacroix too has selected a potentially dramatic moment (the discovery of Hell), but he has focused the drama into an emblematic and carefully poised image, in which the two main figures, Dante and Virgil, stand in the centre of the scene, balanced by the burning city of Dis in the top of the canvas and the writhing, naked sinners drowning in the bottom. Whereas in Dante the conflict between good and evil is depicted in terms of a mounting series of crises which the reader perceives consecutively rather than simultaneously, Delacroix has to achieve a simultaneous visual contrast.

In neither case, therefore, does the painting take as the centre of its pictorial focus an image of what was the moment of climax in the textual narrative: both painters have had to work to recreate a structured and externalized visual equivalent of a cumulative and internal psychological and moral process. The eye has no memory: dramatic tension in painting has to be conveyed in terms of spatial pattern. The images which derive from these naratives are subject to a form of visual proliferation, of imaginative expansion, rather than generating a simple sequential development.

When Delacroix saw Géricault's painting, he felt inspired by this manifestation of the 'sublime'.[4] Géricault had created a composition of extraordinarily disturbing erotic display and morbid violence, with its turmoil of desperate, naked bodies. Later, in *La Barque de Dante*, Delacroix himself transformed Dante's Christian allegory into a painting where naked bodies and burning buildings create an atmosphere of intense, almost baroque hysteria. And yet, in the *Le Radeau de la Méduse* as well as *La Barque de Dante* there is still an obvious concern for academic technique (the composition of both paintings is carefully balanced, the nude figures flex their muscles as if posing for Michelangelo), but academicism is revitalized by a new Romantic energy: Géricault's and Delacroix's nudes are coloured in a strange blend of mannerist chiaroscuro and mingled ochre and leaden flesh tones, which in Géricault's case were the result of most unclassical studies of the rotting pieces of flesh strewn over the floor of his studio. The nudity of both paintings is far removed in its function from the traditional academic model of nudes drawn in life classes and given as set competition pieces (see Germaine Greer's chapter). The classical – or at least mannerist – composition of both pictures is overrun by the Romantic frenzy of the individual figures in the paintings.

What concerns me most, however, in my analysis of the migrations of the Romantic image is the way in which text and image are dialectically related. In 1819, the year of Géricault's triumph, there appeared one of the most shocking and yet witty works of European literature, Byron's *Don Juan*, or rather its first two cantos. In a minor incident in Molière's play, *Dom Juan*, the hero's boat capsizes (offstage) as he and a small group of servants escape from one of his disreputable adventures. This provides the excuse for a farcical interlude where the peasants who save them from drowning are mocked. Yet Byron's Don Juan has a formative experience when his ship goes down, and Baudelaire's Don Juan uses his boat to sail proudly through Hell.

A long section of Byron's Canto II concerns Don Juan's shipwreck.[5] The shipwrecked party, dying in their long boat, first elect to eat Don Juan's dog. Juan initially refuses to partake of his spaniel, for sentimental reasons (Byron himself was a great dog-lover). The passengers then draw lots to choose a victim, and 'the lot fell upon Juan's luckless tutor' (Byron's disrespect for the teaching profession perhaps being exacerbated by his stormy student career at Cambridge). Juan finds himself unable to accept any part of his tutor, largely because of invidious comparisons that his companions might make with his behaviour over the dog. Poetic justice is wrought on the cannibals, for they are swiftly reduced to writhing madness and agony. The survivors are tempted by the plump body of the master's mate, but the latter is saved when they learn that his flesh has been tainted by his intimate relations with some dubious ladies from Cadiz.

Byron's flippant sexual and political iconoclasm were even more outrageous than Géricault's realism. But his references are not only to the *Medusa* affair and Molière's *Dom Juan*. He tempers his outrageous disrespect for current affairs and human suffering by a reference to Dante. One of Dante's damned, Ugolino, spends perpetuity eating the head of his arch-enemy, Archbishop Ruggieri, who had imprisoned him and his sons with no food, forcing Ugolino to eat his sons. Hell for Dante was a place of revenge. Byron defends his cannibals thus:

> Remember Ugolino condescends
> To eat the head of his arch enemy
> The moment after he politely ends
> His tale. If foes be food in hell, at sea
> 'Tis surely fair to dine upon our friends
> When shipwreck's short allowance grows too scanty,
> Without being much more horrible than Dante.

However wrapped in irony, the allusion to Dante allows Byron to remind his squeamish reader that cannibalism is not merely a fashionably shocking anecdote culled from contemporary accounts of the wreck of the *Medusa*, but also a significant allegory, elaborated by the greatest poet and moralist of the Christian tradition (and H.F. Carey's superb blank verse translation of the *Divine Comedy* – from which I quote later in this chapter – also appeared in 1819).[6] The political and the moral are intertwined in Byron, as in Géricault. Byron defended himself from accusations of immortality and sensationalism by arguing that his information was all factual, whether from personal observation or historical documentation.[7] It seems that the *Medusa* affair was one of the accounts that he must have read and used, as well as the personal memoir written by his great-grandfather, mad Jack Byron, who, like Juan, had found himself shipwrecked and reduced to eating the previously discarded paws of a dog.[8]

Through these instantly famous images we may discover an exemplary intersection of several significant nineteenth-century forces: the power of the press and printing in a society of increasing literacy and rapid mechanical reproduction and distribution (particularly when muzzled by an archaic monarchical government); the fashion for medieval literature (often recreated by Walter Scott, but also, in the case of Dante, rediscovered in translation); and the new appeal of oil painting as a medium of mass communication, at a time when the annual Salon – deliberately resuscitated as part of the Restoration government's attempt to revive certain aspects of ancien régime culture – became no longer a simple focus for academic reward, but a locus of display for those imagists whom the State wished to attract by commission to propagate its official imagery, and a market-place for the new bourgeois commerce of pictorial exchange (see the chapters by Greer, Moriarty, Bourdieu for more information on this).

Delacroix's own painting is overtly more controlled, and even more moral, than Dante's savage and ambiguous verse. Phlegyas ferries Dante and Virgil across the Styx, surrounded by damned souls desperate to accompany them. The central figures, looming upright in the boat, are those of Dante and Virgil, and the frenzy that afflicts both Géricault's starving sailors and Byron's poisoned cannibals is relegated by Delacroix to the figures of the damned thrashing about in the water in the foreground. Delacroix has condensed into his picture the central drama of Virgil and Dante sailing erectly but uneasily through the sea of furious sinners. In the top left-hand corner of the canvas the city of Dis burns, fuelled by its blazing mosques. Phlegyas the boatman wrestles with his oar. In Dante's verse, one muddy swimmer, Filippo Argente, protests, only to be first cursed by Dante, then torn apart by the crowd, and finally driven to distraction to the point where he even tries to eat himself. Delacroix has concentrated the series of dramatic confrontations on a single, complex group of water-bound sinners. In the bottom right-hand corner we see two figures trying to eat each other's heads, and these characters are doubtless more reminiscent of Count Ugolino and Arch-bishop Ruggieri from Cantos XXXII and XXXIII than of Filippo Argente trying to eat himself. Delacroix has merged two potentially can-nibalistic scenes of Dante's into one motif. As in Géricault, the anecdotal development of the drama is collapsed into one basic binary opposition, showing in Delacroix's case a wider knowledge of the text beyond the immediate anecdote.

The fact that this painting was admired in Academic circles and acquired by the State suggests that the political origins of the cannibal-ism motif were no longer perceived. Two decades later, in 1840, after another revolution and another disappointing restoration of the mon-archy, Delacroix returned to the same theme, in *Naufrage de Don Juan*. In *La Barque de Dante* the polemical origins of the image had been mediated and transposed. Strangely, however, in the new painting the medieval text, too, has started to slip away. What seems to have hap-pened is that more important, fashionable and prestigious texts have displaced in the public imagination the earlier sources in Dante or Cor-réard and Savigny. The latter writers' pamphlet on the wreck of the *Medusa* is still in the background, as are Dante's Cantos VIII, XXXII and XXXIII. But earlier these were integrated into a composition where anecdote and text were subordinated to a clear visual contrast, pitting the dignified immortals against the frenzied and naked damned; whereas in *Naufrage de Don Juan*, exhibited in the 1841 Salon, Byron's *Don Juan* – perhaps a more readily identifiable narrative, now, than would be a militant pamphlet from a deposed regime, or a momentarily fashionable medieval poem – has moved into the foreground, supplanting the texts that helped generate it. At all events, we seem now to have a more literal illustration of Byron's text. It is the exact moment of the drawing of the lots. The boat's occupants are depicted in varying degrees of collapse, disinterest, agony and despair. As did Géricault, Delacroix has chosen a moment of psychological suspense, rather than a literal depiction of hor-ror. He shows a potential drama, where we read only the beginnings of a process of murder, madness and despair, which he merely suggests pic-torially. Surprisingly, painting seems to need to evoke, as much as depict.

In 1846 Baudelaire wrote a considerable pamphlet on the annual Salon, devoting some significant remarks to Delacroix and his use of colour, and recalling his *La Barque de Dante* of 1822.[9] This vein of in-spiration also fuelled a poem entitled 'L'impénitent' in 1846, but later, in *Les Fleurs du mal*, known as 'Don Juan aux enfers'. In this poem Baude-laire seems to use a Dantesque vision inspired by Delacroix, although the basic situation is obviously inspired by Molière's *Dom Juan* as well. Doubtless it is the fashion for Byron, eclipsing real history and medieval poetry, which gives us the strange focus on Don Juan. It has been argued, persuasively I think, that Baudelaire's title and immediate inspiration were a lithograph by Simon Guérin, entitled *Don Juan aux enfers*, synthesizing the two paintings by Delacroix, *Naufrage de Don Juan* and *La Barque de Dante*.[10] Nonetheless, the characters and basic situation of Baudelaire's poem are borrowed from Molière's *Dom Juan* rather than Byron's parody. Baudelaire has invented an extraordinary vision, where the characters from Molière's play sail through the Hell described by Dante and painted by Delacroix. The literary knowledge of the poet has overlaid the literary sources used by the painters – although the text seems to set up a very visual experience.

Baudelaire's Don Juan encounters naked women aping desire in the most caricatural way:

> Montrant leurs seins pendants et leurs robes ouvertes,
> Des femmes se tordaient sous le noir firmament,
> Et, comme un grand troupeau de victimes offertes,
> Derrière lui traînait un long mugissement.

There are notations here of damnation and torture – but they are attributed to the women in such a way that they themselves appear to be damned in their capacity as Don Juan's victims. Sganarelle asks for his wages, Don Luis accuses Don Juan, and Elvire awaits his smile, but all are disdained by Don Juan who remains unmoved. The reader, however, sees Don Luis tremble and Elvire shiver, apparently craving Don Juan's favour as she 'semblait lui réclamer un suprême sourire'.

There are certainly Dantesque moments in this poem, therefore – the erotically writhing female victims, and the ranks of wandering souls on the river bank ('. . . Don Luis avec un doigt tremblant / Montrait à tous les morts errants sur les rivages') – but they are deliberately ironized by the context, which recalls a farcical scene from Molière's often rather serious and amoral play. Molière's character took an accidental ducking between two seductions, whereas Baudelaire's hero sails determinedly down into Hell. Molière's avenging stone commander has become Baudelaire's and Delacroix's impassive Phlegyas. Don Luis figures as a kind of vaudeville Virgil, and it is the righteous and wronged who suffer in Baudelaire's Hell; his erotic and blasphemous sinner is as superbly unmoved in Hell as he was on earth; indeed Don Juan's unyielding dignity as he crosses to the underworld seems modelled on the stoic impassivity of Dante and Virgil, faced with the suffering of the damned, and the downright hostility of Dante and Virgil to the damned wretches surrounding them in *Inferno* VIII, as imaged in Delacroix's painting:

> Tout droit dans son armure, un grand homme de pierre
> Se tenait à la barre et coupait le flot noir;

> Mais le calme héros, courbé sur sa rapière,
> Regardait le sillage et ne daignait rien voir,

although the disdainful resistance of the damned may yet echo Dante more directly – one thinks of the figure of Farinata, 'disdainful' as he challenges Dante and Virgil in Canto X, 'as in high scorn he held / E'en Hell' – showing how important the knowledge of the original text is for the poet even when drafting a visual image of the moral drama.

But there is a danger, in tracing sources, of making texts appear to be too close a commentary on paintings, and images to be too knowingly an illustration of texts. Baudelaire, who was fascinated by both Dante and Delacroix, teaches us otherwise. As one of the century's leading writers on art, Baudelaire was concerned to formulate a theory of the ways in which the visual and the verbal might relate. (The chapters by Kelley, Scott, and Kearns show how active critics were in helping artists formulate their aims.) He commented on Delacroix's *La Barque de Dante* in his *Salon de 1846*, and a stanza of his programmatic poem, 'Les Phares' (1857), refers to Delacroix:

> Delacroix, lac de sang hanté des mauvais anges,
> Ombragé par un bois de sapins toujours vert,
> Où, sous un ciel chagrin, des fanfares étranges
> Passent, comme un soupir étouffé de Weber.

Baudelaire commented on his own poem in an addition to his critique of the Exposition Universelle of 1855, explaining the lines in these terms:

> *Lac de sang*: le rouge; – *hanté des mauvais anges*: surnaturalisme; – *un bois toujours vert*: le vert, complémentaire du rouge; – *un ciel chagrin*: les fonds tumultueux et orageux de ses tableaux; – *les fanfares et Weber*: idées de musique romantique que réveillent les harmonies de sa couleur.

Although Baudelaire does not explicitly link this stanza of 'Les Phares' with Delacroix's *La Barque de Dante* of 1822, he mentions the painting several times in his article as self-evidently famous and revolutionary.[11] And it is difficult not to see wider connotations looming behind Baudelaire's comments on his own poetic reaction to Delacroix. We are interested in the context and reasons for those particular reds, greens and clouds, inspiring his visions of blood, forest and heaven. And, remembering that Baudelaire had already enthusiastically repeated and endorsed Thiers's appreciation of *La Barque de Dante* in his *Salon de 1846*, it is not far-fetched to note a Dantean subtext to this stanza of *Les phares*.[12] Delacroix's painting itself is not sufficient motivation: Thiers's description of it, reproduced by Baudelaire, merely shows that it captures the moment when Virgil and Dante are ferried across the Styx, and assailed by souls desperate to accompany them, although Dante's green scarf and the blazing red city of Dis might have captured Baudelaire's imagination.

For the lake of blood (and we remember how the poet-persona of Baudelaire's poem 'La cloche fêlée' chokes to death, in a lake of blood apparently produced through his own memories) derives, I would think, from Dante's *Inferno*. It is at first 'a little brook' of blood in Canto XIV, composed of tears of blood flowing from a symbolic wound in age-old humanity; it is a hideous, deafening torrent, roaring down into the abyss of Malebolge in Cantos XVI and XVII, and a river of boiling blood in Canto XII, but a horrifying, frozen lake, Cocytus, in Cantos XXXII, XXXIII and XXXIV, at the very bottom of Dante's Hell, haunted by the fallen angel, Lucifer, where the worst sinners lie frozen and choking.

As for Baudelaire's evergreen wood, no reader of *Inferno* can forget the wood of the suicides, where Dante breaks off a green twig only to find that it bleeds (XIII):

> . . . As a brand yet green,
> That burning at one end from the other sends
> A groaning sound, and hisses with the wind
> That forces out its way, so burst at once
> Forth from the broken splinter words and blood.

On the face of it there is no mystery in Baudelaire's synaesthetic equation of Delacroix's colours with Weber's music; this comparison is already made in the *Salon de 1846*, and in the 1855 commentary on 'Les Phares'.[13] But it is not impossible that there might be, behind the strange fanfares, in their context of wicked angels (i.e., devils), a reminiscence of Dante's vulgar demons of *Inferno* XXI and XXII, one of whom trumpeted 'with sound obscene', demons explicitly described in Baudelaire's contemporary poem, 'La Béatrice'.

These reminiscences allow us to suppose that Baudelaire's reactions to Delacroix are not only Dantesque, but that Delacroix's painting is experienced by him in terms of a reading of Dante's *Inferno* which overflows the specific scenes represented in his painting, and refers to a wider knowledge of Dante's treatment of sin, suffering, suicide, damnation and revolt. But, *mutatis mutandis*, Baudelaire seems haunted by the image of the drowning sinner, and it looks therefore as if his reading of Dante is irremediably affected by its translation through Delacroix's imagery. In 'L'Irréparable' (1855), the lake of boiling pitch from Dante's *Inferno* XXI is recalled in Baudelaire's:

> Peut-on illuminer un ciel bourbeux et noir?
>    Peut-on déchirer des ténèbres
> Plus denses que la poix . . . ?

And similarly in 'L'Irrémédiable' (1857), we find the familiar topos of the fallen Christian angel, struggling in a rather Dantesque mire:

> Une idée, une Forme, un Etre
> Parti de l'azur et tombé
> Dans un Styx bourbeux et plombé
> Où nul œil du Ciel ne pénètre;
>
> Un Ange imprudent voyageur
> Qu'a tenté l'amour du difforme,
> Au fond d'un chauchemar énorme
> Se débattant comme un nageur,

reminding us of the boiling pitch of Canto XXI into which the sinners are thrown by the devils, to swim as best they can, and the frenzied drowning of Delacroix's painting of Canto VIII. We shall have to remember the 'imprudent voyageur' when we come to consider the last poem of *Les Fleurs du mal*, 'Le voyage'.

In 'L'Irrémédiable', Baudelaire's Hell is as much one of relief, through 'La conscience dans le Mal' (the last line of that poem), as one of retrospective punishment. Many of Dante's sinners, too, thus almost willingly reenact in conscious agony the very pleasures and vices that led them to hell – as do Paolo and Francesca, for instance, in *Inferno* V.

Yet Baudelaire's 'Allégorie' is an allegory which parodies such purification of desire. The woman described is the focus of a moral paradox. There is the suggestion that Baudelaire's heroine is suprahuman, but she is also the epitome of debauch and gross appetite; the Dantean Beatrice's divinely radiant eyes have become a crude 'come-on' signal:

> Et dans ses bras ouverts, que remplissent ses seins,
> Elle appelle des yeux la race des humains,

and her appeal is now that of a common, indeed particularly sluttish, prostitute ('Qui laisse dans son vin traîner sa chevelure'), although her appetite for life confers a curious innocence on herself and on her victims:

> Les griffes de l'amour, les poisons du tripot,
> tout glisse et tout s'émousse au granit de sa peau.
> . . .
> Elle croit, elle sait, cette vierge inféconde
> Et pourtant nécessaire à la marche du monde,
> Que la beauté du corps est un sublime don
> Qui de toute infamie arrache le pardon.
> Elle ignore l'Enfer comme le Purgatoire.

171

The paradox is stark. Absolute sexuality appears as a salutory release from sin on a par with its polar opposite, virginal purity. The prostitute is not immoral but amoral, and consolatory, even if not quite redemptive, in Baudelaire's scheme, whereby she would appear to deny the hypocritical separation of goodness and desire which posits man as fallen and needing redemption (the options of 'Enfer' and 'Purgatoire'). She compensates men for the horrors of moralized existence.

Yet Baudelaire's allegorical woman is a complex figure. As bountiful virgin saving humanity, conflated with the generous whore conferring release, she inevitably refers us simultaneously to both the Virgin Mary and Mary Magdalene; she is also crudely emblematic of the nineteenth-century dual morality which creates erotic alibis for purified marital relationships; but she is also like Faust's Gretchen and Dante's own Beatrice, an object of heterosexual desire, whose self-sacrificial accommodation of desire provides forgiveness and release.[14] However, and here Baudelaire is most original, she herself is also, more insidiously, a figure of the desiring subject, her overt acceptance of desire releasing her from Hell and Purgatory:

> Elle ignore l'Enfer comme le Purgatoire,
> Et quand l'heure viendra d'entrer dans la Nuit noire,
> Elle regardera la face de la Mort,
> Ainsi qu'un nouveau-né, – sans haine et sans remords,

just like a kind of female Don Juan. The implication of Baudelaire's 'Satanic' posture being that *both* Hell *and* Purgatory are the creatures of hatred and remorse, of the Christian rejection of sexual desire as corrupt in the first place. Baudelaire's anti-Pauline stance is made explicit – 'Elle a dans le plaisir la foi mahométame'.[15] This Islamic 'faith' in pleasure has to be read against the explicit rejection of a Christian faith in a punitive Hell and Purgatory. Islamic eschatology posits an after-world peopled by 'Houris', angelic concubines who reward earthly virtue with a heavenly version of earthly delights. In the Islamic heaven Baudelaire finds a 'Satanic' riposte to the hypocritical and untenable virtue of Chritian chastity, and his thrust could well be directed at Dante, for whom Mohammed was the most evil sinner and heretic, as can be inferred from *Inferno* VIII, where the blazing, infernal city of Dis is lit by the fires of burning mosques, and from *Inferno* XXVIII, where Mohammed is tortured. Dante's virtual equation of Islam with evil means that Baudelaire's violent rejection of Christian ethics in terms of Islamic sexuality, in a Dantean context, is tantamount to adopting what medieval Christians would have seen as the viewpoint of Satan.

In contrast to the Goethean or Dantean view, which seems to posit the sexual aesthetic as only a medium to salvation and one which leads if unadulterated to damnation (witness the fate of Paolo and Francesca in

*Inferno* V), Baudelaire chooses the diametrical alternative of the Islamic view, which not only accepts sexuality, but uses it as the very essence of a (non-transcendental) salvation. Similarly, in 'Le Léthé' (1857), the Christian eschatology of heaven bringing reward to those who have purified their erotic temptations is upset by Baudelaire's model of heaven, or salvation, being the experience of erotic pacification itself consoling for the agony of life; and the whole topos is again posited in the shape of an inverted Beatrice figure, subverting the Christian ideal of the virgin mother and redeemer through her function as bountiful whore.

Dante's Beatrice insists on the fact that the crossing of the underworld river, Lethe, must bring remorse for sexual desire, rather than convenient forgetfulness, and indeed, in *Purgatorio* XXXI and XXXII, when Dante is allowed to stare at Beatrice's mouth, after gradually becoming able to face her eyes, he gets carried away by his old love and temporarily blinded. Even here Dante's eschatology is orientated towards the transcendence of the amorous, since Beatrice seems to suggest that Dante has drunk of Lethe to make him forget his betrayal of her love, that is, to restore the continuity of his actual sins (*Purgatorio* XXXIII).[16]

In place of the balmy waters of Dante's Lethe, which bring both pure love and the soothing oblivion of death, Baudelaire chooses to drink at the mouth and breasts of the woman:

> L'oubli puissant habite sur ta bouche,
> Et le Léthé coule dans tes baisers.
> . . .
> Je sucerai, pour noyer ma rancœur
> Le népenthès et la bonne ciguë
> Aux bouts charmants de cette gorge aiguë.

A suicidal sexual pleasure is the only release from the agony of life. In 'Le poison' (1857) too, Baudelaire operates a clear reversal of the Dantean topos of the desired woman pouring oblivion, mediated by remorse, in order to soothe desire. Here too, it is sexual pleasure itself which supplies oblivion, to relieve the pain of being; and it is unrepentant orgasm, rather than amorous forgiveness, that sweeps man towards death and infinity, with the role of Lethe daringly attributed to an orgasmic flood of saliva, tossing the damned soul like a drowning man up on to the shore of death:

> Tout cela [wine and women] ne vaut pas le terrible prodige
>    De ta salive qui mord,
> Qui plonge dans l'oubli mon âme sans remords,
>    Et, charriant le vertige,
> La roule défaillante aux rives de la mort!

173

We have noted that Dante explicitly attacks Islam as the utmost trea-
chery in Canto XXVIII of *Inferno*. He sees Mohammed above all as the
betrayer of the church, his body ripped open, foully reproducing within
himself the schism he caused within religion. In a complex way Dante's
schematic vision may find an explicity intertextual riposte in Baudelaire.
Dante's Mohammed is split open like a wine cask, from the chin, via the
chest, to the bowels, with his entrails spilling between his legs (thus insulting at a stroke both Islamic sexuality and teetotalism):

> A rundlet, that hath lost
> Its middle or side stave, gapes not so wide
> As one I mark'd torn from the chin throughout
> Down to the hinder passage: 'twixt the legs
> Dangling his entrails hung, the midriff lay
> Open to view, and wretched ventricle,
> That turns the englutted aliment to dross.
>   Whilst eagerly I fix on him my gaze,
> He eyed me, with his hands his breast laid bare,
> And cried, 'Now mark how I do rip me: lo!'

Baudelaire's allegorical whore in 'Allégorie' is awash in wine ('laisse
dans son vin traîner sa chevelure'), and her grotesque breasts flow out
over her arms ('dans ses bras ouverts, que remplissent ses seins'). Dante
uses a violent and filthy image of smashing into a wine butt, and ripping
open a flatulent belly, in a hideous subversion of alcoholic and sexual
pleasure; Baudelaire uses the overflowing of wine and the opening of the
body to rehabilitate Islamic hedonism, and interestingly uses a notation
of excess of ugliness to signify not immorality but a paradoxical supplement of desire, which overruns everyday morality and the limitations of
moralized beauty.

It is the last poem of the 1861 edition of *Les Fleurs du mal*, however,
which I believe witnesses Baudelaire's profoundest intertextual homage
to Dante, beyond parody and subversion. 'Le voyage' (1859) culminates
in an evocation of Ulysses, who merges with the persona of the author,
as he determinedly plunges into the maelstrom of death in search of experience more satisfying than that of life. This Ulysses is very different
from Homer's, who returns to domestic peace and fidelity. And he differs as much from Goethe's Faust, redeemed from his devilish pact by the
love of the woman he seduced. He is much more like Molière's unrepentant Don Juan or Baudelaire's 'imprudent voyageur', the fallen angel.
But, more especially, he is surprisingly close to Dante's Ulysses.[17] In *Inferno* XXVI Ulysses recounts his last voyage, a compulsive attempt to
sail beyond the limits of the known universe, based on a desire for total
knowledge and experience, seen as stronger than lust for Circe, or even
love for Penelope, a compulsion transcending good and evil. When,

later, Dante's dream figures his own most dangerous temptations as the siren tempting Ulysses with erotic song (*Purgatorio* XIX, 19–25), his reader will remember Ulysses's moving complaint in *Inferno* XXVI:

> ... 'When I escaped
> from Circe ...
>
> . . .
>
> Nor fondness for my son, nor reverence
> Of my old father, nor return of love,
> That should have crown'd Penelope with Joy,
> Could overcome in me the zeal I had
> To explore the world, and search the ways of life,
> Man's evil and his virtue.'

Baudelaire had already used the sailor in 'Un voyage à Cythère' as a figure of the quest to satisfy desire, to the limits of death (he finds on the island of Venus no goddess of love, but the mutilated carcass of his alter ego). In 'Le voyage' the search goes beyond mere physical desire. Baudelaire's sailor leaves the limiting navigation of desire for the dangerous open sea of total experience, beyond life itself:

> Les uns, joyeux de fuir une patrie infâme;
> D'autres, l'horreur de leurs berceaux, et quelques-uns,
> Astrologues noyés dans les yeux d'une femme,
> La Circé tyrannique aux dangereux parfums.
>
> . . .
>
> Nous voulons voyager sans vapeur et sans voile!
>
> . . .
>
> Nous nous embarquerons sur la mer des Ténèbres

Whereas for Dante, shipwreck and death are an unintentional (if not unforeseen and unacceptable) end to the Faustian urge:

> ... 'Joy seized us straight;
> But soon to mourning changed. From the new land
> A whirlwind sprung, and at her foremost side
> Did strike the vessel. Thrice it whirl'd her round
> With all the waves; the fourth time lifted up
> The poop, and sank the prow: so fate decreed:
> And over us the booming billow closed'.

for Baudelaire the shipwreck finally becomes the deliberately sought experience of death and damnation:

> O Mort, vieux capitaine, il est temps! levons l'ancre!
> Ce pays nous ennuie, ô Mort! Appareillons!
>
> . . .

Verse-nous ton poison pour qu'il nous réconforte!
Nous voulons, tant ce feu nous brûle le cerveau,
Plonger au fond du gouffre, Enfer ou Ciel, qu'importe?
Au fond de l'Inconnu pour trouver du *nouveau*!

It transpires that Baudelaire's poetry shows both Dantean and Faustian temptations. In the case of those poems which take up figures from Dante's own verse, we can see that Baudelaire knowingly reworks Dante's themes, images and ethics in a spirit of subversion, working out a position of acceptance of absolutely amoral sexual desire and total experience, overtly rejecting the redemptive perspective in which Dante places these projects – whose attraction Dante recognizes, but whose forces he exploits in the service of goodness.

In the last poem of his masterpiece, *Les Fleurs du mal*, then, Baudelaire returns to the topos of shipwreck which we see, elsewhere in our book, haunting Hugo and Mallarmé. From Géricault, perhaps, comes the morbid depression, from Delacroix the moral search, from Molière and Byron the erotic drive and the flippant atheistic defiance. Baudelaire's Ulysses is no more homogenous than his Don Juan. His erotic nihilism speaks through the various masks of rival texts and images, which become Baudelaire's own, plural, pictorial, polyphonic voice.

## Suggested reading

Barton, Anne, *Byron, 'Don Juan'* (Cambridge: Cambridge University Press; Landmarks of World Literature, 1992).

Baudelaire, Charles, *Les Fleurs du mal*, in *Œuvres complètes*, vol. I, ed. C. Pichois (Paris: Gallimard, Pléiade, 1975).

———, *Salon de 1846*, ed. D. Kelley (Oxford: Oxford University Press, 1975).

Byron, Lord, *Don Juan* (Harmondsworth: Penguin Classics, 1986).

*Byron: A Self-portrait in his Own Words*, ed. P. Quennell (Oxford: Oxford University Press, 1990).

Dante, *The Vision of Dante Alighieri*, trans. H.F. Carey (London: J.M. Dent/ Everyman, 1908).

Delacroix, Eugène, *The Journal of Eugène Delacroix: A Selection*, ed. H. Wellington, trans. L. Norton (Oxford: Phaidon, 1980).

Eitner, Lorenz, *Géricault's 'Raft of the Medusa'* (London and New York, 1972).

———, *Géricault: His Life and Work* (London: Orbis, 1983).

Honour, Hugh, *Romanticism* (Harmondsworth: Pelican, 1981).

Huygue, René, *Delacroix* (London: Thames and Hudson, 1963).

Johnson, Lee, *Delacroix* (London and New York: Weidenfeld and Nicolson, 1963).

Michel, Régis, *Géricault: l'invention du réel* (Paris: Découvertes Gallimard / Réunion des Musées Nationaux, 1992).

Molière, *Dom Juan*, in *Théâtre complet de Molière*, vol. I (Paris: Garnier, 1960)

Pitwood, Michael, *Dante and the French Romantics* (Geneva: Droz, 1985).

Vaughan, William, *Romantic Art* (London: Thames and Hudson, 1978).

# 11

## *Transpositions*[1]

## David Kelley

In his *Salon de 1846*[2] Baudelaire said that the best criticism of a painting might be a sonnet. His own criticism as such always kept to prose, although he may well have been thinking of Gautier's *Salon de 1836*[3] in which one of the articles was indeed composed of poems evoking the work of Corot, Rousseau and Troyat.

Both Gautier and Baudelaire did, however, make extensive use of the visual arts as direct and explicit sources of inspiration for poems. And in the case of both poets, ironically enough, particularly in the case of Gautier, who professed to despise his journalistic activities, and is conventionally known as the principal exponent of 'Art for Art's Sake', there is often a close relationship between their critical texts and their poems.

The relationship between the visual experience of looking at a painting, commenting on it, and transposing that experience into a different art form is nevertheless more complex than is sometimes assumed. Gautier, who did indeed start out as a 'rapin' or art student, seems still to be often regarded as a failed painter who, both in his criticism and in his poetry, contented himself with producing pretty word-pictures. And it has been said of Baudelaire that he was happier with a reality already transformed aesthetically than with the brute object.

But one of the things that characterizes both writers is that their preoccupation with the visual arts involves a particularly acute perception of the specific possibilities of their own art. For Gautier, preoccupied by death and transience, art represented both a means of rendering permanent what is fleeting and of objectifying the fragile dream of the artist. And yet that very fixing of living physical beauty and the artist's inner ideal in painting and sculpture tends at the same time to freeze them, to mummify them, to take away from them those very qualities of vitality and intangibility which make them important to him.

He was thus fascinated by the interplay between dream and reality, art and life. And it is doubtless his fascination which caused him to travel with Nerval to the Low Countries in pursuit of living manifestations of the type of Rubenesque beauty. And this, for him, is part of the importance of writing in relation to the visual arts. For it allows him to play in an ambiguous space somewhere between the stasis of the painting or piece of sculpture and an evocation of the mobility of life.

In 'Le Poème de la femme' from *Emaux et camées*, for example, there is a consistent ambivalence in the writing: is it a real woman adopting for her lover poses from different sculptures and paintings of the past and present, or the construction of a composite ideal woman, created out of evocations of those same works of art? Is the poem of the title the poem which we are reading, or a conventional metaphor for female physical beauty?

> Un jour, au doux rêveur qui l'aime,
> En train de montrer ses trésors,
> Elle voulut lire un poème,
> Le poème de son beaux corps.
>
> (*PC*, III, 7)[4]

One of the ways in which that ambivalence is created derives precisely from the problems of 'describing' visual form. To evoke the shape and curve of a line in a painting, it is sometimes almost necessary to use a verb, as in:

> Et, comme l'odalisque d'Ingres,
> De ses reins cambrant les rondeurs,
>
> (*PC*, III, 9)

where the word 'cambrant' can be perceived simply as a means of suggestively evoking the static but sinuous curve of the woman's back and buttocks in the Ingres painting, but also contains within it an implication of erotically suggestive movement on the part of a living woman. The reader is suspended between an interpretation of the text as a description of a work of art and an evocation of the fleeting mobility of life.[5]

The little device I have just described is indicative, however, of some of the more complex ways in which the relationship between language and painting on the one hand, and on the other, the outside world which they may attempt to represent, is important in what poets do when they base a text on a painting. The visual arts cannot precisely reproduce the world. They work to a very large extent in terms of a series of conventions and signs. But they do also offer a representation of the world which can be apprehended directly by the senses and recognized as representation.

Language works rather differently. Of course, whether written or spoken it can also be apprehended only by the senses. And it can charm by the sounds it makes or its shapes on the page, as Arab and Chinese calligraphers well know. But the sound or shape of words has, in most cases, an arbitrary relationship with what is represented. The ways in which a poem can make an appeal to the sensuous perception of the outside world is an indirect one, working on the mind and imagination.

Both Gautier and Baudelaire were aware of and exploited this. It is obviously impossible to paint a smell or sound. It is even impossible to paint a tactile sensation, although some paintings possess a texture of surface which invites the touch. But through language one can evoke sensations of different orders. French and English are both quite limited in their colour and sound vocabulary. Gradations of hue and intensity, pitch and tone, are very difficult to speak of, except in rebarbative technical terms. What can be done, however, is to use the oblique suggestion of a perception of taste or smell or sound to evoke, with a precision impossible in a non-technical colour language, the particular nuanced colour and texture of a rose petal.

This is demonstrated particularly forcefully in the poem 'Variations sur le carnaval de Venise', also from *Emaux et camées*. The text begins, in fact, by evoking, not a painting but a piece of music, variations on a popular tune produced by the famous violinist Paganini. The music itself cannot of course be reproduced, or even imitated in words, except in the rather banally onomatopoeic line: 'Tra la, tra la, la, la laire!' So Gautier resorts to a series of synaesthetic plays exploiting the evocation of paintings, for example the *Birth of Venus* and Canaletto's views of Venice:

> Une frêle corde qui vibre
> Refait sur un pizzicato,
> Comme autrefois joyeuse et libre,
> La ville de Canaletto!
>
> (*PC*, III, 17)

In this quatrain there is no detailed attempt at description, either of the Canaletto paintings or of Paganini's music. But the comparison of the pizzicato technique with Canaletto's paintings operates in terms of reciprocal suggestion, to evoke both the flecks of light that animate the representations of Venice and the acute points of sound which characterize that particular potential of the violin.

But the point of the poem is of course not simply to recreate in words either music or paintings. Both are used to create a mental image of Venice and its carnival, and more particularly, a sentimental and erotic atmosphere associated with the place and a memory of the past:

> Sur une gamme chromatique,
> Le sein de perles ruisselant,

La Vénus de l'Adriatique
Sort de l'eau son corps rose et blanc.

Les dômes, sur l'azur des ondes
Suivant la phrase au pur contour,
S'enflent comme des gorges rondes
Que soulève un soupir d'amour,

(*PC*, III, 16)

where Gautier plays on the ambivalence of terms like 'chromatique' to refer to the musical scale, uses metaphorically words which relate to visual perception – 'au pur contour' – to evoke musical form, and engages in the game I referred to above, that of exploiting a verb to describe a shape. The domes of Venice swell like the breasts of the Venus (another piece of word-play) rising from the sea.

This use of synaesthetic images, not simply to create either visual or aural sensation, but as a Proustian madeleine *avant la lettre* summoning up the atmosphere of the past and evoking the specific nature of an emotional experience, is probably one of the things Baudelaire learned from Gautier, and one of the reasons for which he made his extravagant dedication of the *Fleurs du mal* to him.

Such a practice is, of course, the core of the theory of metaphor hinted at in Baudelaire's famous sonnet 'Correspondances', and outlined more specifically in his critical writings. It is interesting, however, that the first published text in which the ideas behind this aesthetic are adumbrated concerns painting – namely the chapter on colour in the poet's *Salon de 1846* (OC II, 422–6). Here he evokes a space in nature, attempting as a kind of bravura exercise to avoid reference to the forms of things, in order to suggest that colour and light can in themselves represent the constantly changing relationship of objects with each other, and thus the eternally mobile process – or as Baudelaire would have thought at that time, progress – of the natural world.

Within this text Baudelaire also suggests analogies, not only between colours and sounds, but also between sounds and sentiments. Indeed, probably thinking of Fourier and of Fourierist art criticism,[6] since a fundamental notion in Fourierist thinking is that of the universal analogy between different orders of things, he asks the – rhetorical – question as to whether any analogist has systematized the correspondence between colours and feelings. The theory of metaphor implicit in 'Correspondances,' and more explicitly defined in his critical essays, particularly the *Salon de 1859* and the *Notes nouvelles sur Edgar Poe*, does not particularly emphasize visual perception. On the contrary, it is often the more indefinable sense of smell which seems to be the trigger for the synaesthetic experience. In 'Correspondances', he writes:

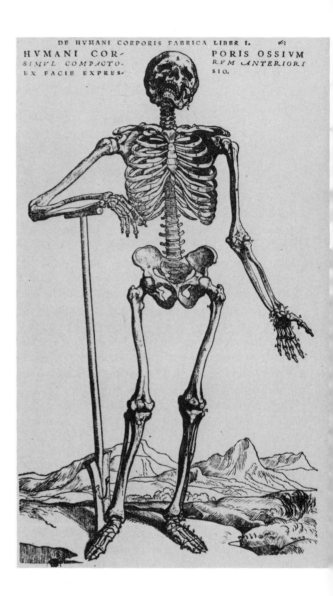

18.  Anonymous engraving, *Le Squelette laboureur*, sixteenth century (possibly after Titian)

Il est des parfums frais comme des chairs d'enfants,
Doux comme les hautbois, verts comme les prairies
– Et d'autres, corrompus, riches et triomphants. . . .
(OC, I, 11)

Here, the poet is playing on tactile sensations, sound and colour to
evoke an unnamed perfume, and through it, ultimately, the quality

innocence opposed to the corrupt, rich and triumphant qualities of the perfumes named in the final tercet. And that play is principally created through the ambiguity of language, – words like 'frais', 'doux' and 'vert', which can refer equally to sensation or to abstract or moral qualities. Similarly, in 'La Chevelure', often thought of as the most accomplished example of Baudelaire's practice of *correspondances*, it is the smell of the woman's hair which is the starting-point for the web of synaesthetic images that evoke and create the voyage to an exotic haven where the soul can drink in perfumes, sounds and colour:

> La langoureuse Asie et la brûlante Afrique,
> Tout un monde lointain, absent, presque défunt,
> Vit dans tes profondeurs, forêt aromatique!
> Comme d'autres esprits voguent sur la musique,
> Le mien, ô mon amour! nage sur ton parfum.
>
> (OC, I, 26)

Where Baudelaire directly draws inspiration from a visual image, that image is not always one that would be thought of as a significant work of art, and the visual information given is often minimal. The poem 'Le Squelette laboureur', for example, is based on an anonymous engraving (fig. 18) from a work of anatomy chanced upon at one of the *bouquinistes* on the banks of the Seine.[7] Only one of the eight quatrains offers any direct description of the image:

> On voit, ce qui rend plus complètes
> Ces mystérieuses horreurs
> Bêchant comme des laboureurs,
> Des Ecorchés et des Squelettes.
>
> (OC, I, 93–4)

Moreoever, the poem could almost be thought of as a deliberate misreading of the image, the function of which is to demonstrate the human bone-structure. The spade and the landscape which excite Baudelaire's interest are principally decorative props – literally perhaps, in the case of the spade. The poet more or less admits as much when he speaks of the gravity and knowledge of the artist adding beauty to the subject. What he does is to interrogate – literally – the image, perceived as the horrifying and clear emblem of an impossible human destiny, asking whether it does not signify that death is not after all the end of suffering, and whether we are condemned in a future life to continue breaking barren ground:

> Qu'envers nous le Néant est traître;
> Que tout, même la Mort, nous ment,

19. Eugène Delacroix, *Le Tasse dans la maison des fous*, 1839 (Sammlung Oskar Reinhart 'Am Römerholz', Winterthur)

20. Théophile Kwiatkowsky, *Les Sirènes*, c. 1846 (Czartoryski Foundation, Muzeum Narodowe, Krakow)

> Et que sempiternellement,
> Hélas! il nous faudra peut-être
>
> Dans quelque pays inconnu
> Ecorcher la terre revêche
> Et pousser une lourde bêche
> Sous notre pied sanglant et nu?
>
> (OC, I, 94)

'Sur *Le Tasse en prison*', based on Delacroix's *Le Tasse dans la maison des fous*, (fig. 19) is rather similar. Again there is relatively little precise visual description:

> Le poète au cachot, débraillé, maladif,
> Roulant un manuscrit sous son pied convulsif,

and

> Ces grimaces, ces cris, ces spectres dont l'essaim
> Tourbillonne, ameuté derrière son oreille,
>
> (OC, I, 168–9)

being the only examples.

Moreover, the second of my two quotations, which refers presumably to the grotesque figures perceived in the painting presumably through the window, alludes principally to auditive sensations – 'ces cris' and 'derrière son oreille'. As in 'Le Squelette laboureur', the image is considered above all as an emblem of the poet's own situation. The intentions of the painter are left behind. The space of the poem is not a visual one but an interior one. Indeed, the spatial limits represented in the painting – the walls of the cell – which confine Tasso are defined as the stifling limits of a reality which confine and constrict the soul in its dreams.

In this sense it is interesting that Baudelaire should have modified the title of the Delacroix picture from *Le Tasse dans la maison des fous* to 'Le Tasse en prison'. The madness manifested by the grimaces, cries and spectres which surge behind his ear and invite his reason into the realm of 'l'étrange et l'absurde', is assimilated to the Real which surrounds the poetic imagination. The terms of madness and sanity are inverted. Tasso is locked within his mind. And, strangely enough, in a poem deriving from a visual source, the principal figure does not see the decor within which he is represented.

Or rather, the decor which he does perceive derives from a different source. For the picture by Delacroix is perhaps not the only visual image present within the poem, and it may even be that the most significant visual source is not explicitly referred to. For Baudelaire follows the initial allusion to the Delacroix picture by the following lines:

185

21.   Giambattista Piranesi, etching from *Carceri d'invenzione, c.* 1745–50 (Trinity College, Cambridge)

[Le poète] Mesure d'un regard que la terreur enflamme
L'escalier de vertige où s'abîme son âme.

And that vertiginous staircase evokes very precisely the work of one of
the most obsessive visual sources for nineteeth-century poets, Piranesi,[8]
and more particularly his series of engravings, the *Carceri d'invenzione*
(fig. 21) or prisons of the imagination, which indeed represent pieces of
fantastic internal architecture, a number of which contain bizarre configurations of steps and stairs. If Baudelaire really was thinking of
Piranesi when writing these lines – and although it is unprovable, I am
convinced of it – the poem is literally a poem about the imagination confined in a prison of the imagination, or perhaps in a representation of a
world which exists only in the imagination.

That one of the visual sources of the poem should be alluded to rather
than stated, even perhaps deliberately censored, need not be surprising.
For in using the visual arts as a trigger, nineteenth-century poets often
played with the seen and the unseen, the stated and the unstated. And
this is certainly the case for Gautier. In 'Symphonie en blanc majeur', he
plays with this in clever ways. The poem is constructed on that characteristic theme in his work to which I have already referred, the
equivocation between art and life. It begins with a reference to the Swan
Women of Scandinavian folklore, and evokes, with a whole series of
bravura images of whiteness a real woman playing the piano in a
musical evening in Paris, who seems to be the living embodiment of
those tales. And if, as Madeleine Cottin has suggested in her edition of
*Emaux et camées*, the poem is in fact inspired by a watercolour by Delacroix, that play becomes even more complex.[9]

But the interplay between life on the one hand, and art, which pre-
serves but mummifies life, relates in an important way to the central
theme of the poem. For the images of whiteness which evoke in a hyper-
bolically galant way the perfection of the real woman are also an image
of sterility, of absence of feeling, and therefore, in a sense, of life. the
'real' woman is strangely 'unreal'. Her resemblance to the Swan Women
makes her a figure of death, since swans only sing before they die:

Sphinx enterré par l'avalanche,
Gardien des glaciers étoilés,
Et qui, sous sa poitrine blanche,
Cache de blancs secrets gelés?

Sous la glace où calme se repose,
Oh! qui pourra fondre ce cœur!
Oh! qui pourra mettre un ton rose
Dans cette implacable blancheur!

(*PC*, III, 24)

The answer to the rhetorical question is of course Gautier himself, through the resources of language. The statement of the absence of pink, for the poet so often the colour of desire and of life, as in the 'Variations sur le carnaval de Venise' referred to above, creates its presence in the mind of the reader. And this is something the visual artist could not do. In a painting, the pink would either be there or not there. It could not be at once effaced and stated, absent and present.

'Les Néréides', a poem from *Emaux et camées* which explicitly refers to a watercolour by the Polish artist Théophile Kwiatkowsky, but which, as the case of Baudelaire's 'Sur *Le Tasse en prison*', possibly also has reference to at least one other work of art, offers an even more telling example of this. After a dazzling, but rather precious evocation of the upper part of the sea-nymphs' bodies:

> Vidant sa nacre, l'huître à perle
> Constelle de son blanc trésor
> Leur gorge, où le flot qui déferle
> Suspend d'autres perles encore,
> (*PC*, III, 85)

the poet goes on to evoke the viscous fish-like tails of the mermaids:

> Se glace d'un visqueux frisson,
> Et le torse finit en queue,
> Moitié femme, moitié poisson.

But what is interesting is that Gautier asks another rhetorical question:

> Mais qui regarde la nageoire
> Et les reins aux squameux replis,
> En voyant les bustes d'ivoire
> Par le baiser des mers polis?
> (*PC*, III, 86)

Here the refusal to perceive imprints on the mind of the reader an image of what is being denied. The watercolour shown in the Salon of 1846 appears to have been lost. But there is, in the museum at Krakow, a painting in oils by Kwiatkowsky entitled *Les Sirènes* (fig. 20) which one might guess to be related to the image referred to by Gautier in his poem. and here, quite clearly there are no 'squameux replis'. It is impossible, because the bottom half of the women depicted in the painting is hidden beneath the water, to see their thighs and calves, or whatever alternative appendages they might have.

In this context it is interesting to look at the critical article in *La Presse* of 8 April 1846 in which Gautier speaks of the Kwiatkowsky water-colour:

Les *Sirènes* de M. Théophile Kwiatkowsky dansent bien sur la crête des flots: leurs corps aux nuances de nacre et de perle se terminent d'une manière originale et poétique par des membres d'eau modelée moitié chair, et qui n'ont pas la monstruosité de ces replis squameux par lesquels finissent les perfides créatures à la voix charmeuse, à l'ascendant irresistible, comme tout ce qui est fatal et mauvais.

Mr Théophile Kwiatkowsky's sirens are dancing with verve on the crest of the waves: their bodies shimmering with the nuances of mother of pearl and pearl are finished in an original and poetic way in liquid limbs modelled somewhere between water and flesh, and which do not betray the horrors of those slimy folds which are the end of those perfidious creatures whose voice enchants, casting an irresistible spell, like all that is fatal and bad.

There is a clear relationship between the prose text and the poem in the references to 'nacre' and 'perle' and' squameux replis'. But there is a very clear and obvious difference. In the article in *La Presse*, Gautier explicitly states the absence of the fishy tails of the conventional siren. The surface of the water – and the surface of the painting perhaps – serves to hide what is frightening about the lower part of the body. Limbs and sea merge in a kind of screen which hides the depths of the sexuality that Gautier finds threatening, as in other poems like 'Cærulei oculi' and 'Tristesse en mer', or even 'Carmen'.

For in *Emaux et camées*, and perhaps in Gautier's poetry as a whole, a 'surface' beauty is important. In 'Bûchers et tombeaux', he expresses very strongly the sense of death which pervades Christian and post-Christian art, and longs for a pagan art – which he knows to be impossible in the present age – constructed of forms and surfaces:

> Le squelette était invisible
> Au temps heureux de l'Art païen
> L'homme, sous la forme sensible,
> Content du beau, ne cherchait rien.
>
> (*PC*, III 72)

This relates to another of the themes of 'Les Néréides', and perhaps suggests a comparison with Baudelaire's 'Sur *Le Tasse en prison*'. The painting from the Krakow museum reproduced here has, in the background, the trireme referred to in the Gautier poem by its absence. The ship which erupts into the tranquil scene of the poem is a modern steamship incompatible with the world of classical mythology, and which causes the Néréides to plunge beneath the waves, fearful that their delicate flesh might be damaged by its brutal paddle-wheels.

There are two ways of interpreting the way in which Gautier has used the Kwiatkowsky picture in his poem. The Krakow painting, *Les*

*Sirènes*, is probably not the watercolour Gautier is specifically referring to in the poem. It could be that the 1846 watercolour did in fact contain an image of a nineteenth-century steamship. Such variants in different versions of paintings were not unknown. The Fourierist painter Papéty produced two versions of his *Rêve du bonheur*,[10] one of which contained in the background an image of a Greek temple, the other, chimneys, the one suggesting an ideal of harmony rooted in the past, the other the idea that it was through the technological developments of industry that a new age of harmony was to be achieved.

This seems likely insofar as the reason that Gautier suggests for his fascination with the Kwiatkowsky image is its bizarre combination of 'fable' and 'réalité'. Indeed, a major theme of the poem is, as I have already hinted, the impossibility of reconciling the plastic beauty of Greek art with the realities of modern life, but, perhaps even more acutely, since he speaks of 'fable' and 'réalité', of reconciling the poetic imagination with bourgeois positivism. For the poem concludes by suggesting that the people on the steamship do not even see the Nereids, doubtless subscribing to the rationalist interpretation of mermaids as the obsessive fantasies of seamen too long deprived of female company:

> Adieu, fraîche mythologie!
> Le paquebot passe et, de loin,
> Croit voir sur la vague élargie
> Une culbute de marsouin.
> (PC, III, 87)

But Madeleine Cottin has suggested, in her illustrated edition of *Emaux et camées*, that Gautier is, in his poem, conflating several images, the Kwiatkowsky watercolour and *Les Sirènes* by Lehmann and *Les Néréides* by Gendron,[11] and that it is from the latter images that Gautier gets the steamboat which allows him to construct the central implications of his poem.

This would suggest a similar process at work to that in the poem by Baudelaire on Delacroix's Tasso painting, where Piranesi's prisons represent an unstated visual reference which complements and complicates the explicit visual source. In any case, it is clear that Gautier's poem is far more than a verbal reconstruction of the painting by Kwiatkowsky to which it makes reference. Its themes are complex and intertwined. But what is perhaps central is a problem of perception, of what is seen and not seen.

Here is the central issue I have been trying to suggest in this chapter. Even in what is perhaps the most direct and locatable instances of relationships between the visual arts and writing, that is, poems explicitly deriving from specific images, those relationships are not simple ones. In both Gautier and Baudelaire, the verse poem which is the culmination of the process ('Les Néréides', for example, in the case of Gautier, 'Le Masque' and 'Danse macabre' in the case of Baudelaire)[12] has often gone through the intermediary stage of journalistic critical comment. But that critical comment is not always very obviously justifiable objectively. For the image which triggers off the poetic imagination does not have to be in itself a particularly rich or significant one. Christophe's *Le Masque* and Kwiatkowsky's *Sirènes* are both fairly banal. The anatomical plate which is the point of departure for Baudelaire's 'Squelette laboureur' has no particular artistic pretensions.

Moreover, what is perceived visually, or what is explicitly described, can be, and can be evoked as, a means of hiding something ill-defined, and sometimes feared, whether it be the image which is unnamed, as in Baudelaire's 'Sur *Le Tasse en prison*' – and perhaps in Gautier's 'Néréides' – or something that the image does not reveal, as is certainly the case in 'Les Néréides'. For the specific power of language, as used in poetry, lies in its indeterminacy, in the indirect nature of the ways in which it refers to the outside world.

## Suggested Reading

Drost, Wolfgang, 'L'Inspiration plastique chez Baudelaire', *Gazette des Beaux-Arts*, 49 (1957).

Fairlie, A., 'Reflections on the Successive Versions of *Une Gravure fantastique*', *Etudes baudelairiennes*, III (1973).

Gautier, Théophile, *L'Art et l'artiste: Actes du colloque de Montpellier, 1982* (Montpellier, 1983).

Leakey, F.W., 'Baudelaire and Mortimer', *French Studies*, VII (1953).

Scott, David, *Pictorialist Poetics* (Cambridge: CUP, 1988).

Snell, Robert, *Théophile Gautier: A Romantic Critic of the Visual Arts* (OUP, 1982).

# 12

# Stendhal's art history and the making of a novelist

## Ann Jefferson

> dans les autres, nous ne pouvons
> estimer que nous-mêmes . . .
> Désormais les jugements des
> artistes sur les ouvrages de
> leurs rivaux ne seront pour moi
> que des commentaires de leur
> propre style.
> Stendhal, *Histoire de la peinture*
> *en Italie*, I, p. 269

There is very little in Stendhal's fiction to suggest the art-lover. If it were not for the existence of the *Histoire de la peinture en Italie* (1817) and the two *Salons* of 1824 and 1827 respectively,[1] and if Stendhal's accounts of his travels in Italy – *Rome, Naples et Florence* (1817 and 1826) and the *Promenades dans Rome* (1829) – did not seem to make the fine arts central to both the goal and the inspiration of the traveller, there would be no way of guessing that this most un-visual of novelists had had any formation as a student of painting and sculpture. He boasted of *Le Rouge et le Noir* that one of its major achievements was to leave the reader 'dans une ignorance complète sur la forme de la robe que portent Mme de Rênal et Mlle de la Mole',[2] and he wilfully and not a little perversely forswore description in depicting the effect of Lake Como on Gina in *La Chartreuse de Parme* with the scornful comment that 'un moderne eût noyé tout ceci dans le paysage, dans un plat d'épinards infini';[3] and yet, as I shall be arguing, the aesthetic of these novels derives in large part from his response to painting. This paradox will need some unravelling, since the dependence of Stendhal's fictional writing upon a painterly aesthetic so palpably renounces the visual form that is usually associated with such a conjunction.

Whether it is in his marginalia, his critical writings or authorial comment in his novels, Stendhal almost always defines the visible in terms of tedium, and that by virtue of a combination of vulgarity, facility and irrelevance. Rejecting Walter Scott in favour of *La Princesse de Clèves*, he remarks disparagingly that 'l'habit et le collier de cuivre d'un serf du moyen âge sont plus faciles à décrire que les mouvements du cœur humain'.[4] The occasional inclusion of the visual in Stendhal's writing is little more than a necessary compromise with the conventional; and his instruction to himself in revising *La Chartreuse*, 'Y mêler des paysages, des circonstances vulgaires, du facile à comprendre',[5] seems to be a concession to readability that implies just this.

This principled avoidance of the visual sets Stendhal at odds with the underlying assumptions of the tradition which he is often regarded as founding; for one of the most characteristic features of nineteeth-century realist writing is the degree of its investment in the visible world. The realist novel was a chronicle of its time largely in its formulation of a social knowledge that is frequently presented as inseparable from the material contents of the world it seeks to reflect. One only has to think of Madame Vauquer's dining-room where moral information is conveyed exclusively through visual channels, from the chipped and murky carafes on the sideboard to the winestains on the serviettes that belong to her *pensionnaires*. For Balzac, objects such as these hold out the promise of a shared reading of social and moral concerns ('la misère sans poésie'),[6] and access to this general social truth is achieved through the novelist's insistent hermeneutic pressure on the visible surface of the world.[7]

If, as I shall be arguing, the visual ultimately leads the way to social understanding in Stendhal, it is by a much more circuitous route than that of Balzac. Initially, however, it would seem that for Stendhal, the visible world comes into focus only in relation to private (as opposed to public or universal) and emotional (as opposed to moral or social) preoccupations. Or, as he records in the *Vie de Henry Brulard*,

> Les paysages étaient comme un *archet* qui jouait sur mon âme, et des aspects que personne ne citait (la ligne des rochers en approchant d'Arbois, je crois, et venant de Dole par la grande route, fut pour moi une image sensible et évidente de l'âme de Métilde).

> Landscapes were like a *bow* playing on my soul, and features which no one mentioned (the line of the rocks as you approach Arbois, I think, coming from Dole on the main road, was for me a tangible and evident image of the soul of Métilde).[8]

The presumption of shared social experience on which Balzac relies so heavily is strikingly absent ('personne ne citait. . .') from an object whose social intelligibility is nil. It is only in Stendhal's inner lexicon that a sky-line could constitute such a tangible image of the beloved.

This kind of response to the visible world may be partly due to the fact that Stendhal seems to have had little natural visual aptitude and, as many critics have observed, his interest in painting was chiefly a peg on which to hang his private concerns and a pretext for expending his emotional energies.[9] The first painting to provoke response of any kind in him was one which he saw less as a visual representation of a certain scene than as a personal promise of happiness and love. This (unidentified) painting which he saw as a child in his art teacher's studio apparently depicted a wooded hillside at the foot of which three nearly naked women were bathing in a stream: 'Ce paysage, d'une verdure charmante ... devint pour moi l'idéal du bonheur. C'était un mélange de sentiments tendres et de douce volupté. Se baigner ainsi avec des femmes aimables! (p. 688). The picture generates a fantasy about the forms that happiness might take and which, he recalls, it was his good fortune to enact one day, many years later in Marseilles.

The private and inward response to art takes precedence over the social and consensual to a degree that at times makes Stendhal appear almost autistic in relation to the visual. This visual autism is paradoxically exemplified by the organization of the unusually illustrated *Vie de Henry Brulard* itself. Carol Mossman has demonstrated brilliantly how the engravings of Italian paintings interleaved into the manuscript (and reproduced in the Pléiade edition) implicitly acquire a particular and quite private meaning in the context of the autobiographical narrative.[10] Although these paintings are, so to speak, in the public domain and thus open to a shared interpretation, Stendhal's silent inclusion of them in his text retrieves them for a private significance which is never spelled out to the reader.

In the case of the numerous *croquis* (sketches), this autism is perhaps even more pronounced: the barely decipherable diagrams function largely as triggers to Stendhal's own memories and as mnemomic devices through which he is able to recall and reexperience the emotions of the past. One instance of such a diagram appears in a brief account of a moment of jealousy provoked by a woman he fleetingly desired as a child (fig.22).

The geography of the emotional scene is offered to the reader as a sub-stitute for its content which Stendhal expects to recover in due course – but for himself, and not for his reader:

A une seconde partie à Berlandet je me révoltai par jalousie: une demoi-selle que j'aimais avait bien traité un rival de vingt ou vingt-cinq ans. Mais quel était l'objet de ces amours? Peut-être cela me reviendra-t-il comme beaucoup de choses me reviennent en écrivant. Voici le lieu de la

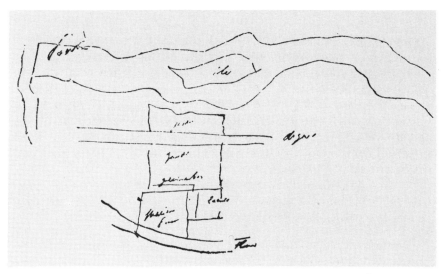

[*Pont. – Ile. – Jardin. – Digue. – Jardin. – Galerie de bois. – Maison Poncet. – Écurie. – Rue.*]

22.  Stendhal, diagram from *La Vie de Henri Brulard c*. 1835–6

scène que je vois aussi nettement que si je l'avais quittée il y a huit jours. (p. 663)

On a second outing to Berlandet, I rebelled out of jealousy: a young lady whom I loved had been kind to a rival aged twenty or twenty-five. But who was the object of this love? Perhaps it will come back to me just as many things come back to me as I write. This is the place where the scene occurred, and I see it as clearly as if I had left it a week ago.

There is a striking disparity between the affective status of the *croquis* for Stendhal on the one hand, and its intelligibility for the wider public on the other. These lines and ciphers speak as much to Stendhal and as little to his reader, as the rocks on the road from Dole. This disparity is further testimony that for him the visual entails a move away from the social intelligibilities and the moral consensus which in Balzac are guaranteed by it.[11]

If we are to understand how, in spite of all this, painting nevertheless acquires a social significance for Stendhal and lays the basis for his practice as a writer, we need now to turn to his *Histoire de la peinture en Italie*. For the writing of this history provided him with the education to become a novelist quite as much as it provided him with an education in the visual arts. The book started life in Italy in 1811 largely as a translation of the Abbé Lanzi's *Storia pittorica dell'Italia dal risorgimento delle belle arti, fin presso al fine del xviii secolo* (first published in 1789).[12]

195

Stendhal was a complete autodidact in the field of art history, and his learning was acquired initially through his acquaintance with the scholarly and voluminous (it ran to six volumes) Lanzi, whose *Storia* Arbelet describes as 'le premier ouvrage d'ensemble, sérieux, complet et impartial sur toutes les écoles de l'Italie' (*L' 'Histoire'*, p. 142). By the time the book was eventually completed in 1817 it was much more than an abbreviated French version of Lanzi, even though Stendhal remained in Lanzi's debt for a good deal of the informative detail of his book and for its historical framework.

Much of this material concerns the kind of visual expertise that Stendhal makes no bones about treating as secondary to what in his view counts as a proper understanding of the arts:

> Il serait ridicule de demander le but moral aux connaisseurs. En revanche, ils triomphent à distinguer la touche heurtée du Bassan des couleurs fondues du Corrège. Ils ont appris que le Bassan se reconnaît à l'éclat de ses verts, qu'il ne sait pas dessiner les pieds, qu'il a répété toute sa vie une douzaine de sujets familiers. . . Huit ou dix particularités sur chaque peintre, et de plus la connaissance de la famille de jeunes femmes, de vieillards, d'enfants, qu'il avait adoptée, font le patrimoine du connaisseur. . . Il n'y a de difficile là-dedans que l'air inspiré (*Histoire*, I, pp. 133–4).

> It would be absurd to expect connoisseurs to know the moral aim of art. On the other hand they are brilliant at distinguishing the broken finish of a Bassano from the melting colours of a Correggio. They have learned that Bassano is recognizable by his bright greens, that he cannot draw feet and that he repeated a dozen familiar subjects throughout this lifetime. Eight or nine characteristics for each painter, and also knowledge about his adoptive family of young women, old men and children make up the connoisseur's inheritance. . . . There is nothing difficult in all this except how to put on a suitably knowing air. (My translation and Wakefield, p. 40)

What his *Histoire* offers is, according to Stendhal, a visual expertise that, unlike the more common form he is so contemptuous of here, opens on to the 'but moral', or the psychological dimension that for him – as for many of his eighteenth-century precursors who wrote about art – was their essence: 'Reconnaître la teinte particulière de l'âme d'un peintre dans sa manière de rendre le clair-obscur, le dessin, la couleur: voilà ce que quelques personnes sauront, après avoir lu la présente histoire' (I, p. 134). Technical know-how becomes a way of reading souls; and the capacity for recognizing the particular spiritual character of a given artist becomes grafted on to the private 'exaltation' that first marked Stendhal's relation to the arts.

This privileging of emotional response on the part of the viewer was a central and uncontested tenet of eighteenth-century aesthetics, but Stendhal differs crucially from his eighteenth-century precursors (Dubos, Rousseau and Diderot) in his choice of a historical rather than a philosophical approach to painting. Philosophy and aesthetics predispose to a universalist line of reasoning; essays on painting and the origin of languages, or entries in the *Encyclopédie* and a *Dictionnaire de musique*, direct thought along a path that leads somewhere very different from that of history.[13] Stendhal's choice of a historical format with its projected division into different 'schools' of painting (projected because Stendhal in fact never got beyond the 'Ecole de Florence'), and within a given school, the distinctions between the contributions of each great master (Leonardo, Michelangelo, Raphael), means that he is constantly confronting specifics. Indeed, it is precisely this capacity to distinguish and to recognize the individual that Stendhal hopes his reader will learn from the *Histoire*: 'Peu à peu ce lecteur distinguera les écoles, il reconnaîtra les maîtres. Ses connaissances augmenteront; il a de nouveaux plaisirs' (I, p. 174). Pleasure is the product here of acumen; but more importantly, the specifics identified by this skill are the point at which art history may cross over into fiction in ways that I shall be going on to explore. The generic form of Stendhal's writing about art with its proclivity towards the particular already opens up a certain novelistic potential within the *Histoire* itself.

There are a number of ways in which the *Histoire* resembles fiction, and the first of these is associated with its semi-fictional narrator. Henri Beyle had yet to adopt the pseudonym Stendhal (a name taken from the German town in which the great eighteenth-century German art historian Winckelmann was born), but he nevertheless created an author-persona for the *Histoire* to whom he ascribes a number of more or less fictional circumstances. For instance, he claims to have spent three years' exile in Tuscany every day of which was devoted to looking at the pictures he discusses in his text, whereas in reality he had spent only three weeks there. Furthermore, most of what he says about the paintings of Cimabue, Giotto and Masaccio comes from Lanzi and is not based on first-hand experience at all.[14] In creating this persona Stendhal may be introducing an element of the fictitious into art history; but, more importantly, he is constructing an identifiable human source for his claims about paintings, and seeking to ground them in the particular experience of a particular individual at a particular time: 'Je puis avoir tort; mais ce que je dirai de Cimabue, de Giotto, de Masaccio, je l'ai senti réellement devant leurs ouvrages, et je les ai toujours vus seul' (I, p. 77). These references to his own responses to paintings and to the circumstances under which he saw them serve to validate what he has to say about them in terms of personal experience rather than objective expertise: 'Ce livre est le résultat d'un séjour de dix années en Italie, il est écrit avec exaltation, mais toujours de bonne foi. L'article de chaque peintre a été fait dans la ville où il est né, et en présence de ses tableaux' (I, p. 314). At times this desire to place both the paintings and the commentary in specific circumstances can lead to unashamedly fictional digressions as when, on the basis of his misreading of an Italian name, Stendhal describes a non-existent château in which Leonardo da Vinci was supposedly born and to which he recounts a totally fictitious visit by himself in pursuit of the appropriate circumstances for appreciating his art:

> Je suis parti de Florence à cheval, à l'aurore d'un beau jour de printemps; j'ai descendu l'Arno jusqu'auprès du délicieux lac Fucecchio: tout près sont les débris du petit château de Vinci. J'avais dans les fontes de mes pistolets les gravures de ses ouvrages; je les avais achetées sans les voir; j'en voulais recevoir la première impression sous les ombrages de ces collines charmantes au milieu desquelles naquit le plus ancien des grands peintres, précisément trois cent quarante ans avant ma visite, en 1452 (I, p. 181).

> I set off from Florence on horseback, at dawn on a beautiful spring day; I followed the Arno downstream until I reached the delightful lake Fucecchio: the remains of the little da Vinci château are just near by. In the holsters of my pistols I had the engravings of his works; I had bought them without seeing them; I wanted to have my first impression of them in the leafy shade of the charming hills amongst which the oldest of the great painters was born, precisely three hundred and forty years before my visit, in 1452.

Much of what Stendhal has to say about Leonardo is taken from Lanzi, Amoretti and Vasari, but this introductory paragraph furnishes the subsequent art-historical commentary with a quite precisely evoked context, whether it is 'le délicieux lac Fucecchio' which provides the setting for the imagined château, or the equally imaginary holsters that contain the engravings. The implication behind this is that authenticity of circumstance counts for more than the authenticity of the aesthetic objects to be contemplated, since Stendhal portrays himself taking engravings to the Leonardo birthplace, rather than visiting the originals in the settings in which they are displayed.

The future novelist is much more to be found in passages such as these than in the rather literary and psychologizing readings of some of the paintings he goes on to produce, which are fully within the tradition of eighteenth-century art-critical writing, and not a mark of any special originality on his part. If the *Histoire de la peinture en Italie* makes Stendhal the novelist that he later became it was not primarily because of the novelistic projections that paintings inspire in the viewer,[15] but because the paintings which are the book's subject matter provoked in Stendhal a sustained and complex meditation concerning the conditions which make both their creation and their viewing possible. These conditions are always local, temporal and particular; and understanding them is a task that is shared by both the art historian and the realist novelist. Stendhal's experience of painting may have been a visual education; but it was above all a lesson in the importance of circumstance, and it was this lesson that formed the future novelist. The specifics which for Balzac constitute the *content* of literary or artistic representation (carafes and serviettes) are for Stendhal displaced on to the *context* within which representations are created and viewed (lake Fucecchio, dawn on a spring morning). In the light of this it becomes possible to see the *croquis* of the autobiography as a further instance of Stendhalian circumstance: the precise character of Brulard's jealousy and the name of the woman who provoked it may have been temporarily elided from memory, but the geographical context, so much of which seems irrelevant to the emotional action, is offered to the reader as circumstantial evidence of their otherwise unelaborated reality.

I shall devote the remainder of my discussion to an exploration of the conditions that enable first the creation, and then the viewing of painting, although in fact this separation is to a large degree arbitrary, since, for Stendhal, the prime determining condition for the arts is the public which receives it. It is because of the importance of their role as circumstance that Stendhal begins the *Histoire* with an account of the character of the Italian people. The 'peinture' whose history he is recounting in this book was brought into being by the existence of 'un peuple riche, rempli de passions, et souverainement religieux', who had the added quality of being able to 'recevoir les plaisirs les plus vifs par quelques couleurs étendues sur une toile' (I, p. 9). He sees the public as the embodiment of a demand for art to which the artist responds, rather than as a force of expression of which the artist is simply the vehicle. It is the nature of the public's demand which determines whether the arts exist at all in a given time and in a given place, which arts will flourish (sculpture in ancient Greece, lithography in modern France), the quality of the work produced, as well as its character. So, for example, if the golden age of Italian painting failed to arrive before the fifteenth century, this was not because of a dearth of artistic talent, but because of the values and outlook of fourteenth-century Florentine society: 'Le malheur de Florence, au quatorzième siècle, n'était pas du tout la malhabileté des artistes, mais le mauvais goût du public' (I, p. 103).

Stendhal's entire conception of beauty is made relative through its dependence on the public which brings it into being. The 'beau idéal' is not some eternal value which different cultures or different artists are more or less capable of approximating (this is, broadly, what Winckel-mann claimed in singling out the Greeks). Rather, the material and social circumstances of each society determine the nature of what appears as beautiful within that society. Consequently, says Stendhal, in ancient Greece where physical strength mattered for the day-to-day survival of its citizens, the idea of beauty was inseparable from the idea of 'force'; but this association has become senseless in a world where physical safety can more or less be taken for granted, and where physical beauty has as a result become synonymous with 'elegance' (II, pp. 135–6). Beauty in Stendhal's thinking is art's response to the implicit demand made by each society to see its own concerns and circumstances reflected in the work that artists produce: 'La beauté dans chaque siècle n'est que l'expression des qualités qui lui sont utiles' *(Salon de 1827,* p.101). Hence, Stendhal's definition of Romanticism as 'l'art de présenter aux peuples les œuvres littéraires qui, dans l'état actuel de leurs habitudes et de leurs croyances, sont susceptibles de leur donner le plus de plaisir possible', in contrast to classicism which 'leur présente la littérature qui donnait le plus grand plaisir à leurs arrière-grands-pères'.[16] Every age has its own idea of beauty, and, since the modern world is unlike both the republics of antiquity and the monarchy of Louis XIV, Stendhal predicts that 'on verra naître un beau *constitutionnel*' (II, p. 137), answering the quite particular needs of the public as it exists in the nineteenth century.

The national and social environment necessary for the arts consists of many elements, but the moral character of a people is the key factor. This extends beyond matters of taste or notions of beauty, since it is above all 'les passions qui font la possibilité comme le sujet des beaux-arts' (I, p. 65). In addition to being both its subject matter and a mark of its effect on the viewer, passions provide what is perhaps the crucial enabling condition for art. Social and political institutions which favour passions are also propitious for artistic production. This means that war is not inimical to the arts ('la guerre ne leur est point contraire, non plus qu'à tout ce qu'il y a de grand dans le cœur de l'homme', I, p. 162), but monarchy is: 'même dans le cas où le roi est un ange [le gouvernement monarchique] s'oppose [aux] chefs d'œuvre, non pas en défendant les sujets de tableaux, mais en brisant les âmes d'artistes. . . . Par les habitudes qu'il imprime, il écrase le moral des peuples' (I, p. 54). Political freedom is not in itself a condition of artistic creation, and there is all the difference in the world between the dreary uniformity of nineteenth-century America where freedom can be taken for granted, and the 'amour furieux pour la liberté et la haine des nobles' (I, p. 117) to be found in fifteenth-century Florence. What counts is more the impassioned desire for liberty rather than the fact of liberty itself.[17] All Stendhal's analyses of social institutions (formal or informal, from government to everyday forms of human exchange) are ultimately based on the degree of potential for human emotion that they contain.

The second enabling condition for painting is the prior existence of other paintings. In other words, the work of precursors provides a necessary context for the painter to produce his own art. This is a commonplace in writing about the fine arts,[18] and in Stendhal's case it is a major justification for the historical approach he takes to his subject matter. So if he starts his account with Cimabue, Giotto and Masaccio, it is not because he finds their paintings intrinsically beautiful, but because their work was vital in preparing the way for their successors: 'Je trouve [les tableaux de Cimabue] déplaisants. Mais la raison me dit que sans Cimabue nous n'aurions peut-être jamais eu l'aimable André del Sarto' (I, p. 78). Precursors provide the painter with a variety of necessary preconditions, some of which are purely technical, such as the achievements of perspective or chiaroscuro. Others have to do with broader principles, so that, for example, Cimabue owes his place as the founder of the Italian tradition to the fact that 'il [osa] consulter la nature' (I, p. 78), thus establishing verisimilitude as a basic aesthetic value. Masaccio's role is almost equally important since, as the inventor of expression, he instituted an essential painterly principle, the portrayal of the inner man through the depiction of externals, demonstrating that 'l'homme n'est rien que par la pensée et par le cœur' (I, p. 128).

The great painter also needs his precursors in order to have an inheritance to overthrow. Invention in the field of the arts is always associated in Stendhal with a 'daring' which is synonymous with a rejection of established convention. Just as Cimabue had dared to reject the lessons of his Greek masters, Michelangelo 'brisa les entraves qui depuis la renaissance de la civilisation retenaient les artistes dans un style étroit et mesquin' (II, p. 180). Similarly, in the modern era David 'dédaign[a] de copier servilement ses prédécesseurs et trouv[a] une nouvelle manière d'imiter la nature' (*Mélanges* III, p. 7). Specifically, the great painter overthrows the achievements of his precursors as institutionalized by the mediocre disciples who inevitably follow him. This explains the distinction that Stendhal makes between the 'Ecole de David' and David himself, and is the basis of his indictment of the *Ecole* as a tyranny requiring of its adherents exact and scientific but utterly passionless representations of bodies without souls.[19] Everything that is valuable in painting for Stendhal is inseparable from this gesture of reversal. The great painter dares both to 'consult nature' and to 'be himself', but the courageous gestures which manifest this daring cannot be performed in a vacuum without tradition.

Neither consulting nature nor being oneself will allow a painter to escape his place in history, and throwing off the shackles of orthodoxy does not mean that anything goes. The degree to which Stendhal sees painters as bound to their circumstances is paradoxically illustrated by the several occasions on which he pauses to consider how a given painter might have painted at a different point in history and under different cultural conditions: 'Si un Michel-Ange nous était donné en nos jours de lumière, où ne parviendrait-il point? Quel torrent de sensations nouvelles et de jouissances ne répandrait-il pas dans un public si bien préparé par le théâtre et les romans!' (*Histoire*, II, p. 190). The form that a particular talent takes is in large part determined by the circumstances under which it realizes itself, and these include both the tradition and the social and cultural context.

For many analysts consideration of the role of circumstance would stop here with the discussion of the production of art. Stendhal is unusual – particularly for his time – in seeing that *response* to the arts is as powerfully bound by circumstances as its creation. Taine, in his 1864 Introduction to the *Histoire de la littérature anglaise,* singles out Stendhal for unreserved praise as the only person (prior to Taine himself) to have approached aesthetic questions in terms of their social and moral context – as Taine himself does when he asks: 'Etant donné une littérature, une philosophie, une société, un art, telle classe d'arts, quel est l'état moral qui la produit? et quelles sont les conditions de race, de moment et de milieu les plus propres à produire cet état moral?'[20] But even Taine was unable to appreciate the full extent of the originality he extols in Stendhal, for his implicit assumption here is that the 'procédés scientifiques, l'art de chiffrer, de décomposer et de déduire' (p. xlv) which Stendhal exemplifies are not themselves bound by the conditions which they analyse in works of art. By contrast, Stendhal makes it clear time and again that response is as much determined by social and cultural context as is the art which is its object.

This insight (which Taine is not the only person to have overlooked in Stendhal) has two principal and complementary consequences. It requires first, that the modern viewer make an active and informed effort to transport himself back to the world in which the work he is contemplating was originally created; and second, that he grasp equally consciously the usually quite unconscious cultural and aesthetic assumptions of his own society in order that they should not stand in the way of a proper appreciation of a culturally distant work of art: 'En lisant les chroniques et les romans du moyen âge, nous, les gens sensibles du dix-neuvième siècle, nous supposons ce qui a dû être senti par les héros, nous leur prêtons une sensibilité aussi impossible chez eux, que naturelle chez nous' (*Histoire* II, p. 327). The natural attitude of the contemporary outlook is a historical impediment to understanding, and cultural anachronism is apt to make for critical blindness.

The first aspect of the question (recreating the assumptions of the past) comes into very sharp focus in Stendhal's discussion of Michelangelo:

Veut-on réellement connaître Michel-Ange? *Il faut se faire citoyen de Florence en 1499.* Or, nous n'obligeons point les étrangers qui arrivent à Paris à avoir un cachet de cire rouge sur l'ongle du pouce: nous ne croyons ni aux apparitions, ni à l'astrologie, ni aux miracles. La constitution anglaise a montré à la terre la véritable justice, et les attributs de Dieu ont changé. Quant aux lumières, nous avons les statues antiques, tout ce que des milliers de gens d'esprit ont dit à leur sujet, et l'expérience de trois siècles. (II, p. 189, my italics).

Do we really want to understand Michelangelo? Then we must become Florentine citizens of 1499. For in Paris we do not force strangers to wear a band of red wax on the thumbnail; and we do not believe in ghosts, astrology and miracles. The English constitution has shown mankind true justice, and God's character has changed. As for intellectual progress, we have classical statues, everything that has been said about them by thousands of clever people and the experience of three centuries (Wakefield, p. 80).

Stendhal is attempting here to itemize what it would take to recreate the world of Michelangelo in a move that is the mental equivalent of the fictitious journey he makes to the Leonardo birthplace. It is a world whose every circumstance, from trivial social practice to fundamentals of religious belief, differs from the modern era. Because of these differences, Stendhal advises the would-be visitor to the Sistine Chapel to try and recreate the conditions of fifteenth-century Florence by undergoing a thorough and intensive course of cultural initiation before setting foot in it: 'Ce genre [de peinture] est difficile à voir; l'œil a besoin d'une éducation, et, cette éducation, l'on ne peut guère se la donner qu'à Rome' (II, p. 215). The modern viewer has to make a considerable effort to close the ideological and aesthetic gap that lies between himself and the fifteenth century, and Stendhal does not underestimate the difficulty involved. In particular, it is hard 'pour nous [qui] avons lu Voltaire à douze ans' (II, p. 191) to imagine the climate of religious terror that marked the age of Savonarola and outside of which, in Stendhal's view, Michelangelo's work cannot speak to its viewers.

Stendhal is also aware that gaps themselves vary with the passing of time, and in the case of Michelangelo it is narrower in the early nineteenth century than it had been in the eighteenth century, whose sensibility was different enough again to put it beyond all possibility of appreciating his work: 'Voltaire ni madame du Deffand ne pouvaient sentir Michel-Ange. Pour ces âmes-là, son genre était exactement synonyme de laid, et qui plus est, du laid à prétention, la plus déplaisante chose du monde' (II, p. 322). This remark has the effect of redirecting the modern gaze back towards its own time in an attempt to understand what it is about the contemporary world that distinguishes it from both the fifteenth and the eighteenth centuries. The nineteenth century finds a satisfaction of its longing for lost energies in fifteenth-century art, but is likely to be limited in its response to that art by its inability to conceive of physical energy except in opposition to spiritual energy.[21] Stendhal is quite precise about the possibilities and the constraints in the nineteenth-century outlook, and this precision might lead one to suppose that cultural and ideological self-knowledge is easily come by. But Stendhal seems to have regarded social self-knowledge as being equally problematic and inaccessible as the elusive personal self-knowledge that prompts the question he asks at the beginning of his autobiographical *Vie de Henry Brulard*: 'quel œil peut se voir soi-même?' (p. 535). Awareness that the cultural lens through which one looks at the world is comprised of quite local and particular assumptions does not of itself enable one to see what those assumptions are. Yet this was the knowledge that Stendhal sought; it is both an essential strategy in his art criticism and its ultimate goal. It is also the raison d'être of his fiction.

In writing his essay on the letters of Président de Brosses ('La comédie est impossible en 1836'), Stendhal identifies particularly clearly the dual form of knowledge which I am suggesting is exemplified by his own work. According to Stendhal, de Brosses's first great merit is to have made known the previously unknown world of Italian *mœurs*:

> Aucun voyageur, que je sache,. . . n'a essayé de nous faire connaître la manière habituelle d'aller à la chasse du plaisir au-delà des Alpes. Ce côté si curieux, mais si difficile, d'un voyage en Italie, est complètement oublié; on remplace ce qu'on devrait dire par d'ignobles exagérations empruntées aux laquais de place, comme les anecdotes sur les grands peintres. La manière dont on cherche le bonheur dans la vie de tous les jours, les habitudes sociales si opposées aux nôtres, sont tout à fait ignorées.[22]

> No other traveller, to my knowledge. . . has tried to show us the habitual way Italians go in search of pleasure. This interesting but delicate subject is usually quite forgotten in accounts of Italian journeys, and is replaced by the discreditable exaggerations of lackeys, and anecdotes from the lives of great painters. Writers totally neglect the way the Italian people look for happiness in everyday life, and their social habits which are so unlike our own (Wakefield, p. 124).

In Stendhal's view this knowledge was not incompatible with the 'anecdotes sur les grands peintres' which he includes in his *Histoire*, but it is worth noting that he describes its acquisition as difficult. He goes on to praise de Brosses for the way in which he simultaneously acquires the even more elusive knowledge of the *moeurs* of the world that he left behind: 'Il peint les mœurs d'Italie, et *par contre-coup* celles de France'

(p. 267, my italics). It is by going outside his own world and discovering another that de Brosses gains access to truths about his own.

The logic of this *contre-coup* means that to know your own world you have to leave it, and leave it to the extent (which Stendhal marvels at in de Brosses, but which is crucial to his own value-system) of being able to appreciate things which lie well beyond its habitual mental and emotional ken:

> une chose incroyable, miraculeuse, à laquelle je ne trouve aucune explication raisonnable, c'est comment un Français de 1739, contemporain de MM. Vanloo, Coypel, Restout, Pierre, etc., etc., contemporain de Voltaire, . . . a pu comprendre non seulement Raphaël et le Dominiquin, que la France ne devait juger dignes de son attention que quarante ans plus tard, mais même le Corrège, de nos jours encore inconnu. Je ne serais pas éloigné de croire qu'en ce genre M. de Brosses avait du génie (p. 269).

> The really incredible, amazing thing is (and I can find no satisfactory explanation for it) that a Frenchman of 1739, the contemporary of MM. Vanloo, Coypel, Restout, Pierre and Voltaire, . . . should have understood not only Raphael and Domenichino (who were not properly appreciated in France until forty years later), but even Correggio, who even today is still hardly known. I am inclined to think that in this matter M. de Brosses was something of a genius (Wakefield, p. 124).

This is a genius to which Stendhal constantly aspires and of which he would no doubt have liked the *Histoire de la peinture en Italie* to be taken as testimony.[23] Stendhal's engagement with painting is quite unlike that of Diderot, Baudelaire or Zola who, in writing about Greuze, Delacroix or Manet were remaining inside their native culture and amongst their own contemporaries. If painting was as essential to Stendhal as I have been suggesting, it was in the first instance precisely because his first serious encounter was with painting of another time (the Renaissance) and another place (Italy). As such, it demanded of him not only a physical but also a mental journey that took him, in every sense, far away from home.

And yet, in the way so characteristic of Stendhal's journeys, it enabled him to return to the point he had set out from: the quest for fifteenth-century Italian *mœurs* is the means whereby he also comes to understand the society of nineteenth-century France. The logic of the *contre-coup* brings both sets of cultural and ideological outlook into complementary focus. Understanding the past necessarily entails a comparison that brings an understanding of the present:

> Au quinzième siècle on était plus sensible; les convenances n'écrasaient pas la vie; on n'avait pas toujours *les grands maîtres à imiter*. La bêtise dans les lettres n'avait encore d'autre moyen de se déguiser que d'imiter

Pétrarque. Une politesse excessive n'avait pas éteint les passions. En tout il y avait moins de métier, et plus de naturel (I, p. 171, Stendhal's italics).

In the fifteenth century people felt things more keenly. Life was not stifled by etiquette, and the Old Masters were not always on hand to be copied. Stupidity among men of letters had no other disguise than to imitate Petrarch. Violent passions had not yet been extinguished by excessive politeness. Everything was less professional and more spontaneous (Wakefield, p. 44).

Renaissance Florence becomes intelligible in the light of – or rather, in contrast to – what it is not, namely Paris of the Restoration. The modern world provides the vantage-point from which to view the past, but then, retroactively, comes into focus when the past, in its turn, is used as a defamiliarizing perspective on it: 'les idées simples d'aujourd'hui alors eussent été surnaturelles' (II, p. 189). This strategy becomes so ingrained in Stendhal's thinking that when he turns his attention to the painting of Paris in the 1820s he constantly invokes other times and other places to provide a framework of reference for understanding the art of the here and now. There is first and foremost his self-presentation as a foreigner (the Prussian M. van Eube de Molkirk) where every remark about contemporary French society is implicitly given an external point of origin. But there are also constant allusions to the arts of the past. So, for example, in order to convey the achievement of Horace Vernet's portrait of the King, Stendhal compares his painting first with what he imagines Rembrandt might have made of the same subject, and then with a hypothetical version by Raphael (*Mélanges* III, pp. 79–80). Moreover, Stendhal even recommends this comparative strategy as part of the education of painters themselves: in the figure of the young Sigalon, he advises them to spend a year in Venice immersed in Italian paintings and the sensibilities of the Italian public.

This was the principle both of Stendhal's education as a novelist and of his practice as a writer of novels. The chronicler of contemporary France could arrive at the elusive knowledge of his own society only by leaving the time and the place to which it applied. As a novelist, Stendhal was a realist chiefly by virtue of being a comparatist. Balzac's realism, by contrast, is based upon an essentialism whose precept (by a nice symmetry) is ascribed to the painter Frenhofer in *Le chef d'œuvre inconnu*: 'persévér[er] jusqu'à ce que la nature en soit réduite à se monterer *toute nue et dans son véritable esprit*'.[24] Stendhal's parallel understanding of the worlds he depicts in his novels is arrived at by means of the principle of comparison, both explicit and implied. So, for instance, the provincial world of Verrières is viewed as if through the eyes of the Parisian tourist, and Paris through Julien's unsophisticated provincial gaze.[25] Nancy is played off against Paris (and vice versa) in *Lucien Leuwen*; and Rome was projected by Stendhal in his plan for the remainder of the novel as yet another comparative focus. And the Italy of *La Chartreuse* is constantly screened through a French perspective whose limits and mistaken assumptions it is one of the author's chief tasks to identify: already in the 'Avertissement' he announces in mock warning to the reader that 'les personnages étant italiens l'intéresseront [le lecteur] peut-être moins, les coeurs de ce pays-là diffèrent assez des cœurs francais' (p. 2).

This comparatist strategy is the principal means available to the novelist for gaining access to the social knowledge that makes his fictions the social chronicles that their status as mirror requires them to be. A hypothetical point of contrast very like the one between Vernet and Rembrandt/Raphael helps to particularize the form that passion takes in Franche-Comté:

> A Paris, la position de Julien envers Mme de Rênal eût été bien vite simplifiée; mais à Paris, l'amour est fils des romans. . . Les romans leur auraient tracé le rôle à jouer, montré le modèle à imiter; et ce modèle, tôt ou tard, et quoique sans nul plaisir, et peut-être en rechignant, la vanité eût forcé Julien à le suivre.

> In Paris Julien's position in relation to Mme de Rênal would have been quickly clarified; but in Paris, love is the child of novels. . . Novels would have outlined the roles they should play, shown them the model to imitate; and sooner or later, although with no enjoyment and perhaps with reluctance, vanity would have obliged Julien to follow it.

And equally, 'Dans une petite ville de l'Aveyron ou des Pyrénées, le moindre incident eût été rendu décisif par le feu du climat' (p. 36). This double comparison with Paris and the Aveyron enables Stendhal to identify what is particular about the way things happen 'sous nos cieux plus sombres', and allows him then to conclude that 'Tout va lentement, tout se fait peu à peu dans les provinces' (p. 37). Once identified, provincial love can, in its turn, offer an implied point of contrast which makes it possible for Stendhal to understand the Parisian love whose depiction he regarded as one of the major innovations of the novel: 'Cette peinture de l'amour parisien est absolument neuve. Il nous semble qu'on ne la trouve dans aucun livre.' And even here in the 'Projet d'un article sur *le Rouge et le noir*', comparative habits reassert themselves, for Stendhal immediately goes on to gloss the concept of Parisian love in relation to its provincial counterpart: 'Elle [cette peinture] fait un beau contraste avec l'amour vrai, simple, *ne se regardant pas soi-même* de Mme de Rênal. C'est l'*amour de tête* comparé à l'amour de cœur' (pp. 724–5, Stendhal's italics). The vocabulary of contrast ('un beau constraste') and comparison ('comparé avec') should by now speak for itself.

To sum up, then: whereas for Balzac the 'immense assemblage de figures, de passions et d'événements' required a perseverance that took the form of a study of 'les raisons ou la raison de ces effets sociaux',[26] Stendhal proceeds towards the same goal by comparing and constrasting different social worlds (just as here I am comparing and contrasting Balzac and Stendhal themselves). Where the two also differ is in the fantasies associated with their common goal. For if Balzac dreams of mastery, Stendhal ultimately dreams of escape. Balzac wishes to marshal all knowledge within the fictional schema of the *Comédie humaine*, and to encompass it under his authorial control. Stendhal, having understood the nature of the world he is living in, its lack of energy, its fearful desire to 'imiter les autres', its 'âmes glacées', wants nothing so much as release from it. While providing their readers with insight into a world which is otherwise too close and too familiar to be grasped, Stendhal's novels also offer the 'happy few' amongst them the means of escape from it. They do so both by describing other worlds (Italy, for example), and by inviting from the reader the autistic, asocial, wordless reverie that the visual arts occasioned for Stendhal himself. The existence of those arts inspired him with a desire for the knowledge that makes him one of the first and finest practitioners of what in the late twentieth century we have come to call cultural history; and yet they simultaneously opened up the possibility of deliverance from the orthodoxies of that culture which we now know as the *doxa*.

## Suggested Reading

Berthier, Philippe, *Stendhal et ses peintres italiens* (Geneva: Droz, 1977).

Bryson, Norman, *Tradition and Desire: From David to Delacroix* (Cambridge: Cambridge University Press, 1984)

Jefferson, Ann, *Reading Realism in Stendhal* (Cambridge: Cambridge University Press, 1988).

Pearson, Roger, *Stendhal's Violin: A Novelist and his Reader* (Oxford: Clarendon Press, 1988).

Wakefield, David, *Stendhal and the Arts* (London: Phaidon, 1973).

# 13

## Victor Hugo, somnambulist of the sea

### Roger Cardinal

Tout est intraduisible.
Henri Michaux,
*Connaissance par les gouffres*

Sometimes a picture arises as an afterthought to a text, amplifying a verbal description and blazing an optical trail towards fresh horizons of meaning. Sometimes a picture comes first, so that when writing takes up the running it starts as no more than a gloss on the image, though it may later produce developments so far-reaching as to make the visual source redundant. The creative genius of Victor Hugo gave rise to a prolix literary œuvre, accompanied by a less known yet scarcely less fertile graphic production, beginning with casual travel sketches in the 1830s and climaxing in the visionary seascapes of the 1850s and 1860s. As one of the foremost exponents of dual-media invention, Hugo uses drawing as a complement to verbal composition, the reciprocity of text and image inhering in a complex cross-play of cues and stimuli. What makes the work across the two media so consistent is their parallel preoccupation with key themes and obsessions, above all Hugo's mythic conception of the artist as an oracular, visionary genius. This chapter seeks to throw light on the macrocosm of Hugo's output during the years he spent in exile on Jersey and Guernsey in the Channel Islands, and proposes a microcosmic focus upon a single emblematic drawing, *Le Bateau-vision* (fig. 23).

The inescapable dominant in Hugo's imagination during these years is the proximity of the surrounding sea. What I am tempted to call his 'oceanic fixation' nourished ways of seeing and imagining which inform his prose works, his verse and his pictures, and give rise to a veritable 'oceanic style' capable of treating *with poetic intensity* anything from the factual detail of a ship's rigging to the most abstruse metaphysical

23.   Victor Hugo, *Le Bateau-vision*, ink and wash drawing, for MS of *Les Travailleurs de la mer, c.* 1865–6 (Bibliothèque Nationale, Paris)

speculations about infinity. Impelled by what some might call megalomania, Hugo elected himself on to a mythic panel of creative geniuses like Aeschylus, Michelangelo, Dante and Shakespeare, those titanic 'hommes océans', of whom Hugo declares that 'c'est la même chose de regarder ces âmes ou de regarder l'océan.'[1]

Now, it can be argued that Hugo's oceanic fixation was in fact a later and more convincing variation of what began as the wilful construction of a 'mythologie de l'exil'.[2] When Hugo first set foot on Jersey in August 1852, he was still gripped by frustration and fury at the coup d'état of the man he had sarcastically dubbed 'Napoléon-le-Petit' (i.e. the self-proclaimed Emperor Napoléon III). The early writings on the island – notably the poems of *Les Châtiments* – teem with angry thoughts about events on the mainland. The writer's bruised persona prompts an operatic truculence of tone, evidenced in the way that, on first reaching port, he feels compelled to redefine the site, privileging disgust over charm so as to launch a self-serving comparison: 'Apparition de Jersey. Cette île charmante, boisée, . . . cet Eden nous apparaît sous la forme d'un monceau de roches arides, et calcinées. . . . *Saint-Hélier ressemble furieusement à Sainte-Hélène'* ('Jersey comes into sight. This charming wooded island, . . . this Eden, appears in the shape of a pile of arid, burnt-out rocks. . . *Saint-Helier looks horrifyingly like Saint Helena'*).[3]

Hugo's self-aggrandizing identification with the exiled first emperor would lapse, once the poet's attention to a mainland audience gave way to more alluring spiritual preoccupations. In an intriguing process of conversion, Hugo steps out of the role of political dissident, and indeed steps outside history, to take on the mantle of the seer or magus, an exceptional person in league with the Eternal and the Infinite. When selecting an earlier and untitled poem for inclusion in 'Au Bord de l'infini', the last sequence of *Les Contemplations,* Hugo deliberately added a more recent date so as to link it to his first visit to the island of Sark in July 1853. The gesture confirms that henceforth Hugo is no longer asking to be compared to Napoleon on Saint Helena but to St. John the Divine, the visionary author of the Biblical *Revelation,* speaking on the isle of Patmos:

> Ecoutez. Je suis Jean. J'ai vu des choses sombres.
> J'ai vu l'ombre infinie où se perdent les nombres,
> J'ai vu les visions que les réprouvés font,
> Les engloutissements de l'abîme sans fond;
> J'ai vu le ciel, l'éther, le chaos et l'espace.
>
> (OC, IX/1, 305)

The poet's recourse to pluralized abstractions, so typical of what I am calling Hugo's oceanic style, reflects an impulse to articulate the incommensurable, to clutch at metaphysical truths hovering beyond material reach. We shall see that the vatic writer, in describing for his audience the apocalyptic chaos of the Infinite, is obliged to use terms which are more and more abstract, less and less tied to the sense of the *visible.* The trend is signalled here in the symptomatic word *'abîme',* the abyss, a key item in a Hugolian lexical cluster of near-cognates – 'gouffre', 'océan', 'ombre', 'nuit', 'mystère', 'infini' and the like – all of which seem to be hurling out of the material and into the metaphysical dimension. It is worth noting that for a long time Hugo's working title for the novel *Les Travailleurs de la mer* was indeed *L'Abîme.*

Hugo's imaginative investment in the supernatural and the occult was reflected in the assiduity of his mediumistic experiments of 1853–5, known as the *Tables parlantes,* in which, taking up the practices of spiritualism, he led a small group of friends on impassioned sorties into the spirit realm, eventually communicating with great writers from the past and even conducting seminars on cosmology with them![4] Although, for various reasons, the séances lapsed when Hugo moved to Guernsey in October 1855, I suggest that there was no loss of momentum in

211

Hugo's project regarding the occult, which was now simply refocused, insofar as the séances were replaced by compulsive meditations upon the sea – that ultimate *abîme* and infinitely versatile symbol of 'l'obscur, l'inconnu, l'invisible' (OC, IX/1, 337). Writing to a friend in Brussels in April 1856, Hugo allows his imagination full rein as he brags about the working room – his 'look-out' – which he has established at the top of his new home, Hauteville House, high above the harbour of St Peter Port. His words ring out as the expression of a self-acclaimed oceanic genius:

> Je vis dans une solitude splendide, comme perché à la pointe d'une roche, ayant toutes les grandes écumes des vagues et toutes les grandes nuées du ciel sous ma fenêtre. J'habite dans cet immense rêve de l'océan, je deviens peu à peu un somnambule de la mer, et, devant tous ces prodigieux spectacles et toute cette énorme pensée vivante où je m'abîme, je finis par ne plus être qu'une espèce de témoin de Dieu. Il y a toujours sur ma strophe ou sur ma page un peu de l'ombre du nuage et de la salive de la mer, ma pensée flotte et va et vient, comme dénouée par toute cette gigantesque oscillation de l'infini.

> I am living in solitary splendour, as if perched upon a jutting rock, with all the great spume of the waves and all the great clouds of the sky beneath my window. I inhabit this vast oceanic dream; bit by bit I am turning into a somnambulist of the sea, and, faced by all these wondrous spectacles and this whole massive body of thought into which I plunge, I end up becoming nothing less than a kind of witness to the deity. There is always some trace of the cloud's shadow and the sea's saliva upon my verse or my page, my thoughts float and come and go, as if set loose by this whole gigantic oscillation of the Infinite.[5]

Solitude, the uninterrupted panorama of sea and sky, the confrontation with the divine and those mighty oscillations which signal cosmic flux, all these programmatic features turn the text into a kind of visionary manifesto, reminiscent of Rimbaud's 'Lettre du voyant', wherein the seer poet outlines his credentials. Access to the mysteries is gained via the tangy immediacy of real sea-spray and winds, yet is corroborated by dreams and sleepwalking, with their connotations of entrancement and hallucination. Indeed, Hugolian oceanic somnambulism is not so different from Rimbaldian *voyance* in that Hugo seems now to find literal perception modulating into reverie or fantasy: the material look-out on Hauteville House becomes a window on to perspectives which are conjectural or symbolic.

I mentioned earlier Hugo's fascination with the model of oceanic genius as incarnated in Shakespeare, in whose honour he penned the rhapsodic *William Shakespeare* in 1863. Soon after, this model was to be complemented and even superseded in the curious figure of Gilliatt, hero of *Les Travailleurs de la mer*. If the factual reality of Shakespeare had at all inhibited Hugo's fantasizing, the fictional characterization now allowed him utter freedom. Gilliatt becomes the Hugolian superman, a giant of enormous physical strength and resourcefulness, 'un homme de mer surprenant' (OC, XXI/1, 567) who steers his longboat through turbulent straits, single-handedly recovers the engine from the shipwrecked steamer *La Durande*, and defeats a fearsome octopus in a fight to the death. Furthermore, Gilliatt is gifted with second sight, and has the clairvoyant capacity to stare out from the 'promontory of sleep' and penetrate 'tout ce mystère que nous appelons le songe et qui n'est autre chose que l'approche d'une réalité invisible' (OC, XII/1, 570).

Moreover, once we learn to follow Hugo's metaphysical logic and to accept his argument from the entranced essay 'Contemplation suprême' that 'c'est au dedans de soi qu'il faut regarder le dehors' (OC, XII/1, 112), we can appreciate the symbolic import of Gilliatt's adventures. His spectacular exploits form a dream allegory in which the apocalyptic confrontation with natural forces represents an initiation into supernatural and spiritual powers. Thus it is that, by invoking what is essentially a Romantic thesis about the coincidence of outer and inner reality, Hugo is able persuasively to ground the equivalence of the ocean and the human sensibility as his metaphoric paradigm. Within the transcendent perspectives of 'contemplation suprême', each mirrors the other, so that Hugolian vision accustoms itself to darting to and fro across the dual network that meshes what is concrete and real with what is abstract and imaginary:

> Le labyrinthe de l'immanence universelle a un réseau double, l'abstrait, le concret; mais ce réseau double est en perpétuelle transfusion; l'abstraction se concrète, la réalité s'abstrait, le palpable devient invisible, l'invisible devient palpable.

> The labyrinth of universal immanence comprises a dual network, the abstract and the concrete; but this dual network is in a state of perpetual transfusion; abstraction concretizes itself, reality abstracts itself, the tangible becomes invisible, the invisible becomes tangible.
> (OC, XII, 1, 120)

It should not be forgotten that there is also a context of concrete daily experience which enframes Hugo's entranced artistry. Of his physical activities, we may pass over his notorious sexual athleticism, yet emphasize his resourceful efforts to explore his surroundings. He made boat trips to local islands, such as Sark, where in 1859 he first set eyes on an octopus, took note of its local name 'devil-fish', and began sketches that would eventuate in *Les Travailleurs de la mer*. On Guernsey itself, he visited archaic sites like the dolmen at Rozel, where he situates his encounter with the spectre in the poem 'Ce que dit la Bouche d'ombre'; he climbed the cliffs, walked along the shoreline with its surrealistic rocks, swam regularly in a cove. These actions take on metaphysical colour once juxtaposed with his ceaseless experience of occult phenomena, including nocturnal rappings and murmurings, ghost sightings, premonitory dreams and the like, many associated with local superstitions (Hauteville House itself was said to be haunted). Hugo's predilection for things spectral can of course be dated back to the trauma of his daughter's death by drowning in 1843; but the sombre tonality of the exile years seems to have been particularly enhanced by news of the deaths of several friends, the hanging of a local criminal in 1854, and Hugo's own very serious illness in 1858.

As regards his writing, Hugo had settled into the prolix routines of the compulsive word-spinner, producing a whole cycle of closely related texts. These years saw the completion of the haunted poems of 'Au bord de l'infini'; of the extravagant monograph *William Shakespeare*; and of a set of visionary essays or metaphysical treatises – Hugo's own *Revelation*, as it were – which include 'Philosophie, commencement d'un livre' (in 1860), 'Promontorium somnii' (in 1863), 'Les Choses de l'infini' (in 1864) and 'Contemplation suprême' (in 1863–4). Finally there was the novel *Les Travailleurs de la mer*, begun on Guernsey in June 1864 and completed seven months later.

Though variable in length and genre, these texts are of a piece in that each is informed by the same model of the creative subject. Whether voiced in the first person singular or in impersonal terms, each work in the cycle transcribes the same expressive outpourings of the entranced 'somnambulist of the sea', the vatic seer who mediates the oceanic voice of the *bouche d'ombre*.[6] These writings are, moreover, contemporaneous with a sequence of ink-drawings, ranging from more or less realistic sketches of local sites or artifacts to spectacular visionary set-pieces in which Hugo demonstrates his mastery as an 'iconographer of darkness'.[7] In my view, this secondary medium of graphic expression was entirely consonant with the literary one which was Hugo's overt forte.

Obviously, a claim for the consanguinity of *all* Hugo's textual and graphic impulses across the exile years cannot be substantiated in a chapter as brief as this. My strategy is therefore to isolate one telling example – the marvellous image of *Le Bateau-vision* – and to appraise its relevance to the text with which it was originally associated, namely *Les Travailleurs de la mer*. Equally I shall bear in mind the wider context of Hugolian graphic and literary production in the period. Baldly put, my case is that the pictorial and the scriptural impulses in Hugo have an almost symbiotic affinity, such that one can shift from one medium to the other and find an uninterrupted continuity of focus. I can only hope that my necessarily selective account will throw some light on Hugo's general habits as a practitioner of the 'art of interference'.[8]

An irresistible reason for considering image/text relations in connection with *Les Travailleurs de la mer* is that it was almost unique among Hugo's manuscripts in comprising original drawings by its author. However, it must at once be pointed out that, contrary to the assumptions of some commentators,[9] Hugo did not improvise these drawings upon the same page as the handwritten text, nor in the margins thereof. (It is true that other Hugo manuscripts do exhibit doodles and marginalia.) Instead, the three dozen images were independently composed, on separate occasions and on different sizes and types of paper; they were carefully pasted on to single sheets which were bound in with the manuscript in May 1866, once it had came back from the publisher in Brussels. There is no doubt that Hugo had accumulated a full stock of drawings by the time he undertook this selection, so that it would be wrong to consider the images as 'illustrations' on the same footing as the engravings by other hands which began to appear in editions of the novel a few years later.

In his facsimile album of the *Travailleurs* drawings, Pierre Georgel reproduces some of these engravings, by contemporary illustrators such as F.N. Chifflart, who prepared the 1869 Hetzel edition, and Daniel Vierge, who worked on the 1876 edition for the Librairie illustrée. Typically, both these engravers like to pinpoint a specific moment in the plot, using a quotation from the text (e.g. 'Le vent soufflait en foudre', or 'Son poing armé s'abattit sur la bête') as an unequivocal anchorage for the image. Two subsequent editions, the Album Méaulle and the Hugues edition, both of 1882, exploit a range of pictorial sources, including Hugo's own drawings, even though many of these last had never been designated by Hugo as belonging to the book. Even so, each engraving is crisply captioned and tied to a specific narrative moment, so that the image always 'mimes' the text rather than speaking independently.[10]

Conversely, Hugo's thirty-six originals contain few clues sharp enough to justify pinning them to specific contexts, and their placement in the manuscript is often so puzzling as to seem haphazard. (As it happens, nearly all the intercalated sheets occur early in the book, well before the maritime adventures of the last sections. Were there any reasoning to these placements, it would have to be that Hugo wanted not to distract the putative reader from the pleasure of visualizing these last independently.) The inference must be that Hugo was not really bothered about *illustrating the plot*, especially when we consider that he had at his disposal several excellent drawings with indisputable links with the novel which he simply ignored.

While conceding that statistics are hardly relevant to an appreciation of the actual visual *impact* of the images, we may note that about a third of the items Hugo chose are caricatures of figures, whether of protagonists like Gilliatt or the villainous Sieur Clubin, or of creatures of legend, such as the sinister-jovial Roi des Auxcriniers, a demonic invention of the artist. About a quarter of the images are of named locations on land, but are more atmospheric than veristic, old Saint Malo, for instance, being shown to be crammed with grotesque architecture. One drawing is a fairly naturalistic representation of the prow of the *Durande*, with its female figurehead. A couple of drawings conjure up aquatic archetypes: the lone seagull, the malefic octopus.[11] In fact, slightly less than half the *Travailleurs* drawings are unequivocal *marines*, although these are surely the most striking in the set. They range from tranquil seascapes, tamely punctuated with steamboats and sailboats, to those devastating tableaux of oceanic turmoil and shipwreck which, in my view, open up a most eloquent dialogue with the oceanic discourse of the novel.

The drawing I reproduce here as my focal specimen was in fact untitled by its author, who stuck it into the manuscript at a fairly random point midway through Part One. (The chapter in question, 'Chance qu'ont eue ces naufragés de rencontrer ce sloop', contains a deliberately off-hand mention of a shipwrecked crew in a longboat, but says nothing about the wreck itself). In its later engraved versions, the image acquired the titles *Tempête. – La dernière lutte* (Méaulle) and *Le Bateau-vision* (Hugues). Pierre Georgel's scruples don't allow him to do more than identify it by the cautiously bracketed formula (*Voilier dans la tempête*), but I propose to follow the lead of Gaëtan Picon and others and to use the evocative *Le Bateau-vision* of the Eugène Hugues edition, which I feel quite appropriate to the pictorial impact.[12]

My chosen image depicts a huge unfurling wave and the hull of a listing ship, with yard-arm and broken-off mast. A clutch of tight black forms silhouetted at the hull's edge could suggest a group of human figures stretching out imploring arms, somewhat as in Delacroix's *Naufrage de Don Juan*, or, as Pierre Georgel hints, Géricault's *Le Radeau de la Méduse*. But I am not entirely convinced that there *are* human figures on board, nor that the Géricault allusion, with its humanly heroic resonances, entirely befits the transcendent mood of the Hugolian scene. Rather than an evocation of any particular disaster in the book, this is a *generic* image of oceanic immensity and power, an apocalyptic vision wherein the minimal allusion to the shape of a stricken vessel serves almost as an ideogram signalling the awesome power of the waves. If ship there is, it is truly a 'vision-ship', the object of a haggard glimpse, a hallucination, a stimulus to non-literal visualization. The waters of the sea are themselves rendered in urgent and emotive strokes. Thick hatching hastily assembled in rough triangles is a shorthand for heavy seas;

216

smudges, spatterings and a few capricious squigglings suggest foam and spume blown in the gale; while dark, swerving lines create a persuasive suggestion of the dynamism of unfurling waves.

Whereas some of Hugo's drawings exhibit a certain finicky naturalism, it doesn't look as if there is much concern here with the true appearances of waves. Rather, using the sign-system at his disposal, Hugo aims to evoke the elements in their capacity to stretch and indeed outstretch the visual imagination. His oceanic tempest is offered to us in, so to speak, its transfigurative moment. While we may recognize 'a sailboat in a storm', the drawing does not aim at realism. Rather it enacts a typical rhetorical gesture of spontaneous symbolization, catching the given and the known at a climax of intensified hyperbole, in that moment of excess when they strain to become something above and beyond themselves. This, I would therefore argue, is really the graphic rendering of an *intuition,* the equivalent of some of Hugo's oracular aphorisms of the type 'Voir le dedans de la mer, c'est voir l'imagination de l'Inconnu' (OC, XII/1, 636). As such, it is nurtured by the same order of metaphysical obsession as the novel, without being reducible to a simple translation thereof.

A secondary, comparatist strategy for appreciating this image is to correlate it with other drawings on similar themes, such as the magnificent *La Durande en pleine vapeur,* with its steamboat advancing through a heavy swell; or F. Méaulle's version of a lost Hugo original, captioned *Sous le flot,* in which heavy seas are about to engulf a foundering ship with a broken mast.[13] Such correlations point towards a recognizable story line which, as it happens, fails to fit the text proper, given that the *Durande* doesn't capsize at sea but is driven on to the Rochers Douvres.

The most telling comparison must surely be with the notorious *Ma Destinée,* a drawing made some seven years before the composition of *Les Travailleurs.*[14] Here Hugo depicts an even more gigantic wave, with the outline of a ship hovering above. This time he provides an explicit symbolic cue in a caption scrawled in capital letters. 'MA DESTINÉE' expresses Hugo's megalomania at its most unabashed, and it may not matter very much whether we take the poet to be saying that his destiny is like that of the ship – of which it is in any case impossible to tell if it is foundering or, alternatively, triumphing over the worst of the storm – or whether we take the wave, with its hollow, horn-like shape suggesting the blaring and howling of the abyss, to be a symbolic equivalent to the vatic voice, the 'mouth of darkness'. For this is above all an image of transcendent power and unearthly sonority, and as such a non-literal emblem of oceanic genius. In this respect I suggest that it transmits back on to *Le Bateau-vision* the deeper colouring of an intense, widening generalization. Ultimately I would see this last as a key image for Hugo, almost a genotype for the entire 'oceanic' cycle. It can stand for everything, even functioning as an indirect self-portrait insofar as, through it, Hugo can persuade us that he is indeed 'l'homme farouche/Ivre d'ombre et d'immensité' (OC, IX/1, 341), the superhuman magus haunted by an abyss which is both internal and external, 'l'immensité qui n'est qu'un œil sublime' (OC, IX/1, 320) – that shape-changing, plurivocal, intermittently communicative yet ultimately unfathomable ocean of artistic genius.

One lesson here is that a drawing can become more eloquent once it is freed of the narrow task of replicating a particular paragraph, and allowed to stand as an iconic proposition within the widest contextual frame. I see *Le Bateau-vision* as the site of an expressive intensity which guarantees its status, firstly, as an outstanding drawing in its own right, and, secondly, as an elective 'look-out' on to a whole cycle of visual and verbal variations. Once we draw back from the specifics of the seafaring yarn, shifting focus from microcosm to macrocosm, we begin to follow an interpretative trail which I think is consistent both with the patterns of Hugo's metaphysics, and with his artistic instincts. The implication is that Hugo used drawings as a great reservoir of metaphoric and metamorphic ideas: perhaps their incidental function was to serve as prompts whenever he needed to sort out the scenery or peripeteia of his narrative; but their more important role was to articulate his boldest intuition, namely the oceanic matrix, conceived as the generative source of art itself.

Hugo's Romantic myth of the transformative, even transcendent ocean inspires many grandiose verse poems of the period, notably 'Horror' and 'Dolor'. But it is in his almost hallucinated, revelatory prose that he makes his boldest attempts to verbalize the inspired conception of 'l'océan, ce grand lyrique'.[15] The hieratic 'Philosophie' contains a long enumeration of the latent contents of the oceanic depths, and defends the equation ocean=poetic imagination by arguing that each possesses the same transfigurative propensity to suck all phenomena into its orbit and to align them in interlinked chains of analogy: 'Analogies vertigineuses!' (OC, XII/1, 23). And in one of several chapters of *Les Travailleurs* where narrative is ousted by passages of oceanic reverie, Hugo praises the ocean as the ultimate poetic cornucopia:

> Il est le récipient universel, réservoir pour les fécondations, creuset pour les transformations. Il amasse, puis disperse; il accumule, puis ensemence; il dévore, puis crée. Il reçoit tous les égouts de la terre, et il les thésaurise. Il est solide dans la banquise, liquide dans le flot, fluide dans l'effluve. Comme matière il est masse, et comme force il est abstraction.

> It is the container for all things, a storehouse for fecundations, a crucible

for transformations. It gathers, then disperses; it accumulates, then spreads it seed; it devours, then creates. Into it all the sewers of the globe flow, and are hoarded up. As iceberg it is solid, as wave it is liquid, as exhalation it is fluid. As matter it becomes mass, while as energy it becomes abstraction.
(OC, XII/1, 677).

Here we see Hugo's obsession with oceanic fluency impelling him to speculate not just on the capacity of water to represent any given *thing*, but to articulate impalpable ideas. The ocean-as-imagination may startle us with its hallucinatory tropes: but there is something even more stunning in its momentum towards an ultimate immateriality. For, having once approached the ocean in the spirit of what Gaston Bachelard would term a 'rêverie en profondeur', Hugo is swept beyond configurations which can still be visualized and into a kind of blind abstraction.

In 'La Mer et le vent', an appendix to *Les Travailleurs de la mer* of which it may truly be claimed that it fulfils the promise of being drenched in 'the sea's saliva', the poet further raises his stakes, forcing his gaze to focus at its widest upon the elective topos. So much so that the ocean is envisaged no longer as simply the crucible of fertile analogy, but as the mechanism of ultimate abstraction. The rhetoric of excess shifts into the register of mathematics, raising to a higher power those 'figures' of poetic value which are now revealed to be abstract numbers:

Les apparences marines sont fugaces à tel point que, pour qui l'observe longtemps, l'aspect de la mer devient purement métaphysique: cette brutalité dégénère en abstraction. C'est une quantité qui se décompose et se recompose. Cette quantité est dilatable: l'infini y tient. Le calcul est, comme la mer, un ondoiement sans arrêt possible. . . . Rien, comme la vue de l'eau, ne donne la vision des nombres.

Marine appearances are so volatile that, if one studies the sea for long periods, its aspect becomes purely metaphysical: brute force degenerates into abstraction. It is a quantity which is broken down and then reconstituted. This quantity can be extended to encompass the infinite. Calculation, just like the sea, is an undulating motion which never falters. . . . Nothing makes us visualize numbers more than the sight of water.
(OC, XII/1, 807)

It is as if, in such passages, we were ourselves witness to the quasi-divine meditations of a disembodied mind. Image by image, phrase by phrase, the Hugolian imagination tries out its elemental equations, tirelessly pressing at its own horizons. Mind is ocean, ocean is mind; it is all infinite, it subsumes everything, and each time we advance, yet another horizon opens up. We are in a transphysical space which is finally un-fathomable:

> Au delà du visible, l'invisible, au delà de l'invisible l'inconnu.
>     Partout, toujours, au zénith, au nadir, en avant, en arrière, au-dessus, au-dessous, en haut, en bas, le formidable Infini noir.

> Beyond the visible lies the invisible, beyond the invisible, the unknown.
>     Everywhere, forever, at the zenith, at the nadir, in front, behind, above, below, on high, deep down, lies the Infinite in all its formidable blackness.
> (OC, XII/1, 108)

Given his oceanic fixation upon depths and distances which defy mortal visualization, it is not surprising that the somnambulistic poet should sometimes stumble, now lapsing into poetic kitsch (how often does Hugo rhyme 'ombre' with 'sombre'?), now into graphic cliché (the chiaroscuro effect). The articulation of a sublime focal point, infinitely distant, at which all things will be resolved within a single titanic abstraction is an enterprise which human resource can only really expect to tackle in the mode of self-reflexive failure. Perhaps Mallarmé's more elided variations on the shipwreck theme represent the next step towards articulating 'les choses de l'infini'.

I take it that Hugo's quest was always for some higher image or mythic configuration that would bind together all the teeming analogical facets of his vision into a single and irrefutable Revelation. To the extent that such a final image might open onto metaphysical abstraction, to the extent that, for mortals, blindness is necessarily attendant upon the hubris of 'contemplation suprême', it fell more to Hugo in his capacity as *writer* to grapple with these giddy themes, given that the idiom of high Romanticism offered at least a stock of reliable tropes for hinting at the unsayable. What Hugo lacked was any real precedent for the iconography of darkness, any conventional devices for figuring the abstract. As a nineteenth-century artist, he remains somewhat in thrall to visible objects, even though (anticipating Redon and Moreau, and beyond them the abstract painters of the next century) he often angled his pen beyond the horizon of the ascertainable.[16]

This is why the drawings, taken as a whole, fall short of the prose in rendering 'le formidable Infini noir', although we may salute *Le Bateau-vision* as at least one valiant attempt to slip the anchor of the visible and to sail, across intense ink and swirling sepia, towards that creative abyss into which mortal eyes can only gaze, as through a glass, darkly.

## Suggested Reading

Blondel, Madeleine, and Georgel, Pierre (eds), *Victor Hugo et les images* (Dijon: Ville de Dijon, 1989).

Georgel, Pierre, *Les Dessins de Victor Hugo pour les Travailleurs de la mer* (Paris: Herscher, 1985).

Picon, Gaëtan, 'Le Soleil d'encre', in *Victor Hugo dessinateur* (Paris: Editions du Minotaure, 1963), pp. 9–26.

Thompson, C.W., Victor Hugo and the Graphic Arts (Geneva: Droz, 1970).

# 14

# *Avatars of the artist: narrative approaches to the work of the painter*

## Patrick O'Donovan

The work of the painter is, among other things, a source of stories. Questions that paintings themselves might be thought to eclipse – the circumstances of their composition, their reception, their place in the culture in which they are produced, the legitimacy of their claims to prestige in the tradition of picture-making – become the object, stated or implicit, of stories that take the painter and his work as their matter. I shall be concerned here with such stories as they are mediated in paintings of the painter, on the one hand, and in a small corpus of texts, on the other, made up mainly of works by Balzac, Zola, and by the Goncourt brothers. Paintings of the painter, which proliferate from the late eighteenth century onwards, have a large role to play in moulding contemporary conceptions of the artist.[1]

In the literary texts, equally, the work of the painter manifests itself as a narrative subject matter of some potency – and of some scope, for many of these stories are also the occasion of striking aesthetic speculations. It is apprehended above all as a process of transformation: in figurative art, the painter effects a transformation of his model or of the subject before him; his work is an agent of transformation, affecting habits of vision, canons of taste, perhaps social attitudes also; he is himself the object of a process of transformation, sometimes unwittingly so. It is above all the imaginary charge of the figure of the painter that triggers a kind of fabulation centred on the artistic process, on its compulsion and its perils: the narrative self-absorption of these works is such that they might be said in the final analysis to keep painting at a distance. One question that might then be said to confront us is this: how readily can the work of the painter be apprehended as anything other than a source of legends?

To such a question, an immediate response might well be made: the painter figures as the hero, so to speak, of countless stories which tend precisely to mythologize his creative role in making pictures. The painter

Zeuxis, the legendary figure who contrived to paint grapes so compelling that birds flew down to eat them, is a case in point.[2] I shall now briefly comment on a painting that exploits a narrative in which he figures, François-André Vincent's *Zeuxis choisissant pour modèles les plus belles filles de Crotone*, first exhibited in the Salon de l'Académie of 1789 and now in the Louvre.

The background to the scene that Vincent depicts is well known. Zeuxis has embarked on a painting of Helen of Troy for the temple of the city of Crotona; here the temple is presented in archaeologically precise detail. In order to paint her, Zeuxis must rely on more than one model, for no single woman can match his ideal conception of the beauty of the figure. The creative process of which he is the master is manifestly of great consequence, but remains nonetheless somewhat enigmatic. In Vincent's painting, we do not see Zeuxis at work at his canvas, which stands facing the artist in the centre of the composition, outside the temple, but on which we see only an outline. Rather, the painter is seated, viewing a young woman divested of most of her clothes who is brought before him; another such figure is being led away to the right, weeping, while Zeuxis's hand is held out in a gesture of admiration as he gazes on the woman offering herself for his appraisal. What are we to infer from this scene? That Zeuxis's response and, in turn, his painting are informed by an idea of beauty that surpasses nature. The outline on the canvas points the way to the accomplishment of the ideal. Vincent's painting depends for its meaning on the fact that stories do attach to the painter: the power of this story lies in its invitation to imagine the yet more exquisite form of the still unmodelled figure of Helen.

Vincent's painting pinpoints a number of the issues with which I shall be concerned: the work of the painter; his relationship with his models; the prestige of ideal classical prototypes. I shall be concerned perhaps most importantly with the ambiguity of beauty – part sacred, part erotic, part substance, part image – as it figures in painting and in stories about painting. Robert Rosenblum has wittily spoken of this work as an illustration of the 'Neoclassic Erotic': he points to Vincent's use of a certain neoclassical erudition to ennoble its straightforward eroticism, and concludes that the painting 'offers, in the most seductive guise, a pictorial demonstration of Neoclassic idealist art theory'.[3] Vincent's painting of the myth of Zeuxis, perhaps because it accords greater prominence by far to the semi-naked model than to Helen, represents in the final analysis a vulgar version of the concept of the *beau idéal*: ideal beauty is not to be found in real models, but in a 'réunion de beautés éparses', a superior assemblage of elements of the imperfect real determined according to the artist's acquired expertise. This notion is nothing other than a commonplace of traditionalist aesthetics and its influence is to be discerned in authoritative sources from the time of the Renaissance onwards: 'I know that our art consists first and foremost in the imitation of nature but then, since it cannot reach such heights unaided, in the imitation of the most accomplished artists'.[4] So seemingly transparent a precept becomes perhaps the most fertile source of myth.[5]

The complexity of understanding not merely the products of the artistic process, but the process itself, is not necessarily mitigated by the production of theory. The claim to universality implicit in academic writing on art becomes, in the latter part of the century, the object of derision.[6] The figure of Pellerin, the painter in Flaubert's *L'Education sentimentale*, points to the perverse effects of theoretical obsession: in order to discover 'la véritable théorie du Beau', Pellerin reads every aesthetic treatise that he can find, confident that this is the way to achieve distinction.[7] But the serpentine path he follows leads only to sterility and indecision. We shall see in considering the Goncourts, for instance, that the prestige of the ideal is the most specific sign of the diminished authority of received theory and of the imminent decadence of art itself.

The radical questions that I mentioned at the outset confront us all the more powerfully: What are the prospects for painting in the modern world? How are we to apprehend the mechanism that brings painting into being? Vincent's painting points to one further response. In this painting, as in another we shall consider in a moment, desire functions as a barely dissimulated emblem of artistic activity. Notwithstanding gestures towards classical erudition in the decor of the painting, the model who stands before the painter is an object of erotic interest. This is the inference to be drawn from Rosenblum's discussion of the painting: the programmatic leaning of this work towards elevation and severity of taste is not without a distinct element of paradox. It is as if the prestige of the canon becomes in part a matter of the desire it arouses. The use of desire to construct an image of the work of the artist becomes an indispensable element of stories of the painter in the nineteenth century. The potentially conflictive conjunction of perfection and of desire imbues the concept of beauty with a measure of ambivalence that comes to characterize it more and more specifically.

A figure who serves, for much of the nineteenth century, to bring these strands of reflection together is Raphael. I should immediately make it clear that I refer here to a mythical Raphael, virtually divorced from the historical figure of the painter. Raphael becomes a mediator between the body and art, and his work infuses each of these poles with something of the sublimeness of the other. Thus, in characterizing the heroine of *La Maison du chat-qui-pelote*, Balzac invokes the grace and the tranquillity of that painter's proverbial compositions.[8] The figure invoked by Balzac is not the paragon of humanist endeavour, the secular creator who stands beyond the reach of propriety and convention;[9] for Balzac as for

24. Jean-Auguste-Dominique Ingres, *Raphaël et la Fornarina, c.* 1814 (Fogg Museum, Harvard University Art Museums)

25. Gustave Courbet, *L'Atelier du peintre*, 1855 (Musée d'Orsay, Paris)

others, Raphael is an artificer, whose art supplants the real. In Raphael's case the boundary between art and the real becomes confused: life is a supplement to the artistic process; La Fornarina, as we shall see, is his mistress as well as his model. The painter stands at once as subject and as object: he is the subject of painting, but, as misogynistic versions of his story tend to suggest, the object of an interpersonal process that culminates in his destruction. Something of the enigmatic charge evoked by the painter can be gauged from Ingres's famous painting of 1814, *Raphaël et la Fornarina* (fig. 24). Perhaps more pointedly than Vincent's painting, this work confronts us with the equivocal standing of the painter and of the relationship between the model and her image.

Ingres's painting is certainly striking. Here we see the painter entwined with La Fornarina, his sole model, who is fully clothed and appears before us, her viewers, as a figure in herself of some interest: she, rather than her portrait, dominates the centre of the painting. This is, first and foremost, an image of disjunction, of divided interest. The painter closely embraces his model, who sits, it appears, on the arm of a chair next to him, and yet he looks away: his head is turned away and he looks towards his still unfinished image of her. Further tensions characterize the painting. The figure in the portrait is semi-naked, and, while the woman herself is clothed, the painter holds his brush, tipped in red, in his hand; he is poised to return to his work. She, by contrast, looks directly outwards; in fact, both the model and the unfinished image on the easel hold our gaze. The image of La Fornarina has a latent erotic interest, intimated by the closeness of the embrace between the two figures and by the directness of her look. The fact that she is clothed points to the hiatus between the woman and the portrait; for La Fornarina is the model for an ostensible painting of herself, rather than of another woman, real or ideal, and the fact that Ingres models his fictive canvas on what he took to be a portrait by Raphael merely adds piquancy to the task of determining what she stands for.[10]

The erotic aspect of the work is in tension with its painterly aspect. Like the painting by Vincent, it brings tradition to bear on its depiction of the work of the painter: the artist's tools are prominently displayed, a major picture in Raphael's canon, the *Madonna della sedia*, appears in the background. The artistic process is mediated with the help of prestigious signs. The association between this painting and those which it invokes casts the relationship to tradition as a relatively stable value: it is as if the picture claims to tell the true story of painting. Yet the painting of the Madonna is abruptly truncated: the frame of the portrait cuts obliquely across it, just as the frame of Ingres's own painting bisects the unfinished work on the easel. The formal device of the painting (or, in this case, the paintings) within the painting thus imparts a certain dynamism to the picture. The portrait used by Ingres as a model determines the composition of his image: the look with which La Fornarina engages us is dictated by the work on the easel. That fractured image projects our gaze back to the model, who glows in the light that permeates the foreground and that illuminates the main figures. The work is structured in such a way as to lead us to consider the transformative work of the painter. It is as if Ingres's painting harnesses the energy of the works (ostensibly by Raphael) that it uses as its models, only to displace these models with the image of the woman. He is, in a sense, merely playing with a commonplace, by evoking the notoriously uncanny quality of Raphael's figures, who appear almost to live and breathe.

Yet the process of painting remains an object of intense interest, as our attention, more vividly than in the case of Vincent's painting, oscillates between the image and the ostensible reality. In the clothed 'model', we come to discern the power of ideal images to give an edge to our apprehension not merely of the real, but of the fleshly. And because the painter holds in his hand a brush, some reference to the specificity of the process of painting is inescapable. Ingres uses the colour red as a version of Raphael's signature and as a means of indicating what *happens* in painting. The fresh red paint on the tip of the brush is the seeming key to the relationship between the diverse elements of the painting: the less-brilliant tint of the canvas on which the painter is working, the scarlet parts of the painter's own apparel which stand out so clearly from the darker garments and from the muted background, the fabric that covers the chair on which the model seemingly sits, and, perhaps most importantly, the faint red glow of her left cheek, the effect in part of the warm light which embraces the whole of the main group and the obliquely positioned canvas. The red in Ingres's painting gives a primacy to the model over her image and directs our interest towards the demands that flesh and painting alike make on our understanding.[11]

In Ingres's painting, the artist becomes an enigmatic figure, but the effects of his work are nonetheless purposive and make a powerful claim on our attention. Now the iconography of the artist in nineteenth-century painting is extremely rich. It is no more than a truism to say that a major part of what is explored in these paintings is the activity of painting itself. It is equally evident that a major function of these paintings is to allow the exploration of new perspectives on painting: thus such works lend themselves to radical reappraisals of the work of the painter and of his standing in the face of his own activity. Before returning to the painter-model relationship, it would be useful briefly to consider this latter question from a different perspective. Where in Ingres's painting, tradition and the canon are dominant points of reference, in certain later works a wider set of issues is explored: the social function of painting, its plasticity, as opposed to its dependence on tradition, the programmatic benefits of a break with the canon and of the

espousal of modernity. I can here invoke only one or two famous paint-
ings of the artist at work which illustrate these tendencies, works such as
Courbet's *L'Atelier* (1855, fig. 25), and Fantin-Latour's *Hommage à
Eug. Delacroix* (1864).

In the homage to Delacroix, the first of his programmatic group portraits, Fantin himself appears. This work seeks to establish the claims to
prestige of modern painting; for the individual painter, the expression of
creative solidarity results in a self-affirmation, leading in turn to a
changed, more critical, relation to received academic canons.[12] Courbet's *L'Atelier* belongs both to this nineteenth-century series of meditations on the condition of the artist and to a body of paintings by the
artist himself that is, as Michael Fried puts it, the effect of an existential
project 'powerfully expressive of having been made by an embodied
being engaged in a particular activity: the production of those very
paintings'.[13] It is in fact a landmark picture. Fried emphasizes a central
facet of the painting: 'the implied dissolution of the boundary between
the worlds of painting and painter-beholder', and deals in particular
with the central group of the artist at work on his landscape, the model,
and the small boy. He demonstrates how elements of the landscape, the
waterfall and the large tree to the right, flow into the figures of the
painter and of the model, such as to create a continuity *of painting* between all three elements of the whole canvas. The act of looking is what
is under scrutiny: the painter figures virtually as the painter-beholder *in*
the landscape painting, his status as an independent beholder of that picture being implicitly neutralized, by contrast with the boy, who
represents the painter as beholder *of* his work.[14]

The contrast with Ingres is significant. There the character of the relationship between the artist and his model is what is at issue; we are
confronted with an account of transformation where the beauty of the
painted model becomes a sign of her disturbing potency, where the
painter is objectively separated from his painting, where canonical signs
obtrude on the image, where the work of the painter is held up for admiration. The painter is poised between different aspects of his life and
work: the painting deals only liminally with the painter as subject of the
process of painting, and points diffusely to ways in which the painter
may come to figure as the object of what painting stands for.

It is this relationship between subject and object that is central to the
multiplicity of transformations which narratives of the painter impose
on their heroes, and it is to these that I shall now turn. Each of these narratives is strongly coloured by rapidly changing perceptions of the
condition of the painter. A sign of this attitude is the conflictive presentation of the relationship between literature and the visual arts in
several of these works: this is a symbolic conflict, where the dissolution

of the doctrine of *ut pictura poesis* is the sign of the loss of aesthetic certainty.[15] Such conflict is on occasion presented in a comic light. In Balzac's *Pierre Grassou*, Bridau reproaches the inept hero:

> 'Tu devrais faire autre chose que de la peinture', dit Bridau.
> 'Quoi?', dit Fougères.
> 'Jette-toi dans la littérature.'[16]

This sense of disjunction is a decisive factor in framing the perception of the visual arts on the part of each of the authors I shall consider; it is especially significant in the reflections of the Goncourt brothers. For the Goncourts, a suspicion of painting is an aid to aesthetic reflection. Thus, for instance, the essentially suggestive ('spiritualiste', in the Goncourts' words) character of writing appears all the more clearly when considered in relation to the purely sensual character which the Goncourts take to be the prime attribute of painting. The setting of the studio is emblematic of the impoverishment of the work of the painter: 'Un atelier, un endroit gai? Un endroit où il y a des peintres et où il n'y a pas de soleil.'[17]

But what the Goncourts stress above all is the anachronism and the sterility of the received academic doctrine of models. They posit a break with tradition as a defining element of any modern artistic undertaking: 'Le dogme académique que le passé inspire l'avenir, est contraire à tous les faits. Les arts qui ont les plus parfaits modèles sont en pleine décadence: je ne citerai que la sculpture.'[18] What is under attack is not the canonical models in themselves, but the means by which these are used to determine our understanding of the artistic process. Now, reflection on the problems of art, and of painting in particular, is a discontinuous but constant element of the *Journal*. Like narratives on painting, such reflection is in part highly self-interested: painting is propitious to the attempt to define the problems of modern writing. Painting can be portrayed in a strong negative light. Conceived of as an art residually influenced by authoritative models, typified by painstaking manual labour, limited to the space of the studio, the work of the painter serves to throw into relief the truly Promethean character of modern literature, committed as it is to openness, originality, plasticity: 'L'artiste peut prendre la nature au posé; l'écrivain est obligé de la saisir au vol et comme un voleur.'

Part of what the writer seeks to appropriate is the mimetic lustre of painting. But the notion of writing that emerges is conceived essentially in terms of the novelistic: a discourse that is delivered of the burden of linearity, that is innovative, heterogeneous, programmatically modern, in contrast to what the Goncourts perceive as the fixity and relative transparency of the hierarchical ordering of the received genres of painting: 'De la peinture au roman, la différence du roman au conte de fée'.[19] For the Goncourts, the story of the painter is all too well known, while that of the writer remains occulted.

The Goncourts' devalorization of painting is in large measure tactical. We shall turn in a moment to their novel *Manette Salomon* as a case in point for an understanding of discourse on painting, because it stands as one of the key nineteenth-century texts dealing with the work of the artist. It should be borne in mind at the outset that the exploitation, by the Goncourts and others, of the figure of the painter is in essence paras- itical on the modernity of the figure of the creative artist, as opposed to that of the artisan. He acquires an ambiguous value: he appears as a dia- bolical sorcerer, an Orpheus venturing into the underworld,[20] but above all as an enigmatic obsessive seeking a lost androgynous completeness.[21] Ancient myths are exploited to obtain a purchase on the elusive figure of the modern artist. As a result the artist engenders a discourse that becomes quite distinctive, rich in symbolic suggestiveness and notable for its exploitation of aphorism, condensation, paradox, antithesis.

A series of articles published by Balzac in 1830, under the title 'Des artistes', illustrates this trend abundantly. For Balzac, the work of the artist is representative of all intellectual endeavour. More particularly, the artist serves to illustrate the essential paradox that attaches to all such activity: the intellectual dignity of his work is obscured by the mat- erial disadvantages and the social disdain from which the artist suffers: 'Nous avons d'abord essayé de faire apercevoir combien était large et durable la puissance de l'artiste, accusant en même temps avec franchise l'état de dénuement dans lequel il passe sa vie de travail et de douleur; méconnu la plupart du temps; pauvre et riche; critiquant et critiqué; plein de force et lassé; porté en triomphe et rebuté.'[22] This situation proves naturally to be prejudicial to the proper reception of the work of the artist. This discursive pattern readily lends itself to conversion into narrative and results in texts remarkable for their symbolic and inter- textual density.

What this highly charged narrative discourse immediately throws into relief is the duplicity of the artist: the artist figures as a subject not neces- sarily present to himself, yet consciously plagued by a sense of limitation, and struggling to discover his identity, a figure of disjunction, at odds with his models, with tradition, with the modern world. This essential motif, though, is itself plural in character. Thus Pellerin, once again, stands as a parodical version of this effect: after experimenting with a plethora of ideologies and of manners, with Fourierism, homo- eopathy, turning tables, Gothic art and humanitarian painting, the one-time idealist becomes, in the 1860s, a photographer.

The myth of mutability is nonetheless an adaptable and economical one: it is the dominant topos of Balzac's stories of the artist. In his *La*

*Maison du chat-qui-pelote*, the relationship between the painter and his model is, once again, vital. Théodore's obsession with an unknown woman generates a painting whose artistic interest derives wholly, it appears, from the feeling that inspires it. When the painter Girodet sees it he concludes that his friend must be in love: 'Tous deux savaient que les plus beaux portraits de Titien, de Raphaël et de Léonard de Vinci sont dus à des sentiments exaltés, qui, sous diverses conditions, engendrent d'ailleurs tous les chefs-d'œuvre.' When this painting is seen by its unwitting object, it is transformed into a token of love; the act of making and viewing the painting seemingly precipitates a happy ending. But this love proves to be perishable. The model, as woman, becomes an equivocal figure, and the narrative tends towards disjunction; it invokes painting as a model of its own writing, but bypasses the scene of violence, that of it own destruction, which painting ultimately generates: 'Il serait odieux de peindre toute cette scène à la fin de laquelle l'ivresse de la colère suggéra à l'artiste des paroles et des actes qu'une femme moins jeune qu'Augustine aurait attribués à la démence.'[23] This act of destruction, and the violence it stands for, are commonplace elements of these stories. In *Sarrasine*, once again, the model is a seemingly perfect object of love; her beauty proves, however, to be radically flawed. The violence that marks the end of this text enables us to apprehend the latent brutality of certain of the others and, more importantly, to grasp the transformative process of which the sculptor here figures as the object.

This process proves to be endowed with a specifically artistic dimension, which is the focus of perhaps the best-known of Balzac's stories of the painter, *Le Chef-d'œuvre inconnu*, a text that ends by identifying the limits of painting. Painting here features as an art of the most potent kind of transformation: Frenhofer's *Belle Noiseuse* is created virtually *ex nihilo*, without the aid of any model. It is, in all appearance, a failure: the figure of the woman is indecipherable, save one perfect foot. But, within this narrative scheme, failure becomes a veiled sign of success; a scene that for Frenhofer amounts to a castastrophic discovery enables two other painters, and most notably the half-fictional, half-historical figure of the youthful Poussin, explicitly to discern the extremes that determine the absolute limits of painting, but also confer on it its peculiar mimetic distinction:

> Porbus frappa sur l'épaule du vieillard en se tournant vers Poussin:
> 'Savez-vous que nous voyons en lui un bien grand peintre?' dit-il.
> 'Il est encore plus poète que peintre', répondit gravement Poussin.
> 'Là', reprit Porbus en touchant la toile, 'finit notre art sur terre.'
> 'Et de là, il va se perdre dans les cieux', dit Poussin.[24]

Success and failure are reversible. In exploring this paradox, Balzac aims to achieve the most potent condensation possible of myths of the painter, with a view to harnessing anew their full symbolic and imaginary potential: their interest self-evidently extends beyond the realm of art, but it must be borne in mind that part of the appeal of these texts, as narrative, lies in their power to illuminate painting. Such a pattern of success and failure becomes, in effect, the dominant narrative matter of nineteenth-century stories of the painter. In the Goncourts' *Manette Salomon* and Zola's *L'Œuvre*, both complex novels, this feature becomes, in the case of the first, the main narrative enigma and, in the second, the problem with which the artist must contend. In Zola's novel, in particular, such a pattern is early on identified as the key to the plot. The eventual self-destruction of the artist is the result of a failed speculation, in terms of which eventual success can only be obtained at the price of initial uncertainty: this is the conundrum that Claude fails to grasp. Zola seizes on this point in the course of his researches. There we see him cite a maxim invoked by the painters among whom he circulates and immediately convert it into the substance of narrative: 'La maxime: il vaut mieux commencer en vieillard et finir en jeune homme, que le contraire. Claude commence en jeune, ébauche très belle; mais la difficulté de finir. C'est en finissant qu'on gâte tout.'[25] The novel itself, in order to obtain its own narrative closure, feeds on the incapacity of the painter. It exploits the relationship between painter and model, and portrays the former as an obsessive: his chastity, seemingly the sign of pure commitment to his work, points in fact to his impotence and becomes the object of a scene of explicit conflict at the end of the novel, in which the model-wife, standing naked before the painter, reveals the dessication of the image he has made of her, and compels him to renounce painting.

Zola's novel brings into view a further avatar of the artist: the painter succumbs to a *passion* for flesh as an object of painting, to an *exaltation* that is the expression of his desire to paint a worthy picture, which together conspire to paralyse him. The desire that painting inspires is essential to this outcome: Claude's death represents a deformed triumph of art over the artist – because he leaves nothing, he becomes the victim of a self-cancelling process. As in *Le Chef d'œuvre inconnu*, it falls to others to draw what purports to be the necessary conclusion to this apocalyptic narrative: ' "Au moins, en voilà un qui a été logique et brave", continua Sandoz. "Il a avoué son impuissance et il s'est tué." '[26] The painter is all but transformed into the witness to the impossibility of his own condition.

*Manette Salomon*, the Goncourts' novel of painters, published in 1867, predates Zola's and anticipates much of its narrative outline (as Edmond, all too characteristically, was the first to point out), but is today much less well known. This is perhaps because its plot appears so much more diffuse; yet this difference is more significant and more telling than it might appear, not least because it enables us to evaluate the relevance of narrative to an understanding of painting. The novel seeks to give a remarkably complete account of the work of the painter: this is the sign of a certain seriousness with regard to painting, and we shall return to this important point at the end of this essay. It is less obviously parasitical on the perceived difficulties of the painter-figure, in part because the narrative doesn't depend as specifically on his destruction. The action revolves around three main figures (the successful orthodox painter, Garnotelle; Coriolis, the failed genius; and Anatole, the artist without a vocation who abandons his career), and follows their destinies from the time of their training onwards. The action of the novel describes a movement from the circumscribed setting of the atelier, in which these characters and a host of others are first assembled, to the wealth of different locations in which the characters are to be found, as the action of the novel branches off in different directions. The Goncourts' working title for the novel was *L'Atelier Langibout*; in the course of its composition this was abandoned in favour of a title which points to each of the centres of interest (the city, the Orient, the studio, the low world that Manette inhabits and the bourgeois milieu to which she aspires) of the novel, but also leaves full scope for the unexpected detours of the plot.[27]

The novel begins by situating the work of the artist primarily in relation to his use of the human body. The relationship between artist and model is the initial focus of attention. Here, the woman is a professional model, and the perfection of her body is represented as quite exceptional: Manette thus becomes the object of a double passion, as model and as woman, and Coriolis's desire to possess her triggers off a conflictive plot that culminates in their marriage and in the decline of his artistic powers. So, in *Manette Salomon*, the body figures to begin with as the stated vehicle of a certain kind of understanding, that of the artist, but the disjunction which comes to affect the relationship between painter and model proves in fact merely to form part of a wider set of transformations which are the true underpinning of the action. Coriolis is the primary figure through whom this effect is explored, in part because of his sensitivity to innovative formal possibilities, and in part because of his progressively more and more dense and diverse exposure to the world.

The painter's work hinges on 'rencontres' with picturesque aspects of the modern world whose most important attribute is their improvised and contingent quality. These are the precise occasions, so to speak, that enable us to apprehend the Promethean dimension of the creative act, a process of theft that the Goncourts themselves identify precisely with the work of the writer: 'Quelquefois, tirant de sa poche un petit carnet grand comme la moitié de la main, il jetait dessus deux ou trois de ces coups de crayon qui attrapent l'instantanéité d'un mouvement.' The success of the artist hinges on 'rencontres soudaines', which both condition and crystallize the 'illumination' which his art purveys.[28] Though Coriolis is largely blind to his own achievement, the frustrated artist remains a figure of infinite potential in pursuit of an artistic project of infinite scope. The novel seeks firmly to establish that failure at the hands of an uncomprehending public is to be regarded as a sign of true artistic attainment; an extremely pointed narrative reversal at the end of the novel evokes such a conclusion, when the success of Coriolis's early works, the effect of pure speculation, signals all at once the canonization and the alienation of the artist.

*Manette Salomon* is an irreducibly equivocal novel,[29] in which painting and literature each appear implicitly to aspire to the condition of the other. Literature is used to promote the values of rapidity, inclusiveness, heterogeneity which, in the Goncourts' view, the traditional genres of painting seem to repudiate; painting is endowed of itself with immense representational prestige and comes to figure as an indispensable element of a continuous dialectic enquiry into the nature of modern artistic practice. Yet the Goncourts are also concerned with painting for and in itself, in ways which their own sardonic aphorisms at the expense of painters tend to obscure. In effect, the use of the visual arts as a means of reflecting on literature gives an unexpected edge to their understanding of painting, and it is with a consideration of this important point that this essay will close.

Towards the beginning of their career as writers, the Goncourts wrote a brief essay on the Exposition Universelle of 1855, in which they conclude that the painter is a slave of chemistry, 'un homme de lettres aux ordres d'essences et de sucs colorants'.[30] Modern painting, from whichever perspective it is viewed, remains unsatisfactory: rather than pursue the stylistic individualism which the Goncourts tacitly posit as the defining condition of literature, painters remain under the limiting influence of canonical models, committed to the depiction of flesh and light. The painting of Delacroix, so remarkable for its *action*, its *mouvement*, itself points to an essential lack of completeness in modern art: his painting, which so markedly evades the *fini* and the *précis*, depends on the evocative, 'spiritualist' quality that is proper above all, in the Goncourts' view, to modern writing.[31] Such comparisons consistently rebound to the disadvantage of painting. In a similar vein, the Goncourts appear to take a strongly prejudicial view of those whom we might now consider to be the most original painters of their day. This is notably true of Courbet: Edmond comments derisively on his self-confidence – 'folle, exagérée, enfantine' – and both brothers react vehemently to what they take to be the irreducible ugliness of his work: 'Le laid, toujours le laid! Et le laid sans son grand caractère, le laid sans la beauté du laid.'[32]

The Goncourts' misapprehension of the most significant trends of the painting of their day is by now notorious; it is to be explained, in part, by the overwhelming influence on their taste of the eighteenth-century painters on whom they wrote at the beginning of their careers.[33] Their writing on painting becomes, however, more compelling and, I think, extremely suggestive if we regard their distaste for the work of, say, Courbet and Manet not simply as an expression of outright disapproval, but as a sign of misrecognition. For the questions raised in their criticism, in the *Journal*, and in *Manette Salomon*, are extremely pertinent to the standing of art in their own period. Like certain painters, the Goncourts sense that painting is exposed to definite transformations, most notably to the reductive threat, as they see it, of photography, all the more powerfully so as the canonical tradition declines in prestige. Coriolis's failure, in large part contingent, points to this difficulty. When he turns to realist painting, he is the victim of a received opinion: 'Il eut encore contre ses tableaux l'idée générale, l'opinion faite que la question de la représentation du moderne en peinture, soulevée par les essais, hardis jusqu'au scandale, d'un autre artiste, était définitivement jugée.' The public refuses to recognize the distinctiveness of this fictive realism, proffered by the Goncourts themselves as the utopian solution to the problems of modern art, a form of realism that shuns the banality of daguerreotype, the cult of ugliness, and that seeks to extract from 'la forme typique, choisie, expressive des images contemporaines, le style contemporain'.[34]

The story of Coriolis gives powerful expression, perhaps above all else, to a desire *for* painting. This desire derives its fervour and its urgency from the very threats which beset painting, and the Goncourts, like the most original painters of their time, are keen to identify and to confront such negative constraints. It is their lucidity that serves to vindicate the novel's narrative approach, its diffuseness, and its extraordinary exploitation of novelistic devices of coincidence, parallelism and reversal. Their lucidity fuels their desire; their desire, in turn, blinds them to the true interest of work pursued in parallel by the painters around them. This is the final bewitching irony of the novel: the desire for painting is displaced from each of the painters and assumed by the narrative which seeks, by virtue of this act of theft, to provide an all the more powerful account of the forces to which the artist is subject and which he must seek to master.

## Suggested reading

Boime, Albert, *The Academy and French Painting in the Nineteenth Century* (London: Phaidon, 1971).

Damisch, Hubert, *Fenêtre jaune cadmium; ou, les dessous de la peinture* (Paris: Seuil, 1984).

Didi-Huberman, Georges, *La Peinture incarnée* (Paris: Minuit, 1985).

Fried, Michael, *Courbet's Realism* (Chicago and London: University of Chicago Press, 1990).

Georgel, Pierre, 'Les transformations de la peinture vers 1848, 1855, 1863', *Revue de l'art*, no.27 (1975).

Milner, Max, 'Le peintre fou', *Romantisme*, no.66 (1989).

# PART IV

# *MODELS OF REPRESENTATION*
## SYMBOLISM AND SELF-CONSCIOUSNESS

# 15

## *The writing on the wall: descriptions of painting in the art criticism of the French Symbolists*
### James Kearns

With the Symbolist movement (1886–95) the relationships between French literature and the visual arts entered a decisive phase.[1] Its short-lived domination of the literary avant-garde coincided with the period in French art when a recently-established modernist trend on the way up passed a long-established tradition on the way down. During these years, the official institutions of French painting and the exhibition of the annual Salon in which they were represented reached the end of their credibility, unable to resist any longer the advance in public acceptance of Impressionism and the impact this painting was having on the conditions in which French art was produced and circulated.[2] The literary Symbolists followed developments in the visual arts as actively as their predecessors had done but they did so in the context of far-reaching changes taking place in the art forms involved. In literature, impelled by Mallarmé's desire to separate 'le double état de la parole, brut ou immédiat ici, là essentiel',[3] the move away from its long-held mimetic ambition to represent the world and towards the production of meaning on the basis of its internal means was under way. In painting, a related emancipation of material forms was expressed when Maurice Denis, one of the founders of the Nabi movement (created in 1888 in response to the arrival in Paris of Gauguin's work produced that summer in Brittany), advised readers to 'remember that a painting – before being a military horse, a nude woman or some anecdote or other – is essentially a flat surface covered with colours assembled in a certain order'.[4]

In the literature of painting, these changing theories of verbal and visual signs necessitated new strategies for exercising the jurisdiction over the visual arts which the literary Symbolists, like their predecessors, believed to be an authentic literary activity and responsibility.[5] The shared imitation of the real by painting and literature had long since legitimized for writers the assimilation of painting by literature but to foreground the expressive potential of the material sign was to call into question a literary discourse on painting dominated by and organized around the description of the pictorial subject.[6] So Thadée Natanson, art critic of the Symbolist *Revue blanche*, wrote in a review of an exhibition of the Nabis that the question which most urgently required an answer was 'what we should understand by this word *subject* which comes up so frequently in discussions about painting'.[7] Since the description of painting always implies assimilation of the system of representation it embodies, the Symbolists faced the problem of adapting the descriptive model to accommodate their pictorial preferences within changing theories and practices of representation in both arts during this period.

Among contemporary painters of the 1890s two reputations dominated the literary Symbolist movement. The first was that of Puvis de Chavannes, 'whose enormous influence at the end of the nineteenth century cannot be sufficiently stressed'.[8] The second was that of Monet, whose series exhibitions of 1891 (haystacks), 1892 (poplars) and 1895 (Rouen Cathedral) secured and increasingly confiscated the victory of Impressionism over the painting associated with the offical Salon.[9] Puvis represented the acceptable contemporary face of the idealist tradition which the Academy had debased, Monet represented the most advanced form of Impressionism. Their convergence in the art criticism of the literary Symbolists was achieved by means of a discourse of reconciliation between realist and idealist traditions which in their view the nineteenth century had separated.[10] In order to reconstruct this discourse, I shall begin in November 1898 when the Paris art world discovered the latest work by two artists now brought together in histories of Symbolist painting but who by that time had experienced very different relationships with the same movement in literature. The works in question were the murals executed by Puvis de Chavannes for the Panthéon in Paris and Gauguin's latest Tahitian paintings exhibited in the Vollard galleries.[11] The art critic of the Symbolist *Mercure de France* compared the two achievements in terms which illustrate that movement's characteristic readings of the visual image.

On 30 November 1898 visitors to the Panthéon in Paris were able to see *in situ* the frescoes commissioned from Puvis de Chavannes and completed shortly before his death the previous month. The two works, *La Ravitaillement de Paris par Sainte Geneviève* and *Sainte Geneviève veillant sur Paris endormi*, were hailed as the painter's spiritual testament, a fitting summary of his renewal of French history painting. Puvis had adapted the original commission to emphasize the meeting of real and supernatural represented by the saint's intercession between God and the people of Paris. The siting of this lesson in the temple of the Republican ideal, formerly the church of Saint Geneviève, had its place in the wider political and cultural context of the 1890s when the Republican government was pursuing its policy of improved relations with the Catholic Church which would lead to the *ralliement* and when the Catholic and the classical revivals were relaying and extending Symbolism's challenge to naturalism.[12] The fact that Puvis had died so soon after completing the work gave added poignancy to the murals' association of art and faith.

In his distinctive mural style Puvis broke with trompe-l'œil practices of volume, depth, modelling and naturalist colour associated with nineteenth-century realism. He used the mural's flat surface and strong panoramic effect to emphasize linear rhythms and spatial relationships across the surface and his pale colour harmonies were integrated with the surrounding stone. For the greater part of his career his use of similar procedures in easel painting had not won critical acclaim since it was generally assumed that easel and mural painting involved quite different economies, procedures and objectives.[13] By the 1890s these reservations had ceased. Avant-garde painters such as Seurat and Gauguin saw his work as one example of the possibilities opened up by the idea of painting as a decorative patterning of the picture-surface.[14] The literary Symbolists stressed what they saw as his timeless, universal themes expressed through a non-naturalist treatment of subject and their support for his work marginalized the doubters, notably Huysmans.[15] Puvis's reputation achieved new heights in the 1890s because he gained this audience among the literary and artistic avant-garde without forfeiting his growing success with traditionalists who saw him as the heir to the Italian fresco painters of the pre-Renaissance and with supporters of the classical revival who saw him as the heir to Poussin.[16] By the time of his death he had become unofficially France's *peintre national*.

In his Panthéon commission Puvis applied his mural technique to a text in which were accumulated centuries of narrative. It celebrated a supposed golden age of faith, a community of religious feeling co-incident with the origins of national life. The historical accounts of the saint's organization of supplies to the besieged city in AD 450 made available to the painter a well-thumbed anthology of figures, gestures, expressions and attributes. Puvis made a selection which he pared down and filtered through linear rhythms and tonal harmonies to eliminate the local colour and incidental detail which might limit the universality of the theme. The Symbolists were more familiar with the theme than the mural technique, more conversant with its verbal extensions than its material means, but their contacts with his supporters among the painters ensured that they recognized the need to integrate the two in their appreciation of his work. This appreciation reflected the extent to which it facilitated the complicity of verbal and visual signs.

In the *Mercure de France* of January 1899, André Fontainas praised the Panthéon murals in terms which illustate the forms this complicity took. His short review applies a conventional format. It is in three parts, opening with a description of the subject followed by a brief account of its essential formal values and closing with a summary of the general meaning of the work. The description of the subject had always been art criticism's primary task.[17] Initially its compositional procedures were designed to enable the reader to 'see' the painting but with the increase of reproductions and of access to exhibitions this objective was superseded by that of demonstrating the extent to which the language of art criticism could reproduce painting's formal presentation of a subject and make explicit the meanings which in the painting remained implicit. In the murals and in the description events unfold from left to right. In both the saint is placed in the centre. The nouns recreate the presentation of community, the adjectives the range of emotional attributes. One detail – 'vêtues du voile blanc et le cierge aux doigts' – is sufficient to place the reading on the allegorical level the murals invite.

Once this verbal reproduction of the visual is secured the description moves to its second stage, the moment at which the critic recognizes that the verbalization of the visual has limits, in this case those of 'cette harmonie pâle, tendre et précise' in which the blues and violets of the landscape espouse the pinks of the cityscape and figures. This concession is, however, provisional. No sooner is the formal autonomy admitted than it is transcended in stage three by the revelation of the work's hidden meanings to which the painter has given access but which it is the critic's task to actualize. According to Fontainas, Puvis has abolished the local colour of conventional illustrated hagiography and created a more authentic mystical history, an ideal, timeless landscape of the soul – 'un chant silencieux ... le songe des temps lointains' – where the critic's discourse is once again on home ground.

In the relationship between Puvis's choice of subject and the formal system through which he represented it, the literary Symbolists identified a practice which displayed recognizably modern pictorial values such as flatness and simplification but which did not challenge more familiar procedures for translating the visual into discourse. He had found the means to anchor the idea of community in the sacred, to portray an ordered timeless world by creating colour harmonies and linear rhythms which led the spectator across and into the scene, between background and foreground, giving a sense of the contemplation through which the hidden patterns of history might come to the surface.[18] But these visual means were in turn anchored in his historical subject, derived from written texts and, therefore, preprogrammed for reinsertion in the critical narrative. Underpinning the relationship between subject and form in his work was the most familiar rhetorical model of all, that which held together visible sign and hidden meaning. Allegory after all had long been the basis for the relationship between verbal and visual.[19] In theory, the Symbolists considered allegory to be devoid of aesthetic value, so culturally coded that sign and meaning were coextensive and artistic language had no space within which to engage the spectator's imagination.[20] Puvis's work retained allegory's exegetical value but his formal procedures reinstated just sufficient distance between sign and signified to open up a decorative space in which the critic was able to write timeless narratives.

For the art critic of the *Mercure de France*, the open but directed legibility of Puvis de Chavannes served as the model for figure-painting. His review which closed with his homage to the Panthéon murals opened with his sympathetic but negative assessment of Gauguin's work shown the same month in the Vollard galleries.[21] Here Fontainas defined the programme expected of a painter of the Tropics as 'the idea of a warm, luxurious and primitive land, with expansive, thick vegetation, deep, clear springs, violent contrasts of light and air and peopled by a serious, slightly precious, backward race' (236). This programme directed the critic's reading of the 'brutal opposition of full, rich and vibrant tones' in Gauguin's landscapes. It was a different matter, however, in the case of the Tahitian figure where this correlation of meaning and form had to confront the predominance which figure traditionally enjoyed in the production of meaning. So Fontainas brought to the figure-painting the culturally-inscribed late nineteenth-century Parisian male's erotic fantasies of Tahitian women and regretted the absence of 'mysterious dancers moving slowly amidst the dense landscape' or 'bathers naked in a glorious and strangely radiant vegetation'. Faced instead with the 'dry, colourless, rigid' forms of the figures shown in *D'où venons-nous? que sommes-nous? où allons-nous?* he fell back on a charge which had been levelled against Gauguin from the earliest days of his contacts with the literary Symbolists, that his figures were the result of ill-digested philosophical ideas derived from poets and unsuited to his temperament.[22] The art of Puvis had shown that abstract ideas such as those expressed in the title of *D'où venons-nous . . .* required 'some material allegory' with which to narrate them.

Gauguin replied to Fontainas in a letter in which he explained his work in terms themselves largely derived from an earlier article on his work by the minor Symbolist poet Achille Delaroche.[23] Delaroche had described Gauguin's work as a musical poem, one which anchored Gauguin's colours and figures in the alternative, non-discursive tradition of landscape which had been 'so luminously formulated by Baudelaire' (37). The much-criticized violent, monotonous and arbitrary tones, the inelegant figures could now be seen to be the undifferentiated, non-hierarchical elements of a suggestive decor which opened a 'new door on to the infinite and the mysterious'. The painting as illustrated text was replaced by painting as 'intimate correlation of theme and form', the plastic equivalent of the artist's experience of the general and mysterious force of nature. 'If he represents jealousy it is by a blaze of pinks and violets in which the whole of nature seems to participate' (37). Delaroche gave Gauguin's own definition of Symbolist painting philosophical credibility and freed his paintings from the narrative closure of Puvis's conservative figurative system. He based his description to Fontainas of the fusion of figure, objects and landscape in *D'où venons-nous* . . . upon them. In a later letter, to Charles Morice, he summarized the lesson of this exchange with Fontainas: 'Puvis explains his idea, yes, but he does not paint it.'[24]

In his study of *L'Art impressionniste*, published in 1892, Georges Lecomte included a chapter on Puvis de Chavannes. Lecomte's praise for Puvis's 'poèmes de signification idéale' (188) in a book on Impressionism was less surprising then than it appears now. In 1876 Mallarmé had defined Manet's open-air work as the revelation 'in the clear and durable mirror of painting' of 'that which perpetually lives yet dies each moment' and referred to Puvis as one of the 'other great talents' of modern painting.[25] At the time, Mallarmé's idealist interpretation of Impressionism was an isolated one, marginalized by that painting's naturalist supporters who argued that it represented the external world more truthfully than had been possible hitherto because it described the role of light and atmosphere and rejected academic theories of composition and hierarchy of subjects. It is clear that during the 1880s Mallarmé communicated his account of Impressionism to his regular Tuesday evening visitors.[26] When he emerged towards the end of the decade as the dominant figure of the Symbolist movement, his account reasserted itself against the naturalist one. The turning-point came with the Monet-Rodin exhibition of 1889 in which Monet showed 145 works in the most important retrospective of his work to date.[27]

In his preface to the exhibition catalogue Mirbeau defined Monet's role in terms which implicitly located the painter in the succession to Manet as Mallarmé had described him. Just as Manet had shown life 'with its perpetual metamorphosis and its invisible action rendered visible . . . this struggle ever continued between surface and space, between colour and air . . . ' (p.75), so for Mirbeau Monet was 'the painter who had taken furthest the expression not only of the visible, but also of the invisible . . . who had painted all the fluidities of light and the infinite reflections in which it envelops objects and beings'. According to the critic, Monet's work demonstrated his continuous refinement of a pictorial method evolved to express 'une interprétation exacte et émue de la

nature' (14). By perfecting the means to recreate the envelope of luminous atmosphere which bathed all objects, he had produced decorative
designs which represented the point of balance between visual truth and
subjective interpretation and so enabled the spectator to transit between
the visible unity of the perception and the hidden, mysterious unity of
the perceived. In the sort of metonymic transfer destined for a bright
future in the Monet literature, Mirbeau argued that the unity of the pattern signified the unity of the patterned, the mystery of the atmospheric
envelope that of the enveloped, the infinite reflections the infinity of the
reflected. Naturalist truth, subjective interpretation and visual language
formed a seamless continuum and Mirbeau's translation of it established
Monet as a Symbolist painter.

The 1889 exhibition was the artistic and commercial breakthrough
for which Monet had waited for years but it severely jeopardized that of
another painter with similar designs on the Symbolist movement. With
the failure of his own exhibition held between June and October of the
same year, Gauguin was forced to recognize the fact that the type of
description of Monet's painting which Mirbeau had made available
would marginalize his own more radical work within the literary group
and that therefore it had to be countered.[28] The result of this strategy
was the article published in March 1891 by Albert Aurier, art critic of
the *Mercure de France*, announcing the existence of a Symbolist movement in painting, nominating Gauguin as its leader and describing his
work as a fundamental break with Impressionism, now dismissed as no
more than 'une variété du réalisme, un réalisme affiné, spiritualisé, dilet-
tantisé, mais toujours le réalisme'.[29]

In his article Aurier listed the five characteristics of Symbolist painting
– 'ideist', 'symbolist', 'synthetist', 'subjective' and 'decorative' in des-
cending order of priority from finality (the expression of the Platonic
Idea) to means (the decorative). The definition of the decorative restated
the four preceding characteristics in ascending order of priority to illustrate the steps which led from material surface to Platonic Idea. The
essential element was the elimination of the mimetic relationship betwen
the object represented and its counterpart in the natural world. The
formal arrangement of lines and colours was designed to display the new
relationship between sign and signified. It was in effect Denis's definition
of painting quoted above with the reference to the pictorial subject removed and Platonic ideas inserted in its place.

Within the Symbolist movement Aurier's authority derived not only
from the eloquence of his attack on the naturalist aesthetic of which Impressionism was in his view the extension but also from the prose poem
with which he opened his article and in which he gave a demonstration
of how to write this non-naturalist function of the decorative as it was
displayed in Gauguin's work, *Vision après le sermon*.[30] The short first

paragraph defined the Biblical subject in the narrative mode of the fairy tale appropriate to the Breton peasant-women represented and which assimilated the decorative features of non-naturalist perspective ('Loin, très loin . . . ') and colour ('vermillon rutilant'). The second narrated the Symbolist means, guiding the spectator through the signs (women, Bretons, prayer) and the forms (the pronounced lines of bonnet and dress, the purple hill) and culminating in the conditionals and questions which denied the naturalist legibility of the image. The third narrated the Symbolist finality, the realization of the pure Idea of the divine Voice, materialized in language throughout the insistent accumulation of nominative clauses introduced by 'c'est . . .', the linguistic counterpart to the spatial unfolding of formal elements across the picture-surface. It culminated in the details with which it began, the circularity emphasizing the transfer from naturalist to ideal level. Aurier adopted the rhetoric of the sermon to narrate the vision which it produced and which Gauguin's painting displayed.

Despite the respect within the Symbolist movement for Aurier's undoubted familiarity with the formal premisses of Gauguin's work, for his Neoplatonism and for the quality of his exercises in *transposition d'art*, he failed to impose Gauguin as the leader of Symbolist painting because the rival claims were stronger. The assimilation of the figural within the allegorical legibility of figure-painting (Puvis) or within a familiar narrative of landscape as interstate between the visible and the invisible (Monet) represented a compromise between the meanings derived from the pictorial subject for which Symbolist art critics possessed well-practised rhetorical strategies and those derived from the formal system for which they did not. No sooner had Aurier's article appeared than Monet cut the ground from under it when he held his first series exhibition, the sequence of fifteen haystack paintings shown in the Durand-Ruel galleries on 4–18 May 1891. The serial phenomenon gave a new dimension to the reception of Monet's work and in particular facilitated its Symbolist annexation. Each painting appeared to recount a particular moment of light and atmosphere but the series actively encouraged narratives of transcendence on the theme of the present's relationship to the eternal. Each painting could demonstrate the partnership betweeen the human and the natural embodied in the relationship between the stacks on the one hand and on the other the houses and barns placed on the horizontal behind them,[31] but the series transformed this partnership into a timeless statement of man's place in the natural order of things. The individual haystack was a massive, reassuring presence in the natural scene, but the series showed that it was only a pretext for the demonstration of Monet's methods of picture-making.

Since the subject of each picture was the same, to compare one with another was inevitably to focus on the system of painterly traces by which the surface was assembled.[32] Such explicit evidence of the working of paint actively solicited strategies for sublimating its material presence into the immaterial reality of an idealized poetic landscape. The topos of unity within diversity was the most familiar and Camille Mauclair showed its efficacy in his description of 'these fifteen identical and yet so varied studies of haystacks, now bathed in the dawn light, now ablaze in the heat of the midday sun, now buried beneath snow, now drowned in exquisite twilights. . . '.[33] For the Symbolist imagination, the potentially unlimited extension of the serial effect created the same ideal landscape of the soul that we have seen Fontainas describing in the Puvis murals. To translate it, Mauclair used the linguistic series ('tantôt' + participle) into which he incorporated via metaphor the general colour unity of the picture. The following year, reviewing the second series exhibition, that of the poplars, he found them transfigured 'jusqu'à l'idéal', endowed by Monet's working of paint with a 'mysterious *meaning* which makes them suddenly participate in the symbolic universe of which poets dream'.[34] In doing so, he confirmed the conjunction of the work of Puvis and Monet established the previous year by Mirbeau, who had written that Monet was 'with Puvis de Chavannes, the one who addresses himself the most directly, the most eloquently, to poets'.[35]

For the literary Symbolists, the legibility of the figure-painting of Puvis de Chavannes, like that of Monet's landscapes, owed its prestige to the compromise these works made possible between traditional narratives of human history and modern, material signs. It enjoyed its high point in 1895, firstly in the album of homages in prose and verse presented to Puvis de Chavannes in the course of the banquet held in January of that year in honour of his seventieth birthday and again in the critical reaction to Monet's new series, that of Rouen Cathedral, which went on show in the Durand-Ruel galleries in May.[36] But the critical convergence between the work of these two artists in Symbolist definitions of painting was also an important element in the emerging reputation of an artist identified by Impressionists such as Pissarro and Symbolists such as Gauguin and Denis as a major formative influence on their respective groups: Paul Cézanne.

Cézanne had not exhibited in Paris since 1877, with the result that he was both unknown and famous, his reputation sustained by word of mouth. One who had written about him in the recent past was Huysmans who in *Certains* published a short analysis which is significant in being the first to locate in Cézanne's still-life work his essential orginality and its lesson for modern art.[37] The first two paragraphs are given over to a description of his still lifes in general in which Huysmans

26.  Paul Cézanne, *Jug and Fruit*, 1893–4 (Berggruen Collection, on loan to The National Gallery, London)

attempted to define the relationship between process and result, between Cézanne's very visible handling of paint and the powerful effect of visual truth which this produced.[38]

Huysmans began by presenting characteristic features of the Cézanne still life: composition, the distribution of light and the arrangement of objects and fruit on tablecloths, and colour, pigment trowelled and thumbed on to the canvas with a violent physicality for which Huysmans offered a verbal analogy in 'rebroussées par des roulis de pouce'. The result when seen close to dissolved into 'un hourdage furieux de vermillon et de jaune, de vert et de bleu', but when viewed from the correct distance gave a display of paint and of fruit which were both 'au point'. This idea of the correct distance was by 1889 a commonplace of art literature, particularly that relating to the Impressionists, and here Huysmans legitimized it further by incorporating it within the still more respectable one of the transformation of matter by the will of the artist.[39] The gulf between the focused, driven energy of picture-making and the ripe, mouth-watering fruit 'destinés aux vitrines des Chevet' was briged by Cézanne's colour. The painter had overthrown conventional academic composition in which still lifes 'enlevées en des repoussoirs de bitume, sur d'inintelligibles fonds' used artificially exaggerated shadow

248

to highlight the objects depicted.[40] One example served to illustrate it, that of the bluish tints which in the tablecloths faintly echo those of the cast shadows of the fruit to establish across the surface of the painting relationships which lock together gesture and the truthful representation of light on the surface of objects.

The still lifes of Huysmans's Cézanne were, therefore, a synthesis of artifice and nature. Huysmans sought the explanation of this synthesis in the role of colour but was unable to elucidate the mystery of these 'tons étranges et réels', of these 'taches d'une authenticité singulière'. But at least the impulsion of colour gave him a means of access to Cézanne's still-life work.[41] Other elements he could see but not explain. His description of 'des fruits de guingois dans des poteries saoules' showed his recognition that Cézanne's organization of space was part of the figural system too but, unable to relate it to any constructive critical topos, he fell back on the rhetoric of *A Rebours*. Cézanne was an artist 'aux rétines malades' whose work was possessed by 'une fièvre de couleurs gâchées'.

It is difficult to evaluate the impact of this reading of Cézanne on the literary Symbolists. By 1890 Huysmans's art criticism was a declining force not only because it was identified with the decadent movement that Symbolism had supplanted but also because his repeated attacks on Puvis de Chavannes, linked to his support for Gustave Moreau, had weakened its credibility among a group which had reversed the priority attached to these two painters. On the other hand, there was very little competition in the Cézanne literature. In 1890, Émile Bernard, a cofounder of the Nabis, had written a short essay on the painter.[42] His reference to Cézanne's 'compotiers de guingois' suggests that he had read *Certains* but it is now inserted after others ('pommes arrondies comme au compas, poires triangulaires') which reveal a wider but still ambiguous grasp of the expressive function of Cézanne's formal system. He describes the napkins as 'rageusement pliées' but does not say by whom, Cézanne or the now absent user at the end of the meal. For Bernard, Cézanne 'ouvre à la peinture cette surprenante porte: la peinture pour elle-même' and he assimilates it to definitions of the flat surface and its links to those of primitive art current within the Nabi group.[43]

In November 1895, the dealer Vollard, encouraged by Pissarro, organized a major exhibition of Cézanne's work.[44] The contrasting responses to his work from the art critics of the two major Symbolist reviews are an indication of the growing divorce between developments in painting and the capacity of the literary tradition of writing on the visual arts to describe them. In the *Revue blanche*, Natanson, who, thanks to his close links with the Nabis, was familiar with current technical debates, recognized that Cézanne's still lifes involved the relationships between colours and geometrical forms displayed on the picture-surface.[45] He described them in ways clearly related to the Goncourts' description of Chardin's still lifes ('pommes, poires, oranges, citrons s'adossent à des gobelets . . . se dressent en pyramide . . . '), but recognized that this description was incapable of distinguishing them from the innumerable academic still lifes which cluttered up the annual salon, that it omitted 'l'essentiel, l'impénétrable et le plus précieux de ces objets, *tout ce reste qui n'est que peinture*' (Natanson's italics). He attempted a second description ('cernures des fruits accentuant les ronds ou les angles . . . ') but again concluded that the established discourse of the visual arts could not deal with the range of tones and values and their relationships to arabesque in Cézanne's work ('Mais combien dénués paraissent après les mots . . . '). This combination of material signs was for Natanson the discreet or forceful charm of painting which discourse could not possess.

In the *Mercure de France*, Mauclair was faced with the same problem and his first short response to the Cézanne exhibition illustrated his difficulty.[46] He saw the work of 'this solitary initiator of Impressionism "dernière manière"' (by which he meant Gauguin, whose art he loathed) as an example of what he called the 'rustic and anti-intellectual' tendency of modern painting.[47] He had been campaigning with increasing vigour against it for over a year. When he came to analyse Cézanne's still life at greater length he did so in terms of the idealization of Chardin which had been one of the major reevaluations of the artistic field during the Second Empire.[48] Chardin still lifes revealed 'the permanent life of the inert' in which humble, familiar objects 'begin to think, feel, respond, recite their individual poem'.[49] In Cézanne's objects there was no life, no intimacy, no 'histoire'. Mauclair was prepared to put up with Cézanne's 'usual failings' in technique but not with the lack of 'psychology' in his still life. To the painter's work he applied a modernized version of the traditional academic hierarchy of subjects. Landscape provided the greatest scope for narrative extensions and therefore occupied the summit. The future of still life lay in its potential to bask in the reflected glory of landscape's poetry of the natural world. Natanson knew how irrelevant this discourse was to a form of painting whose primary objective was to display the means and ends of constructing through paint.

Symbolist literature and the visual arts shared a wide range of subject matter (swans, angels, parks, lakes, veils, Wagnerian themes and characters, and so on) on which were exercised the forms of reading which have been my subject here. These shared subjects are Symbolism's local colour but it is the manner of reading which points to the significant underlying developments taking place in art theory and practice during this period. The literary Symbolists approached painting in the context of changing attitudes to the nature and status of the pictorial subject. They had at their disposal the description of the imagination of colour bequeathed to them by Baudelaire and the example of the Goncourts' attempts to reproduce in literature the sensuous impact of painting's engagement with its objects.[50] Such models as these were, however, of only limited use when the Symbolists were confronted with the task of interpreting forms of painting which challenged the traditional bases of representation more radically than before. A theoretical awareness of the expressive potential of the material sign provided a path into the painting, but once inside, the tendency was still to organize these signs into the hierarchical zones of information which the eye searched out as it negotiated its familiar tracks across and into the image, still to integrate the imagination of colour into narratives of figure or landscape.

Whether the object of painting was thought to be Aurier's Platonic Idea or the silent landscapes of the soul to which the Puvis figures and Monet landscapes gave access, the descriptive method remained for the most part reductive, able to isolate segments of meaning but unpractised in describing the ways in which paintings were built up by the working of pigment. Cézanne's still lifes and Gauguin's Tahiti paintings demonstrated the limits of this descriptive method. From the turn of the century, it would share the demise of the Salon system from which it was derived, as art criticism became more professional in order to respond more effectively to the increased diversity and more rapid turnover of trends within painting's avant-garde.[51] In this respect the Symbolist movement marks the final major flourish of the literary genre of art criticism founded by Diderot's *Salons*. In 1896, in his preface to the catalogue of the posthumous exhibition of the work of Berthe Morisot, Mallarmé returned to the sources of the new painting to define a new form of art literature, one in which the shared promotion of verbal and visual signs on behalf of which he had intervened twenty years before in defence of Manet would attain its true dimension.[52]

## Suggested reading

*La Critique d'art en France 1850–1900*, ed. J.-P. Bouillon (Saint-Etienne: CIEREC, 1989).

Florence, P., *Mallarmé, Manet and Redon: Visual and Aural Signs and the Generation of Meaning* (Cambridge: Cambridge University Press, 1986).

Gamboni, D., *La Plume et le pinceau: Odilon Redon et la littérature* (Paris: Editions de Minuit, 1989).

Halperin, J.U., *F. Fénéon and the Language of Art Criticism* (Ann Arbor: UMI Research Press, 1980).

Herbert, R.L., *Impressionism: Art, Leisure and Parisian Society* (New Haven and London: Yale University Press, 1988).

Kearns, J., *Symbolist Landscapes: The Place of Painting in the Poetry and Criticism of Mallarmé and his Circle* (London: Modern Humanities Research Association, 1989).

*The New Painting: Impressionism 1874–1886* (San Francisco: The Fine Arts Museums of San Francisco, 1986).

*La Promenade du critique influent: Anthologie de la critique d'art en France 1850–1900*, ed. J.-P. Bouillon et al. (Paris: Hazan, 1990).

Scott, D., *Pictorialist Poetics: Poetry and the Visual Arts in Nineteenth-Century France* (Cambridge: Cambridge University Press, 1988).

Shiff, R., *Cézanne and the End of Impressionism* (Chicago and London: University of Chicago Press, 1984).

Steiner, W., *The Colors of Rhetoric: Problems in the Relation between Modern Literature and Painting* (Chicago and London: Chicago University Press, 1982).

# 16

# *Rimbaud: the shaping of a vision*

## Roger Little

Once it was clearly established, in the course of the nineteenth century, that the attribute of poetry was distinct from the technique of verse, it was possible for poets to allow the shaping of their texts to respond to visual stimuli, whether from the real world or from existing art works. Without going as far as Mallarmé in *Un coup de Dés* . . . or, later, Apollinaire in his *Calligrammes*, Rimbaud displays, in his use of prose for poetry in *Illuminations* for example, a concern for form no less responsive to his object than they, however much less obvious to the reader's eye. His approach to the literary imitation of reality must be understood to go beyond a concern with narrative alone. Each text espouses its object to the point where it becomes an equivalent object incorporating an expression of the poet's relationship with what he has seen and felt. The decorative is therefore relinquished in favour of the organic, integrated and hidden in often surprising and stimulating ways.

This study will first show how rewarding the investigation of selected examples and features can be, revealing some patterns of form unexpected in the usual use of prose for the communication of messages and ideas. Rimbaud's subversion of our lazy assumptions about the potential of prose for poetry will then be linked to a pattern of subversiveness apparent in his earlier writings. That pattern will finally be associated with 'now-you-see-it-now-you-don't' visual metaphors drawn from physics and popular imagery (for which Rimbaud expressed fondness) and which seems both to encapsulate a singularly appropriate image of his preoccupations and to suggest a way of reading his elusive and fascinating work.[1]

The very title *Illuminations* is, at least in some of its principal meanings, a programme for an instructive approach. We do not know whether the word is to be understood in English or in French, nor even indeed if it is the title Rimbaud intended. There is a general consensus, however, that it is an appropriate title for the collection, the primary

sense being visionary flashes of insight, supported by a strong con-
notation of the jewel-like intensity of medieval illuminated manuscripts.

Rimbaud never lets us rest easy. Form is not fixed even though he may
use certain narrative paradigms such as the riddle in 'H', the wondrous
tale in many a text, lists in 'Solde' and 'Dévotion', travelogues and
descriptions elsewhere. If 'Conte' does indeed, with whatever ironies,
tell a story, such a title as 'Sonnet' (the second part of 'Jeunesse') challenges our expectations by heading a text in prose. It is an invitation to
decipherment. We are impelled to seek ways in which features of a sonnet might be present in the text; and because the syntax and sense seem
so unclear, we explore the overall structure and the details of the phonetics more closely. Because we are not then disappointed, we are not
only duly compensated for our efforts but also willing to give Rimbaud
his due for consciously contructing his text. Analysis shows that the persistent view of him as a wild wordsmith is untenable.

'Sonnet' consists of three sentences, the first two of almost equal
length and the last approximately as long as the first two together:

> *Homme* de constitution ordinaire, la chair n'était-elle pas un fruit pendu
> dans le verger; – ô journées enfantes! – le corps un trésor à prodiguer; – ô
> aimer, le péril ou la force de Psyché? La terre avait des versants fertiles en
> princes et en artistes et la descendance et la race vous poussaient aux
> crimes et aux deuils: le monde votre fortune et votre péril. Mais à présent
> le labeur comblé, – toi, tes calculs, – toi, tes impatiences – ne sont plus
> que votre danse et votre voix, non fixées et point forcées, quoique d'un
> double événement d'invention et de succès une raison, – en l'humanité
> fraternelle et discrète par l'univers, sans images; – la force et le droit réflé-
> chissent la danse et la voix à présent seulement appréciées.

The opening sentence is a question, addressed to a normally constituted
man, but ends with a series of exclamations which disrupt the inter-
rogative flow. The second is a statement, clipped after the colon by a
verbless element. The third, a series of statements, is dislocated and re-
directed at various turns by subsidiary phrases or clauses in an
accumulation which seems both self-reflective through its repetitions
and bewilderingly tumultuous in its effects. Yet one feature stands out as
a clear realization of the title: the 'turn' of the sonnet, as between octave
and sestet, on 'Mais à présent'.[2] And the reader looks to the repetitions
of word and sound as a life-raft for his or her intelligence of the text and
is not disappointed. Indeed, the patterns which emerge show shifts of
tone and emphasis and an increase in intensity which mirror, however
obscurely, the increase in syntactical complexity. A cluster of [ɛʀ]
sounds informs the opening lines: 'ordinaire', 'chair', 'verger', 'terre',
'fertiles'. The sound does not reappear until 'fraternelle' and 'l'univers'
towards the end. Likewise [ɔʀ] sounds are grouped at the beginning

('ordinaire', 'corps', 'trésor', 'force', plus the reversed form [RO] in 'prodiguer') but more thinly scattered later on ('fortune', 'forcées', 'force').

More remarkable, however, are the cases of phonemes which recur in-
tensively only in the second half of the text (in the case of [wa]: 'toi',
'toi', 'voix', 'point', 'quoique', 'droit', 'voix') or with far greater fre-
quency there: [ã] in 'pendu' and twice in 'enfantes' develops into [sã] in
'versants' and the second syllable of 'descendance' before shifting to [ãs]
in the last syllable of the same word and figuring massively, like [wa], in
the last sentence in 'à présent ce', 'impatiences', 'danse', 'invention',
'sans images' (voiced), 'danse' and 'à présent seulement'. Repetitions of
whole words support this increased intensity in the latter half, the more
so as they all involve the insistent phonemes to which attention is
drawn: 'à présent', 'danse', 'voix' and 'force', only the last being picked
up from the first half of the text. Only 'péril' is repeated within the first
two sentences, though it 'rhymes' with 'fertiles' and includes the [e]
sound which clusters towards the end of the opening sentence and in the
last: 'verger', 'journées', 'prodiguer', 'aimer', 'péril', 'Psyché', 'péril',
'présent', 'fixées', 'forcées', 'l'humanité', 'réfléchissent', 'présent', 'appréciées'. To present all the details of related sounds (such as 'prince' and
'race' playing around [ãs]) would be inappropriate here: the patterns
already traced show clearly enough how Rimbaud's poetic sense led him
to shape his phonetics to compensate for the bewilderment that his syn-
tactic and semantic obscurities might cause.

If the phonetic armature is as tightly organized as in a traditional sonnet, it seems legitimate to seek ways in which the text might be divided
into octave and sestet and even into individual lines. One such hypothetical presentation, with the 'rhyming' pattern indicated, might be as
follows:

| | |
|---|---|
| *Homme* de constitution ordinaire, la chair | a |
| n'était-elle pas un fruit pendu dans le ver- | a |
| ger; – ô journées enfantes! – le corps un trésor | b |
| à prodiguer; – ô aimer, le péril ou la for- | b |
| ce de Psyché? La terre avait des versants fertiles | c |
| en princes et en artistes et la descendance | – (e) |
| et la race vous poussaient aux crimes et aux deuils: | – |
| le monde votre fortune et votre péril. | c |
| Mais à présent le labeur comblé, – toi, tes calculs, – | |
| toi, tes impatiences – | e |
| ne sont plus que votre danse et votre voix, non fixées et | |
| point forcées, | f |
| quoique d'un double événement d'invention et de succès | {f} |
| + une raison, – en l'humanité fraternelle et discrète | |
| par l'univers, sans | {e} |

images; – la force et le droit réflechissent la danse       e
et la voix à présent seulement appréciées.             f

However approximate some of the rhymes (such as those in curly brackets), the dispositions shows graphically at least how tightly the prose is organized while at the same time benefiting from the very fluidity of prose in its game of hide-and-seek with the reader.

Another approximation to a prose sonnet in the *Illuminations* may help to suggest that 'Sonnet' is not an isolated example of the poet's using appearances as a foil for his exploration of a higher reality. The syntax of 'Mystique' is more conventional and the careful balancing of features more evident than in 'Sonnet', but it confirms this balance in the phonetic structure in support of the meaning:

> Sur la pente du talus les anges tournent leurs robes de laine dans les herbages d'acier et d'émeraude.
>
> Des prés de flammes bondissent jusqu'au sommet du mamelon. A gauche le terreau de l'arête est piétiné par tous les homicides et toutes les batailles, et tous les bruits désastreux filent leur courbe. Derrière l'arête de droite la ligne des orients, des progrès.
>
> Et tandis qui la bande en haut du tableau est formée de la rumeur tournante et bondissante des conques des mers et des nuits humaines,
>
> La douceur des étoiles et du ciel et du reste descend en face du talus, comme un panier, contre notre face, et fait l'abîme fleurant et bleu là-dessous.

We are formally alerted to the fact that these are not ordinary prose paragraphs only by the comma at the end of the third phrase, but it is sufficient to make us investigate the structure more closely than we might otherwise have done. Indeed, the very balance and consistency of the presentation, with its emphasis on curvature ('tournent', 'mamelon', 'courbe', 'tournante' and 'conques', which thereby influences our apprehension of 'pente', 'ligne', 'bande' and 'panier') and careful positioning of features evoked ('Sur la pente', 'dans les herbages', 'au sommet', 'A gauche', 'Derrière l'arête de droite', 'en haut du tableau', 'en face du talus', 'là-dessous'), makes this comma more surprising and provocative. The repetition of words is no less marked than in 'Sonnet', though more evenly spread across the text. Three are repeated without change: 'talus', 'l'arête' and 'face'; three others shift to the adjectival form of the present participle: 'tournent' – 'tournante', 'bondissent' – 'bondissante' and 'fleurie' – 'fleurant'. The reader's eye is guided from the centre of the landscape first to the left, then to the right, then upwards, and finally downwards in a grand sweep encompassing the universe. The movement is logical and all-embracing, as befits the investigation of the allegorical picture of heaven and earth, good and evil, which is described.

Closer investigation of the final line reveals a particular phonetic organization which can only be described as palindromic. Around the pivotal word 'panier', working backwards and forwards, one finds echoing pairs of words: 'comme' – 'contre', 'face' – 'face', 'fleurie' – 'fleurant' and finally 'La douceur' – 'là-dessous'. The eye follows the descent from the sky towards the abyss with the curvature of the basket which acts as a crucible or a concave mirror for the vision. The principal semantic feature which escapes this phonetic balance occurs equidistantly from 'panier' and commands closer attention: 'des étoiles et du ciel et du reste' is mirrored by 'l'abîme'. The formulation invites us to consider three possible meanings of 'abîme' which correspond to the tripartite presentation of the night sky. Firstly there is a physical gulf below the poet's gaze; secondly there is 'the deep', the sea; thirdly, in recognition of the fact that 'le ciel' means heaven as well as the sky, is the moral notion of the abyss of hell.

Once again the organization proves exceptionally tight, a fitting climax to a text whose length and shape readily suggest a prose sonnet, even to the point where the last two lines form separate 'tercets'. If the 'quatrains' are less manifest, it is rather because Rimbaud is once again hiding his game: the natural division of sense in relation to the spatial disposition of the references comes not after 'émeraude' but after 'mamelon'. A line break at that point would have made the 'sonnet' form all too obvious.

Whether we should take Rimbaud's reference to a picture literally is uncertain, but its style is suggested by the presence of angels (unless they are sheep, with their 'robes de laine', envisioned as such), by the mineral brilliance of the colouring ('d'acier et d'émeraude', 'flammes'), by the pitting of man's evil on the left against rays of hope rising to the right, by the speech scroll ('la bande' with its conch-like ends) at the top of the picture, carrying the angels' or the painter's message as a 'rumeur' literally 'tournante et bondissante' on the canvas or parchment. There is something medieval or, at the latest, quattrocento about its allegorical basis which seems unmistakable, and its colouring could well lead us to look for it among illuminated manuscripts.

While the title of *Illuminations* would justify such a search, it is not in high art that Rimbaud expresses an interest. François Boucher (1703–70) warrants a passing mention in 'Fête d'hiver'. Otherwise, reference is restricted in Rimbaud's writings to such painters as he knew in Paris. The most extended comment he makes on the subject, in the 'Alchimie du verbe' section of *Une Saison en enfer*, leads us firmly in the direction of popular art:

Depuis longtemps je me vantais de posséder tous les paysages possibles, et trouvais dérisoires les célébrités de la peinture et de la poésie moderne.

> J'aimais les peintures idiotes, dessus de portes, décors, toiles de saltim-
> banques, enseignes, enluminures populaires; la littérature démodée, latin
> d'église, livres érotiques sans orthographe, romans de nos aïeules, contes
> de fées, petits livres de l'enfance, opéras vieux, refrains niais, rhythmes
> naïfs.

Only recently has criticism begun to take a serious interest in popular
culture. Rimbaud's stated preference for popular over high art subverts
traditional critical assumptions. As usual, however, we have to take a
poet's declarations about himself with a grain of salt: in his adolescent
revolt, he could afford to be lofty about high culture because he had so
thoroughly absorbed and mastered it at school.

It is not my purpose here to trace individual sources of inspiration for
Rimbaud's poems – the many recent editions of his work cater well for
that legitimate interest[3] – but rather to suggest a cast of mind and a con-
sequent manner. The expression of the particular kind of ambivalent
relationship that Rimbaud has with his subject matter and with his
reader changes as his poetry evolves. His apprenticeship, not surprisingly, includes pastiche, whether of French or Latin poets. He then
develops an interest in parody analogous to the art of caricature and
with a keen sense of the obscene.[4] Such areas of interest cannot but involve duplication of reference and duplicity of manner, and Rimbaud
raids the polysemy of language to sustain the balance between the re-
ferentially obscene and the ostensibly anodine. The experience of such
writing continues to inform the *Illuminations*, many of which appear as
conundrums to the uninitiated.

I should like to propose two visual metaphors of that conundrum
which help to throw light on the nature of Rimbaud's writing. Each involves seeing and not seeing, almost but not quite simultaneously, with
time and memory therefore performing a function similar to that which
is required by the reading of ambivalent or even contradictory meanings
into a text.

The first is stroboscopic lighting, familiar to those who go to the
theatre or discos, but also used by psychiatrists provoking their patients
to crisis point. At certain rates of change from light to dark, a continuous but different turning speed will be perceived, as is well known
from fast-moving wheels apparently rotating slowly forwards or even
backwards on the cinema or television screen. Such interplay between
the discontinuous and the non-discontinuous (i.e. the continuous of the
third kind) is closely analogous to our sense of Rimbaud's poetic vision.
We are conscious both of the flickering interruptions of light and of the
different reality to which the phenomenon gives rise, both of the dynamism and of the ambiguity. The stroboscope, invented around 1830,
gave rise to the diorama, with which Rimbaud would undoubtedly have

been as well acquainted as were the *pensionnaires* of Balzac's 'maison Vauquer', and eventually to the cinema. That a sequence of still images should give rise to moving pictures had not lost its almost magical fascination in Rimbaud's day.

A singularly apposite example of this effect may be found in 'Marine', one of the two free-verse poems in *Illuminations*:

> Les chars d'argent et de cuivre –
> Les proues d'acier et d'argent –
> Battent l'écume, –
> Soulèvent les souches des ronces –
> Les courants de la lande,
> Et les ornières immenses du reflux,
> Filent circulairement vers l'est,
> Vers les piliers de la forêt, –
> Vers les fûts de la jetée,
> Dont l'angle est heurté par des
> tourbillons de lumière.

The careful interweaving of references to land and sea grants a line to each to begin with and then, in lines 5, 6, 8 and 9, has each appear as an attribute of the other. The sequence of images has speeded up. The dynamic seventh and closing lines seem to relate to either or both, as befits a seascape seemingly painted, as would be usual, from dry land, setting the sea off against features of the shore. The swirling interactions are nonetheless even more complex than at first they appear, since 'char' could mean a vessel as well as a cart, and 'les souches des ronces' not merely bramble-stumps but also nests of rays (the fish). Rimbaud seems so aware of this effect that the last line is almost a straight translation of the Greek roots of 'stroboscope': στρόβος, 'a whirling round', and σκοπεῖν, 'to observe, to look at'.

The second, and related, metaphor drawn from the visual field is more directly linked with popular traditions. It is perhaps most familiar to us in playing-cards, where all the cards, and the court figures most colourfully, are so designed as to be legible from either end. Nowadays, the topsy-turvy heads and trunks are identical, but this has not always been the case, nor is a single figure an absolute requirement (fig. 27(i)). We are aware of the coexistence of the upside-down form but have to use our memory to carry its features over into our reading of the whole, just as with the stroboscope our total perception is dependent on creating non-discontinuity out of discontuity and being simultaneously aware of both. Ernst Gombrich draws attention at the beginning of his *Art and Illusion* to the ambivalent image 'Rabbit or Duck?' drawn from the humourous weekly *Die fliegenden Blätter*, which can be read as either creature depending on the importance attached to certain features of the

27. (i) *left* 'Ace of Hearts', traditional playing card

(ii) *above* 'Ci-devant duc d'Aiguillon. Passe salope', satirical print, exhibited at *Taking Liberties. Satirical Prints of the French Revolution*, Chester Beatty Library, Dublin, in 1989

(iii) *below left* 'Cherchez et vous trouverez! Officiers prussien et autrichien', *devinette d'Epinal*

(iv) *below* 'Montrez à ces gamins que, s'ils se croient à l'abri des regards du proviseur et du censeur, ils se trompent', *devinette d'Epinal*

drawing and notably on the extent to which, as the gaze swithers between one interpretation and another, the two shapes jutting out to the
left are seen as ears or beak. Gombrich's comments are germane to the
present argument:

> . . . we are compelled to look for what is 'really there', to see the shape
> apart from its interpretation, and this, we discover, is not really possible.
> True, we can switch from one reading to another with increasing rapid-
> ity; we will also 'remember' the rabbit while we see the duck, but the
> more closely we watch ourselves, the more certainly will we discover that
> we cannot experience alternative readings at the same time.[5]

The psychoanalyst might wish to press the point and see in Rimbaud's
double-takes something that Freud discovered through his observation
of his grandson responding 'Fort' when an image struck him and 'Da'
when it disappeared. His interpretation of this relating to the lost
mother-figure will doubtless appeal to those who seek the origins of
Rimbaud's attitudes in his strained relations with his mother, but that
would be matter for another study.

Popular imagery and caricature have used the tête-bêche form over
the ages to symbolize duplicity and show the interplay between appearance and reality (fig. 27(ii)) or merely to relish the fun of the fair.[6] The
popular French prints known as 'images d'Épinal', to which Rimbaud
refers directly in 'L'éclatante victoire de Sarrebrück',[7] gave rise, towards
the end of the nineteenth century, to what are known as 'devinettes
d'Épinal', in which there are either reversible heads (fig. 27(iii)) or more
complex visual games in which the eye has to hunt for hidden features
(fig. 27 (iv)).

My argument is less that Rimbaud's is a topsy-turvy world (though to
some it may well appear to be) than that the 'now-you-see-it-now-you-
don't' qualities of stroboscopic effects or of 'devinettes d'Épinal' and
their like are analogous to the fascination he had with words in general
and with the potential of verbal ambiguity in particular. Our difficulty in
reading him is adumbrated by Gombrich's observation: 'Illusion . . . is
hard to describe or analyse, for though we may be intellectually aware of
the fact that any given experience *must* be an illusion, we cannot, strictly
speaking, watch ourselves having an illusion.'[8] Rimbaud is not indulging
idly in illusionism, but his fondness for an interactive multiplicity of
meanings and bravura effects of semantics, of structure and of phonetics
is integral to his style, where obscurity seems an essential partner for
brilliance.

The mastery as well as the attendant difficulties increase as his writing
develops. Pastiche and parody necessarily relate to a model: we know
we have to take account of that model, and that its existence is integral
to the total effect achieved. In such cases, because of the passage of time

and taste, we may need instruction (as we do for Lewis Carroll or W.S. Gilbert) about the text parodied. Likewise, an obscene sub-text is precisely that: inseparable from the text which both bears and conceals it. Again, light must be thrown on period slang, that most transient and least well recorded of sociolinguistic phenomena, and on meanings of words which have slipped, sometimes out of sight, over the years, for us to appreciate Rimbaud's intentions and achievement. Our reading of the texts must be double (at least) to take account of the poet's artful ambivalences.

Structurally, Rimbaud's sleight of hand may be seen at the closure of many of the *Illuminations*: rarely do endings conclude. They invite us rather to reread the text in a new light and so make it stand outside the temporal, sequential assumptions of narrative. We have seen how 'Marine' closes in a whirl of light which requires us to reconsider the coloration of what precedes. The same is true of 'Les Ponts', where 'Un rayon blanc, tombant du haut du ciel, anéantit cette comédie'. This final word seems curiously at odds with the description that has preceded and makes us investigate more closely the way in which the picture is animated. Seen first in terms of a black and white drawing, the poem offers its first non-visual reference more than halfway through, when muted minor chords lend a musical equivalent to the grey tones. Light is then made to fall on 'une veste rouge', as if the sunrise had singled it out for attention, rather as Monet's near-contemporary 'Impression: soleil levant' (1872), which gave its name to Impressionism, lends colour to such details in the early mist. With the increase in colour comes a crescendo in the music, emblematic of the three estates of the *ancien régime*: 'airs populaires', 'concerts seigneuriaux' and 'hymnes publics'. Blue appears in the water thanks to the revolution of the light, so the shaft of white light at the end logically completes the tricolour and lends the text an unsuspected sociopolitical and historical dimension which legitimizes the use of the word 'comédie'. The shadowy figures, whose presence is not stated but implied, emerge from the grey background to force a rereading of the text and bring the picture to life.

Time and again, Rimbaud's poetic closures throw us back provocatively upon our ignorance and thereby alert us to unsuspected readings. Negatives abound as the blank page reasserts its right not to explain. 'Après le déluge', 'Conte', 'Vies', 'Ouvriers', 'Jeunesse' and 'Dévotion' end on explicitly negative formulations which challenge our assumptions about what we have read. Elsewhere, the sense may be negative (or at best ambiguous) even if the syntax is not; such is the case in 'Parade', 'A une raison', 'Matinée d'ivresse', 'Aube', 'Nocturne vulgaire' and 'Angoisse'. Questions and defiant claims leave us in suspense or make us bridle and search for a justification. At every turn, Rimbaud toys with our expectations and deploys his panoply of ambiguity and ambivalence in the texts and their microstructures. Their challenge to our assumptions about form and meaning, however daunting, is invigorating in the extreme, the more so as they straddle high and popular linguistic and more broadly cultural traditions.

An exceptional quality of control is required to master such material, hence the importance of demonstrating that despite certain appearances Rimbaud does indeed possess a supreme poetic intelligence. He knew well that expectations were best subverted if interest was to be sustained, and he did so by engaging in those aspects of language neglected by communicative prose: phonetic and structural patterns redundant and indeed obtrusive in the conveyance of a message, semantic ambivalences and ambiguities disruptive of logic and obstructive to clarity. Gestures towards the fixed forms of prose or even the sonnet, as we have seen, are two-edged, not to say two-fingered. It is hardly surprising that they proved unsustainable: they reflect the wilful brilliance of youth. The fluctuating, probing nature of the stroboscope and the topsy-turvy model of the 'devinettes d'Épinal' seem apt visual analogies for their characteristic qualities, metaphors of metaphor which can be instructive when a more straightforward approach proves difficult or impossible.

## Suggested reading

Fabre, Daniel, *Carnaval ou la fête à l'envers* (Paris; Gallimard, 1992).

Gombrich, Ernst, *Art and Illusion: a Study in the Psychology of Pictorial Representation* (London: Phaidon, 3rd edn, 1968).

Hackett, C.A., *Rimbaud: a critical introduction* (Cambridge: Cambridge University Press, 1981).

Little, Roger, *Rimbaud: 'Illuminations'* (London: Grant and Cutler, 1983).

Murphy, Steve, *Le Premier Rimbaud ou l'apprentissage de la subversion* (Lyon: CNRS, Presses universitaires de Lyon, 1990).

———, *Rimbaud et la ménagerie impériale* (Lyon: CNRS, Presses universitaires de Lyon, 1991).

Rimbaud, Arthur, *Œuvres*, ed. Louis Forestier (Paris: Laffont, 1992).

# 17

# Sex and the occult in
# Symbolist art and literature

## Timothy Mathews

## *Introduction: pleasure, performance, vision*

This essay deals with the vicissitudes of a theme stretching from the Romantic avant-garde in France through to the new European Modernism gravitating around Paris in the early twentieth century. One of its principal elements is theatricality, viewed as a heightened enaction of ways in which our identities are constructed, and given to us in a perpetual exchange of roles: those of performer and spectator. This implies a disquieting mobility and even eclecticism in the make-up of the social persona. The layers of interaction involved include the political, the moral, the aesthetic. The Latin verb *occulare* signifies 'to hide from view', and the sense that the psyche is constituted as hidden, as removed from efforts to categorize it and shape it, is one of the focal points of this theme. An integral element of it is sexuality, and particularly the sense that sexuality is at once intimate, unique *and* part of the public space, of the socialized arena of gaze and countergaze – the sense that sexuality is performed.

Freud's thinking is immersed in the vicissitudes of a pleasure principle propelled by sex. This principle is one of survival. But a 'principle' also signals the method used to interpret it, it inaugurates the coercion involved in applying a method as well as in accepting its conclusions. For Freud, pleasure is part of an economy of sexual disparity that involves 'unpleasure' and pain. The pleasure principle, in Freud's thought, provides the boy and the girl each with their own reward – each incompatible with the other's – for giving up the mother in the Oedipal drama, for accepting positions in society and in a discourse which privileges the image. In this setting, the image acts as a space where the retentive embrace of the mother's body is both given up and recalled as a memory that may not be named. The fragile reward offered in this space is a sexed ego struggling continuously for its position centre-stage, for domination of the voices that have socialized it, and trained it to relativize its desires in pursuit of permissible forms.

But in 1920, with *Beyond the Pleasure Principle*, Freud embarks on a new turn in his theory: a desire for a 'beyond' directed at his own theory, and at the tautology in theory of description and prescription. A silent pursuit of decomposition emerges in Freud's writing and in his account of the survival of the ego: the pursuit of an end to alienated relations determined biologically by sexual difference and disparity. Beyond the pleasure principle lies the mirage of a halt to the ways in which sexual desiring, gender and social identity are psychically pre-set by the incompatible positions that make up family relations. It is this glorious delusion of a death implanted in the social as well as the bodily self that I want to go on to explore.[1]

Symbolist art precedes Freudian thinking and writing and, unlike avant-garde movements of the twentieth century such as Surrealism, it is therefore not propelled by an explicit response or indeed challenge to Freudian notions. Freud's own thought, on the other hand, is consistently nourished retroactively by artists from the past, ranging from Sophocles, to Michelangelo and Leonardo, to Shakespeare, to Goethe and Heine. This is not so much a sign of appropriation as of continual modification and development of an intellectual and clinical experience – and an equally powerful sign of the capacity of the arts to trouble and disturb theoretical entrenchment. In what ways might the residue of Freudian notions in contemporary culture in turn nourish a reading of representations of sex in fin de siècle art? For such representations abound obsessively in these works. And what relation might there be, in this art so predominantly male-oriented in its production, between the interplay of sex and death and the interplay of sex and the occult?

The affinity to each other of these two overlapping pairs of notions is exemplified in Gérard de Nerval's *Aurélia*, published in 1853 after the author's suicide.[2] It is an account of the narrator's folly, and of a potentially irreversible disintegration into madness. Death is a state which, on one level in the text, the narrator actively desires and pursues, for to him it represents an access to his allocated place in the world of the Spirits – and in particular, a place where he will be reunited with his dead lover, a former actress. His passage to his place in this other, non-material world of physical and metaphysical union is announced to him by a vision or a hallucination of his own double – thought of as the harbinger of his journey from the world of the living to that of universal spiritual integration. Drawn from the mystical thinking of Swedenborg, and drawn on in the metaphysical and aesthetic speculations of Balzac and Baudelaire as well as of Nerval, the *Doppelgänger* as a mystical Hermes and

Siren combined was to become a source of morbid and obsessional fascination in the work of the Norwegian Symbolist painter Edvard Munch. In Nerval's text, the mad desire for a place in cosmological infinity is barred by our own language, by the opacity of its signs and their labyrinthine etymology. The narrator suffers acutely from what he comes to think of as his own unique incapacity to read linguistic signs as hieroglyphs activating the magic of universal sense, and capable of unveiling the paths of Genesis itself.

This occultist pursuit of union, of the Word and of the Deity beyond the myths of It, is eventually experienced by the narrator as transgressive, as a fault in him that has the effect of darkening the sign still further rather than unveiling its revelatory power. His promised voyage in the ethereal depths of spirituality and temporality is ultimately represented as a Don Juanesque Descent into Hell. The punishment for seeking to embrace the Deified Body of the actress he loved, in fact of seeking to embrace the Deified Image projected on the other side of the footlights and of the social arena of human exchange, is a series of apocalyptic hallucinations seeming to testify to the consequences of his own cosmic guilt. If he is to lay to rest these violent scenes of paranoid delusion, the narrator must accept, as Beckett a century later imagines Proust doing, that the only conceivable Paradise is a Paradise lost. Signification emerges as Purgatory itself, but also as a realm of dialogue, and the narrator seems to sense in the end that Purgatory and a blind waiting experienced in dialogue must be accepted as a gift if he is not to drown in fantasm and insanity. Nerval's own suicide seems still to send a morbid signal that this is a gift he could not accept.

*Aurélia* concentrates a number of dominant French nineteenth-century literary investigations of the psyche, its grafting on to expression and the problems of reading forms and signs that this grafting gives rise to. European artists later in the century such as Georges Seurat, Edvard Munch and Gustave Moreau become still more absorbed in exploiting the revelatory powers of imagistic surfaces and aesthetic forms, and in challenging their limits. Such investment in aesthetic effects is characteristic of the formalist revolt of Cubism some thirty years later, and of Expressionism beyond that. In common with such later approaches, the work of fin de siècle artists remains in a confrontational dialogue with mimesis. The interaction which it stages of myth and icon, on the one hand, and formal examination of the two-dimensional image on the other still involves examinations of how to represent experience; this examination now involves ever more mobile boundaries between inner and outer experience.

The fin de siècle aesthetic involves seeking out an integration of what an image makes apparent and blots from view simultaneously. This imaged interaction is a socialized one, it is the image of the self, which this art becomes embroiled in seeking grandly to put to death. Representations of sexual desire in European art of the period encourage this pursuit of occultist, mystical transcendence of social discourse. Ironically, these representations involve images of theatrical performance – for this performance is a loaded one. It is predominantly male figures which occupy the position of artist and of the spectator, and female ones the position of elusive image, object of the desiring gaze. Perhaps a signal of fin de siècle Decadence emerges in precisely this inability to think consistently against Oedipus, coupled with an anxiety and a discomfort at thinking through him and with him.

## Muses, Vamps and Madonnas

In 1896, the artist Lucien Lévi-Dhurmer, much admired by the Belgian Symbolist poet Georges Rodenbach and the fin de siècle novelist Pierre Loti, drew a startlingly transgressive version of the classical, academic subject of Salome. It is entitled *Salomé embrassant la tête de Saint Jean*; the title is the source of the picture's shocking effect, rather than a benign explanation of the subject on offer. Without the title, the picture's impact might engulf heterosexual viewers in its eroticism, in the way it melts the distinction between public and private. The grainy texture of the combination used of pastel and charcoal is absorbing in its decorativeness, and at the same time in its capacity to wipe out all decorative features from the surface other than that of the interplay of light and dark and the mobile frontier between them. There is a halo-like radiance appropriately emanating from the figure of St John, but this potential symbolism is itself embroiled and thus undermined in the sensuality of the surface texture. The darkness from which emerge the heads of St John and Salome shows them both to be symmetrically drawn to each other, and the structural epicentre of the image shifts from the dissipated halo to the dark and concentrated space between their mouths, watched over on either side by their eyes that are closed. It is almost possible to feel and hear their breath.

The composition of the picture is such that the body of St John would be imagined hidden, Salome on top and all the politics of sexual dominance evaporated. But the shock of reading the title shatters this illusion. In realizing that the body of St John is not hidden by the composition but absent from it, not there, it is now unambiguously, undecoratively, verbally apparent that Salome is literally embracing the 'severed head' with all the bloody tendrils that might be hanging from it, and that she now epitomizes the figure of the violent 'femme fatale', mythical emasculator of men, source of all menace and danger to men, however fascinating. The flimsy signal of sexual emancipation provided by Salome's position in sex is now nothing more than an ironic indicator of the picture's place in the mythology and drama of male sexual anxiety.

This oscillation between extremes is typical of male representations of women in European art of this period: an oscillation between decorativeness, on the one hand, danger on the other; on the one hand spiritual expansion, on the other violence, perversion or death. Dante Gabriel Rossetti's *Daydream* (1872–8), with its idealization of Jane Morris, its eclectic, affirmative styling combining the neoclassical and the hyperrealist, and supported by arabesques of a reference-resisting kind, is a striking example of the decorative in the exploitation of the female image at the hands of the male artist of this period.[3] The dominant associations in this imagery of danger and perversion, on the other hand, are exemplified in Franz von Stuck's *Le Péché*, with its gleaming white female torso shrouded in the dark and menacing forms of a python.[4] Edvard Munch's *Madonna*, whch he began in 1895 and reworked in 1902, fuses both these elements in this representation of women; but he does so in a thematic and formal play that disrupts the predictable antagonism of the way these two elements – idealization and terror – interrelate.[5]

This work resonates with Munch's own pre-Expressionist fascination with the spiritual and the erotic as well as the corruptible elements of death which he shares with Nerval and Baudelaire before him, and which made him a natural gravitater to the salon of Mallarmé and to Paul Gauguin whom he met there. In the manner of von Stuck's *Le Péché*, the Madonna's torso is naked and captures the eye, and here too the torso is encircled in dark colours and shapes. But in this picture, the shapes are the swirling ones specific to Munch's own stylistic obsessions – not only encircling but effusive; these shapes are moulded to the contours of the body which in this way seems to enact some continuation from the public and the visible into the realm of psycho-sexual intimacy and secrecy. The outlines and the surface of the body are worked on, worked at and worked away; and the corruptibility of the body visible is turned to the profit of forbidden fruits of creation and salvation. For the sensuality of this Madonna is not so much menacing, as in *Le Péché*, or idealized, as in *Daydream*, as blasphemous. The foetus in the corner of the painted frame is very real-looking, molecular, rather than angelic or heavenly; this frame-in-the picture is itself decorated with spermatozoid shapes: the Conception, far from Immaculate, is sexual and visceral. But the message of this toying with blasphemy is far from univocal. Is the spiritual being granted human form, brought to within the dimensions of the human form and the human imagination? Or is the desperate hubris of such a pretension being displayed, along with its cost in with-drawal, shame and morbidness?

## The decorative; inner visions

The critic and philosopher Albert Aurier, in an article entitled 'Le Symbolisme dans la peinture: Paul Gauguin', which was published in the *Mercure de France* in March 1891 and acted as a kind of manifesto, gives decorativeness a pivotal role to play in shaping the new art of the moment. The constituent qualities of this decorativeness, as he sees it, are 'idéiste', 'symboliste', 'synthétique' and 'subjectif'.[6] But Aurier's evocative account of decorative, Symbolist art might seem to comprise too many eclectic components to work effectively as a definition. The decorativeness of Gauguin's *Le Christ jaune* (1889), with its emphasis on colour and fluidity in the two-dimensional space, in many ways seems to have little in common with, say, the decorative features of Pierre Puvis de Chavanne's *Le Pigeon Voyageur* (1871) or his *L'Espérance* (1872).[7]

Puvis de Chavannes's pictures might strike us now as disconcertingly static and ponderous, schematic, overtly allegorical, and frankly two-dimensional. And yet artists who differ from one another as much as they differ individually from Puvis de Chavannes, and including Georges Seurat as well as Gauguin, bear witness to what they owe to his work. Gauguin makes a practice, in fact, like many other artists, of examining and intertextually reworking in his own image-making the styles of other artists – not only that of Puvis de Chavannes but also, for example, Cézanne and van Gogh. The composition of his *Tahitian Pastoral* (1898), its return to a mode of construction that is not bound by the perspectival illusion that dominates European painting since the Renaissance, seems to work in just such an intertextual dialogue with Puvis de Chavannes's *Inter Artes et Naturam* of 1890.[8]

The perturbation of the illusion of depth is one of the salient features in the impact of Puvis de Chavannes's work, and one which particularly signals the appeal of this work to other artists of the period. In *L'Espérance* of 1872, hostile two-dimensionality both heightens and undermines the allegorical effect of the picture. The allegory, on one level, could not be more obvious. The title of the painting combines with the olive branch it depicts, held out to her right by the figure in white which dominates the composition, to suggest the offer of peace and goodwill, and in particular a desire for an end to the brutality of the Franco-Prussian War and its aftermath. But at the same time, the artifice itself of this allegory, the unnaturalness of the woman's pose in support of it, the sharp outline of her white dress against the overwhelmingly green background all draw the attention to the surface itself of the picture, rather than to its functioning as an allegorical sign. The female figure of peace strikes the eye as plaquetted on to the surface of the picture, or conversely as a white shape cut out of that surface, which heightens the effect of drawing attention to the organizational play on the picture's two-dimensional space. This effect of flattening perspective is enhanced by the position of the cluster of masonry in the background – perhaps a ruined city, or a graveyard. The hand with the olive branch might – but only might – be pointing in its direction, and might have the power to summon this scene of desolation as evidence in its case for peace. The formal organization of the picture both supports and undermines its allegorical content. Peace, the fertility of the harvest and a virginal sense of new beginning are *formally* – not now purely thematically or didactically – located in the realm of the unreal.

This does not necessarily imply that such aspirations are unattainable or fanciful – on the contrary. This is a challenge thrown down to the implicit violence with which our responses, our images of what lies ahead of us, are categorized and set against each other along the battle-lines of the orthodox and the permissible. It is a still more extreme, post-Romantic invitation to unclog the imagination, and its power to re-form the perceptible world according to the unpremeditated workings of its own processes and of its own art. But at the same time, this studied lack of premeditation and of pre-setting is highly self-conscious. The artifice that it makes a virtue of is made up of a network of historical and cultural pointers which both extend its powers and sketch in its limitations. Puvis de Chavannes delights in studied stylistic confusion, often staging figures in poses derived from Hellenistic sculpture within a spatial organization reminiscent of fifteenth-century Italian painting. In *L'Espérance*, such deliberate, artificial shuffling of cultural signals unties and reties the hinging of the spatial and temporal dimensions; these now form two wings beating oddly together in the picture's probing of the hidden realms of the imagination, and of the hidden structures of how we perceive.

There is not a naive antagonism, then, in this work between the imagined and the real, or between the perceptible and the inner worlds. Social and socially resistant elements not only interpenetrate in Symbolist art, they vie with each other in a vain struggle for ascendancy. This expressive tension, this systematic disruption of logical opposition, echoes and develops the irredeemably ironic foundation of much of the nineteenth-century aesthetic sensibility of Romanticism and post-Romanticism in France: the relativized idealism of Musset's drama, the artificial visionariness of Baudelaire's poetics, the lyrical historicism of

28. Georges Seurat, *Une Baignade, Asnières*, 1883–4 (National Gallery, London)

Flaubert's narratives. Moreover, this oscillation between potentially in-compatible levels of response seems to be the feature of Puvis de Chavannes that was most admired and exploited by his contemporaries. The style and manner of Georges Seurat in many ways might seem to be at odds with those of Puvis de Chavannes. The latter is concerned with the static, the posed and the outlandishly allegorical, the former with the explosion of outline and the kaleidoscopic, scientistic screening of colour and its component relations. But Seurat pays homage to what he suggests Puvis de Chavannes has made possible in art in his own *Paysage avec 'Le pauvre pêcheur' de Puvis de Chavannes* (1881).[9] There is a jux-taposition of styles in this picture, made up of Seurat's own shimmering landscaping, and the allusion in the corner to Puvis de Chavannes's *Le pauvre pêcheur* with its own taste for the static and the geometrical. The effect is dialectical rather than oppositional, admiring rather than satirical.

The dialogue between these two artists suggests an approach to com-position and the composite that allows a swerving of focus away from the perceptible world and towards the psychic impulses and pressures which form it. Comparing Puvis de Chavannes's *Le Chant du pâtre*

(1891) with Seurat's earlier and well-known *Une Baignade, Asnières* (1883–4) brings this out explicitly.[10] Once again, to our contemporary eye, the disparities seem more striking than the interconnections. The later painting by Puvis de Chavannes is classical in motif and in stylistic allusion, minimalist in colour differentiation, whereas Seurat's earlier one is resoundingly of the present moment, suburban, and plural both in content and composition. But the poses of the figures are the first element in the paintings that draws them together. Massive, static, or at least exaggeratedly caught-in-the-act, in both pictures they emphasize the two-dimensionality of the painted surface, the artificiality of the compositional procedure at large. This exposure is evident on a number of levels in each work. In the *Chant du pâtre*, the curiously flat perspective, as in *L'Espérance*, does allow some sense of depth. But this is a depth that refuses to place the shepherd securely either in the middle distance, or in relation to the mountains and the lake behind him. These distances have been made imaginary ones as we look, they involve time as well as space – the time spent in imagining the sound of the notes of the shepherd's song, in bringing it to our mind's ear from the indistinct distance in the picture, as well as across the distances dividing the cultures and mythologies of antiquity from our own.

In *Une Baignade* (fig. 28), the poses are more natural, less theatrical-looking, but the construction of the group is in many ways at odds with this style, being as mannered and overt as the composition in *Le Chant du pâtre*. All the figures are seen in profile, even the figure lying down is leaning on one elbow with her shoulders turned flatly towards the viewer. The poses of the seated figures seem to echo each other – an effect itself mirrored in the disposition of repeated patches of black and orange colours. There is even a diagonal line across the flatness of the picture separating water from land, and almost dividing the social from the natural: only two bathers, and a distant sail, the other human beings on land. But this division is transgressed, it is not and cannot be kept intact. The picture, beginning with the suburban setting signalled in the title, sets about exploring the ways in which categories take root and exposing the mobility of the borderlines between them. On the thematic level, the city-dwellers' day-out ambience extends only so far as to emphasize the shortness of the trip and the imminence of the return to suburban amorphousness and diffuseness. On the level of form and composition, the figures themselves are massive, and yet because they are seen so resolutely in profile, the effect is one of silhouetting and of levelling.

Such ambivalence on the level of form stretches to the basis of Seurat's compositional process and of his self-presentation as a colourist and as an artist. Colour and its painterly textures are self-consciously dramatic features in the initial impact that Seurat plans for his paintings, and which he makes sure of by publicizing his debt to the discoveries of Chevreul regarding the prismatic composition of light. Science comes to the aid of artists, apparently, in understanding the properties of light, in decomposing it and uncovering the complementary colours which are its constituent features. But this bridge-building between science and the arts is not some attempt to remove image-making from the unpredictability of subjective impulse. Quite the reverse. Seurat's pictures are not scientifically de-composed, but artificially com-posed – and composed in such a way as to confuse boundaries rather than to propel us into the realm of rationalist objectivity. The overt reference to science in Seurat's exploitation of colour in effect forms part of a 'scientistic' mirage that projects an image of *subjective* perception. Light is still not there other than in the actuality or the memory of reflections and refractions. Seurat's painterly treatment of its physical properties reactivates this oscillation between the assimilated image and its disintegration in time, or between the glimpsed and the half-remembered. Once again, frontiers between categories are made volatile rather than stable. Analytical approaches are not to be easily uncoupled from impressionistic ones.

In effect, Seurat's appeal to a scientific understanding at the level of the image is subverted and fragmented in the 'pointilliste' constitution of this image itself. Such emphasis on the component parts of light and of the representation of it in paint does not divert attention away from the effects of a specific text to the general principles of its functioning. On the contrary, it seeks to reconstruct our outlook in terms of the subjective, the intimate and the inward. The figure and the memory of Baudelaire and of his own ironic artifice form a dominant and all the more amorphous network of influence that itself surfaces as a kind of 'pointilliste' web. From within this web, the writing of another 'poète maudit' – Paul Verlaine himself, who comments on that notion of the poet in his short literary portraits entitled *Les Poètes maudits* (1884) – can be seen as a literary counterpart of Seurat's pursuit in painting of an analytic formalism that would penetrate the inner recesses of subjective sensibility.[11] His references to colour in the poems of *Romances sans paroles* (1874) are such that they cease to function purely as a qualification of objects, and instead turn towards the evocation of psychic states. The title 'Green', from its foreignness onwards, spurns description in favour of presenting colours and objects as the setting of a mood and of a symbolic offering.[12]

'Crépuscule du soir mystique' from the earlier work *Poèmes saturniens* (1866) is a formalist tour de force, a text constructing circles and spirals that envelop the reader in their own sensations, associations and textures.[13] Verlaine uses all the aural armoury of prosody to fashion a hothouse of rhyming and assonantal refraction. The poem is a verbal distillation of visual and olfactory sensation into a set of signals, at once formal and physiological, that raise the curtain on a subjective and inward enmeshing of sensation and memory. Each reader reactivates individually this corporeal temporality in allowing himself or herself to be submerged by the text and its echoes.

And yet for all this appeal to the subjectivity of the reader and the multiple access to the poem that this seems to provide, Verlaine's poetics seem oddly, almost perversely closed, hermetically sealed off. The very circularity of the syntax of 'Crépuscule du soir mystique' – leaving the reader where he or she began with the merging of 'Le Souvenir avec le Crépuscule' – confirms this, even in its act of turning public language inside out and moulding it to our most intimate sense of self. But this circularity, in the here and now of reading Verlaine's poem, is valued for its capacity to withdraw poet and reader alike from a painful engagement with society and its bruising attacks on individual importance and autonomy. Verlaine exploits the notion of 'le poète maudit', of the poet as social outcast, but misreads its dynamism, the untenable no-man's land it places the writer in as well as the reader who engages with the idea. Baudelaire characterizes this no-man's land in terms of the crowd and the way it establishes and at the same time destabilizes individual uniqueness and subjectivity. But in Verlaine's poetry, the position of outcast is kept distinct and intact by the very sophistication of Verlaine's own poetic artifice. To be immersed in this position, we are led to believe, is in itself to make a statement about the vulgarity and materialism of public life. The openness of Verlaine's verse to the anfractuosities of sensation and of the psyche ultimately forms a paradoxical mirage: it depends for its life on a perverse closure, a prediction and a foreclosing of its own effects, a scene-setting in which the poet is in advance anointed Orphic prophet by his own devoted readers.

Perhaps this inward-looking elitism, or this elitism of the inner world, is characteristic of many Symbolist and Decadent poets including Jean Moréas, Stuart Merrill and many others as well as Verlaine himself. Certainly the later writings of Rimbaud, from *Une Saison en Enfer* onwards, are an aggressive and desperate attempt to break free from this potentially asphyxiating and fetid narcissism. Like the 'pointillisme' of Seurat, the exploration of subjective sensibility carried out in the half-tones of Verlaine's metres and versification is an invocation of the stimuli provided specifically by aesthetic forms and surfaces. But each of these two forms of art suggests a quite different understanding of the purpose of its own existence. In Verlaine, it seems that intimate subjectivity can be delved into by artificially circumscribing it and valuing it in opposition to a culture of commodity exchange and materialism; whereas in Seurat's paintings such categories are not left intact – on the contrary, their potential fixity and complacency are explosed. The armoury of spatial composition, projected and magnified through the

29.   Paul Gauguin, *Hina Tefatou* [*La Lune et la Terre*], 1893 (Museum of Modern Art, New York)

artificial explosion of light, produces images whose impact, by oscillating on the formal level between the pointed or the punctual and the impressionistic overview, straddles on the the the thematic level the inner world of private perception and the public world of vision in all its diversity, slipperiness and *otherness*. The emphasis in these aural and visual impressionisms on the formal impact of the image and of image-making places them in a dialogue poised on a knife-edge: on the one hand, an elitist self-regard; on the other, an irreparable confusion of the private and the public, the intimate and the coercive, the creative and the enforced.

# Coda: Totem and the Body

Like Munch's *Death and the Maiden*, Gauguin's *Hina Tefatou [La Lune et la Terre]*, painted in Tahiti in 1893, shows a naked woman erotically embracing a male figure who is not living[14] (fig. 29). Sex and death in the case of Munch's image; sex with a totem in Gauguin's. In each case, the woman in the heterosexual emblem is naked, the male icon clothed in all its cultural and public reverberations. How is the gendered gaze channelled across the image? Might a male viewer desire the female body in the picture, and see in it the whole range of objects in heterosexual desire made exotic and all the more mysterious and alluring? For all Gauguin's work from the South Seas is destined, even if only in Gauguin's own lonely fantasy, for the Parisian, Western European public. Or does this well-dressed male viewer see himself embodied in the male god, adorned with adoring female worshippers, and yet destined to remain unmoved and immovable, locked within the symbolism assigned to him in the phallic drama? Might the female viewer reject this enacted and enforced projection of phallic images and phallic desire on to her body? Or conversely, might she see enacted phallic formation ingrained in the psyche, imprinted on the skin and in this and every posture of the female form? Is it possible for a male heterosexual viewer to speculate otherwise? What about the homosexual gaze or perusal of such an image?

The picture continually projects incompatible readings of itself, while at the same time suggesting that one kind of reading might predominate. On the one hand, there is Tahitian imagery involved, but on the other, this image takes its place in the history of colour in French painting, particularly in the nineteenth century, ranging backwards through Impressionism to Delacroix. In the pool there is liquid water, but its surface also acts as firm ground. The shapes of leaves form abstract, decorative, mental arabesques, and yet resolutely refuse to take us beyond this specific allusion to the experience of watching leaves. Inner recesses of the mind and body are evoked and seemingly placed beyond conscious recall, silencing all structure, but the picture dis-covers even there an erotic charge and a magnetic appeal in relating to orthodoxy iteslf. The gendered gaze confronts sexual antagonism in the picture and *because of* this antagonism, an ability to *imagine* the other – the other sex, other sexualities, other cultures, the other at large – is recovered. And yet *in* this imagining and *because* of it, purchase on difference is eroded, and we drift back and plunge into a silenced, totemized in-corporation of otherness – or is it a warding off of it?

Gauguin's is an eclecticism by which immobilizing categories melt brilliantly and magnificently, and yet which for all that exposes primal desires and structures still intact – '*D'où venons-nous? Que sommes-nous? Où allons-nous?*' . . .[15] This is a farewell to culture and simulta-neously a gorging on all cultures. It is an embracing of Rimbaud's impossibly grand projection of revolt, of his vision of each individually sexed person finding the gift of a paradoxical, altruistic self-regard through which to 'posséder la vérité dans une âme et un corps'.[16]

## Suggested reading

Delevoy, Robert L., *Symbolists and Symbolism* (Skira/Rizzoli, 1978).

Freud, Sigmund, *Beyond the Pleasure Principle* in *On Metapsychology: The Theory of Psychoanalysis*, Pelican Freud Library XI (London: Pelican, 1984).

Lucie-Smith, Edward, *Symbolist Art* (London: Thames and Hudson, 1972).

Nerval, Gérard de, *Aurélia* (Paris: Livre de Poche, 1972).

Rimbaud, Arthur, *Une Saison en Enfer* in *Œuvres*, ed S. Bernard (Paris: Gallimard, 1960).

Russell, John, *Seurat* (London: Thames and Hudson, 1989).

Verlaine, Paul, *Fêtes Galantes, Romances sans paroles*, précédé de *Poèmes saturniens* (Paris: Poésie/Gallimard, 1972).

# 18

## *Valéry and Rodin: Orpheus returning*

## Peter Collier

At first sight Auguste Rodin and Paul Valéry appear to belong to different worlds. The Romantic visionary fell out of fashion well before the refined neoclassical contemporary of T.S. Eliot made his mark. Yet there is evidence of interaction in Valéry's signature in 1898 of a motion of support for Rodin's ill-fated monument to Balzac, spurned by the very committee of the Société des gens de lettres who had commissioned the sculpture. And we know that the twenty-year-old Valéry spent two years, between 1890 and 1892, writing Symbolist poetry under the wing of Mallarmé, during which period Mallarmé was in close contact with Rodin.[1] It can hardly be a coincidence, and they can hardly have been ignorant of the conjunction, if both produced a major work entitled *Orphée* (fig. 30) during the same period, 1891–2, whether or not unconscious forces were driving them independently towards their choice of the same theme, the theme which calls into question the activity of the artist himself, or the cultural force of fashion leading them to use the same myth, that of Orpheus, as their medium. But first and foremost, the choice of Orpheus, the lyric poet who enchanted the guardians of Hell with his song, yet whose need to view his love caused Eurydice's death, suggests the aspiration of poetry and sculpture to music, as well as the tragic destiny of the self-conscious artist. Both artists in fact found their Orpheus extraordinarily obsessing and intractable. Rodin's kept him busy from 1884 to 1894, whereas Valéry, the younger, later starter, took from 1891 to 1926 before he finally laid his Orphic ghost.

Rodin's *Orphée* started as part of his enormous Gates of Hell project, Orpheus being one of Dante's damned,[2] tormented by the Furies. In a new plaster which Rodin completed in 1892, he abandoned the Furies, attributing an ambiguous role to Eurydice, who seems to float ominously over the head of an Orpheus torn by the effort of holding her up while still clinging to his lyre.[3] The moment chosen is the return of Orpheus and Eurydice from the underworld, or rather the decisive and

30.  Auguste Rodin, *Orphée*, bronze, s.1014, 1892 (Musée Rodin, Paris)

tragic moment of the return, when he loses Eurydice in the very act of looking round to make sure that she is still there. Rodin simplified his subject by removing Eurydice and her column at an unknown date.[4] Had he looked at her as long as he could bear? It is tempting enough to compare this tortured sculpture with the death-throes of the relationship between Rodin and Camille Claudel, as one critic does.[5] But as late as 1894 Rodin showed himself able to respond to a commission from the United States, by producing another variant of the sculpture, restoring Eurydice.[6]

It is the 1892 version, where we see Orpheus alone with his tree and his lyre, which was cast in bronze and is conserved to this day by the Rodin museum.[7] The Furies have gone, Eurydice has gone, and our attention is concentrated on the person of Orpheus with his gestures and feelings, bereft of the distraction of the narrative context. With a movement that is half destructive, and half creative, Orpheus seems either to brandish his lyre or to tear at a piece of Greek column. Against his flank there rises a tortured tree. Eurydice having died a second time, Orpheus is now alone, living in Thrace, as described by Ovid, who tells how the trees came to settle beside him to listen to his song.[8] Later, however, the Thracian women, spurned by Orpheus who seems to have developed contrary passions, attack him with rocks and branches, although these are warded off by the magical power of Orpheus's lyric art, delaying the moment of death, when the rocks will weep and the trees lose their leaves.[9] The sculpture, then, seems to connive knowingly at ambiguity, conflating the friendly tree supporting Orpheus with the torn branch used as a weapon and the weeping, leafless branch, just as the lyre seem at one and the same time to figure a massive rock hanging threateningly over Orpheus's head, an enchanted rock held hanging in the air through the magic of his song, and the lyre itself, massive, square, powerful, and yet aerial.

The symbolism of this strikingly modernist piece, then, is flagrantly not a unitary symbolism, but a shifting, self-questioning symbolism, where each motif as we focus on it seems to mutate into some contradictory alternative. And what is also striking in this sculpture, and most different from the vigorous Romantic figures created by François Rude or the suavely erotic images fashioned by Clésinger or Pradier, is its brazenly disparate textures. Rodin's sculpture refuses stylistic unity: the figure of Orpheus is relatively smooth, and his gestures fairly realistic, he is more or less attached to a roughly sketched tree, whose crude wood barely emerges from its stone husk, and Orpheus's lyre, a bizarrely tentative cube anticipating Picasso, evokes neither a realistic representation of Orpheus's lyre, nor a conventional symbol of his art, but above all a dramatic staging, a sign of the effort to create. The poet's body is stylized, its flesh polished smooth as stone, leaving to the tree the task of expressing the latent tension, as it emerges in quasi-human fashion from its stone straitjacket, drawing our attention to the act of seemingly arbitrary creativity which shapes the human body as it does the wood, using the raw material of inanimate resisting matter. The lyre, neither realistic like the figure of Orpheus nor expressive of its material and its function (as the branch of the tree could be seen to be), brutally formalist to the point of being almost abstract, shows the scars of the act of creation. The whole ensemble of three ostentatiously ill-assorted pieces draws attention to the tentative process of creation that is sculpture ('Un artiste a frappé des milliers de coups rebondissants, lents interrogateurs de la forme future' [An artist has struck a thousand glancing blows, slowly seeking out its hidden future form'], as Valéry was to say in his essay 'Au sujet d'Adonis'). And perhaps it also shows the destructive force of creativity: even without the wrenching away of Eurydice's head by Rodin, the 'not-waving-but-drowning' posture of the figure clinging to the wreckage might remind us of a version of the myth where after Orpheus's death his head alone, still singing, floats across the sea to be washed up on the shore at Lesbos.

Speaking of the textural differences of his 1894 American commission Rodin declared that the unfinished parts were intentionally left unfinished, to give his sculpture 'atmosphere'.[10] Making due allowance for Rodin's theoretical casualness we could go further, for 'atmosphere' hardly does justice to the tension created between the polished and the rough (a typical Rodin technique, apparent for instance in *Aurora* of 1895, where a smooth female head struggles free of a mass of hair entangled in stone which she is unable to shed, a self-hypnotizing Medusa, evoking the resistance of matter to mind, the fleshly envelope weighing down thought, and the poem of the same name by Valéry where the mind is caught in the quicksand of its own process). The search for 'atmosphere' is of course a typically Symbolist ambition, as epitomized in Mallarmé's notorious goal to 'peindre non la chose mais l'effet qu'elle produit'.

In fact this artistic Orpheus is most like a sculptor, the arms raised to deliver some inspired blow to the rock, and his lyre – a heavy chunk of inchoate Greek statuary, as well as a shapeless mass of marble wrenched from a cliff by the vision of some Michelangelo or Rodin – figures the birth of the work in the imagination, as it struggles to emerge from its cubic confines. Thus we are led to reinterpret this sculpture not as an emotional expression of the tragic separation from Camille Claudel, but as performance, moving beyond symbolism towards expressionism or even abstraction (as did the painting of his contemporaries Gauguin, Van Gogh, Cézanne and Monet), a self-reflexive dramatization of the drama of creativity. The sculptor Orpheus aspires to carve out his own forms and accede to a polished state, but in the rough-hewn tree he projects his emotional, imaginative and intellectual fears, fantasies and doubts, expressing his power without being able to attain formal mastery of his material: and we think irresistibly of Van Gogh during the same period. For almost a decade, from 1891 to 1898, Rodin fought his convervative public, and struggled with his own conflicting lyrical, visionary and formalist urges in the effort to create the new expressionist form of his *Balzac*. In the heavy and yet aerial lyre, evoking some Greek column collapsing under its own weight, does he perhaps figure the struggle in his own imagination to disentangle himself from the neoclassical representational projects which potentially haunt all lumps of plaster and all blocks of marble?

In 1891, the twenty-year-old Valéry cannot have been unaware of the ongoing obsessions of France's greatest sculptor, the master of the *Bourgeois of Calais*, the hero of a one-man show at the Exposition Universelle of 1889, and the co-victor with Monet of a triumphal two-man show in Paris the following year. Valéry and Rodin dined together at the table of Mallarmé in 1891, the year when the whole group turned out to speed Gauguin on his way to the Pacific, and the year of the official declaration of a Symbolist movement in painting (see James Kearns's chapter above). The aspiring Valéry launched his own figure of Orpheus in March 1891 at the end of a lyrical yet mannered article entitled 'Paradoxe sur l'architecte',[11] where Orpheus is lauded as the exemplary creator, a musician rather than a writer, or at the very least a symbolist poet, trying to move beyond language in order to attain to the pure structure of music or architecture. This Orpheus was written at a crucial moment for Mallarmé's young protégé. Despite his precocious success, soon afterwards, in Autumn 1891, he underwent an emotional crisis in Genoa which led him eventually to decide to abandon the writing of poetry, a quasi-definitive decision which he was to uphold for a good twenty years.[12] We may well suspect that such an enormous creative crisis must have lasted longer than the alleged single Pascalian 'nuit de Gênes' (did Valéry enjoy the ambiguous meaning of the French name for his mother's native city – 'torture' and 'embarrassment'?) and have roots that were intellectual as much as emotional.

At all events, the choice by Valéry of the poet Orpheus in 'Paradoxe sur l'architecte' was already emblematic. In this first attempt at an Orphic posture, the previously bland poet of vaguely symbolic scenes evokes a lost age when architecture expressed an inspired human vision: 'In days gone by, in the Orphic age, the spirit breathed across the face of the marble; the ancient walls were full of human life, and architecture bodied forth man's dreams.'[13] But although Valéry preaches the superiority of architecture and music over poetry, it is a superiority still expressed through the poetic work of 'analogy' – which Baudelaire before him and Proust after him were to favour – 'for subtle analogies link the unreal, fugitive edifice of dreams to the solidity of art through which imaginary forms are fixed in porphyry beneath the sun'.[14] The ideal creator envisaged by Valéry, then, is more of an architect and a musician than a poet. He is a sculptor, like Rodin's Orpheus, 'a carver of words, a builder of phrases, an architect concerned with the musical synthesis of his work'.[15] He is a creator of plastic and rhythmical form as much as of linguistic symbols. Architecture, like music, seems to break through to the world of Platonic forms and express emotions and ideas directly without having to pass through the filter of language.

This choice of the exemplary mythical poet by the aspiring writer in 1891, at the apogee of the short-lived Symbolist movement, is instructive, for it helps us to realize that the very ideal of Symbolism entails a questioning of the role of language, shown first of all in Valéry's theory of harmony and structure, and then in his desire to find an adequate form through which to express that theory by going beyond the linguistic symbol, judged too impure. For the artist, like the poet, instead of symbolizing in a one-to-one fashion, already announces the end of Symbolism through his tendency towards self-reference. Orpheus becomes author of himself as much as symbol of something else:

Il évoque, en un bois thessalien, Orphée, sous les myrthes; et le soir antique descend. Le bois sacré s'emplit lentement de lumière, et le dieu tient la lyre entre ses doigts d'argent. Le dieu chante, et, selon le rythme tout-puissant, s'élèvent au soleil les fabuleuses pierres, et l'on voit grandir vers l'azur incandescent, les murs d'or harmonieux d'un sanctuaire.

Il chante! assis au bord du ciel splendide, Orphée! Son œuvre se rêvet d'un vespéral trophée, et sa lyre divine enchante les porphyres, car le temple érigé par ce *musicien* unit la sûreté des rythmes anciens à l'âme immense du grand hymne sur la lyre! . . .

In a wood in Thessaly, within a myrtle grove, he calls forth Orpheus; and the age-old night then falls. The sacred wood fills gradually with light, as the god runs silver fingers down his lyre. The god sings, and, obeying his omnipotent rhythm, stones from fables rise towards the sunlight, as reaching to the glowing azure sky appears a golden harmony of sanctuary walls.

Singing, seated on the edge of heaven in its splendour, is Orpheus! His work is cloaked in twilight glory, and his lyre divinely charms the porphyry, for the temple built by this *musician* marries securely with traditional rhyme the swelling soul of a great hymn sung on the lyre!

I would agree with William Stewart[16] that the tide of this inspired prose seems to take on the form of verse as if to match the action of Orpheus himself, but at the same time I believe that the superficial maintenance of the form of prose, resisting lyrical effusion, makes us feel the speaker resisting the full power of poetic rhetoric, as its elements are forced to conform to the more down-to-earth gait of prose. We remember that if Orpheus's exquisite art can save himself and his beloved at first from death, he is nonetheless vulnerable to passion, which leads him towards death, dismemberment and fragmentation. During the 1880s, the publication of Rimbaud's *Illuminations* and Laforgue's experiments in 'vers libre' had started to threaten the status of regular prosody, as noted excitedly by Mallarmé himself in his essay 'Crise de vers'. Soon after Valéry's ambiguous performance in prose poetry, however, partly on the insistence of the young prodigy's admirers, Pierre Louÿs and André Gide[17] (but also, perhaps, partly from a feeling that the prestige of his master Mallarmé derived not from his prose poems but from his sonnets), he rewrote his disguised verse in the form of a declared sonnet published in *La Conque*, 3, of 1 May 1891:

Il évoque, en un bois thessalien, Orphée
Sous les myrtes, et le soir antique descend.
Le bois sacré s'emplit lentement de lumière,
Et le dieu tient la lyre entre ses doigts d'argent.

Le dieu chante, et selon le rythme tout-puissant,
S'élèvent au soleil les fabuleuses pierres
Et l'on voit grandir vers l'azur incandescent
Les hauts murs d'or harmonieux d'un sanctuaire.

Il chante, assis au bord du ciel splendide, Orphée!
Son œuvre se revêt d'un vespéral trophée
Et sa lyre divine enchante les porphyres,

Car le temple érigé par ce *musicien*
Unit la sûreté des rythmes anciens
A l'âme immense du grand hymne sur la lyre! . . .

As the prose falls effortlessly into verse (except for an awkward lack of rhyme between lines 1 and 3) the only difference in the wording is the minimal insertion of a single word – 'hauts' – in the eighth line, repairing a break in metre which was invisible when the poetry was disguised as prose.[18] But the change in context is all-important. The text, previously isolated, now seems immediately to refer not to the architect but to the mythical poet, the poet who charmed the natural world and is integrated into its form. And yet, in a more subtle, structural way, the architecture of the sonnet form does refer us back to the poet as architect. 'Il évoque', whose subject was some hypothetical visitor wondering at the architecture of music, first meant 'he (the viewer) is led to think of'. Now, as it emerges abruptly and self-sufficiently at the start of a contextless poem, the work seems to create an Orpheus as subject, narrator of himself, creator of his own myth. In the first version, 'la lyre' seemed to allude to architecture, but in the sonnet it refers naturally to poetry (although, surreptitiously, through rhyme, rhythm and assonance, we are nonetheless aware of the nature of the poet as musical architect). In this second 'Orphée', detached from the generative voice which belonged to an admirer of musical architecture, the subject immediately becomes a poet himself, echoing the Orpheus that he evokes. The sense seems to be that poetry has the power to instil divine form into its landscape, and when 'Le dieu chante, et selon le rythme tout-puissant, s'élèvent au soleil les fabuleuses pierres', we understand that it is the rhythm of the verse which creates a precious world, as the music of Orpheus moves stones to create a temple.[19]

Yet, if Valéry continued for a time to refer to the character of Orpheus, the Orpheus who creates harmonic forms was quickly to become the Orpheus dismembered by the Maenads. On 7 November 1891 Valéry sent Gide his 'Bathylle de Lesbos'[20] where he evokes 'Orphée antique mort par les mains furibondes'. In November 1891 he also published some 'pages inédites' in which he marked out even more clearly his distance from the ridiculous Orphic pretence of certain poets, who 'grow their hair long and set themselves up on the horizon as Orpheus, raising their lyres to the heavens and rolling their eyeballs – because they have managed to hew out a hexameter and create clusters of similar consonants in the same line'.[21]

Valéry's inspired creative drive, then, seemed to have been no more fulfilled by the Orphic sonnet than by the architectural prose. His crisis seems to antedate the night in Genoa. Valéry did go on to write a few poems after his Genoese crisis, but it is interesting to see how, although he continued to use the sonnet form, he tended to abandon the mythographic pose. 'Anne' (1893) and 'Eté' (1896) seem to push the poet's search uneasily, through a still oblique and allusive language, towards the subjects of Impressionist painting, taking their topics from everyday life – the nude on the bed, the female bather on the beach – rather than from the Symbolist's inventory of enigmatic objects and mythological subjects. There is still the suggestion of a mysterious world of ideas and sensations available through intermittent formal correspondences. But these poems take on a modernist power from their assumption of the performative. In 'Eté' the interchange of sound and colour, light and touch (a feature of 'transposition' discussed by David Kelley in his chapter above) is acted out in the very construction of its metaphors, as happens in many paintings by Monet, where qualities and substances seem to be exchanged:

31.  Claude Monet, *Falaise à Etretat, La Manneporte, I*, 1883 (Metropolitan Museum of Art, New York)

> Eté, roche d'air pur, et toi, ardente ruche,
> O mer! Eparpillée en mille mouches sur
> Les touffes d'une chair fraîche comme une cruche,
> Et jusque dans la bouche où bourdonne l'azur,

> Summer rock of limpid air and burning hive
> The sea dispersed in fleeting flies
> Among the tufts of flesh whose jug-like
> Coolness fills our mouths with humming blue,

while in 'Anne' the subjective desire and objective gaze of the speaking subject, and the fluctuating consciousness of the enigmatic woman before him, are echoed in the sumptuously reverberating, almost impenetrably hypnotic interrelations of the poem's material sonorities, exemplified later in: 'Dormeuse, amas doré d'ombres et d'abandons' from the poem's final version of 1920.

It took ten years before Valéry was able openly to confront his Orphic temptations, and say of Gluck's *Orpheus* in 1901: '*Orpheus* grabbed hold of me, especially the first and the fourth act. It was able to strike deep down inside me at an ancient, abandoned seam. I remembered the *Orpheus* which I had myself once sung, and wanted to be ... when I attributed a divine power to my imagination and my will. ...'[22] Thus there is little doubt that Valéry's 'Orpheus' is the inspired, creative self that the analytic and critical Valéry can no longer abide after his Genoese renunciation. And this disingenuous rejection of his own identification with Orpheus was to last another twenty years before he was tempted momentarily to admit its perspective back into his newly reborn and reworked poetic enterprise. During the rewriting of 'Aurore' in 1920 he included an eighth stanza, mentioning Orpheus, which contains the line: 'Je suis cette créature / Dont la fatale nature / Est de créer à son tour'.[23]

Yet when Valéry finally came to terms with his Symbolist past in publishing his *Album de vers anciens* in 1920, we may wonder, as does William Stewart, why this considerable poem, admired and praised in public by Gide and Mallarmé, is alone excluded from the collection. For if Valéry had abandoned and indeed rejected his Orphic stance, he had nonetheless in 1920 caressed the project of a lyrical drama on Orpheus and Euyridice, a composition where Orpheus would symbolize love, which would finally become entitled *Amphion*.[24] But it is no doubt also true that the figure of Orpheus, the poet who builds a world and in so doing constructs himself, but who is torn apart as a result of the passions he turns his back on, is still too tender a subject to be presented as 'vers anciens' ('antique' or 'former' verse). After all, the other poems of the Symbolist nineties which Valéry served up carefully repolished in the 1920 volume seemed to be pleasantly distant: 'ils ne représentent pas mes pensées'.[25] We must suppose then that 'Orphée' would have run the risk of representing what he secretly felt and thought, but did not like to admit to himself.

And indeed, when the new version did finally appear in the *Album de vers anciens*, not in the first edition of 1920 – which publication seemed almost a recantation, after Valéry's attempt to return to poetry through the reinvigorated style of *La jeune Parque* in 1917 – but in the second edition of 1926, published by the man who had become meanwhile, with the publication of *Charmes* in 1921, the greatest living French poet, we discover a different Orpheus, who is able at last to come to terms with his problems, and assume himself and his destiny:

> ... Je compose en esprit, sous les myrthes, Orphée
> L'Admirable! ... Le feu, des cirques purs descend;
> Il change le mont chauve en auguste trophée
> D'où s'exhale d'un dieu l'acte retentissant.

Si le dieu chante, il rompt le site tout-puissant;
Le soleil voit l'horreur du movement des pierres;
Une plainte inouïe appelle éblouissants
Les hauts murs d'or harmonieux d'un sanctuaire.

Il chante, assis au bord du ciel splendide, Orphée!
Le roc marche, et trébuche; et chaque pierre fée
Se sent un poids nouveau qui vers l'azur délire!

D'un Temple à demi nu le soir baigne l'essor,
Et soi-même il s'assemble et s'ordonne dans l'or
A l'âme immense du grand hymne sur la lyre!

This Orpheus is a sombre Orpheus. The 'doigts d'argent' have disappeared. A whole vocabulary of falsely naive devotion has disappeared ('fabuleux', 'divine', 'vespéral'); the song has become painful ('une plainte inouïe'); the equivocal act of creation inspires 'l'horreur'. Maria Teresa Giaveri notes the disappearance of the conventional local colour ('thessalien' ['Thessaly' was an odd choice instead of 'Thracia' in the first place], 'antique', 'porphyres'), and the new dynamism of the scene.[26] There is certainly a thematic reference in 'ce poids nouveau qui vers l'azur délire' to the difficulties and responsibilities of painful creation for Orpheus, and, moreover, for the speaking subject who 'composes' or stages him, all the more so since he is apparently stricken with fragmentation and disorder, as he is obliged to 's'assembler' and 's'ordonner' in the lyre, that is, in the act of composition. But what I find even more striking is a kind of performative heaviness which seems to be articulated by the subject; the very sounds stagger: in a single line ('Le roc marche, et trébuche; et chaque pierre fée') the plosive [k] disintegrates into a fricative [ʃ] thrice repeated before being reconstituted as [k], yet this recomposition is immediately followed by the collapse of the plosive [p] this time into a fricative [f], while twice the mute [ð], offending the rules of classical prosodic elegance and symbolist smoothness, runs breathlessly into an initial vowel [marche/et; trébuche/et], not to mention the rather un-French clash of terminal and initial consonants [roc/marche]. We have come a long way from 'la sûreté des rythmes anciens'; there is no longer any *'musicien'*, emphasized or otherwise, although Orphée has now been allowed to rhyme.

Thematically again, the tragic aspect of creation appears. Orpheus, placed against the heavens without being able to join them, resembles Narcisse, insofar as, if he sings, 'il rompt le site tout-puissant'. Like Narcisse, who will lose his beautiful reflection if he breathes on the surface of the water, Orpheus destroys the landscape around him, if he tries to create. Valéry is suggesting an art which rejects realistic description, but

one which also stages a creative violence that destroys the natural relation between the artist and his environment. Fitfully, Valéry
inaugurates modernist art, with moments where his text becomes
creation and interrogation of the self, explores itself as process rather
than posing as finished object. All of Valéry's mature aesthetic thinking,
as much on the fine arts as on writing, tends to confirm this preference
for the moment of creativity over the finished object.

Thus the 'Je' who composes is no longer the mythical god but the contemporary writer, dramatizing his own attempts at symbolic creation.
Certainly Valéry, in Daniel Moutote's fine phrase, reunites the 'disjecta
membra' of language, and 'reconstitutes the myth of the poet as essential
builder, erecting with his rhythmical blocks a temple which realizes in its
form what is sung of in myth on the figurative lyre of Orpheus',[27] but it
is rather the aspect of *deconstruction* which wins; not, however, as
Moutote suggests, through the soaring flight of language, but through
the performative awkwardness of language, and through the force of the
gaze turned inwards on itself. The 'Je' which 'composes' the poem loses
ground in favour of a figure who himself becomes decomposed.

Perhaps even after thirty years' work it is not an unequivocally successful poem. I find it difficult to agree that the adjectives are all as
'impressive' as James Lawler finds them,[28] since they seem here and there
to lack that subtly balanced ambiguity which marks the adjectives in
most of Valéry's mature poetry (although we must make an exception
for the excellent and subtle 'inouïe', meaning simultaneously both 'unheard' and 'unheard of'). For me the poem is haunted by a mixture of
blandness and overemphasis ('admirable', 'auguste', 'retentissants',
'splendides', 'éblouissants', 'immense'), and virtual repetition ('d'or'/
'dans l'or'; 'chante'/'chante'), despite an effort to replace some of the
Symbolist commonplaces with formulae which move towards expressionism (the act which 's'exhale', the weight which 'délire'). The last line
seems to fall rather flatly, when the newly self-reflexive tone of the poem
seemed to prepare the reader for a less straightforward dénouement.
There is nonetheless a tightening of internal phonetic echoes ('change'
comes to underline 'chante'; 'horreur' comes to reinforce the relations
among 'Les hauts murs d'or harmonieux'). I would agree with Lawler
that the 'legendary description in the Parnassian style has given place to
a poem which endeavours to convey the very sensation, *in actu*, of
creative experience',[29] but I do not think that the effort creates any impression of triumph: it is a poem which unfolds a critical vision of its
own formulation, but which is finally unable systematically to put into
practice the programme of its own subversive destructive force.

Yet its success may be seen to lie in its foregrounded conflict and dis-
sonance of styles, as in the case of Rodin – perhaps, one might say, 'after
Rodin'. The smooth lies alongside the rough, the polished is negated by

the tortured. The issue is perhaps not quite what Lawler suggests, that the poem is not a finished enough machine[30] – on the contrary, in some ways it remains too finished a machine, still haunted by the need for closure, despite its disturbing indications of self-critical doubt and openness.

Ned Bastet notes a passage in Valéry's *Cahiers* where Valéry says: 'Orpheus: O my familiar deity! With every problem I turn towards you. Without hesitation. (Just think, in my free spirit you play the part of an idol.)'[31] Here we might note a revealing lapsus, for it is in turning to gaze at one's idol, in Orphic or Narcissistic terms, that one makes it disappear. And yet it is that gaze of Orpheus turning back upon himself, without closing his eyes, and without disappearing, no longer ignoring or repressing the ambitions and the agonies of the creative self, transforming the very process of the production of meaning into a slowly self-regarding form, that announces the hard-won success of the mature Valéry. The great poems of *Charmes* would confidently subsume the processes of intellectual doubt and imaginative hesitation and use them as a compositional principle. Like Rodin, Valéry had to develop a form that rejected the Symbolist image, in order to create a modernist work, where the process of symbolic representation is called into question. Valéry's and Rodin's twin figures of Orpheus both enact the failure of symbolic meaning, but turn that failure into the founding performative gesture of modernist art.

## Suggested reading

Butler, R., *Rodin: The Shape of Genius* (London and New Haven: Yale University Press, 1993).

Elsen, A., *In Rodin's Studio* (Oxford: Phaidon, 1980).

Grunfeld, F., *Rodin. A Biography* (Oxford: OUP, 1989).

Houston, J.P., *French Symbolism and the Modernist Movement* (Baton Rouge and London: Lousiana State University Press, 1980).

Kermode, F., *Romantic Image* (London: Ark Paperbacks, 1986).

Lehmann, A.G., *The Symbolist Aesthetic 1885–95* (Oxford: Blackwell, 2nd ed., 1968).

Mossop, D., *Pure Poetry: Studies in French Poetic Theory and Practices* (Oxford: OUP, 1971).

Nash, S., *Paul Valéry's Album de vers anciens: A past transfigured* (Princeton: Princeton UP, 1983).

# 19

# Dancing with Mallarmé and Seurat (and Loie Fuller, Hérodiade and La Goulue)

## Mary Ann Caws

Le bâton directeur attend pour un signal.
Stéphane Mallarmé, 'Plaisir sacré'

Seurat may be seen in the line of great theoretician-painters, like Leonardo and Poussin, say his recent commentators; in any case, he dies at thirty-one, having had time for just one change of theory and style. The early Seurat paintings, which can be heavy in tone like *La Baignade*, are concerned with the relation of colours, as in the theories of the Frenchman M.E. Chevreul[1] and the American Ogden Rood.[2] But in the years 1886–91, the years of *La Parade*, *Chahut* and *Le Cirque* (uncompleted at his death in 1891), he becomes far more interested in the work of Charles Henry, particularly Henry's 'Introduction à une esthétique scientifique',[3] the predecessor of his significant *Cercle chromatique, éléments d'une théorie générale de la dynamogénie* (not published until 1888–9, but already in preparation in 1886).[4] In his writings, Henry deals with the harmonic relation of lines, their angles, their 'agreeable directions', and their potential to express emotions.[5]

All three of these late Seurat pictures, *La Parade*, *Chahut* and *Le Cirque*, are formally static in their staging, even as their matter includes an ongoing performance – the first and third about the circus, and the second about a very particular sort of dance, odd and transgressive. Given the passion of Mallarmé for things performed, visible from the time of his first version of 'Le Pitre châtié' of 1864, staged in a circus metaphor, through the *Notes sur le théâtre* of March 1887, the essays in *Crayonné au théâtre* of April 1887,[6] including 'Planches et feuillets', and the prose poem called 'La Déclaration foraine' which appeared in August 1887,[7] and for the specific performance of dance, especially in the *Ballets* of 1886[8] and *Les Fonds dans le ballet* of 1893,[9] it proved tempting to reflect on, and compare, his own written relation to performance and staging with that which Seurat illustrated in his late

32.   Georges Seurat, *Chahut* , 1889–90 (Rijksmuseum Kröller-Müller, Otterlo)

works.[10] In situating his mental theatre by place and feeling ('*Situant un lieu*'),[11] Mallarmé studies himself as scribe and as potential spectator. That is also my point of view, as the scribe of this chapter, and the spectator of the double-bill performance.

Now in relation to Seurat, the particular staging I want to examine is that of *Chahut* (fig. 32), the strange painting of 1889–90, thus roughly contemporaneous with Mallarmé's most profound reflections on the questions of dance and staging. Given the spatial compression of Seurat's last canvases, and the verbal compression of Mallarmé's expression, I have not wanted to range beyond these narrow limits. Roger Fry says of *La Parade* that 'it is as though Seurat had not only painted the "Grecian Urn" but had written Keats's poem on it all in a single action, for, certainly, here far more than in any Grecian urn, and without external aid, we feel that '"this silent form doth tease us out of thought as doth eternity"'. The most literal facts, Fry continues, are transmuted into the 'purest, most abstract of spiritual values'.[12]

In approaching *Chahut* with an eye on Mallarmé, seeing his own eyes trained on the dancer Loie Fuller, I am not so much thinking of pure and abstract values as of a passion for the representational: it is of the latter and its spirited pursuit that I hope I am keeping the spirit.

## *Just looking*

The dancer, says Mallarmé famously in his essay 'Crayonné au théâtre', is not a woman, but a metaphor so successful in its shorthand inscription, so incisive and complex, that her act can only be described as a poem:

> A savoir que la danseuse *n'est pas une femme qui danse*, pour ces motifs juxtaposés qu'elle *n'est pas une femme*, mais une métaphore résumant un des aspects élémentaires de notre forme, glaive, coupe, fleur, etc., et *qu'elle ne danse pas*, suggérant, par le prodige de raccourcis ou d'élans, avec une écriture corporelle qu'il faudrait des paragraphes de prose dialoguée autant que descriptive, pour exprimer, dans la rédaction: poème dégagé de tout appareil du scribe.[13]

> Let's agree that the dancer *is not a woman dancing*, for these closely associated reasons – she *is not a woman*, but a metaphor summing up one of the basic aspects of our form, a sword, a cup, a flower, and so on, and *that she does not dance*, suggesting, by the marvel of shortcuts or leaps, with a bodily writing that it would take whole paragraphs of dialogic and

descriptive prose to express in writing: a poem disengaged from any scribal apparatus.

De-individualized, never standing for anyone specific but always an emblem, the dancer not as woman but as sign represents in her semiotic presence what Wallace Stevens could later call the 'poem of the mind in the act of finding what will suffice'.[14] Even the floorboards are treated by Mallarmé with an incantatory lyricism, as the mise-en-scène speaks for the depth and width of the imagination. This is Mallarmé high on what he most believes in and most convincingly celebrates: the theatre of his own mind. He links, with a youthful enthusiasm, fury to beauty of figure, and purity to the intensity of sign:

> Quand, au lever du rideau dans une salle de gala et tout local, apparaît ainsi qu'un flocon d'où soufflé? furieux, la danseuse: le plancher évité par bonds ou dur aux pointes, acquiert une virginité de site pas songé, qu'isole, bâtira, fleurira la figure.[15]

> When, at the rise of the curtain in a gala local performance, the dancer appears, like an angry snowflake blown in from where? the floorboards avoided by leaps and bounds, or hard on the points, take on a virginity of place never yet dreamt of, that the figure will isolate, build, bring to blossom.

The floorboards do not *remain* virgin, they rather become virgin, purified by the way in which the figure as sign isolates them from the everyday, pointing and leaping, writing – rapidly, lightly – to construct the mental architecture in a minimal breath of a flourish, no heavier than a snowflake.

The figure who concretizes most exactly Mallarmé's mental theatre as dance is that most celebrated dancer with circling veils, her filmy costume as magic as music: Loie Fuller, the heroine of Whistler's imagination as of Mallarmé's. The spell she casts is a 'transition de sonorités aux tissus', with her various techniques of 'exagération, les retraits de jupe ou d'aile, instituant un lieu. L'enchanteresse fait l'ambiance, la tire de soi et l'y rentre, par un silence palpité de crêpes de Chine' ('a transition of sounds to fabric . . . exaggeration, the withdrawing of skirt or wing, instituting a place. The enchantress creates the atmosphere, drawing it from and back into herself, in a silence throbbing with crepe').[16] What she produces is a *free staging*, the opposite of any permanent backdrop, stultifying in its paralysis. Her dance is 'centrale, car tout obéit à une impulsion fugace en tourbillons' ('central, for everything obeys a fleeting, spinning impulse').[17] Her whirling stages the poem, and upstages anything else.

Seurat's celebration of the dance, in the peculiar painting of 1888–9 called *Chahut*, certainly seems not to be about veils, sonorities or the

gauzy withdrawals of wings or skirts as in Loie Fuller's dance. La Goulue, the best-known performer in this dance originally thought to be so
vulgar that it was unlawful even to mention it, as Jean-Claude Lebensztejn points out, is certainly a far distance form the delicacy of Loie
Fuller.[18] Richard Thomson's *Seurat* discusses at length the setting and
meaning of the café-concert, the way in which 'Seurat's attitude to the
chahut's public expression of promiscuous sexuality is to be found in
both the painting's subject and its means of representation'.[19] Seurat's
deliberate evocation of the posters of Chéret brings into the scene this
democratic and egalitarian art, aimed at the crowd. But in this painting
and the allied paintings and sketches, composed in his studio, Seurat is
rehearsing, says Thomson, 'a trenchant, melancholy irony at odds with
his brash and vulgar subject', and developing a sense of alienation between the audience and the on-stage performers, further intensified by
the orangey-blue haze of its surface and the repetitive movements. This
is scarcely the place of Mallarmé's Symbolist-nuanced and elitist theatri-
calizations, his theatre of the mind, although Thomson points out, as
have others, what an important role such repetitive effects play in
Symbolist writing. In *Chahut*, the two female dancers, perfectly aligned
with their male counterparts, raise their skirts indeed, but there is
neither Mallarmé's tenuous crêpe nor silence, nor is enchantment exactly the word for the feeling produced. The whole thing is noisy, edgy,
tense. The place it institutes is as much of a *formal sign* for us as it is for
the master Mallarmé, and is just as noticeably significant of the mindset
of the artist as is the Loie Fuller dance to that of the poet: it is a key
work, no less so than the latter's essays on the dance and the theatre.

If Mallarmé sees the action of the dance in a whirl – 'ce dégagement
multiple autour d'une nudité, grand des contradictoires vols' ('this
multiple clearing around a nudity, serving as a focus of flights in contradictory directions'), Seurat's bizarre arrest of attention is upon a set of
contradictions also, analysed most intricately by Lebensztejn and by
Robert Rey.[20] Lebensztejn shows Seurat's interest in the 'visible des regards invisibles' as the spectator included in the canvas looks away from
the direction in which the skirts of the female dancers are lifted, in the
visual echo of the lines of the legs, the dark double-bass, the baton of the
conductor, and the flute at the bottom left-hand corner. Rey shows the
force of the diagonals, its 'fatiguing balance' of right angles and its 'carefully regulated turbulence', drawing his own grid across the painting to
show the triangle at the lower left. This last is the 'Egyptian triangle'
dear to Charles Henry, whose study of angles and circles and directions
was so important to Seurat. He translated these theories into simple language for Camille Pissarro, using them in his late works: a study of
angles in *Chahut* and, in *Le Cirque*, a study of inscription in a circle.[21]

Among his important discussions, we should include Henry's theory of dynamic force or 'dynamogènes'. This theory is based on the nervous irritation provoked in the specatator by certain 'arresting phenomena' discovered in the physiological experiments of Brown-Séquard.[22] The tug between nervousness or the dynamic of the diagonal and the static freeze of the figures accounts at least in part for the fascination of the work; as Rey puts it, we have the feeling that when the baton of the conductor comes down, 'it will cause all of these legs to lower simultaneously, as though by means of an invisible crank rod.'[23] This is a snazzy set-up all around, with us all positioned as spectators, waiting, and the profits about to roll in the coffers.

## Clowning around

For Mallarmé, the theatre is written in nature so everyone can see it, participate in it. There are not, separately, spectators and actors: we are all both, if we choose. It is, sooner or later,

> un Livre, explication de l'homme. . . . Cette œuvre existe, tout le monde l'a tentée sans le savoir; il n'est pas un génie ou un pitre, qui n'en ait retrouvé un trait sans le savoir. Montrer cela et soulever un coin du voile de ce que peut être pareil poème, est dans un isolement mon plaisir et ma torture.[24]

> a Book, the explanation of man. . . . This work exists, everyone has tried it without knowing it; there is no genius or clown who hasn't found one of its traces unconsciously. Showing that and lifting one corner of the veil from what such a poem can be is in isolation my pleasure and my torture.

Let me underline the juxtaposition between the genius and the clown, for they are interdependent: 'ou un pitre. . . '. This clown exists, as well as this Book of a work, and he does not exist only in that most wonderful circus poem 'Le Pitre châtié':

LE PITRE CHÂTIÉ

Yeux, lacs avec ma simple ivresse de renaître
Autre que l'histrion qui du geste évoquais
Comme plume la suie ignoble des quinquets,
J'ai troué dans le mur de toile une fenêtre.

De ma jambe et des bras limpide nageur traître,
A bonds multipliés, reniant le mauvais
Hamlet! c'est comme si dans l'onde j'innovais
Mille sépulcres pour y vierge disparaître.

Hilare or de cymbale à des poings irrité,
Tout à coup le soleil frappe la nudité
Qui pure s'exhala de ma fraîcheur de nacre,

Rance nuit de la peau quand sur moi vous passiez,
Ne sachant pas, ingrat! que c'était tout mon sacre,
Ce fard noyé dans l'eau perfide des glaciers.

### THE CLOWN CHASTISED

Eyes, lakes with my simple passion to be reborn
Other than the actor, evoking with gestures
For feather the ugly soot of stage lights,
I have pierced a window in the canvas wall.

Clear traitor swimming with my legs and arms
Leaping and bounding, denying the wrong
Hamlet! as if I created in the wave
A thousand tombs in which to virgin disappear.

Joyous gold of the cymbal fists have inflamed,
Suddenly the sun strikes the barrenness pure
Exhaled from my coolness like mother-of-pearl.

Stale night of the skin when you swept over me,
Ungrateful! Ignorant of my whole consecration,
That grease paint drowned in faithless glacier water.[25]

In a first draft of this poem the poet plays clown to the muse:

J'ai, Muse – moi, ton pitre, – enjambé la fenêtre
Et fui notre baraque où fument tes quinquets.[26]

He exists boldly in Seurat's own *Parade* and his *Cirque*. In the first painting, he is centre-stage, performing, and we watch. In the last one, he is looking, with his back to us, a baton or stick in his left hand and his right one pulling back a curtain: *so that we can see*. These clowns are geniuses at directing attention where it is supposed to go: in the final version of the Mallarmé poem, instead of simply stepping over the window to the outside in some simple performance beyond the circus, he really tears apart the tent to make his outside move, ridding himself of the actor as hesitating-Hamlet who is stuck with those stage lights.

To be born again, further out, means being other than the

. . . histrion qui du geste évoquais
Comme plume la suie ignoble des quinquets

and he wants to be, must be other. The circus is left behind for another staging, as the clown gives way to the dancer, as the figure of indentificatory desire. Mallarmé, once identifying himself with Hamlet – that 'latent lord who cannot become' – and ex-clown, has a cross-dressing fantasy which will endure. He longs not just to stage the dance, but to belong in it. The focus is so intense as to feel myopic: such is the concentration on these points.

## A sticky business

In my view, this is Seurat's masterpiece: *Chahut* includes it all. It has everything: the flautist in the left corner, with his flute the diagonal echo of the contre-bass and the dancers' legs, keeps both hands on the stick (no body, no face, just the essential stick), perfectly situated in the all-important left-side triangle Seurat liked to accentuate. Directly above him, to his left, the orchestra leader, whose moustache flips up like the flickering ribbons on the female dancers' ankles and the moustache of the male dancer matched to the smile of the female dancer, only needs one hand on his stick but points it knowingly at the dancer's skirt opening, whereas the first female dancer has placed her fan directly to complete the swirl of her skirt and the second skirt, forming a circle in strong and erotic opposition to the diagonals so patently the focus of all eyes.[27]

Mallarmé could not have wished for a better example of his emblematic icons: her fan like his texts-upon-a-fan, the conductor's stick, and above all, the score of the centrally placed musician of the double-bass, with his back to us, reading, as it were, in an open book. The silly-faced smiling behatted and eyeless man to the lower right, balancing the flautist and the conductor to the left, plays his own clown role. The direction is marked, just as Henry insisted, and yet the action is static, as he also required, the legs at their full height, ready for descent – but nothing is halfway. Seurat's emphasis on the static comes also from a Turkish or Persian painter's manual lent him by Gauguin, in which he underlined, among others, the following phrase: 'Everything in your work should breathe the calm and peace of the soul. You should also avoid *poses in movement*. Each of your figures ought to be in a *static* position.'[28] And, strangely enough, here they are.

## Circling away

Above all, the dance is transgressive, spectacular, and keeps its legs and its motion removed. The central figure with its back to us, like the *Rückenfigur* so much a part of the German Romantic paintings, of Kaspar David Friedrich in particular, keeps the observer included in the painting and yet distant from it. We are close and far away.[29]

This is true also of the isolation felt in the solitary figures of Seurat's work with the conté crayon: his mother embroidering or reading, his father dining by candlelight, a seamstress – these are hieratic and emblematic of a solitude which the isolation of the performers from the spectators included and outside the painting does nothing to contradict, even in the mad dance of the Chahut.

We see a group of performers on the stage and around it: four dancing, one conducting, and two playing (one facing away, the other cropped out except for the flute), and that peculiar spectator at the bottom right, eyes hidden by his rakish hat, just his leering smile showing under his nose: these are the stagey elements, and as for the audience, they are only dimly seen under the skirts in the central whirl. What they see, we cannot. There is no meeting of the eyes, for everyone is looking in some other direction. Every direction is symbolic, said Charles Henry,[30] for whom lines and directions dominated everything else: his score was complex. The influence that all this working-out of direction was to have upon the futurist movement in Italy and the vorticist movement in England, both with their lines of force and their centralizing whirl, is no less complex, but this is not the place to expand on that.[31]

The transgressive sense is already present in just this complexity of direction and lines of sight, as well as in the formal techniques with which the presentation is made: cropping (the two hands only), reversal (the turned back), concealment (the hat over the eyes), all this balanced against display (skirts awhirl) and diagonal energizing of the forbidden scene – this, for the end of that last century, is rated X.

## I get a kick out of you

But La Goulue, and the Chahut, were high-kicking demonstrations of a joyous mood. Close to the poster gaiety and spritely appeal of the posters of Jules Chéret, Seurat's up-springing, high-swinging lines, his dancing ribbons in the *Chahut* have the same zip, the same 'tongue-inflame' form as Chéret's representation of the Folies-Bergère, *Les Girard* of 1877, in which the costumed gentlemen do the high-kicking, and the lady dances between their legs, more demurely than in Seurat's *Chahut* ten years later, where the skirts and the ironic smiles soar sky-high.[32] The flickering of the forms is parallel, and a free-wheeling spirit.

The kick of *Chahut* seems genderless, androgynous, as if the dancers male and female were both representing the possibilities indicated by the score, held open in the V shape that Mallarmé associates elsewhere with the idea of the Book, erotic in its red edging full of gilt. Book open, legs open, but much seemingly cropped off or misdirected: this is Seurat, doing his Mallarmé act for us without knowing it, and even as he seems in full control of the scene. We are following his lead and his lines, as he is thinking Egyptian, painting his figures in profile and his forms flat, keeping to the static pose.[33]

When Mallarmé was working on his own masterpiece, the *Noces d'Hérodiade* which he left behind him, he asked – as he was choking[34] – that his inheritors should destroy the fragments of the manuscript: 'Croyez-moi,' he said, 'c'eût été très beau.' He gave Salomé the name of her father Herod, transforming it to the feminine mode: this last dancer and doer, who does a ritual dance with John the Baptist's severed head between her thighs, is the most violent and erotic of performers, joining the sexes and celebrating death as the ultimate high point towards which the text leads. She is nothing if not strong. I am suggesting that Mallarmé's own crossing-over upon the points that the ballerina makes provides his extraordinary sighting of the ballet with that same kind of tension, like energy about always to be released, seen at a remove but close-up: all those contradictions in the flight and sight-lines that complicate his dance of the text. In the dance that I am comparing to Mallarmé's own staging of desire, from Loie Fuller and La Cornalba to Hérodiade, both male and female spectators are watching, both male and female are dancing, and the score is still open. Nor are the details to be overlooked: the fact that the male dancer's moustache is topologically similar to the female dancer's smile provides a setting, a small visual detail to go along with the accidental but symbolically significant linguistic detail about the dance represented; that the term 'chahut', as Lebensztejn points out, has been of both genders before settling down to the male one; and that Seurat leaves off the article altogether, a fact many commentators seem to ignore. Those dancers kicking high above everyone's line of sight are clearly of both sexes, as are the readers on whom Mallarmé's own sights never ceased to be trained.

This is, it seems to me, one of the most energizing modes we could have wished for such a performance: double-sexed, provided with a vigorous cropping device and a stick or two well handled, knowing the score, this dance turns out to be about all of us, kicking high.

# Framing by the light

Finally, how should we set apart the static scene and yet retain its energy? 'La scène libre' which was Mallarmé's goal requires an androgynous performer and an androgynous spectator to project energy on to the stage. One of the techniques Seurat found the most appealing, and to which he devoted a great deal of study, was that of the 'lustral': the study of lighting and its theoretical as well as practical side, as they were developed by the German physicist Heinrich-Wilhelm Dove (1803–98) and transmitted through Ogden Rood's writing.[35]

If we look at the extraordinary frame set around *Chahut*, to its left and above, we see the tulip forms of the gas-lamps Seurat used to stare at in his walks, seeing about them a halo: they combine, strangely, the natural or flower form, with a highly mannered construction, nature and culture merging. The verticality of the pole sets off the stage all the more, but it is this lustral effect that Seurat develops through *Le Concert* and brings over to this formal setting, as repetitious as the steps of any dance, and as transforming to the spirit. Mallarmé was lustrally inclined: for him, there was no higher compliment than the luminous one – 'lumineux à l'éblouissement'.[36]

So to frame with light was to frame for the spirit as for the understanding: nothing more could be expected of the painter. Seurat was able to transform those smoky stage-lights which Mallarmé's clown-as-poet first fled when he left Hamlet behind to go beyond, outside the stage, beyond the 'suie ignoble des quinqets' into a non-imprisoning border. What are not left behind are those orbs at the beginning of 'Le Pitre châtié', the introductory and shocking unpoetic 'Yeux', the eyes that set that poem and Mallarmé's future stagings beyond the circus into the space of spectacle. Forever, the spectacle will demand and create a privileged if ironized space in which to recite that 'poem freed from any scribe's apparatus'. In a utopian recreation, a new virginity is possible, and will take place within the staging, upon the boards and the page ('planches et feuillets'). Now the particular high kicks of the dancers have become the metaphor they are aiming toward – and Mallarmé the dancer he dreamt of – in this double feature of a theatre of the mind.

## Suggested reading

*French 19th-Century Painting and Literature*: with special reference to the relevance of literary subject-matter to French painting, ed. Ulrich Finke (Manchester: Manchester University Press, 1972; New York: Harper and Row, 1978).

Lebensztejn, Jean-Claude, *Chahut* (Paris: Hazan, 1989).

Kermode, Frank, *Romantic Image* (New York: Ark, 1986).

Mallarmé, Stéphane, *Œuvres complètes*, ed. Henri Mondor et G. Jean-Aubry (Paris: Gallimard/La Pléiade, 1945).

Russell, John, *Seurat* (New York: Praeger, 1965).

Seurat, Georges, *Correspondances, Témoignages, Notes inédites, Critiques*, ed. Eric Darragon (Paris: Acropole, Coll. Ecrits sur la Peinture, 1991).

*Seurat in Perspective*, ed. Norma Broude (Englewood Cliffs: Prentice-Hall, 1978).

# Notes

*Chapter 1: Structures of cultural production in nineteenth-century France*

1. See Pierre Bourdieu, *La Distinction: critique sociale du jugement* (Paris, 1979).
2. On the reciprocal influence of art and literature in the conquest of this autonomy, see Bourdieu's chapter below (pp. 30–39).
3. For different versions of the position that 'literature' as an isolatable cultural category emerges round about the beginning of the nineteenth century, see Raymond Williams, *Marxism and Literature* (Oxford, 1977), pp. 47–50, 51–2; Marc Fumaroli, *L'âge de l'éloquence: rhétorique et 'res literaria' de la Renaissance au seuil de l'époque classique'* (Geneva, 1980), pp. 17–20; Michel Foucault, *Les Mots et les choses* (Paris, 1966), pp. 307–13). The catalogues of early nineteenth-century *cabinets de lecture* often include history, travel and educational writings under the heading of 'littérature' – and exclude novels; sometimes novels are counted as part of *belles-lettres*, but very commonly classed separately (Françoise Parent-Lardeur, *Lire à Paris au temps de Balzac: Les Cabinets de lecture à Paris, 1815–1830* [Paris, 1981], p. 34). In discussing 'literature' here I shall exclude theatre, as a distinct cultural sphere.
4. On the origins of the Académie, see Nicolaus Pevsner, *Academies of Art, Past and Present* (London, 1940).
5. On the politics of the Salon, see Thomas Crow, *Painters and Public Life in Eighteenth-Century Paris* (New Haven, 1985).
6. Elizabeth Gilmore Holt, *The Triumph of Art for the Public 1785–1848: The Emerging Role of Exhibitions and Critics* (Princeton, 1979), p. 11.
7. The Académie itself was dissolved in 1795, and recreated as the Section des Beaux-Arts of the Institut de France. It became an Académie again under the Restoration. Its educational role was hived off into the Ecole des Beaux-Arts, with which it was at times institutionally linked (Holt, pp. 43–4, 211–12).
8. Holt, pp. 6, 390–1; on the relation between the Académie and the juries, see pp. 91–2, 212.
9. The figures are in Holt, pp. 41, 485.
10. See the extract from Etienne Delécluze's report on the Salon of 1847 in Holt, pp. 463–6. An important case of political censorship under the Second Empire was Manet's *Execution of Maximilian*: the artist was informed that if he submitted it, as he planned to in 1869, it would be rejected by the jury. See John House, 'Manet's Maximilian: History Painting, Censorship and Ambiguity', in *Manet: The Execution of Maximilian*, ed. Juliet Wilson-Bareau (London, 1992), p. 100. House sets the banning of Manet's painting, and of his lithograph of the subject, in the general context of Second Empire censorship.

11.   Holt, p. 462; John Rewald, *The History of Impressionism*, 4th ed. (London, 1973), p. 79.
12.   On the Académie's promotion of landscape, and its contribution to the emergence of a new 'aesthetics of the sketch' that valorizes spontaneity and originality, see Boime, *The Academy and French Painting in the Nineteenth Century*, 2nd ed. (New Haven and London, 1986), particularly pp. 133–85.
13.   Harrison C. White and Cynthia White, *Canvases and Careers: Institutional Change in the French Painting World* (New York, 1965), p. 83. For an account of the impact of railways on Impressionist painting, see Robert L. Herbert, *Impressionism: Art, Leisure, and Parisian Society* (New Haven and London, 1988), pp. 196–8, 219–29.
14.   T.J. Clark, *The Absolute Bourgeois: Artists and Politics in France 1848–1851* (London, 1973), p. 101.
15.   See Ann Jefferson, *Reading Realism in Stendhal* (Cambridge, 1988), p. 32.
16.   Boime, *The Academy*, p. 26.
17.   On lithography, see White and White, pp. 79–82, and Albert Boime, 'Entrepreneurial patronage in nineteenth-century France', in *Enterprise and Entrepreneurs in Nineteenth- and Twentieth-Century France*, ed. Edward C. Carter II, Robert Forster and Joseph N. Moody (Baltimore and London, 1976), p. 161. On its relationship to Daumier's painting, see Clark, *The Absolute Bourgeois*, pp. 99–123.
18.   Theodore Zeldin, *France 1848–1945: Taste and Corruption* (Oxford, 1980), pp. 108–9; Linda Nochlin, *Realism* (Harmondsworth, 1971), p. 182.
19.   Nochlin, *Realism*, pp. 44–5, 164.
20.   Nochlin, pp. 167–9. On the representation of the city, see T.J. Clark, *The Painting of Modern Life: Paris in the Art of Manet and his Followers* (London, 1985), pp. 23–78; Herbert, *Impressionism*, pp. 1–32.
21.   House, p. 91. On State patronage under the July Monarchy, see Boime, *The Academy*, pp. 11–14.
22.   Boime, *The Academy*, pp. 15–21.
23.   House, p. 90. House shows, nonetheless, that despite the declining influence of the ideal of 'high art' history painting, history painting remained a central focus of artistic debate.
24.   See Clark, *The Absolute Bourgeois*, pp. 32–71.
25.   White and White, p. 78; Zeldin, p. 111.
26.   On all this, see White and White, pp. 83–8.
27.   White and White, p. 92. Extreme specialization was in itself no novelty: it was a fact of artistic production in seventeenth-century Holland. But in France, the Académie system had served to delay the subjection of art to the laws of the capitalist market.
28.   On Bonheur, see Linda Nochlin, *Women, Art, and Power, and Other Essays* (London, 1991), pp. 170–5. Whitney Chadwick, incidentally, has argued that images of animals, especially horses, high-spirited beasts controlled and sold by men, could function as images (not necessarily conscious ones) of women's condition in the mid-nineteenth century (*Women, Art and Society* [London, 1990], pp. 181–6).
29.   On the emergence and workings of this system, see White and White, pp. 94–9, to which what follows is heavily indebted.
30.   White and White, pp. 9–10.
31.   Zeldin, p. 112.
32.   Baudelaire, *Salon de 1846*, in *Curiosités esthétiques, L'Art romantique*, ed. H. Lemaître, Classiques Garnier (Paris, 1990), pp. 97–102; see also the attack on anti-bourgeois rhetoric in the *Salon de 1845*, ibid., pp. 4–5.
33.   White and White, p. 95. On Durand-Ruel, see Boime, 'Entrepreneurial patronage', pp. 168–70, and also the interview with Durand-Ruel quoted in *The Impressionists at First Hand* ed. Bernard Denvir (London, 1987), p. 90.

34. Zeldin, pp. 111–12.
35. White and White, p. 99.
36. Baudelaire, p. 194. The passage goes on to argue that 'cette glorification de l'individu a nécessité la division infinie du territoire de l'art': the specialization of painters to particular genres mentioned above (p. 18) could be seen as one form of this division.
37. Compare *Salon de 1846*, p. 101, and *Salon de 1845*, p. 18.
38. White and White, pp. 94–5.
39. White and White, pp. 126–7; Boime, 'Entrepreneurial patronage', p. 185. See the letters from Degas to Durand-Ruel, reproduced in *The Impressionists at First Hand*, ed. Denvir, p. 141.
40. White and White, p. 2.
41. Rewald, pp. 79–89.
42. The critical reaction to *Le Déjeuner sur l'herbe* is analysed in Clark, *The Painting of Modern Life*, pp. 94-5. As House points out, Manet's *Execution of Maximilian* was specifically designed with the Salon in mind (p. 91).
43. Rewald, pp. 302–6; pp. 309–40.
44. On the political and economic constraints of the book trade, and the resulting crisis of the late 1820s, see *Histoire de l'édition française*, ed. Henri-Jean Martin and Roger Chartier, 4 vols. (Paris, 1982–6), especially II, pp. 528–35, 538–9, 552–7, 597–8, 612–13 and III, pp. 130–2, 176. On the *cabinets de lecture*, see II, pp. 614–21, and, for more detail, Parent-Lardeur, *Lire à Paris au temps de Balzac*. On Balzac's own analysis of the book trade, see Roland Chollet, 'Un épisode inconnu de l'histoire de la librairie: la Société d'abonnement général', *Revue des sciences humaines*, 141 (1971), pp. 55–109.
45. See *Histoire de l'édition française*, III, pp. 368–97.
46. Ibid., III, pp. 135–6.
47. Ibid., III, pp. 128–9.
48. For a summary of the respective contributions to literacy of the ancien régime and the later period, see François Furet and Jacques Ozouf, *Lire et écrire: l'alphabétisation des Français de Calvin à Jules Ferry*, 2 vols. (Paris, 1977), I, pp. 54–8.
49. See *Histoire de l'édition française*, III, pp. 25–45.
50. Chollet, pp. 69–73, 82.
51. On technical innovations, see *Histoire de l'édition française*, II, pp. 554-61, and *Histoire générale de la presse française*, ed. Claude Bellanger et al., 5 vols. (Paris, 1969–76), II, pp. 15–22.
52. *Histoire de l'édition française*, III, pp. 180–1.
53. *Histoire de l'édition française*, III, pp. 128–9, 132.
54. *Histoire de l'édition française*, III, pp. 140.
55. *Histoire de l'édition française*, III, pp. 138–42.
56. Zeldin, pp. 145–6; F.W.J. Hemmings, *Culture and Society in France, 1789–1848* (Leicester, 1987), pp. 138–40; Parent-Lardeur, *Lire à Paris au temps de Balzac*, pp. 166–7. For a detailed account of the Press under the Restoration, see *Histoire générale de la presse française*, II, pp. 33–90.
57. *Histoire générale de la presse française*, II, pp. 114–24.
58. Stendhal, *Le Rouge et le Noir*, ed. P.-G. Castex, Classiques Garnier (Paris, 1973), pp. lviii–lxv; Flaubert, *Madame Bovary*, ed. C. Gothot-Mersch, Classiques Garnier (Paris, 1971), pp. ix–x.
59. On the *roman-feuilleton*, see *Histoire générale de la presse française*, II, pp. 121–2, and Hemmings, pp. 309–16 (and compare p. 248).
60. *Histoire de l'édition française*, III, pp. 144–5.
61. Zeldin, p. 127. On unofficial art schools, see also White and White, pp. 26, 114–16; on the importance of finish in Académie doctrine, see Boime, *The Academy*, pp. 20–1, and on the relevant technological changes see above, pp. 16–17.

62. Griselda Pollock, *Vision and Difference: Femininity, Feminism and the Histories of Art* (London, 1988), pp. 67–9, 81.
63. Jefferson, *Reading Realism in Stendhal*, pp. 27–33.
64. George Sand, *Indiana*, ed. Béatrice Didier, Collection Folio (Paris, 1984), p. 37.
65. Walter Benjamin, *Charles Baudelaire: A Lyric Poet in the Era of High Capitalism* (London, 1973), pp. 145–51.
66. Baudelaire, *Salon de 1859*, in *Curiosités esthétiques*, pp. 317–19.
67. Quoted in Holt, p. 45.
68. White and White, pp. 98–9.
69. Boime, 'Entrepreneurial Patronage', p. 144.
70. *Histoire de l'édition française*, III, pp. 140–3.
71. Walter Benjamin, 'The Author as Producer', in *The Essential Frankfurt School Reader*, ed. Andrew Arato and Eike Gebhardt (New York, 1978), pp. 255–69 (p. 257).
72. Christopher Prendergast, *Balzac: Fiction and Melodrama*, (Cambridge: Cambridge University Press, 1978) pp. 94–7.
73. Balzac, *Illusions perdues*, in *La Comédie humaine*, ed. P.G. Castex (Paris: Gallimard, Pléiade, 1977), V, pp. 328, 365, 346.
74. For a penetrating exploration of the problems raised by this self-reflexivity, see Prendergast, *The Order of Mimesis* (Cambridge, 1986), pp. 83–119.
75. *Illusions perdues*, p. 407.
76. Ibid., p. 490.
77. Prendergast, *The Order of Mimesis*, p. 108.
78. On Courbet's uses of material from popular culture, see T.J. Clark, *Image of the People: Gustave Courbet and the 1848 Revolution* (London, 1973), pp. 138–40, 157–60.
79. Clark, *Image of the People*, pp. 139–40.
80. Quoted in Holt, p. 368.
81. Quoted in Clark, *Image of the People*, p. 189, n. 81.
82. Clark, *The Absolute Bourgeois*, p. 158. Nothing is more likely than that such pictures would have been rejected by the Salon jury; but Courbet was profiting from the rule introduced only in 1849 that the winning of a certain grade of Salon medal guaranteed admission to future Salons (see White and White, pp. 89–90).
83. 'Artist, art dealer, and patron share a common set of assumptions about the work-as-commodity, independent of their peculiar aesthetic appraisals of the object'; (Boime, 'Entrepreneurial patronage', p. 165). 'It is not enough to say that [Manet and his followers] were bourgeois artists; it needs stressing, rather, that their practice as painters – their claim to be modern – depended on their being bound more closely than ever before to the interests and economic habits of the bourgeoisie they belonged to' (Clark, *The Painting of Modern Life*, p. 260).

*Chapter 2: The link between literary and artistic struggles*

1. This chapter uses some of the results of research which I undertook regarding the 'symbolic revolution' brought about by Manet, and whose primary results (on the Académie and the Academic eye) were published in P. Bourdieu, 'L'Institutionalisation de l'anomie', in *Les Cahiers du Musée national de l'art moderne*, vols. 19–20 (1987), pp. 6–19.
2. In referring here to the revolutionary role of Manet (as elsewhere to that of Baudelaire and Flaubert), I would not wish to encourage a vision of the genesis of social

fields which might be too naively discontinuist. If it is true that one can actually pin-point the moment when the slow process of *emergence* (as Ian Hacking so rightly terms it) of a structure undergoes that decisive transformation which seems to lead to the perfection of that structure, it remains no less true that in each movement of this continuous and collective process one can distinguish the emergence of a provi-sional form of the structure, which is already capable of directing and controlling the phenomena which can arise there and thus contribute to the more complex and subtle elaboration of the structure. However, for present purposes I will content myself with borrowing from Aristotle, by way of an antidote to the illusion of there being a first moment of beginning, a question which could in fact act as a somewhat ironic formulation of the false problem which has given rise to so much fruitless debate on the priority attributed to the birth of the artist as opposed to the writer. Exactly how does a retreating army stop retreating? At what moment, precisely, can one say that it has stopped retreating? Is it at the moment when the first soldier stops, or the second, or indeed the third? Or is it in fact only when a sufficient num-ber of soldiers have stopped retreating, or even when the very last of the fleeing troops has stopped his flight? For in fact it cannot rightly be said that it was with him alone that the army ceased to retreat: because it had actually started to stop fleeing quite some time before that.

3.   C. Baudelaire, *Œuvres*, 2 (Paris: Gallimard, La Pléiade, 1944), p. 312.

4.   J.C. Sloane, *French Painting between the Past and the Present: Artists, Critics and Traditions, from 1848 to 1870* (Princeton: Princeton University Press, 1951), p. 77.

5.   E. Zola, *Mes Haines* (Paris: Ed. Fasquelle, 1923), p. 34.

6.   C. Pissarro, *Lettres à son fils Lucien* (Paris: Albin Michel, 1950), p. 44.

7.   D. Gamboni, *La Plume et le Pinceau* (Paris: Minuit, 1989).

8.   It is significant that Gide explicitly evokes the backwardness of literature with regard to painting in order to exalt the *roman pur*, devoid of all meaning (the same novel, in fact, invented by Joyce, Faulkner and Virginia Woolf): 'I have often asked myself, by what prodigy of nature painting was so far ahead of literature, and why it was that literature should have let itself get left behind. What discredit has what we used to consider the "topic" in painting fallen into today! A "fine subject" only makes people laugh. Painters no longer dare risk a portrait unless they avoid any re-semblance to the original. If we manage to bring this off – you can can count on me for that – I give it less than two years for tomorrow's poet to consider himself dis-honoured if someone understands what he means. Yes indeed, my lord: would you care to wager on it? All meaning, all significance will be deemed anti-poetical. I pro-pose to work for the cause of illogicality.' (André Gide, *Les Faux-monnayeurs* (Paris: Gallimard, Folio, 1978), p. 30.

9.   Analyses of essence and formal definitions cannot, in fact, disguise the fact that the assertion of the specificity of the 'literary' or the 'pictorial', and of their irreduc-ibility to any other forms of expression, is inseparable from the assertion of the field of production's autonomy, which it simultaneously implies and reinforces. Thus the analysis of the pure aesthetic disposition that is elicited by the most advanced forms of art is inseparable from the analysis of the progress towards autonomy of the field of production. Similarly, epistemology cannot be separated, either in deed or in law, from the social history of science.

10.   E. Zola, *Mes Haines*, pp. 68 and 81. The logic behind the transfer to literature of categories invented for application to painting can be seen clearly in the statement made with reference to Hugo, which no doubt defines the *modern* aesthetic as radical subjectivism, as opposed to the absolutism of the *academic aesthetic*: 'There must be no trace of literary dogma: each work stands, by itself, and demands to be judged separately, in its own right' (Zola, p. 98). Artistic activity is not governed by

any preexisting rules, and cannot be measured by any transcendent criteria. It produces its own rules, and carries with it the yardstick of its own appreciation.

11.  In order to make it easier to understand the link between Zola's political commitments and the stand he took regarding aesthetics, it is clearly necessary to renounce the common image which all too easily associates political militancy with an accusatory naturalism. Naturalism is not opposed to symbolism as much as people think, or at least, not in the way that people usually think. Over and above their mutual opposition to the canons of the prevailing aesthetic, which leads them to defend the same painters, Zola and Mallarmé also share the 'artistic' style of writing, which is associated with a practice shrewdly distanced from 'popular' language and slang.

12.  For a development of the notion of 'Reason of State' as a specific kind of reason (which is as irreducible with regard to 'ethical reason' as it is to 'theological reason'), see E. Thuau, 'Raison d'Etat et pensée politique à l'époque de Richelieu', thesis (Paris: University of Paris, 1966).

*Chapter 3: 'A tout prix devenir quelqu'un': the women of the Académie Julian*

1.  Quoted by Colette Cosnier, *Marie Bashkirtseff: Un portrait sans retouches* (Paris: Horay, 1986), pp. 220–1.

2.  Charlotte Yeldham, *Women Artists in Nineteenth-Century France and England: Their Art Education, Exhibition Opportunities and Membership of Exhibiting Societies and Academies, with an Assessment of the Subject Matter of their Works and Summary Biographies* (New York and London: Garland Publishing Inc., 1984), vol. 2, p. 205.

3.  For the sake of consistency and brevity, married women who exhibited under more than one surname will be indicated with the married name followed by the single name, e.g. Virginie Demont Breton. This form is slightly more usual than the other way about (as in Elisabeth Vigée LeBrun), but there is in fact no uniformity in late nineteenth-century practice.

4.  *La Gazette des Femmes*, no. 48, 10 Nov. 1878, p. 2.

5.  Carolus-Duran and Jean-Jacques Henner trained many women, including thirty Americans, between 1872 and 1887 (H. Barbara Weinberg, *The Lure of Paris: Nineteenth-Century American painters and their French Teachers*[New York, 1991], pp. 189 and 218–19). The best-known of their American women students was Elizabeth Nourse, who attended the Académie Julian for a few weeks in 1887. In 1890 she became a member of the opposing camp, by joining the Société Nationale des Beaux-Arts, of which she became sociétaire in 1904 (M. A.H. Burke, *Elizabeth Nourse, 1859–1938: A Salon Career* [Washington: Smithsonian Press for the National Museum of American Art and the Cincinnati Art Museum, 1983], pp. 31–2. Burke's statement, that Julian 'had been the first to offer art training in Paris exclusively for women', is of course wrong).

6.  Nélie Jacquemart won medals at the Salons of 1868, 1869, 1870 and 1878; obit., *Chronique des Arts*, 18 May 1912, p. 157; see also *Gazette des Beaux-Arts*, vol. 1 (1869), pp. 501–2; *Revue Internationale de l'Art et de la Curiosité*, vols. 3–4 (1870), p. 3427; J.A.K. Castagnary, *Salons de 1857–1870* (Paris, 1892), p. 427; T. Veron, *De l'Art et des artistes de mon temps: Salon de 1877* (Paris, 1877), p. 268; *L'Art*, vol. 3 (1878), pp. 182, 292; M. Du Seigneur, *L'Art et les artistes au Salon de 1880* (Paris, 1880), p. 62.

7.   There is another 'Intérieur d'atelier' by Marie Amélie Cogniet in the museum at Lille, unseen by this writer.

8.   Female exhibitors in the Salons of the 1830s acknowledge masters relatively seldom. Abel de Pujol, whose career foundered after promising beginnings, may have preferred not to be known as principally a teacher of women.

9.   For a reproduction of the version in the Musée Marmottan, see G. Greer, *The Obstacle Race* (London, 1979), p. 44, and Yeldham, vol. 2. Another version may be seen in the Musée de Valenciennes.

10.   See Greer, p. 313. All three of these paintings are in the Musée des Beaux-Arts, Orléans.

11.   Martine Hérold, *L'Académie Julian a cent ans* (Paris, 1968), p. 4; Catherine Fehrer, 'New Light on the Académie Julian and its Founder (Rodolphe Julian)', *Gazette des Beaux-Arts*, mai–juin 1984, p. 215.

12.   *Gauloises*, Sept. 1874, no. 9, p. 34.

13.   *La Gazette des Femmes*, vol. 10, no. 3 (10 Feb. 1883).

14.   *The Artist*, 1 May 1880, p. 154.

15.   *L'Académie Julian*, vol. 3, no. 2 (December 1903), p. 3, an interview with Gabrielle Réval, reprinted from *L'Echo de Paris*.

16.   May Alcott Nieriker, *Studying Art Abroad and How to do it Cheaply* (Boston, 1879), p. 48. Alcott says however that many ateliers were 'overcrowded, badly managed, expensive or affording only objectionable company'. What Alcott means by objectionable [female] company is not clear. Some women who worked as models sought training as painters; though one hopes that Miss Alcott was not referring to the large number of Jewish women who sought art training, the possibility may not automatically be discounted.

17.   Though Lemaire, whose hospitality Proust enjoyed on countless occasions, greatly assisted Proust by agreeing to illustrate *Les Plaisirs et les jours* for him (Ronald Hayman, *Proust: A Biography* [London, 1990], p. 83), John Cocking, in his article on 'Proust and painting', in *French 19th Century Painting and Literature* (Manchester, 1972), did not see fit to mention her at all.

18.   Yeldham, I, pp. 345–50.

19.   Louise Jopling, *Twenty Years of My Life 1867–87* (London, 1925), describes her sixteen months with Chaplin, 'whose studio for women was the fashion just then' (1867–8); according to her his was then the only atelier 'where the students were all women' (p. 4). Unfortunately, Jopling does not see fit to mention any of the other women who studied there with her.

20.   Ellen Wilson, *American painter in Paris: A Life of Mary Cassatt* (New York: Farrar Straus, Giroux, 1971), pp. 19, 22; E. John Bullard, *Mary Cassatt, Oils and Pastels* (Oxford: Phaidon, 1976), p. 12.

21.   See also J. K. Huysmans, *L'Art Moderne: Salons 1879–1882* (Paris, 1883), p. 57, and Valerie E. Morant, 'Charles Josue Chaplin, an Anglo-French artist, 1825–1891', *Gazette des Beaux Arts*, vol. CXIV, Oct. 1989, p. 1449.

22.   For an explanation of this curious term, the reader is referred to George Moore, 'Meissonnier and the Salon Julian', *Fortnightly Review*, vol. XVIII, new series, 1 July to 1 Dec. 1890, p. 54; ' . . . to draw by the character, as we had hitherto been content to do, was but the infancy of art, whereas to draw by the "masses" was its manhood and apotheosis. So we went to France to learn to draw by the "masses" . . .'.

23.   Cosnier records that Bashkirtseff applied to be taught by Bonnat and was refused on the grounds that the students' atelier was unsupervised.

24.   It is only fair to point out that after 1887 Beaury-Sorel's work was treated rather more kindly; by that time however the network of influence of the Académie Julian was so well developed that we may suspect that the reviewer in *L'Art* (vol. 2,

1887, p. 10) who remarked that portraits by Beaury-Sorel and Louise Breslau, another Julian of the Bashkirtseff period, were better than those of Bonnat and Carolus-Duran was a part of it.

25.   Collart's rural genre pieces were widely praised; see for example *Gazette des Beaux-Arts*, 1865, vol. 19, p. 8; 1869, vol. 4, p. 56; 1872, vol. 6, p. 54.

26.   Cosnier, p. 220.

27.   Mary L. Breakell, 'Marie Bashkirtseff: The Reminiscence of a Fellow-Student', *Nineteenth Century and After*, vol. 52 (July–Dec. 1907), p. 110.

28.   Julian's ateliers were always so crowded that, to avoid quarrels, spaces for tabourets and easels had to be marked out with chalk and strictly adhered to. Cecilia Beaux found painting impossible, there being no room to wield brushes (*Background with Figures*, p. 122).

29.   This was probably not Alice Beckington, a Julian who went on to teach at the Pennsylvania Academy of Fine Art for many years, unless her birthdate is given wrongly as 1868, nor can it be Alice Beek, who spent six years at the Académie Julian, if she was in fact born in Rhode Island in 1876. The other possibility is Alice (Mrs Clifford) Barney or perhaps Alice Brisbane.

30.   Ibid., 113. 'Mlle de V.' is probably Marie de Villevieille, a Julian who exhibited at the Salons of 1881 and 1882.

31.   *L'Académie Julian*, vol. 2, no. 3 (Jan. 1903), p. 4.

32.   Breakell does not positively identify all the individuals depicted in the painting, which she clearly had not seen in many years.

33.   Cosnier, p. 221.

34.   According to Anna Klumpke, *Memoirs of an Artist*, ed. L. Whiting (Boston, 1940), p. 20, at this time the women of the atelier worked from the draped model in the morning and the nude only in the afternoon. When Bashkirtseff demanded that the women be allowed as the men were to work from the nude all day Julian agreed, but only, one suspects, for this one atelier.

35.   George Moore, 'Meissonnier and the Salon Julian', *Fortnightly Review*, volume XVIII, new series, 1 July to 1 Dec. 1890, p. 46.

36.   William Rothenstein, *Men and Memories: Recollections of William Rothenstein 1872–1900* (London, 1931), p. 39.

37.   Martine Hérold, *L'Académie Julian a cent ans*, p. [1].

38.   In 1890, Marie Adelaide Belloc, in a curiously inaccurate article on 'Lady Artists in Paris' in *Murray's Magazine*, vol. VIII, pp. 371–84), affects to be undecided on the point: 'it may or may not be true that M. Julian has hitherto been the Warwick of the Salon Jury, and with the aid of his two thousand old pupils, decided whose pictures were to be admitted to the galleries of the Palais de l'Industrie. There may have been a very strong clique who believed in and voted for Julian, his students and his masters' (p. 374). Belloc may have been influenced by George Moore's account of the schism that resulted in the formation of the Société Nationale des Beaux-Arts. The same cannot be said of Alice deWolfe Kellogg, who wrote home in the Spring of 1888: 'Our enthusiasm for the Salon is decidedly dashed by the undeniable fact – hardly concealed at all – of the all-powerful potency of 'influence' and wire-pulling. We all feel that the fact of going in as pupils of Julian did more than half toward gaining our acceptance' (quoted in Weinberg, p. 224).

39.   In April 1877, *Le Moniteur des Arts* announced: 'Le banquet annuel offert a M. Léon Cogniet par ses élèves aura lieu le 29 avril courant, chez Lemardelay, rue de Richelieu, 100 (MM. Barrias, Bonnat, Jean-Paul Laurens, Maillart et Tony Robert-Fleury commissaires). On souscrit dès à présent chez M. Julian, 27, galérie de Montparnasse, passage des Panoramas, de huit à onze heures du matin.' These annual banquets, which, like the balls for 'Artists and Models' were not attended by female élèves, bien entendu, had begun years before and continued until the end of Cogniet's life.

40. L. Etienne, *Le Jury et les exposants* (Paris, 1863), p. 41.
41. Julian continued to exhibit in the Salons, without distinction, until 1878.
42. A persistent belief that these gentlemen offered their services free of charge (see, for example, M. Riccardo Nobili, 'The Academie Julian', *Cosmopolitan*, vol. 8, no. 6, April 1890) appears to be without foundation.
43. A. S. Hartrick, *A Painter's Pilgrimage through Fifty years* (Cambridge, 1939), p. 10.
44. Ibid., pp. 22–7.
45. Moore, 'Meissonnier and the Salon Julian', p. 49.
46. Lovis Corinth, *Legenden aus der Künstlerleben* (Berlin, 1908), p. 64.
47. Jacques Lethève, *La Vie quotidienne des artistes français au XIXe siècle* (Paris, 1968), p. 23.
48. Weinberg (pp. 225–6) identifies one of these women as Ellen Maria Carpenter, who claimed to have been taught by Lefebvre and Robert-Fleury on her second visit to Paris in 1873. Weinberg quotes also Albert Rhodes, who encountered six or seven women in Julian's atelier in 1873. Elizabeth Jane Gardner too claimed to have been one of Julian's first women students (Lida Rose McCabe, 'Mme Bouguereau, Path-finder', *New York Times Book Review and Magazine*, 19 Feb. 1922, p. 16).
49. May Alcott Nieriker, *Studying Art Abroad*, p. 48. The argument that it was the Americans who forced the revolution in women's art education in France was put forward in an article in *The Times* for 18 Oct. 1891 (Yeldham, vol. 2, p. 19, n. 353).
50. Sotheby's (London) sale, 8 Feb. 1989, lot no. 51. In August 1880, *La Gazette des Femmes* reported the marriage of Lucien Doucet to Lola de Ruiz of Philadelphia: '[ils] se sont connus et remarqués dans l'atelier de leur maître commun, M. Jules Lefebvre.' Later observers insist that women and men Julians had no opportunity to meet, only the maître, the patron and the colour-dealer ever gaining admittance to the women's ateliers.
51. However, when Royer as a student painted a picture for the Salon in which he showed the men's atelier during the repose of the female model, Julian, fearing an *équivoque*, persuaded him to paint another subject though barely three weeks remained before the submission date (*L'Académie Julian*, vol. 2, no. 4, Feb. 1903, p. 3).
52. In 1873 Gardner was thirty-six, Carpenter forty-two.
53. Lethève, p. 9.
54. The confusion in contemporary accounts is well-nigh impenetrable: Riccardo Nobili thought that in 1889–90 there were nine ateliers, five for men and four for women, Belloc that there were seventeen, seven 'given over to ladies'; Lucy Hooper (*Cosmopolitan*, 1892) that there were three ateliers, in the passage des Panoramas, the rue de Berri and a new one in the rue Fromentin, with a thousand students of whom three or four hundred were women. The truth seems to be as J. Sutherland described it in 'An Art Student's Year in Paris: Women's Classes at Julian's School', in *Art Amateur*, vol. 24, no. 2, Jan. 1895, that when one studio 'became full to overflowing, the newcomers were relegated to a deserted atelier in the nearest street'. Some of the confusion can be explained by the geography of the passage des Panoramas itself, being as it were the mews of the rue Vivienne, with many different and tortuous entrances to the same buildings, so that, as Hooper relates, it was easy for concerned Parisian mammas to be reassured that their 'treasured girls' need have no contact whatsoever with any members of the life-class (Hooper, 62).
55. Some evidence for the inferiority of the women's models is to be found in a letter of March 1891 by Eleanor Cunningham Bannister, then a student at the Académie Julian, quoted in Weinberg, p. 228.
56. Belloc, p. 377. All the masters who taught women charged them much more, sometimes three times as much, as men were expected to pay (see Weinberg, p. 226).

57. Hooper, pp. 61–2.
58. Sutherland, p. 52.
59. Later that year *Le Moniteur des Arts* announced art classes to be run by another of Chaplin's pupils, the Algerian, Mme Marie Mathieu, who offered drawing from life, as well as porcelain and fan painting. Though Mme Mathieu's classes were announced in editorials of *La Gazette des Femmes* as well, she is not acknowledged as a teacher by any artist of note.
60. *L'Académie Julian*, vol. 12, nos. 3 and 4, Jan.–Feb. 1913. Julian had eventually married Amélie Beaury-Sorel. The marriage was childless. Beaury-Sorel took to signing her work Julian Beaury Sorel; her portrait of Jean Paul Laurens which used to be in the Luxembourg is therefore listed by many authorities as by a man of that name.
61. Jopling, p. 5.
62. Alcott, p. 47.
63. Cosnier, p. 147.
64. For Robert-Fleury's effect on women, see also Belloc, p. 375.
65. *L'Académie Julian*, vol. 5, no. 3, Jan. 1906, p. 3.
66. E.Œ. Somerville, 'An Atelier des Dames', *The Magazine of Art*, vol. 9, 1886, p. 153.
67. Maximilienne Guyon; interview reprinted in *L'Académie Julian*, vol. 3, no. 2, pp. 2–3. Guyon won a third class medal at the Salon of 1888, a second class medal in 1889 and a travelling scholarship in 1894. Within days of the original publication of the interview with Gabrielle Réval in November 1903, she was dead. On 10–11 January not only her paintings, but all her personal effects were sold up, probably to pay her creditors (sale catalogue in the Witt Library).
68. The story of this struggle is succinctly told in Yeldham, vol. 1, pp. 55–62.
69. Susan N. Carter, *The North American Review*, no. CCCCXXX, Sept. 1892, p. 384.

*Chapter 4: Writing the arts: aesthetics, art criticism and literary practice*

1. Baudelaire cites Mrs Crowe in the section 'Le Gouvernement de l'imagination' of his *Salon de 1859*. For her influence on Baudelaire, see his *Œuvres complètes*, ed. Claude Pichois, 2 vols (Paris: Gallimard, Pléiade, 1975–6), II, pp. 1393–4.
2. *Cours de philosophie . . . sur le fondement des idées absolues du Vrai, du Beau et du Bien* (Paris: Hachette, 1836), p. 280.
3. *Cours d'esthétique* 2nd edn, ed. Ph. Damiron (Paris: Hachette, 1863), p. 254.
4. *Journal 1822–1863*, ed. André Joubin and Régis Labourdette (Paris: Plon, 1980), p. 373 (hereafter *Journal*).
5. *Essai sur la nature, le but et les moyens de l'imitation dans les beaux-arts* (Paris: Didot, 1823), p. 40 (hereafter, *Essai*).
6. See Emile Bergerat, *Théophile Gautier peintre: Etude suivie du catalogue de son œuvre peint, dessiné et gravé* (Paris: Baur, 1877).
7. 'Chronique des Beaux-Arts', *Le Figaro* (11 Nov. 1836), cited in I.J. Driscoll, 'The Role of Transposition d'art in the Poetry of Théophile Gautier' (PhD, Cambridge, 1971), p. 1; see also Robert Snell, *Théophile Gautier: A Romantic Critic of the Visual Arts* (Oxford: Clarendon Press, 1982).
8. See also Armand Moss, *Baudelaire et Delacroix* (Paris: Nizet, 1973).
9. Cited in Albert Cassagne, *La Théorie de l'art pour l'art en France* (Geneva: Slatkine, 1979; first pub. 1906), p. 360.
10. *Salon de 1847* (Paris: Hetzel Warnod, 1847), p. 10.
11. See chapter III, 'Visual Sources', in David Scott, *Pictorialist Poetics: Poetry and*

*the Visual Arts in Nineteenth-Century France* (Cambridge: Cambridge University Press, 1988), pp. 38–70.
12. 'Notice sur Baudelaire' cited in Cassagne's *La Théorie de l'art pour l'art en France*, p. 434.
13. *Petit Traité de poésie française* (Paris: Librairie de l'Echo de la Sorbonne, 1872), p. 8.
14. *L'Art du 18e siècle et autres textes sur l'art*, ed. J-P Bouillon (Paris: Hermann, 1967), p. 212; hereafter *L'Art du 18e*.
15. *Œuvres complètes*, ed. H. Mondor and G. Jean-Aubry, (Paris: Gallimard, Pléiade, 1945), p. 386.
16. Letter to Camille Mauclair in Mallarmé, *Correspondance*, IX, ed. L.J. Austin (Paris: Gallimard, 1983), p. 385.

*Chapter 5: The problem with colour. Three theorists: Goethe, Schopenhauer, Chevreul*

1. Le. R. P. Castel, *L'Optique des couleurs* (Paris, 1740), pp. 20, 21, 23.
2. 'The Recent Progress of the Theory of Vision', in *Popular Lectures on Scientific Subjects by Hermann von Helmholtz*, trans. E. Atkinson (London: Longmans, Green and Co.; new impression, 1904), vol. I, pp. 237–8.
3. Schelling, *Werke*, ed. Manfred Schrötter (Munich: C. H. Beck, 1956–), 3. Ergänzungsband [vol. 9], *zur Philosophie der Kunst, 1810–1850*, p. 171.
4. Kant, *Critique of Aesthetic Judgement*, para. 14.
5. Baudelaire, *Salon de 1846*, in *Œuvres complètes*, ed. Cl Pichois, 2 vols (Paris: Gallimard, Pléiade, 1975), vol. II, p. 418.
6. Ibid., p. 493.
7. See for example the *Dictionnaire de l'Académie Impériale des Beaux-Arts*, 1858, the article 'Coloris', which leaves nothing to the most excited Freudian imagination.
8. References in this article are to the following texts and editions and are given in parentheses: Goethe, *Theory of Colours*, trans. Charles Eastlake (1840), republished with an introduction by Deane B. Judd (Cambridge, MA, and London: MIT Press, 1970). Schopenhauer's *Vision and Colours* is not available in English; references are therefore to Schopenhauer, *Sämtliche Werke*, Bd I (Leipzig: Brockhaus, 1937), in my own translation. A useful French translation is to be found in Schopenhauer, *Textes sur la vue et sur les couleurs*, introduction et notes par Maurice Elie (Paris: Vrin, 1986). A synopsis of Schopenhauer's views is to be found in 'On the Theory of Colours', in *Parerga and Paralipomena: Short Philosophical Essays by Arthur Schopenhauer*, trans. E.F.J. Payne, 2 vols (Oxford: Clarendon Press, 1974), vol. II, pp. 177–200. I refer to Chevreul's *De la loi du contraste simultané des couleurs* in the facsimile edition (Paris: Léonce Laget, 1969), in my own translation. A full English version is available in *The Principles of Harmony and Contrast of Colours* by M. E. Chevreul, trans. Charles Martel, 2nd ed. (London: Longman Brown, Green and Longmans, 1855).
9. *The Oxford Companion to Art*, ed. Harold Osborne (Oxford: Clarendon Press, 1970), p. 259 (article on 'Colour').
10. Baudelaire, *Œuvres complètes*, vol. II, pp. 458, 460.
11. Ibid., p. 424.
12. Roger de Piles, *Cours de peinture par principes* (Geneva: Slatkine Reprints, 1969; reprint of 1708 Paris edition); see especially the sections 'Le Coloris' and 'Le Clair-obscur' – pp. 303, 367–8, for example.

13. Castel, *L'Optique des couleurs*, pp. 39–40.
14. *Popular Lectures*, vol. 2 (1903); see Lecture III, 'On the relation of optics to painting: (i) Form, (ii) Shade, (iii) Colour, (iv) Harmony of Colour'.
15. Charles Blanc, *Grammaire des Arts du Dessin*, 2nd ed. (Paris, 1870), p. 601.
16. *Du Dessin et de la Couleur*, par Bracquemond (peintre et graveur) (Paris, 1885), pp. 45, 100.
17. For an extended account of this controversy as it affects ideas about painting, the reader is referred to Martin Kemp's brilliant study, *The Science of Art* (New Haven and London: Yale University Press, 1990), particularly Part III, 'The Colour of Light', pp. 261–334.
18. For an account of Aristotelian theory, its relation to Aristotle's *De Coloribus*, and its variations, see Kemp, chapter VI, 'The Aristotelian Legacy'.
19. See E. Heller, 'Goethe and the idea of Scientific Truth', in *The Disinherited Mind* (London: Bowes and Bowes, 1975), especially pp. 22, 23. See also Werner Heisenberg, 'The Teachings of Goethe and Newton on Colour in the Light of Modern Physics', in *Philosophic Problems of Nuclear Science*, trans. F. C. Hayes (London: Faber and Faber, 1952), pp. 60–76.
20. *Opticks* (New York: Dover Publications, 1952), p. 123.
21. Ibid., pp. 31, 32, 113–21 (especially), 158, 297.
22. See the notes to Eastlake's translation (note N, p. 389); and see Helmholtz, 'On Goethe's Scientific Researches', in *Popular Lectures*, vol. 1, pp. 35–8.
23. Helmholtz, p. 49.
24. Jubiläums-Ausgabe, XL, 61, quoted by Heller, p. 23.
25. Ibid., p. 159.
26. For Goethe there is no such thing as pure transparency: 'Transparency itself, empirically considered, is already the first degree of the opposite state. The intermediate degrees from this point to opaque white are infinite' (61).
27. *Œuvres complètes*, vol. II, p. 424, 'La couleur es donc l'accord de deux tons. Le ton chaud et le ton froid, dans l'opposition desquels consiste toute la théorie, ne peuvent se définir d'une manière absolue: ils n'existent que relativement.' In any pair of opposite colours, one is cold and one is warm of course, as in Goethe's diagram (p. 84, fig. 5).
28. Bracquemond, p. 85, See also Blanc, p. 611: 'L'individualité de la couleur disparaîtra avec l'individualité de la forme' (along the line of demarcation between two juxtaposed coloured surfaces – as Chevreul demonstrated).
29. *Œuvres complètes*, especially pp. 472–4 ('De l'éclectisme et du doute'); pp. 477–9 ('De quelques douteurs'); pp. 490–2 ('Des écoles et des ouvriers').
30. See Schopenhauer's letter to Goethe of 11 November 1815. The Schopenhauer-Goethe correspondence can be consulted in Paul Deussen's edition: A. Schopenhauer, *Sämtliche Werke*, 14. Bd (München: Piper, 1929).
31. Newton of course knows that colour is a sensation and that the rays are only 'coloured' in vulgar parlance (*Opticks*, pp. 124, 125). And he was, in *Opticks*, fairly open-minded about the minimum number of colours of the right 'intensity' required to reconstitute white, though he doubted a proper white could be produced from two (pp. 156, 157).
32. See *On the Fourfold Root of the Principle of Sufficient Reason*, translated by E.F.J. Payne (La Salle, Illinois: Open Court, 1974), pp. 112–13.
33. See Maurice Elie in the introduction to his French translation of *Vision and Colours*, p. 26.
34. *Fourfold Root . . .* , p. 79.
35. Ibid., p. 79.
36. Ibid., p. 81.
37. Baudelaire, *Œuvres complètes*, vol. II, p. 424.

38.  See Baudelaire's distinction between 'coloristes', 'harmonistes' and 'contrastés', ibid., p. 421.

39.  The full extent of Chevreul's conservatism is to be seen in his paper, 'De l'Abstraction considérée relativement aux Beaux-Arts et à la Littérature' (Extrait des *Mémoires de l'Académie de Dijon*) (Dijon, Imprimerie J-E Robutot, 1864): sculpture is the most abstract and ideal art, representing the *form* of objects, painting only represents *appearance*. Statuary has an *absolute* quality: nothing can be added or taken away without spoiling it. The same is not true of painting: two equally beautiful paintings of Venus, one with blond hair, one with brown, would immediately divide the opinion of spectators! (pp. 12–14).

40.  Heinrich Wölfflin, *Principles of Art History* (New York: Dover Publications, 1950), p. 21.


*Chapter 6:   Book illustration*


1.  Préface to *Sous les rideaux*, by Edouard Thierry and Henri Trianon (Paris: A. Belin and Lachapelle, 1834), quoted by Champfleury, *Les Vignettes romantiques* (Paris: Dentu, 1883), p. 6.

2.  Walter Benjamin, 'The Work of Art in the Age of Mechanical Reproduction', in *Illuminations* (1970), pp. 219–53.

3.  A good explanation of the technique is found in Eric de Maré, *The Victorian Woodblock Illustrators* (London: Gordon Fraser, 1980), pp. 42–3; see also John Jackson and W.A. Chatto, *A Treatise on Wood Engraving, Historical and Practical* (London, 1839; 2nd ed. 1861).

4.  Jules de Rességuier, 'Mœurs. Un samedi au Louvre, septembre 1823. Exposition des produits de l'industrie', in *La Muse française* (1823–4), éd. Jules Marsan (Paris, 1907), p. 215.

5.  Echoes of this economic 'war' appear until the end of the century in the histories of nineteenth-century book illustrations; see for instance Henri Bouchot, *Les Livres à vignettes du XIXe siècle* (Paris: Edouard Rouveyre, 1891).

6.  Ambroise Firmin Didot, *Essai typographique et bibliographique sur la gravure sur bois* (Paris: Firmin Didot, 1863), col. 282.

7.  Branston, Nichols, Laing, Jackson, Sears, Orrin Smith, Williams, Gowland, Scheeres, Timms, Sargent, Gray, Folkard, Benworth, Wright, Clis, Clint, Quartley, Stadler, Hart, Linton, Whithead, Etherington, Smeeton; Pierre Gusman, *La Gravure sur bois en France au XIXe siècle* (Paris: Editions Albert Morancé, 1929), p. 23.

8.  Birouste, Godard fils, Maurisset, Brugnot, Thiébaut, Pouget, Laisné, Cherrier, Lacoste, Beugnot, Dujardin . . . .

9.  Paul Dupont, *Histoire de l'imprimerie* (Paris: chez tous les libraires, imprimerie Paul Dupont, 1854), vol. 2, p. 373 (from the statistics published by the chamber of commerce of Paris in 1847).

10.  'Siderography' was invented in the late eighteenth century by Jacob Perkins; the invention was improved in successive steps, described by Basil Hunnisett, *Steelengraved Book Illustration in England* (London: Scolar Press, 1980), pp. 12–15.

11.  As the Bank of England did not adopt his system, the American Perkins established a firm in London in 1820 with Fairman and Heath, and turned, among other engraving activities, to book illustration.

12.  Hunnisett, p. 30.

13.  'Fisher and Virtue had offices in Paris. Longman used agents, who were Rittner and Goupil in Paris' (Hunnisett, p. 161).

14.  This was particularly the case for 'keepsakes' as they derived from French and German book-forms (the 'almanach' and the 'Taschenbuch').
15.  *Paris-Londres Keepsake français 1837. Nouvelles inédites illustrées de vingt-six vignettes gravées à Londres par les meilleurs artistes* (Paris: Delloye, Desmé et Cie, 1837).
16.  'Célestin Nanteuil', in *Histoire du romantisme* (Paris: Charpentier, 1877), p. 52.
17.  'Notre but', *L'Illustration*, n°1, 4 mars 1843, p. 1.
18.  Discussing the future of photography and its derivatives, which threatened the art of engraving, Henri Delaborde considered that 'illustration' did not belong to the realm of 'art'; he wrote in 1859: 'Que l'imagerie, les illustrations de livres à bas prix, tout ce que l'on pourrait appeler la gravure industrielle finisse par disparaître à peu près complètement, cela est vraisemblable, mais il n'y aura pas là d'atteinte grave portée à l'art.' 'La photographie et la gravure', *Revue des Deux-Mondes*, 1er avril 1856, pp. 617–38, reprinted in André Rouillé, *La Photographie en France, Textes et controverses: Une anthologie 1816–1871* (Paris: Macula, 1989), p. 236.
19.  Nicole Felkay, *Balzac et ses éditeurs 1822–1837: Essai sur la librairie romantique* (Paris: Promodis, 1987).
20.  In an open list, which ended with 'etc.' or 'et les artistes les plus distingués'.
21.  For the first volume of *Les Français peints par eux-mêmes* (Paris: Curmer, 1841), 39 authors, and 2 illustrators, Gavarni and H. Monnier, are listed in the dedication signed 'l'éditeur reconnaissant'.
22.  Aristide Marie, *Alfred et Tony Johannot, peintres, graveurs et vignettistes* (Paris: Floury, 1925).
23.  Annie Renonciat, *J.-J. Grandville* (Paris: ACR, 1985); Philippe Kaenel, 'Autour de J.-J. Grandville', *Romantisme* (1984), pp. 43–61.
24.  Annie Renonciat, *Gustave Doré* (Paris: ACR, 1983); Exp. Strasbourg, *Gustave Doré* (1983).
25.  He was to become very famous in the second half of the century as a painter; in 1836 Hetzel paid ten francs for his drawings, according to Emile Bayard, *L'Illustration et les illustrateurs* (Paris: Delagrave, 1897).
26.  L. Carteret, *Trésor du bibliophile romantique et moderne 1801–1875* (Editions du Vexin français, 1976), vol. III, p. 152 (reprint of the 1928 edition).
27.  Martyn Lyons, *Le Triomphe du livre: Une histoire sociologique de la lecture dans la France du XIXe siècle* (Paris: Promodis, 1987), p. 38 and notes 68 and 72.
28.  Ségolène le Men, *Les Abécédaires français illustrés au XIXe siècle* (Paris: Promodis, 1984), and 'Mother Goose illustrated: from Perrault to Doré', *Poetics Today*, 13;1 (spring 1992), pp. 17–39.
29.  Variations on this theme of reading may be also found in the caricatures of the Republican Daumier, who showed a child reading in front of his painted allegory of the Republic for the competition of 1848 (Marseille, Musée des Beaux-Arts).
30.  See, in *Histoire de l'édition française*, vol. III, ed. Roger Chartier and Henri-Jean Martin (Paris: Promodis, 1985), the articles by Claude Savart ('le livre religieux'), Jean Glénisson ('Le livre pour la jeunesse'), Anne Sauvy ('Une littérature pour les femmes'), Anne-Marie Thiesse ('le roman populaire').
31.  Michel Melot, 'Le texte et l'image', in *Histoire de l'édition française*, p. 287.
32.  Françoise Parent-Lardeur, *Les Cabinets de lecture. La Lecture publique à Paris sous la Restauration* (Paris: Payot, 1982).
33.  Réjane Bargiel and Ségolène Le Men, *L'Affiche de librairie au XIXe siècle* (Paris: Réunion des Musées Nationaux, 1987).
34.  Book catalogues are kept in the Département des Imprimés of the Bibliothèque nationale, under the code number Q10.
35.  One of the three heroes is called 'Mr Puff'.
36.  See my article, '*Mœurs aquatiques*, une lithographie de Grandville expliquée par Balzac', *Gazette des Beaux-Arts*, Feb. 1988.

37. As was stated in the title of one of his collections.
38. In the later volumes, lithography was replaced by photography.
39. *Les Vignettes romantiques.*
40. Recalled later by Victor Pavie and Théophile Gautier, and Adèle Hugo in her *Victor Hugo raconté par un témoin de sa vie*: the most famous 'cénacles' were centred around Nodier, who organized the 'soirées de l'Arsenal' to which the brothers Johannot belonged, and around the homes of Hugo and Devéria, who were close friends and neighbours, and frequently met Louis Boulanger and David d'Angers; younger artists, architects and poets held their 'little cénacle' in the 'impasse du Doyenné', close to the Louvre; in the same way, on the other side of the River Seine, the 'studio' of the young Grandville, a corner of his small apartment, blended this early Bohemian life with the 'cénacle' atmosphere.
41. Charles Asselineau, 'Préface de la première édition', *Bibliographie romantique*, 2nd ed. (Paris: Rouquette, 1874), p. xviii.
42. Porret was a wood-engraver who started in the field of popular imagery in Lille; his social background was representative of the origins of French wood-engravers, who came from the provinces, and were often associated with popular imagery.
43. Henri Zerner and Charles Rosen, *Romanticism and Realism: The Mythology of Nineteenth-Century Art* (New York: Viking, 1984). 'The fingerprint: a vignette', pp. 1–5, and 'The Romantic Vignette and Thomas Bewick', pp. 73–96.
44. This theme appears frequently in the illustration, with metaphorical undertones about the definition of the vignette as an image.
45. Opened in 1789.
46. Pierre-Louis Duchartre and René Saulnier, *L'Imagerie parisienne* (Paris: Gründ, 1944).
47. The invention of the feuilleton may be related to the success of *Gil Blas*, as it occurred one year later, along with that of the Balzac novel *La Vieille Fille* in Girardin's journal *La Presse*.
48. In *Les Français peints par eux-mêmes*, for instance, the 276th instalment gave the frontispiece of the first four volumes.
49. *La Gloire de Victor Hugo*, ed. Pierre Georgel (Paris: Réunion des Musées Nationaux, 1985).
50. *L'Histoire des contes* (Paris: Fayard, 1992).
51. In the etymological sense of the first occurrence of a recurrent image.
52. *Le Triomphe du livre: Une histoire sociologique de la lecture dans la France du XIXe siècle* (Paris: Promodis, 1987).
53. Claude Witkowski, *Monographie des éditions populaires: les publications illustrées à 20 centimes, les romans à quatre sous 1848–1870* (Paris: J.-J. Pauvert, 1971).
54. Significantly, the text is about a newspaper 'feuilleton', but it refers rather to the illustrated book, as 'feuilletons' were not usually illustrated.
55. *Journal d'Eugène Delacroix* (Paris: Plon, 1895), 13 Jan. 1857, vol. III, 1855–63, p. 223.
56. Along with that of 'portraits de genre' in the history of painting.

*Chapter 7: 'Telle main veut tel pied': Balzac, Ingres and the art of portraiture*

Except where stated to the contrary, references to Balzac's novels are to the Pléiade edition of *La Comédie humaine*, 12 vols. (Gallimard, 1976–81), hereafter abbreviated to *Pl.* All references to Baudelaire's art criticism are to Baudelaire, *Critique d'art*, suivi de *Critique musicale*, edited by Claude Pichois with an introduction by Claire Brunet, Collection Folio/Essais (Gallimard, 1992), hereafter abbreviated to *Critique d'art*. Place of publication is London for English-language publications and Paris for publications in French, unless otherwise stated.

1.   *Pl.*, IV, pp. 386, 435.
2.   *Pl.*, II, p. 316.
3.   *Pl.*, II, p. 1207.
4.   *Pl.*, IV, p. 377.
5.   *Pl.*, II, p. 152.
6.   *Critique d'art*, p. 61 (*Le Salon de 1845*).
7.   Compare Hélène Toussaint, *Les Portraits d'Ingres* (Editions de la Réunion des Musées nationaux, 1985), p. 23.
8.   Charles Du Bos, *Journal 1924–25* (Corrêa, 1948), p. 280.
9.   See Graeme Tytler, *Physiognomy in the European Novel: Faces and Fortunes* (Princeton, NJ: Princeton University Press, 1982), a work that has proved invaluable in providing pointers for the present essay.
10.   *Critique d'art*, p. 355 (*Le Peintre de la vie moderne*).
11.   Ibid., p. 116 (*Le Salon de 1846*).
12.   Sainte-Beuve, *Œuvres*, ed. Maxime Leroy, 2 vols. (Paris: Gallimard, Pléiade, 1956–60), I, p. 649.
13.   Sainte-Beuve, *Causeries du Lundi*, 3rd ed. 15 vols. (Garnier, n.d.), I, p. 282; quoted by Richard M. Chadbourne, *Charles-Augustin Sainte-Beuve* (Boston, MA: Twayne, 1977), p. 157.
14.   Irving Babbitt, *The Masters of Modern French Criticism* (London: Constable; Boston and New York: Houghton Mifflin, 1913), p. 148.
15.   Sainte-Beuve, *Port Royal*, ed. Maxime Leroy, 3 vols. (Paris: Gallimard, Pléiade, 1953–5), I, p. 130.
16.   Chadbourne, pp. 155–6.
17.   Sainte-Beuve, *Œuvres*, I, p. 867.
18.   Sainte-Beuve, *Causeries du Lundi*, XI, p. 486.
19.   *Pl.*, III, p. 431. Compare Henry James, *Literary Criticism: French Writers, Other European Writers*, The Library of America (Cambridge: Cambridge University Press, 1984), p. 54.
20.   In his 1826 lectures, quoted in G.W.F. Hegel, *Aesthetics: Lectures in Fine Art*, translated by T.M. Knox, 2 vols. (Oxford: Clarendon Press, 1975), I, p. 165, n.1.
21.   See Tytler, p. 104.
22.   Hegel, *Aesthetics*, II, p. 748.
23.   Philip Conisbee, *Painting in Eighteenth-Century France* (Oxford: Phaidon, 1981), pp. 111, 128.
24.   Sainte-Beuve, *Nouveaux Lundis*, 14 vols. (Lévy, 1865), IV, p. 163.
25.   Quoted by Tytler, p. 108, where the artist is, however, confused with Georges de la Tour.
26.   Gautier makes a similar claim for Meissonier's portraits in *Les Beaux-Arts en Europe 1855*, 1ère série (Lévy, 1855), p. 72.
27.   Théophile Gautier, *Fusains et Eaux-Fortes* (Fasquelle, 1907), pp. 248-9 (the article originally appeared in *L'Evénement*, 1848).
28.   *Critique d'art*, p. 61 (*Le Salon de 1845*).
29.   Ibid., p. 247 (*Exposition Universelle (1855)*).
30.   Ibid., p. 356 (*Le Peintre de la vie moderne*).
31.   The phrase belongs to Robert Snell, *Théophile Gautier: A Romantic Critic of the Visual Arts* (Oxford: Clarendon Press, 1982), p. 100.
32.   Quoted by Snell, p. 127.
33.   *Critique d'art*, p. 119 (*Le Salon de 1846*).

34. Quoted by Tytler, p. 71.
35. *Critique d'art*, p. 119 (*Le Salon de 1846*).
36. Théophile Silvestre, *Histoire des artistes français et étrangers*, 1ère série (Blanchard, n.d.), p. 31.
37. [A. Le Go], 'La *Revue de Paris* au Salon', 2ème article, *Revue de Paris*, 48 (1833), pp. 211–17 (pp. 211–13).
38. Gautier, 'Le Salon de 1833', *La France littéraire*, VI (1833), pp. 139–66 (p. 154).
39. Gautier, *Les Beaux-Arts en Europe 1855*, p. 164.
40. Gautier, *Portraits contemporains* (Charpentier, 1874), pp. 108, 114.
41. *Pl.*, II, pp. 1057–8. (Compare Tytler, p. 202).
42. *Pl.*, II, p. 328.
43. Ibid., p. 312.
44. In their novel *Renée Mauperin* (1864).
45. Silvestre, p. [1].
46. *Critique d'art*, p. 61 (*Le Salon de 1845*).
47. Malcolm Easton, *Artists and Writers in Paris: The Bohemian Idea, 1803–1867* (Arnold, 1964), p. 25.
48. *Pl.*, IV, p. 75.
49. See Dorette Berthoud, *Vie du peintre Léopold Robert* (Neuchâtel: La Baconnière, 1934); and Sainte-Beuve, *Causeries du Lundi*, X, p. 428.
50. See Olivier Bonard, *La Peinture dans la création balzacienne* (Geneva: Droz, 1969), p. 149, and Balzac's letter to Mme Hanska of 17 January 1846. The engraving was much appreciated by Robert himself (see Sainte-Beuve, *Causeries du Lundi*, X, p. 439).
51. Sainte-Beuve, *Causeries du Lundi*, X, pp. 423–4.
52. The depiction of Mme Firmiani may require the talents of an Ingres, but Balzac insists 'il y avait tout dans cette femme' before going on to compare her with Jeanne d'Arc, Agnès Sorel, and Eve, as well as with Byron's Doña Julia and Haidée.
53. *Pl.*, VII, p. 58.
54. *Pl.*, II, p. 328.
55. Ibid., p. 300.
56. Compare Du Bos, *Journal 1924–25*, p. 281.
57. Du Bos, *Journal VI – Janvier 1930–Juillet 1931* (La Colombe, 1955), p. 173.
58. Edmond About, *Voyage à travers l'Exposition des Beaux-Arts* (Hachette, 1855), p. 126.
59. Silvestre, pp. 27, 32.
60. Edmond and Jules de Goncourt, *La Peinture à l'Exposition de 1855* (Dentu, 1855), p. 33.
61. Sainte-Beuve, *Œuvres*, I, p. 756 (portrait of Racine).
62. Gautier, *Les Beaux-Arts en Europe 1855*, p. 165.
63. Jacques Rivière, *Etudes* (Gallimard, 1924), p. 36 (essay dated 1911).
64. Charles Du Bos, *Approximations* (Plon, 1922), p. 162. On Flaubert and Ingres, see Alison Fairlie, 'Flaubert and some painters of his time', in Fairlie, *Imagination and Language* (Cambridge: Cambridge University Press, 1981), pp. 355–78 (p. 361).
65. In addition to the documentation contained in vol. II of *Pl.*, see Patrick Berthier's edition of the novel, Collection Folio (Gallimard, 1980); P. Berthier, 'Balzac lecteur de Gautier', *L'Année balzacienne 1971*, pp. 282–5; and Edmond Brua, 'Gautier aide de Balzac', *L'Année balzacienne 1972*, pp. 381–4.
66. Gautier, *Les Jeunes-France* (Charpentier, 1885), p. 31.
67. See Marc Thivolet, 'Caricature' in the Encylopaedia Universalis.
68. *Critique d'art*, p. 216 (*Quelques caricaturistes français*).
69. About, p. 126.

70.   Gautier in *La France industrielle*, April 1834 (quoted by Snell, p. 99; cf. ibid., p. 229, for the original French text).
71.   On Girodet and Lavater, see George Levitine, 'The Influence of Lavater and Girodet's *Expression des sentiments de l'âme*', *The Art Bulletin*, XXXVI (1954), pp. 33–44.


*Chapter 8:   The model's unwashed feet: French photography in the 1850s*

1.   Peter Galassi, *Before Photography: Painting and the Invention of Photography* (New York: Museum of Modern Art, 1981), p. 12. A striking alternative account, rejecting any hint of technological determinism, has been made by Jonathan Crary, *Techniques of the Observer: On Vision and Modernity in the Nineteenth Century*, an 'October' Book (Cambridge, MA, and London: MIT Press, 1990).
2.   *From Today painting is dead: The Beginning of Photography* (London: Arts Council of Great Britain, 1972), p. 5. Josef Maria Eder's *Geschichte der Photographie* (1905), frequently reprinted in translation, tells the story from a technological point of view.
3.   These developments are very suggestively argued in Crary, *Techniques of the Observer*.
4.   Helmut and Alison Gernsheim, *The History of Photography from the Camera Obscura to the Beginning of the Modern Era* (London: Thames and Hudson, 1969); and the early documents reproduced in André Rouillé, *La Photographie en France: Textes et Controverses: une Anthologie 1816–1871* (Paris: Macula, 1989), and in *Classic Essays on Photography* ed. Alan Trachtenberg, with notes by Amy Weinstein Meyers (New Haven, CT: Leete's Island Books, 1980), pp. 5–26.
5.   Helmut and Alison Gernsheim, *L.J.M. Daguerre: The History of the Diorama and the Daguerreotype* (London: Secker and Warburg, 1956), which has a useful bibliography.
6.   'Le Daguerréotype ne comporte pas une seule manipulation qui ne soit à la portée de tout le monde. Il ne suppose aucune connaissance du dessin, il n'exige aucune dextérité manuelle. En se conformant, de point en point, à certaines prescriptions très simples et très nombreuses, il n'est personne qui ne doive réussir certainement et aussi bien peu que M. Daguerre lui-même' (Rouillé, p. 40).
7.   Gail Buckland, *Fox Talbot and the Invention of Photography* (Boston: David R. Godine, 1980).
8.   Janet E. Buerger, *French Daguerreotypes*, with a Foreword by Walter Clark (Chicago and London: University of Chicago Press, 1989), p. 6; see also Stefan Richter, *The Art of the Daguerreotype*, with an Introduction by Helmut Gernsheim (New York: Viking Press, 1989).
9.   Ruskin quoted in Aaron Scharf, *Art and Photography* (London: Allen Lane, The Penguin Press, 1968), pp. 69–70; Morse quoted in Van Deren Coke, *The Painter and the Photograph from Delacroix to Warhol* (Albuquerque: University of New Mexico Press, 1964; rev. ed. 1972), p. 7.
10.   Poe, 'The Daguerreotype', *Alexander's Weekly Messenger*, 15 Jan. 1840, quoted in Trachtenberg, ed., *Classic Essays on Photography*, pp. 37–8.
11.   Buerger, *French Daguerreotypes*, p. 3.
12.   Anne McCauley, 'Of Entrepreneurs, Opportunists, and Fallen Women: Commercial Photography in Paris, 1848–1870', in *Perspectives on Photography: Essays*

*in Honor of Beaumont Newhall*, ed. Peter Walch and Thomas F. Barrow (Albuquerque: University of New Mexico Press, 1986), pp. 67–97.

13. François Loyer, *Paris Nineteenth Century: Architecture and Urbanism*, trans. Charles Lynn Clark (New York: Abbeville Press, n.d.), ch. 4.

14. Eugenia Parry Janis, 'Demolition Picturesque: Photographs of Paris in 1852 and 1853 by Henri Le Secq', in *Perspectives on Photography*, pp. 33–66.

15. Delécluze quoted in Scharf, *Art and Photography*, pp. 96–7; pictures at Courbet's exhibition in Jack Lindsay, *Gustave Courbet: His Life and Art*, 2nd imp. (London: Jupiter, 1977), p. 138.

16. Eugenia Parry Janis, *The Photography of Gustave le Gray* (Chicago: Art Institute of Chicago and University of Chicago Press, 1987), ch. 5

17. Reproduced in Parry Janis, *Le Gray*, p. 30.

18. Reproduced in André Rouillé, *La Photographie en France*, p. 105.

19. Exhibited at the Metropolitan Museum of Art in the winter of 1980–1; reproduced in *After Daguerre: Masterworks of French Photography from the Bibliothèque Nationale* (New York: Metropolitan Museum of Art, in association with Berger-Levrault, Paris, 1980), plate 17. Was the bruise a chemical trace of Berthier's processing? It would have appeared to be a bruise to contemporaries. Weston J. Naef, in the accompanying essay in *After Daguerre*, attributes such 'overlooked details' as bruises, birthmarks and dirty soles to the inexperience of photographers working with the nude (p. 37).

20. Reproduced in André Rouillé, *La Photographie en France*, p. 420.

21. It is reproduced in Nigel Gosling, *Nadar* (London: Secker and Warburg, 1976), p. 69. See also Jerrold Seigel, *Bohemian Paris: Culture, Politics, and the Boundaries of Bourgeois Life, 1830–1930* (New York: Viking Penguin, 1986), Ch. 2.

22. Parry Janis, *Le Gray*, p. 33.

23. Quoted in Scharf, *Art and Photography* pp. 89–90.

24. The rights of mirrors: Fernand Desnoyers, 'Du Réalisme', *L'Artiste*, Dec. 1855, pp. 197–200; quoted in *Documents of Modern Literary Realism*, ed. George J. Becker (Princeton: Princeton University Press, 1963), pp. 80–8; on Louis Napoleon, see Scharf, *Art and Photography*, p. 101.

25. Aguado reproduced in *A History of Photography: Social and Cultural Perspectives*, ed. Jean-Claude Lemagny and André Rouillé, trans. Janet Lloyd (Cambridge: Cambridge University Press, 1987), p. 40; Pierson in Helmut Gernsheim, *The History of Photography*, vol. II, *The Rise of Photography 1850–1880: The Age of Collodion* (London: Thames and Hudson, 1988), p. 219.

26. Baudelaire, 'The Exposition Universelle, 1855', in *Art in Paris 1845–1862: Salons and Other Exhibitions*, trans. and ed. Jonathan Mayne (London: Phaidon Press, 1965), p. 129.

27. Twelve portraits of Dallemagne, about 1866, reproduced in *After Daguerre*, entry 48.

28. Such as Paul Pretsch's 'Don Quichotte dans son cabinet', 1857.

29. Roger Cardinal, 'Nadar and the Photographic Portrait in Nineteenth-Century France' in *The Portrait in Photography*, ed. Graham Clarke (London: Reaktion Books, 1992), pp. 6–24.


## Chapter 9: Manet's textual frames

1. Baudelaire, *Œuvres complètes*, ed. Y.-G. Le Dantec and Claude Pichois (Paris: Gallimard, Pléiade, 1961), p. 1571. The quatrain was included on the third state of the etching exhibited in the print section of the Salon des Refusés; see *Manet, 1832–*

*1883*, ed. Françoise Cachin and Charles S. Moffett (New York: Metropolitan Museum of Art, 1983), pp. 152–4.
2.   See David Alston, 'What's in a Name? "Olympia" and a Minor Parnassian', *Gazette des Beaux-Arts*, XCI (1978), pp. 148–54.
3.   Emile Zola, *Ecrits sur l'art*, ed. Jean-Pierre Leduc-Adine (Paris: Gallimard, 1991), p. 157.
4.   Theodore Reff, 'Degas and the Literature of his Time', in *French Nineteenth-Century Painting and Literature*, ed. Ulrich Finke (Manchester: Manchester University Press, 1972), p. 203.
5.   See Wendy Steiner, 'Intertextuality in Painting', *Representations*, III, no. 4 (1985), pp. 57–67: 'no art is as dependent on subtexts from another art to complete its own meaning as is painting' (p. 62).
6.   Zola, *Ecrits*, p. 152.
7.   See Michael Moriarty's essay in this volume (pp. 15–29).
8.   See Dario Gamboni, *La Plume et le pinceau: Odilon Redon et la littérature* (Paris: Editions de Minuit, 1989).
9.   Cited by Reff, pp. 197–8 and n. 71
10.   *Manet: Three Studies in Artistic Conception* (Lund: Gleerup, 1954), p. 55.
11.   See George Mauner, *Manet, 'Peintre-Philosophe': A Study of the Painter's Themes* (Pennsylvania State University Press, 1975).
12.   In *Pièces sur l'art* (1934), cited by Lois Boe Hyslop and Francis E. Hyslop, 'Baudelaire and Manet: A Re-appraisal', in *Baudelaire as a Love Poet and Other Essays* (Pennsylvania State University Press, 1969), pp. 87–130 (p. 88); this useful synoptic account has been updated in Lois Boe Hyslop, *Baudelaire: Man of his Time* (New Haven and London: Yale University Press, 1980), pp. 47–61.
13.   Cited by A. Tabarant, *La Vie artistique au temps de Baudelaire* (Paris: Mercure de France, 1942), p. 68.
14.   See Anne Coffin Hanson, *Manet and the Modern Tradition* (New Haven and London: Yale University Press, 1977), pp. 54–5.
15.   *The Painting of Modern Life: Paris in the Art of Manet and his Followers* (Princeton: Princeton University Press, 1984), pp. 139–44.
16.   *Manet: 'Olympia'* (London, 1976), p. 89.
17.   See Christopher Prendergast, *Paris and the Nineteenth Century* (Oxford: Blackwell, 1992), p. 181.
18.   *Manet, 1832–1883*, p. 180 (my italics); in the same mode, see Hyslop (1980): 'in his discussions with Manet, [Baudelaire] must have expressed his ideas about the nude figure'; 'Manet must have been encouraged by Baudelaire to turn to scenes of contemporary life' (p. 53).
19.   Clark, *The Painting of Modern Life*, p. 85.
20.   'The Impressionists and Edouard Manet', in *Documents Stéphane Mallarmé*, ed. C.P. Barbier (Paris: Nizet, 1968), I, pp. 66–86 (p. 71).
21.   *Manet, 1832–1883*, p. 180.
22.   *Manet, 'Olympia'*, p. 91.
23.   *Manet and the Nude: A Study of Iconography in the Second Empire* (New York, 1981), p. 169 (my italics).
24.   As Clark notes, 'the link between *Olympia* and Baudelaire was rather rarely made in 1865' (*The Painting of Modern Life*, p. 296, n. 145).
25.   These connotations were also evident in Manet's lithograph for Champfleury's *Les Chats*, in 1868; see Reff, *Manet: 'Olympia'*, p. 100.
26.   Reff, 'Degas and the Literature of his Time', p. 185 and n. (p. 225).
27.   The richest analysis of the painting remains Sandblad's (*Manet: Three Studies in Artistic Conception*, pp. 17–68).
28.   See, for example, Kathleen Adler on *L'Evasion de Rochefort* (1881): 'the six

men . . . are Baudelairean modern heroes in dark suits and hats even in these extra-ordinary circumstances, revealing another facet of "the epic side of modern life"'; in *Manet* (Oxford: Phaidon, 1986), p. 129.

29.   *Art Journal*, 38, no. 2 (winter 1978), pp. 107–13; in the same tenuous vein, see Larry Ligo, 'Manet's Frontispiece Etchings: his Symbolic Self-Portrait Acknowledges the Influence of Baudelaire and Photography upon his Work', *Gazette des Beaux-Arts*, 108 (1986), pp. 66–74.

30.   Reff claims that the etching *Cat and Flowers* (1869) 'may in fact have been conceived as a homage to the recently deceased poet; (*Manet: 'Olympia'*, p. 102).

31.   See Claude Pichois and François Ruchon, *Iconographie de Charles Baudelaire* (Geneva: Cailler, 1960), item 123.

32.   See *Manet, 1832–1883*, pp 156–60; Sandblad, pp. 18–19; Jean Adhémar, 'Le Portrait de Baudelaire gravé par Manet', *Revue des arts*, II (1952), pp. 240–4; and *Album Baudelaire*, ed. Claude Pichois (Paris: Gallimard, 1974), p. 236.

33.   See Joël Dalançon, 'Le Poète et le peintre (1870–1885): les enjeux sociaux et culturels d'un face à face', *Romantisme*, 66 (1989), pp. 61-73.

34.   For the fullest discussion, see Hollis Clayson, *Painted Love: Prostitution in French Art of the Impressionist Era* (New Haven and London: Yale University Press, 1991), pp. 67–75.

35.   See Janice Best, 'Portraits d'une "vraie fille"': *Nana*, tableau, roman et mise-en-scène', *Les Cahiers naturalistes*, 66 (1992), pp. 157–66.

36.   See Theodore Reff, 'Manet's Portrait of Zola', *Burlington Magazine*, 117 (1975), pp. 35–44.

37.   Originally published in the *Revue du XIXe siècle* on 1 Jan. 1867; subsequent references are taken from the text reprinted in Zola's *Ecrits sur l'art*, pp. 137–69.

38.   Mauner, *Manet: 'Peintre-Philosophe'*, p. 149.

39.   See my 'L'Accueil critique à l'œuvre de Zola avant *L'Assommoir*', *Les Cahiers naturalistes*, 54 (1980), pp. 214–23.

40.   *Correspondance*, 8 vols., ed. B.H. Bakker et al. (Montréal: Presses de l'Université de Montréal, 1978–), I, pp. 496–7.

41.   Henri Mitterand, 'Le musée dans le texte', *Les Cahiers naturalistes*, 66 (1992), p. 15.

42.   See the special issue of *La Revue de l'Art*, vol. XXVI (1974), devoted to pictorial signatures, which include Jean-Claude Lebensztejn, 'Esquisse d'une typologie', pp. 46–56; and Claude Gandelman, 'The Semiotics of Signatures in Painting: a Peircian Analysis', *American Journal of Aesthetics*, III, no. 3 (1985), pp. 73–108.

43.   The self-consciousness of this technique is attested to by Manet's use of his signature for perspectival purposes in his portrait of Duret (1868) and in *Le Fifre* (1866), as well as the more literal indexing of his own name by Mallarmé's hand in the 1874 image of the poet.

44.   See my 'Zola, Manet and *Thérèse Raquin*', *French Studies*, XXXIV (1980), p. 283.

45.   'Manet's Portrait of Zola', p. 41.

46.   See two important articles by Nicole Savy: '*Aut pictura, poesis*: Baudelaire, Manet, Zola', *Romantisme*, 66 (1989), pp. 41–50; and 'Un étranger vu par Manet: Emile Zola', *Les Cahiers naturalistes*, 66 (1992), pp. 23–32.

47.   See Adler, *Manet*, p. 100; and Alan Krell, 'Manet, Zola and the "Motifs d'une exposition particulière" 1867', *Gazette des Beaux-Arts*, 99 (1982), pp. 109–15.

48.   See *Manet, 1832–1883*, p. 282.

49.   See S.L. Faison, 'Manet's Portrait of Zola', *Magazine of Art*, 42 (1949), pp. 163–8.

50.   An ambition sustained in his dedication of *Madeleine Férat* to Manet in 1868.

51.   In 'Pauvre Belgique', *Œuvres complètes*, p. 1429.

*Chapter 10: Newspaper and myth: migrations of the Romantic image*

1. A. Corréard et H. Savigny, *Naufrage de la frégate 'La Méduse'*, 5e édition (Paris, 1821).
2. *Dante et Virgile aux Enfers* was exhibited in the 1822 Salon; it was hung in the Luxembourg until 1874; since when it has been in the Louvre. See C. Baudelaire, *Salon de 1846*, ed. D. Kelley (Oxford: Oxford University Press, 1975), p. 196.
3. See R. Michel, *Géricault, l'invention du réel* (Paris: Découvertes Gallimard/ Réunion des Musées Nationaux, 1992).
4. See E. Delacroix, *The Journal of Eugène Delacroix: A Selection*, ed. H. Wellington, trans. L. Norton (Oxford: Phaidon, 1980), p. 27.
5. Lord Byron, *Don Juan* (Harmondsworth: Penguin Classics, 1986), p. 108–29 (Canto II, stanzas 27–111).
6. Dante, *The Vision of Dante Alighieri*, trans. H.F. Carey (London: J.M. Dent/ Everyman, 1908).
7. Lord Byron, *Byron: A Self-portrait in His Own Words*, ed. P. Quennell (Oxford: Oxford University Press, 1990), p. 661.
8. *Don Juan*, pp. 596, 600 (notes to Canto II, stanzas 71 and 137).
9. *Salon de 1846*, in C. Baudelaire, *Œuvres complètes*, ed. Claude Pichois, 2 vols (Paris: Gallimard, Pléiade, 1975–6).
10. *Œuvres complètes*, vol. I, pp. 867–8, vol. II, pp. 300, 440
11. *Œuvres complètes*, vol. I, pp. 854–5; vol. II, pp. 427, 595.
12. Ibid., vol. II, pp. 427–8.
13. Ibid., p. 440.
14. M. Shapiro, *Women, Earthly and Divine in the 'Comedy' of Dante* (Lexington: University Press of Kentucky, 1975), captures Dante's ambiguity neatly: 'Relieved of her sexuality, a woman may elevate man as well as herself and become the bearer of his salvation. . . . Subject to the contingencies of her physical being she becomes the figure of malicious temptation' (p. 68).
15. This line – 'Elle a dans le plaisir la foi mahométane' – embarrasses the editors of the Pléiade edition. They say 'L'expression ne va pas de soi, même si on considère qu'elle est appelée par la *sultane* du vers précédent. Nous comprenons: une foi aveugle, entière, une soumission parfaite' (I, 1066). I disagree.
16. I agree here with P. Armour, 'Purgatorio XXVIII', in D. Nolan (ed.), *Dante Commentaries: Eight Studies of the Divine Comedy* (Dublin: Irish Academic Press, 1977), pp. 115–41, who argues that oblivion for Dante in Lethe is oblivion from *infidelity*.
17. For an interesting commentary on Baudelaire's use of Dante's Ulysses, see L. Pertile, 'Baudelaire, Dante e il mito di Ulisse', in *Rivista di Letteratura moderne e comparate*, XXXVI, 2 (Pisa: Pacini, 1983), pp. 109–22. For a more comprehensive treatment of the whole question of Baudelaire's knowledge and use of Dante, see P. Collier, 'Baudelaire and Dante', *Studi Francesi*, n. 102, anno XXXIV, fascicolo III, pp. 417–35.

*Chapter 11: Transpositions*

1. This chapter does not attempt to deal with the 'transposition d'art' in an exhaustive way, but simply to propose, using a limited number of examples from Baudelaire and Gautier, some of the possibilities it offers the poet.
2. Baudelaire, *Salon de 1846*, in *Œuvres complètes*, ed. Claude Pichois, 2 vols

(Paris: Gallimard, Pléiade, 1975–6), vol. II, p. 418. Subsequent page references to Baudelaire will be to this edition (abbreviated *OC*).
3.   Published in *La Presse*.
4.   References to Gautier poems are to: Théophile Gautier, *Poésies complètes*, ed. René Jasinski (Paris: Nizet, 1970); abbreviated *PC*.
5.   Many of my remarks on Gautier owe much to Joan Driscoll's unpublished Cambridge Ph.D. thesis, 'The Role of the "Transposition d'art" in the Poetry of Theophile Gautier', 1971.
6.   See in particular the article on Delacroix by Désiré Laverdant in *La Phalange* of 1845, and my article 'L'Art, harmonie du beau et de l'utile', *Romantisme*, vol. 5 (1973), pp. 18–36.
7.   Claude Pichois notes (*Œuvres complètes*, I, 1023) that Baudelaire may well have come across this engraving while looking for ideas for *Les Fleurs du mal*. It probably comes from Vesale's *De corporis humani fabrica libri septem* (Basel, 1543) and was engraved after a drawing by Titian. See J. Prévost, *Baudelaire, essai sur la création et l'inspiration poétiques* (Paris: Mercure de France, 1964), p. 166. Prévost's chapter on Baudelaire and art is a piece of pioneering work in the study of Baudelaire and the visual arts.
8.   See Luzius Keller, *Piranèse et les romantiques français* (Paris: Corti, 1966), p. 200. Piranesi (1720–78) provided, through his engravings of fantastic architecture, an almost obsessive source of imagery for the major Romantics.
9.   Théophile Gautier, *Emaux et camées* (Paris: Minard, 1968), p. 45.
10.   One of the versions of this painting, shown at the Salon of 1843, had been enormously successful.
11.   *Emaux et camées*, p. 99.
12.   The relevant prose texts are in *Salon de 1859* (*OC*, II, 678–80). Baudelaire quotes his own poem 'Danse macabre'.

## Chapter 12:   *Stendhal's art history and the making of a novelist*

1.   *Histoire de la peinture en Italie*, vols. I and II, edited with an introduction by Paul Arbelet, *Œuvres complètes*, ed. Victor Del Litto and Ernest Abravanel, Cercle du Bibliophile (Paris, 1969), tomes 26–7. *Salon de 1824* and *Salon de 1827* in *Mélanges III. Journalisme*, ed. Ernest Abravanel, *Œuvres complètes*, tome 47. This also contains the *Idées italiennes sur quelques tableaux célèbres* written jointly with the Genevan painter Abraham Constantin under whose name it was published in 1840. All references will be to these editions. David Wakefield's selection of Stendhal's writings on the arts, *Stendhal and the Arts* (London, 1973), contains translations from all these texts, and where possible I shall be referring to this translation in the English version of my longer quotations.
2.   'Projet d'un article sur *Le Rouge et le Noir*', in *Le Rouge et le Noir*, ed. P.-G. Castex, Classiques Garnier (Paris, 1973), p. 715.
3.   *La Chartreuse de Parme*, ed. A. Adam, Classiques Garnier (Paris, 1973), variant from the Lingay version, p. 593.
4.   'Walter Scott et la Princesse de Clèves', in *Mélanges II. Journalisme*, ed. Victor Del Litto, *Œuvres complètes*, tome 46 (Paris, 1972), pp. 221–4 (p. 221).
5.   'Annotations de Stendhal', *La Chartreuse*, p. 577.
6.   Balzac, *Le Père Goriot*, in *Œuvres complètes*, ed. Marcel Bouteron (Paris: Gallimard, Pléiade, 1935), tome II, pp. 851–2.
7.   As Peter Brooks has so clearly demonstrated in *The Melodramatic Imagination* (Yale, 1976).

8.   *Vie de Henry Brulard*, in *Œuvres intimes*, ed. Victor Del Litto (Paris: Gallimard, Pléiade, 1982), vol. II, p. 542. Unless otherwise indicated, all translations are my own.
9.   As Paul Arbelet says, 'Le génie du peintre ne sera jamais pour Stendhal qu'un moyen de s'exalter lui-même' ('Préface' to *Histoire de la peinture en Italie*, pp. i–ii).
10.   Carol Mossman, 'Iconographie brulardienne: les figures d'une écriture', *Stendhal Club*, 112 (1986), pp. 339–53.
11.   For an extensive discussion of the diagrams and memory, see Michael Sheringham's thought-provoking 'Visual autobiography: diagrams in Stendhal's *Vie de Henry Brulard*' in *Paragraph*, vol. 11, no. 3 (1988), pp. 249–73.
12.   For further details about the origins of Stendhal's *Histoire* and about his debt to Lanzi, see Arbelet's 'Préface' and his *L'*Histoire de la peinture en Italie*' et les plagiats de Stendhal* (Paris, 1914). My own account is indebted to Arbelet.
13.   See Diderot's *Essais sur la peinture* of 1766, the article *Génie* and the 'Recherches philosophiques sur l'origine et la nature du beau', all in the *Œuvres esthétiques*, and Rousseau's *Essai sur l'origine des langues* and the *Dictionnaire de musique*. In this connection see also Dubos's *Réflexions critiques sur la poésie et sur la peinture* (Paris, 1719).
14.   See Arbelet's note on the subject, *L'*Histoire*'*, vol. I, p. 320. The fictional persona Stendhal invents for the *Salon de 1824* is an even more elaborately invented figure: a German with the somewhat preposterous name of M. van Eube de Molkirk.
15.   See Philippe Berthier, *Stendhal et ses peintres italiens* (Geneva, 1977) for this view.
16.   *Racine et Shakespeare*, ed. Roger Fayolle (Paris: Garnier-Flammarion, 1970), p. 71.
17.   For discussion of ideas about the link between freedom and art in the late eighteenth century and the early nineteenth century, see A.D. Potts, 'Political attitudes and the rise of historicism in art history', *Art History*, vol. I, no. 2 (1978), pp. 191–213. I am grateful to Iain Pears for drawing this article to my attention, and also for his expert comment on a number of the issues I have discussed here.
18.   See Norman Bryson's discussion of the assumptions behind this view in *Tradition and Desire: From David to Delacroix* (Cambridge, 1984). Stendhal relies heavily on Vasari, whom Bryson cites as a characteristic instance of the received view of tradition.
19.   See the *Salon de 1824* for this.
20.   Hippolyte Taine, *Histoire de la littérature anglaise*, 8th ed. (Paris, 1892), pp. xliii–xliv.
21.   For a discussion of nineteenth-century views of the paintings of the past in the context of a history of taste, see Francis Haskell, *Rediscoveries in Art: Some Aspects of Taste, Fashion and Collecting in England and France* (London, 1976). Again, I am indebted to Iain Pears for drawing this to my attention.
22.   In *Mélanges II. Journalisme*, pp. 265–78 (p. 267).
23.   He implicitly ascribes a small amount of this genius to himself through the fact that he is able to read de Brosses at all, since he wonders whether the letters will find readers in the modern world which is itself so different from the one in which de Brosses wrote: 'La gravité empesée et hargneuse de 1836 pardonnera-t-elle à la gaieté de la bonne compagnie de 1739?' (p. 270).
24.   Balzac, *Short Stories*, ed. A. W. Raitt (Oxford, 1964), p. 68. My italics.
25.   See 'The uses of reading', in my *Reading Realism in Stendhal* (Cambridge, 1988), for a fuller discussion.
26.   'Avant-propos' to the *Comédie humaine*, tome I, p. 7.

*Chapter 13:   Victor Hugo, somnambulist of the sea*

1.   'William Shakespeare', in Victor Hugo, *Œuvres complètes*, edition directed by Jean Massin (Paris: Club français du livre, 1967–70), vol. XII/1, p. 159. Subsequent references to this edition appear as *OC*, with volume and page numbers.

2.   The phrase is Pierre Albouy's: see his *La Création mythologique chez Victor Hugo* (Paris: Corti, 1985), p. 318.

3.   Letter to Paul Meurice of August 1852, quoted in Jean-Bertrand Barrère, *La Fantaisie de Victor Hugo. Tome 2. 1852–1885* (Paris: Editions Klincksieck, 1972), p. 17.

4.   Transcriptions of the *Tables parlantes* texts, rapped out in code by the table, are to be found in *OC*, IX/2, 1166–1490. A resourceful and witty analysis of Hugo's mediumism is to be found in Charles Duits's *Victor Hugo: Le grand échevelé de l'air* (Paris: Pierre Belfond, 1975).

5.   This version, quoted in Barrère, p. 151, was adapted by Hugo from an original letter to Franz Stevens (in *OC*, X/2, 1235).

6.   In her unpublished MA thesis 'Romantic Ecstasy: A Comparative Study of Hugo and Keats' (University of Kent, Canterbury, 1986), Maria Zarpetea insists on the affinity between Hugo's conception of the poet-magus and Mircea Eliade's model of the *shaman*, the ecstatic intermediary between the everyday and the supernatural realm.

7.   The coinage is Max-Pol Fouchet's: see his *Victor Hugo: L'Imagier de l'ombre* (Arles: Actes Sud, 1985).

8.   I borrow the term from Mary Ann Caws, whose *The Art of Interference: Stressed Readings in Verbal and Visual Texts* (Cambridge: Polity Press, 1989) scans many varied instances of word/image clashes and fusions.

9.   For example Victor Brombert, in *Victor Hugo and the Visionary Novel* (Cambridge Mass.: Harvard University Press, 1984), p. 149.

10.   For a discussion of all these editions, see Pierre Georgel's *Les Dessins de Victor Hugo pour les Travailleurs de la mer* (Paris: Herscher, 1985).

11.   I regret that I lack space to discuss the octopus as icon and as focal myth – the 'devil-fish' associated with the ocean, the monstrous, the evil, the inhuman, the unknowable, the unconscious, and so forth. Of some relevance to my present theme is the fact that Hugo's manuscript drawing involves a visual pun insofar as the octopus's tentacles trace the shapes of Hugo's initials: octopus = V.H. = tentacular genius . . . ? One might add that if sepia is an octapod secretion, the lurid depiction of an octopus in sepia pigment offers a strong metonymic prompt to the associative mind: octopus as inky configuration or calligram, draughtsman's or writer's inkwell as dark cavern heaving with metamorphic energy . . . .

12.   *Le Bateau-vision* was executed in 1865 or early 1866, in black and sepia inks with wash on cream-coloured drawing paper. It measures 193 × 255 mm, an average format for Hugo, who never ventured into large-scale graphics, and indeed never painted on canvases. Along with the rest of the manuscript illustrations, it was removed from its binding for restoration purposes, and, once framed for display in 1985, now enjoys the status of an independent artwork. Full technical details are given in Pierre Georgel, *Les Dessins de Victor Hugo* . . .. The expanding bibliography of Hugo's pictorial output need not be given here, beyond mention of the nigh-exhaustive gathering of monochrome reproductions in the Massin *Œuvres complètes* (vols XVII/1 and 2; and XVIII/1 and 2); of *Victor Hugo dessinateur* (Editions du Minotaure, 1963), with its fine preface by Gaëtan Picon; and the selective albums of Jean-François Bory (1980), Jacqueline Lafargue (1983) and Pierre Seghers (1983).

13.　See illustrations in *OC*, XVIII/2, figs 712 and 755. A fine colour reproduction of the first drawing is in Pierre Georgel, plate 11.

14.　See reproduction in *OC*, XVIII/2, fig. 738. Though Hugo declined to insert it in the manuscript, the Méaulles and Hugues editions originated the tradition of appending it to the *Travailleurs* set.

15.　The phrase comes from Hugo's working notes for *William Shakespeare* (OC, XII/1, 337). Victor Brombert discusses Hugo's oceanic reveries in terms of a conception of the natural world as a divine palimpsest or poem (*Victor Hugo and the Visionary Novel*, pp. 166–7); while Alfred Glauser similarly envisions the oceanic *gouffre* as an immense ink-blot, an 'espace scriptural' whose aquatic formations spawn infinite meanings (see his *La Poétique de Hugo* [Paris: Nizet, 1978], pp. 35–8). Such discussion could be productively applied to the drawings.

16.　Jean-Pierre Reynaud examines Hugo's struggle to surpass orthodox representation by experimenting in 'l'évanouissement des images' through the extinguishing of contours. See his 'Le Contour et l'infini', in *Victor Hugo et les images*, ed. Madeleine Blondel and Pierre Georgel (Dijon: Ville de Dijon, 1989), pp. 212–22.

*Chapter 14:　Avatars of the artist: narrative approaches to the work of the painter*

1.　On this point, see Robert Rosenblum, *Jean-Auguste-Dominique Ingres*, rev. ed. (London: Thames and Hudson, 1990), p. 82.

2.　On Zeuxis and the myth of the essential copy, see Stephen Bann, *The True Vine: On Visual Representation and the Western Tradition* (Cambridge: Cambridge University Press, 1989), p. 27.

3.　*Transformations in Late Eighteenth-Century Art* (Princeton: Princeton University Press, 1967), pp. 22–3. Rosenblum reproduces Vincent's painting (see his fig. 19).

4.　Giorgio Vasari, *The Lives of the Artists*, trans. George Bull (Harmondsworth: Penguin, 1965), p. 31.

5.　On the commonplace value of the story of Zeuxis and the Crotonian women in the articulation of the Renaissance concept of the *beau idéal*, and on the debates it launches on the place of nature in painting, see Erwin Panofsky, *Idea: A Concept in Art Theory*, trans. Joseph J.S. Peake (New York: Harper and Row, 1968), pp. 57–9, 65–6, and 109–10.

6.　On the role of a figure such as Quatremère de Quincy in perpetuating academic values, see Albert Boime, *The Academy and French Painting in the Nineteenth Century* (London: Phaidon, 1971), pp. 6–8 and 178–9.

7.　See *L'Education sentimentale*, ed. P.M. Wetherill (Paris: Garnier, 1984), pp. 36–7.

8.　*La Comédie humaine*, ed. Pierre-Georges Castex, 12 vols (Paris: Gallimard, 1976–81), vol. I, p. 43. All further references, giving volume and page number, are to this edition.

9.　On the displacement of pictures of Raphael with a serious social and didactic purpose by often frivolous images of romance, see Francis Haskell, *Past and Present in Art and Taste: Selected Essays* (New Haven and London: Yale University Press, 1987), pp. 93–7.

10.　The portrait of the Fornarina used by Ingres, now attributed in fact to Giulio Romano, is discussed and illustrated by Rosenblum, in *Jean-Auguste-Dominique*

*Ingres*, p. 82; Rosenblum points out also that the image of the painter in Ingres's painting is based on a self-portrait of Raphael.

11.   This conundrum is the object of a brilliant discussion by Georges Didi-Huberman, who presents 'la Peau' as the Other of painting and who analyses the equivocal quality of the act of painting, and of *finishing* in particular; see *La Peinture incarnée* (Paris: Minuit, 1985), pp. 13–15, 22, 26.

12.   For an account of the *Hommage à Eug. Delacroix* as an affirmation of the religion of art, see Douglas Druick and Michel Hoog, *Fantin-Latour* (Ottawa: National Gallery of Canada, 1983), p. 174. This aspect of Fantin-Latour's work is the object of a brief but sensitive discussion on the part of Pierre Georgel, in 'Les transformations de la peinture vers 1848, 1855, 1863', *Revue de l'art*, no. 27 (1975), pp. 62–77 (p. 75).

13.   *Courbet's Realism* (Chicago and London: University of Chicago Press, 1990), p. 49.

14.   This is the burden of Fried's highly perceptive and fluent analysis, in *Courbet's Realism*, pp. 155–64.

15.   On this point, see David Scott, *Pictorialist Poetics: Poetry and the Visual Arts in Nineteenth-Century France* (Cambridge, Cambridge University Press, 1988), pp. 5–19.

16.   *La Comédie humaine*, VI, 1099.

17.   *Journal: mémoires de la vie littéraire*, ed. Robert Ricatte and Robert Kopp, 2nd ed., 3 vols. (Paris: Laffont, 1989), vol. I, p. 316.

18.   *Journal*, II, p. 1.

19.   *Journal*, II, p. 165; I, p. 416.

20.   On this, and other, mythological transformations, see again Didi-Huberman, *La Peinture incarnée*, in particular pp. 66–9.

21.   This is the complaint of Henry James's H – in 'The Madonna of the Future', as he sits before his blank, yellowing canvas; see *The Complete Tales of Henry James*, III, ed. Leon Edel (London: Rupert Hart-Davis, 1962), p. 48.

22.   'Des artistes', in *Œuvres complètes*, XXXVIII, ed. Marcel Bouteron and Henri Longnon (Paris: Conard, 1956), p. 140.

23.   *La Comédie humaine*, I, p. 54, pp. 92–3.

24.   *La Comédie humaine*, X, p. 437. On the importance of this theme, see Hubert Damisch, *Fenêtre jaune cadmium; ou, les dessous de la peinture* (Paris: Seuil, 1984), p. 18.

25.   *Carnets d'enquête: une ethnographie inédite de la France*, ed. Henri Mitterand (Paris: Plon, 1986), p. 252. The finished novel repeatedly stresses the beauty of Claude's *ébauches* and the difficulties he encounters in completing his paintings; see *Les Rougon-Macquart: histoire naturelle et sociale d'une famille sous le second Empire*, IV, ed. Henri Mitterand (Paris: Gallimard, 1966), pp. 27, 33, 258–9.

26.   *Les Rougon-Macquart*, IV, p. 363.

27.   On the genesis of the novel, see Robert Ricatte, *La Création romanesque chez les Goncourt: 1851–1870* (Paris: Armand Colin, 1953), pp. 305–7.

28.   *Manette Salomon* (Paris: UGE, 1979), pp. 307–8. The significance for the figure of the writer of the notion of the *rencontre* is the object of an illuminating essay by Anne-Marie Christin, 'Matière et idéal dans *Manette Salomon*', *Revue d'histoire littéraire de la France*, 80 (1980), pp. 921–48.

29.   This point is implicit in Alain Buisine's engaging analysis of the structuring role of colour in the novel, in 'L'impossible couleur: l'impressionnisme et la critique d'art', *Word & Image*, 4 (1988), pp. 131–8.

30.   *La Peinture à l'Exposition de 1855* (Paris: Dentu, 1855), p. 6.

31.   See ibid., pp. 41–5.

32.   *Journal*, II, pp. 775, 109.

33.   On this point, see Jean-Louis Cabanès, 'Les Goncourt et la morbidité, catégorie esthétique de *L'Art au XVIIIe siècle*', *Romantisme*, no. 71 (1991), pp. 85–92.
34.   *Manette Salomon*, pp. 322–3.


*Chapter 15:   The writing on the wall: descriptions of painting in the art criticism of the French Symbolists*

1.   See in my bibliography the books by Florence, Gamboni, Halperin, Kearns, Scott; see too articles by Abastado, Forestier, Németh, Ashton and the editor in *The Symbolist Movement in the Literature of the European Languages*, ed. A. Balakian (Budapest: Kultura Hungary, 1982).
2.   See in my bibliography *The New Painting: Impressionism 1874–1886*.
3.   Mallarmé, *Œuvres complètes*, ed. H. Mondor and G. Jean-Aubry (Paris: Gallimard, Pléiade, 1945), p. 368.
4.   In a two-part article published in 1890; see 'Définition du néo-traditionnisme', in *Théories 1890–1910. Du symbolisme et de Gauguin vers un nouvel ordre classique* (Paris: Floury, 1912), pp. 1–13 (p. 1). On Symbolist painting, see R. Goldwater, *Symbolism* (New York: Harper and Row, 1979); W. Jaworska, *Gauguin et l'école de Pont-Aven* (Neuchâtel: Ides et Calendes, 1971). On the Nabis, see *The Nabis and the Parisian Avant-Garde*, ed. P.E. Boyer (New Brunswick and London: Rutgers University Press, 1988).
5.   See D.H.T. Scott, 'Towards the Materiality of the Sign: Aesthetics and Poetics in Nineteenth-century France', in *French Literature, Thought and Culture in the Nineteenth Century: A Material World*, ed. B. Rigby (London: Macmillan, 1993), pp. 128–47.
6.   In 1892 M. Denis considered the crucial distinction in contemporary art to be that between what he called the mystical, allegorical tendency, defined as the search for expression via the subject, and the symbolist tendency, defined as the search for expression by form. He was quoting Gauguin's definition of his own Symbolist work as the plastic equivalent of the painter's feelings. See P.L. Maud (pseud. M. Denis), 'Notes d'art et d'esthétique', *La Revue blanche*, 2 (June 1892), pp. 364–5.
7.   'Un groupe de peintres', *La Revue blanche*, 5 (Nov. 1893), pp. 339–40.
8.   M. Denis, 'L'Epoque du symbolisme', *Gazette des Beaux-Arts* (March 1934), pp. 165–79 (p. 166). On Puvis, see *Puvis de Chavannes 1824–1898*, catalogue of the exhibition held in the Grand Palais, Paris, 26 Nov. 1976–14 Feb. 1977 (Paris: Editions des Musées Nationaux, 1976).
9.   On Monet's series paintings, see particularly J. House, *Monet: Nature into Art* (New Haven and London: Yale University Press, 1986); P. H. Tucker, *Monet in the 90s: The Series Paintings* (New Haven and London: Yale University Press, 1989); S.Z. Levine, *Monet and his Critics* (New York and London: Garland Publishing, 1976).
10.   Rémy de Gourmont stated that Impressionist and Symbolist painting were complementary, for the latter required a basis in nature while the former could not be satisfied with a naturalist ambition alone ('Les premiers salons', *Mercure de France*, 5 [May 1892], p. 61).
11.   For information on the Panthéon murals, see the Puvis catalogue referred to above (note 8), pp. 241–6. On the Gauguin exhibition, see the catalogue of the 1989 Gauguin exhibition held in the Grand Palais, Paris (Editions de la Réunion des Musées Nationaux, 1989), pp. 378–84.
12.   See M. Ozouf, 'Le Panthéon', in *Les Lieux de mémoire. I. La République*, ed. P. Nora (Paris: Gallimard, 1984), pp 139–66.

13.   See A.B. Price, 'L'esthétique décorative de Puvis de Chavannes', in the Puvis exhibition catalogue, pp. 21–8.

14.   The idea had gained ground primarily via the critical response to Impressionism. See Levine, *Monet and His Critics*, p. 463, for an index to the use of this term in the Monet literature.

15.   Throughout the 1880s, from his comments in 'Le Salon officiel de 1880' to those in *Certains*, published in 1889, Huysmans had consistently attacked Puvis's pale colours and flattened forms. See *L'Art moderne/Certains*, Préface by H. Juin (Paris: UGE, 10/18, pp 144–7, 286–9).

16.   See R. Marx, *Maîtres d'hier et d'aujourd'hui* (Paris: Calmann-Lévy, 1914), pp. 178–9.

17.   See the important series of articles by B. Vouilloux: 'Le tableau: description et peinture', *Poétique*, 65 (Feb. 1986), pp. 3–18; 'La description du tableau dans les *Salons* de Diderot', *Poétique*, 73 (Feb. 1988), pp. 27–50; 'La description du tableau: la peinture et l'innommable', *Littérature*, 73 (Feb. 1989), pp. 61–82; 'La description du tableau: l'échange', *Littérature*, 75 (Oct. 1989), pp. 21–41.

18.   For a discussion of the relationship between these themes and practices in Puvis's work of the 1860s and 70s, see C. Mitchell, 'Time and the Idea of Patriarchy in the Pastorals of Puvis de Chavannes', *Art History*, 10, 2 (June 1987), pp. 188–202.

19.   See Vouilloux, 'La description du tableau dans les *Salons* de Diderot', pp. 30–2.

20.   Hence the speed with which Péladan's *Salons de la Rose-Croix* were rubbished in the Symbolist reviews. In the *Revue Blanche* of June 1895, Natanson described that year's exhibition as 'lamentable' (8, p. 336). G. Comès, in 'Le *Mercure de France* dans l'évolution des arts plastiques 1890–1895', *R.H.L.F.* (1992), 1, pp. 40–55), describes Y. Rambosson's support for Péladan's Salons as the 'triomphe de l'art mystico-larviste' (51). It may be the reason he did not last long as art critic on the *Mercure* following Aurier's death.

21.   See above, note 8.

22.   In 1891, Fénéon had described Gauguin as 'the prey of writers'. See his *Œuvres plus que complètes*, ed. H. Halperin, 2 vols. (Paris and Geneva: Droz, 1970), I, p. 1752.

23.   'D'un point de vue esthétique à propos du peintre Paul Gauguin', *L'Ermitage*, 8 (Jan. 1894), pp. 35–9.

24.   *Lettres de Gauguin à sa femme et à ses amis*, ed. M. Malingue (Paris: Grasset), p. 300 (letter dated July 1901).

25.   'The Impressionists and Edouard Manet', *The Art Monthly Review* (London, 30 Sept. 1876), in *Documents Stéphane Mallarmé*, ed. C.P. Barbier, 7 vols. (Paris: Nizet, 1968–80), I (1968), pp. 66–86 (pp. 86, 84).

26.   See T. Natanson, 'Edouard Manet d'après Mallarmé', in *Peints à leur tour* (Paris: Albin Michel, 1948), pp. 94–109.

27.   For full details, see the exhibition catalogue, *Claude Monet-Auguste Rodin. Centenaire de l'exposition de 1889* held in 1889–90 in the Rodin Museum, Paris. It reproduces (47–57) in facsimile Mirbeau's preface, written in collaboration with the painter. It was, therefore, part of a deliberate strategy on Monet's part to widen his audience in response to changes taking place in the literary field. As a result of the success of Monet's exhibition, Gauguin would take the same strategic decision later the same year.

28.   On the failure of the Volpini exhibition and Gauguin's campaign to be adopted by the literary Symbolists, see Kearns, *Symbolist Landscapes*, pp. 11–14.

29.   'Le Symbolisme en peinture: Paul Gauguin', *Mercure de France*, 2 (March 1891), pp. 155–65 (p. 157).

30.   I have republished the text of this prose poem in an appendix to *Symbolist Landscapes*, pp. 169–70.

31.  See in this respect Tucker, *Monet in the 90s*, pp. 90–1.

32.  Tucker (pp. 88–9) gives examples of the sort of formal comparisons between individual paintings which their participation in a series could hardly fail to stimulate: 'What do the oranges and reds describe in the stacks in plates 23 and 24 or the reds and greens in plate 30? . . .'

33.  *La Revue indépendante*, 19 (May 1891), pp. 267–9 (p. 268).

34.  *La Revue indépendante*, 23 (April 1892), pp. 417–18.

35.  'Claude Monet', *L'Art dans les deux mondes*, 16 (7 March 1891), pp. 183–5 (p. 184).

36.  On the Puvis banquet, see Kearns, pp. 158–63; on Monet's 1895 exhibition, see Tucker, pp. 187–99 and Levine, *Monet and His Critics*, pp. 177–222.

37.  See *L'Art moderne/Certains*, pp. 308–9.

38.  For the most penetrating analysis of this relationship in the context of the theories of sensation upon which contemporary critics drew, see Richard Shiff, *Cézanne and the End of Impressionism* (Chicago and London: University of Chicago Press, 1984).

39.  J. Dupont, in 'La couleur dans (presque) tous ses états' (*Huysmans: Une esthétique de la décadence*, ed. A. Guyaux and R. Kopp [Paris: Honoré Champion, 1987] pp. 155–66), states that the correct distance was 'un topos de la critique depuis les interventions célèbres de Baudelaire et de Zola' (p. 163). In fact it was present from the outset in the founding texts of Salon writing. Diderot used it in his Salon of 1765, also to describe still life, that of Cézanne's great predecessor, Chardin. See *Œuvres esthétiques*, ed. P. Vernière (Paris: Classiques Garnier, 1965), p. 491. The Goncourts had repeated it in their study of Chardin: *L'Art du dix-huitième siècle*, ed. J.-P. Bouillon (Paris: Hermann, 1967), p. 83. Huysmans had himself used it in 1881 to describe a Cézanne landscape (*L'Art moderne/Certains*, p. 237).

40.  In 1880 Huysmans had praised a Caillebotte still-life in the same terms: 'Ici, nul repoussoir . . .' (*L'Art moderne/Certains*, p. 111), but Caillebotte's *facture* was 'simple', with none of the violence of colour or handling which interested Huysmans in Cézanne.

41.  See the article by J. Dupont referred to above (note 39) for an effective wider analysis of Huysmans's approach to colour in painting.

42.  'Paul Cézanne', *Les Hommes d'aujourd'hui*, 8, 390 (1890), pp. 1–3.

43.  See J. Wechsler, *The Interpretation of Cézanne* (Ann Arbor: UMI Research Press, 1981), pp. 14–16.

44.  For Pissarro's views on the exhibition, see *Correspondance de Camille Pissarro*, ed. J. Bailly-Herzberg, 5 vols. (Paris: Editions du Valhermeil, 1980–91), vol. 4 (letters 1169, 1171, 1175, Nov. 1895), pp. 112–22.

45.  'Paul Cézanne', *La Revue blanche*, 8 (Jan.-June 1895), pp. 496–500 (p. 500).

46.  'Choses d'art', *Mercure de France*, 17 (Jan. 1896), pp. 129–30.

47.  See Kearns, pp. 42–6, 145–7.

48.  See J. Kearns, 'No Object too Humble? Still Life Painting in French Art Criticism during the Second Empire', in *French Literature, Thought and Culture in the Nineteenth Century*, pp. 148–68.

49.  C. Mauclair, 'Psychologie de la nature morte', in *Trois crises de l'art actuel* (Paris: Charpentier, 1906), pp. 181–94 (p. 189).

50.  See Scott, 'Towards the Materiality of the Sign', pp. 136–41.

51.  1889 had seen the creation of the 'syndicat de la presse artistique française'. See J. Jurt, 'Huysmans entre le champ littéraire et le champ artistique', in *Huysmans: Une esthétique de la décadence*, pp. 115–26 (p. 126).

52.  'Berthe Morisot', in *Œuvres complètes*, pp. 533–7. I have analysed this text in 'Mallarmé and Morisot in 1896', *Australian Journal of French Studies*, XXXI, 1 (1994, forthcoming).

## Chapter 16: *Rimbaud: the shaping of a vision*

1. I have presented several of these ideas before on different occasions and in different contexts. For a general study, readers may wish to refer to my book *Rimbaud: 'Illuminations'*, Critical Guides to French Texts 29 (London: Grant and Cutler, 1983). Relevant articles I have published include 'Rimbaud's "Mystique": Some Observations', *French Studies*, XXVI (1972), pp. 285–8; 'Rimbaud's "Sonnet"', *Modern Language Review*, 75 (1980), pp. 528–33; '"H": l'énigme au-delà de l'énigme', *Revue des Sciences Humaines*, LVI, 184 (oct.–déc. 1981), pp. 129–44; 'Réflexions sur les effets de forme et de style dans les *Illuminations*', in *Minute d'éveil: Rimbaud maintenant* (Paris: CDU et SEDES réunis, 1984), pp. 159–66; 'Quelques choses vues dans les *Illuminations*: retraverser "Les Ponts"', in *Rimbaud à la loupe: Parade Sauvage: Colloque N°2, Cambridge 10–12 septembre 1987, Hommage à C.A. Hackett*, 1990, pp. 172–7; 'Forever Alien: The Prose Poem', *PN Review*, 81 (Sept.–Oct. 1991), pp. 34–5; 'The Shaping of Modern French Poetry: Cratylian Nostalgia', *PN Review*, 82 (Nov.–Dec. 1991), pp. 27–9; 'The Shaping of Modern French Poetry: Rainbow Rimbaud', *PN Review*, 84 (March–April 1992), pp. 41–4; and 'Stroboscopies rimbaldiennes', in *Parade Sauvage: Actes du colloque du centenaire de la mort de Rimbaud* (Charleville-Mézières, septembre 1991), Charleville-Mézières: Musée-Bibliothèque Rimbaud, 1992, pp. 270–77.
2. A further feature, first drawn attention to by André Guyaux and myself, is that the manuscript of the text comprises fourteen lines. His 1983 Classiques Garnier edition of the collection (and Steinmetz's 1989 'GF Flammarion' one) reproduce these fourteen lines but unfortunately have to use a smaller and different typeface for the text, thereby singling it out for special attention. Guyaux's 1985 edition (Neuchâtel: La Bacconière) presents all the texts line by line according to the manuscripts (where these are available in some form). There is no evidence that Rimbaud intended his texts (with the exceptions of 'Marine' and 'Mouvement') to be other than sequential prose, partly no doubt to create just the kind of surprise which we are investigating here.
3. Since Antoine Adam's edition of Rimbaud's *Œuvres complètes* (Paris: Gallimard, Pléiade, 1972), the principal relevant editions have been: *Illuminations*, ed. Nick Osmond, 'Athlone French Poets' (London: Athlone Press of the University of London, 1976); *Œuvres*, ed. Suzanne Bernard and André Guyaux, Classiques Garnier (Paris: Garnier 1983; rev. ed. 1987); *Illuminations*, ed. André Guyaux, (Neuchâtel: La Baconnière, 1985); *Œuvres poétiques*, ed. C.A. Hackett, 'Lettres françaises' (Paris: Imprimerie nationale, 1986); *Œuvres, III: Illuminations, suivi de Correspondance (1873–1891)*, ed. Jean-Luc Steinmetz, 'GF Flammarion' (Paris: Flammarion, 1989); *Œuvres*, ed. Louis Forestier, 'Bouquins' (Paris: Laffont, 1992).
4. This aspect of Rimbaud's writing has been extensively explored by Steve Murphy in a series of important recent studies: *Le Premier Rimbaud ou l'apprentissage de la subversion* (Lyon: CNRS, Presses Universitaires de Lyon, 1990); *Rimbaud et la ménagerie impériale* (Lyon: CNRS, Presses Universitaires de Lyon, 1991); *Chant de guerre parisien: essai d'archéologie symbolique*, in *Parade Sauvage: Bulletin*, 7 (septembre 1991); *Arthur Rimbaud: Un Cœur sous une soutane*, 'Bibliothèque sauvage', 2 (Charleville-Mézières: Musée-Bibliothèque Arthur Rimbaud, 1991).
5. E.H. Gombrich, *Art and Illusion: A Study in the Psychology of Pictorial Representation* (London: Phaidon, 1960; 3rd ed. 1968), p. 5. For 'Rabbit or Duck?', see ibid., fig. 2, p. 4.
6. For example, two clowns playing at 'pet-en-gueule' figure on an eighteenth-century Dijon carnival banner reproduced in Daniel Fabre's delightful *Carnaval ou la fête à l'envers*, Coll. Découvertes (Paris: Gallimard, 1992), p. 69 (appropriately,

for its sexual inference). More philosophically, the traditional symbol of the Chinese yin-yang principle, a circle divided equally by an S-shaped line between black and white complementarities, represents the totality of the universe divided between day and night, male and female etc.

7.   For a black and white reproduction of the 'image d'Épinal' entitled 'Prise de Sarrebrück', see Rimbaud, *Œuvres*, ed. Bernard and Guyaux; and for the same in colour, see Murphy, *Rimbaud et la ménagerie impériale*, fig. 35.

8.   Gombrich, p. 5.

*Chapter 17:   Sex and the occult in Symbolist art and literature*

1.   Sigmund Freud, *Beyond the Pleasure Principle*, 1920; in *On Metapsychology: The Theory of Psychoanalysis*, Pelican Freud Library 11 (London: Pelican Books). In alluding to an inescapable sexual disparity emerging in Freud's account of the psyche, I am referring to Freud's description of incompatible processes of identification undergone by the girl and the boy in accepting places in the Oedipal structure that are biologically as well as socially determined. The boy abandons his hold on the mother and identifies with the position of the father. The girl, on the other hand, has an extra psychic manoeuvre to perform. In addition to those performed by the boy, she has to return her identifying embrace to the position of the mother if she is to accept the conditions of her own body. In such a state of affairs, Freud wonders how there can be any relation between the sexes at all, and Lacan after him affirms a fundamental lack of relation between the sexes. Sigmund Freud, *Female Sexuality*, 1931, in *On Sexuality*, Pelican Freud Library, 7; and *On Femininity*, in *New Introductory Lectures*, Pelican Freud Library, 2. See also Jacques Lacan, *Encore*, Le Séminaire, XX (Paris: Seuil, 1975).

2.   Gérard de Nerval, *Aurélia*, in *Œuvres*, édition de H. Lemaître (Paris: Classiques Garnier, 1986); and in *Aurélia*, suivi le *Lettres à Jenny Colon*, de *La Pandora* 3t de *Les Chimères*, édition établie et commentée par Béatrice Didier, introduction de Jean Giraudoux (Paris: Livre de Poche, 1972).

3.   This picture is reproduced in Robert L. Delevoy *Symbolists and Symbolism*, trans. Barbara Bray, Elizabeth Wrightson and Bernard C. Swift (Geneva: Skira and New York: Rizzoli International, 1978), p. 35.

4.   *Symbolists and·Symbolism*, p. 104.

5.   Edvard Munch, *Madonna* (1895/1902) is reproduced in J.P. Hodin, *Edvard Munch* (London: Thames and Hudson, World of Art series), p. 72.

6.   In addition to *Mercure de France*, 1891, see *Symbolists and Symbolism*, p. 82.

7.   Paul Gauguin, *Le Christ Jaune* (1889), is reproduced in Belinda Thomson, *Gauguin* (London: Thames and Hudson, World of Art series, 1987), p. 107. Henceforth this book will be referred to as Thomson. Pierre Puvis de Chavannes, *L'Espérance* (1871), and *Le Pigeon voyageur* (1871), are reproduced in *Symbolists and Symbolism*, p. 36 and p. 24 respectively.

8.   Paul Gauguin, *Faa Iheihe (Tahitian Pastoral)* (1898), and Pierre Puvis de Chavannes, *Inter Artes et Naturam* (1890), are reproduced in Thomson, p. 184 and p. 196 respectively.

9.   Seurat's painting is reproduced in John Russell, *Seurat* (London: Thames and Hudson, Word of Art series, 1989), p. 31.

10.   Pierre Puvis de Chavannes, *Le Chant de pâtre* (1891), is reproduced in *Symbolists and Symbolism*, p. 158.

11. Paul Verlaine, *Les Poètes maudits*, préface de François Boddaert (Cognac: Le Temps qu'il fait, 1990).
12. Paul Verlaine, 'Green', *Romances sans paroles*, in *Fêtes galantes, Romances sans paroles*, précédé de *Poèmes saturniens*, édition établie par Jacques Borel (Paris: Gallimard, Poésie, 1973), p. 148.
13. *Poèmes saturniens*, p. 54.
14. Edvard Munch, *Death and the Maiden* (1891), is reproduced in Hodin, p. 60.
15. Paul Gauguin, *D'où venons-nous? Que sommes-nous? Où allons-nous?* (1897), is reproduced in Thomson, p. 180.
16. Arthur Rimbaud, 'Adieu', *Une Saison en Enfer*, in *Œuvres*, édition de S. Bernard (Paris: Garnier, 1960), p. 241.

## Chapter 18: *Valéry and Rodin: Orpheus returning*

1. Cf. L.J. Austin, 'Les premiers rapports entre Valéry et Mallarmé', in *Entretiens sur Paul Valéry. Actes du colloque de Montpellier des 16 et 17 octobre 1971*, textes recueillis par D. Moutote (Paris: PUF, 1972), pp. 39–50; F. Grunfeld, *Rodin. A Biography* (Oxford: OUP, 1989), pp. 271, 275, 283–5, 326–7, 379).
2. A. Elsen, *In Rodin's Studio* (Oxford: Phaidon, 1980), p. 179.
3. Elsen, plate 100.
4. Elsen, p. 179.
5. Elsen, p. 179.
6. Grunfeld, p. 343.
7. Bruno Jarret's photograph represents Rodin's *Orphée* (1892), bronze no. S. 1014 (dimensions 145.7 × 103.5 × 115.5) in the Musée Rodin in Paris. I am grateful to them for permission to reproduce this illustration.
8. Ovid, *Metamorphoses*, trans. M.M. Innes (Harmondsworth: Penguin, 1955), p. 247. If Suzanne Nash's *Paul Valéry's Album de vers anciens. A past transfigured* (Princeton: Princeton UP, 1983), which confirms Valéry's recourse to Ovid in composing his 'Narcisse', does not mention 'Orphée', it is doubtless because her study focuses on the first edition of the 'Vers anciens', that of 1920, where 'Orphée' is absent, since it was only restored in the 1926 edition.
9. *Metamorphoses*, pp. 268–9.
10. Grunfeld, p. 343.
11. Published in *L'Ermitage*, seconde année, no. 3, pp. 129–33, in March 1891. Cf. P. Valéry, *Œuvres*, ed. J. Hytier (Paris: Gallimard, Pléiade), tome I, 1957, p. 19; tome II, 1980, pp. 1402–5 [henceforth: PV I or II].
12. PV I, p. 20
13. PV II, p. 1402.
14. PV II, p. 1403.
15. V.J. Daniel, '*Eupalinos*, rencontre de thèmes anciens', in *Entretiens sur Paul Valéry* (D. Moutote, 1972), p. 116.
16. Stewart, 'Le Thème d'Orphée chez Valéry', in *Entretiens sur Paul Valéry*, ed. E. Noulet-Carner (Paris: Mouton, 1968), pp. 164–5.
17. PV II, p. 1405.
18. PV I, p. 1541.
19. W. Stewart, pp. 165–6.
20. PV I, pp. 1594–5.
21. *Chimère*, no. 4; PV I, p. 1609.
22. PV I, p. 28.
23. PV I, p. 1658.

24. Stewart, pp. 166–70.
25. Nash, p. 11.
26. M.T. Giaveri, *L'Album de vers anciens di Paul Valery*. *Studio sulle correzioni d'autore edite ed inedite* (Padova, 1969), pp. 48–9.
27. D. Moutote, 'La poésie grecque dans l'œuvre de Paul Valéry', in W. Ince, ed., *Colloque Paul Valéry*. *Valéry et la littérature du passé* (Southampton: Southampton University/London: Grant and Cutler, 1984), p. 57.
28. J. Lawler, 'The Technique of Valéry's "Orphée"', *Journal of the Australasian Modern Language Association*, no. 5 (Oct. 1956), p. 57.
29. Lawler, p. 62.
30. Lawler, p. 63.
31. Stewart, p. 165.

*Chapter 19: Dancing with Mallarmé and Seurat (and Loie Fuller, Hérodiade and La Goulue)*

1. M.E. Chevreul, *De la loi du contraste simultané des couleurs* (Paris: Gauthier-Villars et fils, 1889).
2. Ogden N. Rood, *Students' Textbook of Color* (New York, 1881). Seurat would have known his work as O.N. Rood, *Théorie scientifique des couleurs* (Paris: Librairie Germer Baillière et Cie, 1881).
3. In *La Revue contemporaine*, 25 Aug. 1885.
4. See Norma Broude, in a note, p. 39, of her valuable edition of *Seurat in Perspective* (Englewood Cliffs: Prentice-Hall, 1978).
5. See Robert J. Goldwater, 'Some Aspects of the Development of Seurat's Style', *The Art Bulletin*, 23 (June 1941), pp. 117–30. Excerpts of this are given in *Seurat in Perspective*, pp. 84–92.
6. In *La Revue Indépendante*, April 1887, and then to appear in *Divagations* of the same year.
7. In *L'Art et la mode*, on 12 Aug. 1887.
8. Published in *La Revue indépendante* of 1 Dec. 1886, and then the second part of *Notes sur le théâtre*.
9. Appearing in the *National Observer* of 13 March 1893, under the title: 'Considérations sur l'art du Ballet et la Loie Fuller'.
10. In his *Seurat* (New York: F.A. Praeger, 1965), John Russell juxtaposes the two: see pp. 155, 176.
11. Stéphane Mallarmé, *Œuvres complètes*, ed. Henri Mondor and G. Jean-Aubry (Paris: Gallimard, Pléiade, 1945).
12. Roger Fry, 'Seurat's *La Parade*', *The Burlington Magazine*, 55 (Dec. 1929), pp. 289–93, excerpted in *Seurat*, ed. Broude, pp. 62–4; the quotation is from p. 64.
13. Mallarmé, *Œuvres complètes*, p. 304.
14. Wallace Stevens, 'Of Modern Poetry', in *The Palm at the End of the Mind*, ed. Holly Stevens, (New York: Random House, 1971), p. 174.
15. Mallarmé, p. 308.
16. Mallarmé, p. 309.
17. Mallarmé, p. 309.
18. It was for this delicacy that Fuller was adored by Mallarmé – and by Whistler, whose sketch of the whirling Fuller is admirable in its own characteristic light touch, even lighter here, like a kind of spinning fog.
19. Richard Thomson, *Seurat* (Oxford: Phaidon, 1985). See in particular the pages

on 'The Modern City and the Critical Metaphor', pp 185–221, in which he discusses the dancer, the café-concert, and the circus.

20.   Jean-Claude Lebensztejn, '*Chahut*', in *Seurat: Correspondances, Témoignages, Notes inédites, Critiques* (Paris: Ecrits sur la peinture, Acropole, 1991) p. 235; Robert Rey, 'The Renaissance of Classical Sensibility in French Painting at the End of the Nineteenth Century' (Paris: Les Beaux-Arts, 1931), excerpted in *Seurat in Perspective*, ed. Norma Broude (Englewood Cliffs: Prentice-Hall, 1978), pp. 65–70.

21.   Seurat encountered the theories of Charles Henry in *La Revue contemporaine*; for his reaction to them and their importance, see Eric Darragon, in his edition of *Seurat: Correspondances . . .*, pp. 103–4.

22.   See Charles Henry, 'La Dynamogénie et l'inhibition' of 1884, part of his *Cercle chromatique*, an essay excerpted in *Seurat: Correspondances . . .*, p. 203.

23.   Rey, 'The Renaissance of Classical Sensibility', p. 67.

24.   Mallarmé, p. 875–6.

25.   Mallarmé, p. 31. The translation given is from *Stéphane Mallarmé: Selected Poetry and Prose*, ed. Mary Ann Caws (New York: New Directions, 1982).

26.   Mallarmé, p. 1416.

27.   Thomson describes the entire *raison d'être* of the *chahut* as one of immodest display, pointing out the dancers' availability, citing as instances the splits done by the dancers in *le grand écart*, and the quadrille, where the high kicks frequently revealed the absence of underwear (*Seurat*, p. 206) The dancers La Goulue and Grille d'Egout were the most famous performers.

28.   Quoted in Robert Herbert, 'Seurat's Drawings', in *Seurat*, p. 135.

29.   Peter Collier reminds me of the odd and peripheral trapeze and green ballet-shoes in the corner of Manet's *Bar Aux Folies-Bergère*. So many side-stagings: what has once caught our eye, even at a remove, stays in our memory, making its own transgression upon our present focus.

30.   Félix Fénéon, speaking of the importance of Henry's theories to Paul Signac, in *La Plume*, 1 Sept. 1891, p. 299. He is quoted by William Innes Homer, who maintains that the same could be applied with equal force to Seurat and to his reception of Henry's theories. *Seurat and The Science of Painting* (Cambridge: MIT Press, 1964), excerpted in *Seurat*, ed. Broude, pp. 135–54; the quotation comes from p. 146.

31.   See the indications of André Salmon, sketched briefly in a piece called simply 'Georges Seurat' printed in *The Burlington Magazine*, 37 (Sept. 1920) and excerpted in *Seurat*, pp. 60–61.

32.   See Robert L. Herbert, 'Seurat and Jules Chéret', *Art Bulletin*, 40 (1958), pp. 156–8, reprinted in *Seurat*, ed. Broude, pp. 111–15.

33.   For the Egyptian side of things, see Umbro Apollonio, 'Les Dessins de Seurat', 1950, quoted in *Seurat: Correspondances . . .*, ed. Darragon, pp. 85–6.

34.   In his preface to Mallarmé's *Igitur* and other writings, Yves Bonnefoy associates the final cutting off of sound and breath in the poet's own throat with the beheading of John the Baptist. Mallarmé thought the very *name* 'Hérodiade' gem-like enough to gleam in the centre of a page and make it poetry.

35.   An idea of what the lustral came to mean can be sensed in Roland Rood, *Color and Light in Painting*, ed. George L. Stout (New York, 1941).

36.   Mallarmé, 'Crayonné au théâtre', p. 111.

# Notes on contributors

**Pierre Bourdieu** is Professor of Sociology at the Collège de France. His many works include *Distinction* (Routledge, 1984) and *Les Règles de l'art* (Minuit, 1992).

**Roger Cardinal** is Professor of Literary and Visual Studies at the University of Kent. His books include *Expressionism* (Paladin, 1984) and *The Landscape Vision of Paul Nash* (Reaktion Books, 1989).

**Mary Ann Caws** is Professor of English, French and Comparative Literature at the Graduate School of the City University of New York. She has addressed the relations between texts and images in *The Eye in the Text* (Princeton University Press, 1981), *The Art of Interference* (Princeton University Press, 1989), *Women of Bloomsbury* (Routledge, 1990) and in several other books.

**Peter Collier** is a Fellow of Sidney Sussex College, Cambridge. The author of *Proust and Venice* (Cambridge University Press, 1989), he has also edited a number of collections of interdisciplinary essays including *Visions and Blueprints* (Manchester University Press, 1988) and *Modernism and the European Unconscious* (Polity, 1990).

**Germaine Greer** is a Fellow of Newnham College, Cambridge. Her many books include her path-finding study of women artists: *The Obstacle Race* (Secker and Warburg, 1979).

**Eric Homberger** is Reader in American Literature at the University of East Anglia. He has written on topics as diverse as photography and American politics. His study of nineteenth-century New York society is forthcoming from Yale University Press.

338

**Bernard Howells** is Lecturer in French at King's College, London. His publications include studies of Baudelaire's aesthetics and Camille Claudel.

**Ann Jefferson** is a Tutorial Fellow in French at New College, Oxford. Her books include *The Nouveau Roman and the Poetics of Fiction* (Cambridge University Press, 1980) and *Reading Realism in Stendhal* (Cambridge University Press, 1988).

**James Kearns** is Lecturer in French at the University of Exeter. He is the author of *Symbolist Landscapes* (Modern Humanities Research Association, 1989) and a number of articles on the relationship between literature and the visual arts.

**David Kelley** is a Fellow of Trinity College, Cambridge. His books include the critical edition of Baudelaire's *Salon de 1846* (Oxford University Press, 1975) and *Unreal City* (Manchester University Press, 1985).

**Ségolène Le Men** is a CNRS Research Fellow at the Musée d'Orsay. Her publications include *Les Abécédaires français illustrés* (Promodis, 1984), *L'Affiche de librairie au XIXe siècle* (Réunion des Musées Nationaux, 1987), and *Les Français peints par eux-mêmes* (Réunion des Musées Nationaux, 1993).

**Robert Lethbridge** is a Fellow of Fitzwilliam College, Cambridge. His publications include *Maupassant: 'Pierre et Jean'* (Grant and Cutler, 1984) and *Zola and the Craft of Fiction* (Leicester University Press, 1990).

**Roger Little** is Professor of French and a Fellow of Trinity College, Dublin. He has written extensively on modern poetry. His books include *Rimbaud: 'Illuminations'* (Grant and Cutler, 1983) *Études sur Saint-John Perse* (Klincksieck, 1984) and *André Frénaud entre l'interrogation et le vide* (Sud, 1989).

**Timothy Mathews** is a Fellow of Trinity Hall, Cambridge. He is the author of *Reading Apollinaire* (Manchester University Press, 1987) and co-editor of the Bloodaxe Contemporary French Poets series.

**Michael Moriarty** is a Fellow of Gonville and Caius College, Cambridge. He is the author of *Taste and Ideology in Seventeenth-Century France* (Cambridge University Press, 1988) and *Roland Barthes* (Polity, 1991).

**Patrick O'Donovan** is a Fellow of King's College, Cambridge, He has published work on Stendhal, Flaubert and the Goncourt brothers.

**David Scott** is Associate Professor of French and a Fellow of Trinity College, Dublin. He has written on Symbolist poetry and Paul Delvaux. His many publications include the seminal work on 'transposition', *Pictorialist Poetics* (Cambridge University Press, 1988).

**Michael Tilby** is a Fellow of Selwyn College, Cambridge. His publications include *Gide: 'Les Faux-Monnayeurs'* (Grant and Cutler, 1981) and *Beyond the Nouveau Roman* (Berg, 1990).

# Index

341

344